Effective Communication in Organizations

MICHAEL FIELDING
M A, B Ed (Cape Town); M A (Leeds)

In association with
THE INSTITUTE OF MARKETING MANAGEMENT

Marketing means Business

First published in 1993
Revised first edition 1995
Second edition 1997

Copyright © Juta & Co, Ltd
PO Box 14373, Kenwyn 7790

This book is copyright under the Berne Convention. In terms of the Copyright Act 98 of 1978, no part of this book may be reproduced or transmitted in any form or by any means (including photocopying, recording, or by any information storage and retrieval system) without permission in writing from the publisher.

ISBN 0 7021 4236 0

Cover design by Joy Wrench, Cape Town
Typesetting by Zebra Publications, Cape Town

Printed and bound in South Africa by
The Rustica Press, Ndabeni, Western Cape
D5999

Preface

This book was designed specifically to cover the business communication syllabuses of the following institutions:
- the Institute of Marketing Management (IMM),
- the Institute of Administration and Commerce (IAC), and
- the South African Institute of Chartered Secretaries and Administrators (CIS)

It also caters for the needs of technikon students in business communication, and for students working on their own or attending classes to prepare them for the examinations. Each chapter ends with discussion points and exercises. Answers to all these are given.

The approach to business communication is both theoretical and practical. The book gives detailed advice on the preparation of twenty types of messages in business — spoken as well as written. Each type of message is backed up with an example.

The book covers the following important aspects of business communication:

- The process of communication
- Communication flows within organizations
- Small-group communication
- Formal meetings
- Interpersonal communication
- Interviews
- Preparation of spoken and written messages
- Communicating with tables, graphs and bar charts
- Writing case studies
- Writing summaries and comprehension tests
- Mass communication and public relations
- Grammar, sentence structure and punctuation

The material for all of the above was designed to cover the syllabuses of the various institutes, technikons and private colleges.

Contents

PART 1

1 Introduction to the Study of Communication in Organizations   **3**

    Summary 3
    Key points 3
    Introduction 4
    Contexts in organizations 5
    External environment 5
    Communication activities. 6
    Major functions for communication 7
    Downward, sideways (lateral) and upward communication 7
    The subject of the book 8

2 The Process of Communication   **11**

    Summary 11
    Key points 12
    Communication models. 13
    Intercultural communication 19
    Differences between one-way and two-way communication 20
    Levels of communication in organizations. 20
    Implications for communication. 22
    Need for a supportive climate 22

    Questions: Part 1 . . . . **23**

PART 2

3 Communication in Organizations   **27**

    Summary 27
    Key points 28
    Communication makes organizations possible 29
    What is an organization? 29
    Characteristics of organizations. 31

Theories about organizations — a brief overview.................. 34
Culture and climate in organizations 36
Theories of motivation in companies — a brief overview 38
Messages in organizations 42
Intercultural communication in organizations................... 54
A definition of culture 54

Questions: Part 2.. 58

PART 3

4 Small-group Communication   63

Summary 63
Key points 64
Introduction 65
Stages of group development................................... 71
Leadership in groups 71
Ineffective groups 75
Conflict in groups... 76
References.. 79

5 Formal Meetings   81

Summary 81
Key points 81
Differences between formal meetings and small groups 82
Aspects of formal meetings 82

Questions: Part 3.. 93

PART 4

6 Interpersonal Communication   99

Summary 99
Key points 100
The importance of effective interpersonal communication in
organizations.. 101
Intrapersonal communication and perception 101
Interpersonal communication................................. 103

7 Active Listening — 109

   Summary 109
   Key points 110
   Active listening 111

8 Non-verbal Communication — 115

   Summary 115
   Key points 116
   Introduction 117
   Reference 128

9 The Interview — 129

   Summary 129
   Key points 130
   Introduction 131
   The special nature of interviews 132
   The panel interview 139
   The job application 140

   Questions: Part 4 146

PART 5

10 The Rhetorical Situation — 153

   Summary 153
   Key points 153
   The rhetorical situation 155
   What is a message? 155
   Analysing the needs of your audience 157
   Deciding on your purposes 158

11 Planning and Organizing Messages — 161

   Summary 161
   Key points 162
   Introduction 163
   Planning information 166
   Choosing an appropriate style: ensuring unity, coherence and
   the right emphasis 169

12 Choosing an Effective Vocabulary — 177

Summary 177
Key points 178
Introduction 179
Functions of words 181
Choosing a vocabulary for professional messages 183

13 Style, Tone and Jargon — 189

Summary 189
Key points 190
Introduction 191

14 The Elements of Readability — 201

Summary 201
Key points 201
Introduction 202
Calculating a fog index................................... 206

Questions: Part 5.. 209

PART 6

15 Oral Messages — 217

Summary 217
Key points 218
Introduction 219
Formats for a talk and a report 219
Preparing a talk or oral report........................... 222
Complete horizontal outline for talk.................... 224
Presenting the talk or report 226
Using audio-visual aids 227
Audience response and questions 231

16 Using the Telephone Effectively — 235

Summary 235
Key points 236
Introduction 237
Telephone as first point of contact 237
A telephone user's rights 240

CONTENTS

Callers' techniques 241

Questions: Part 6 .... **242**

PART 7

17   Written Messages in Organizations   247

Summary 247
Electronic mail and its effects on communication in organizations 253
Key points 254
Effect of the personal computer and the Internet on communication 255
Key points 256
Reports 258
Letters 283
Memoranda 306
Proposals 309
Notices and circulars 315
Writing instructions 318
The press release 327
Essays and articles for in-house journals 330
Telegrams and telexes 335
Advertisements 338
The electronic office 342
What is e-mail? 347
Effect of the personal computer and the Internet on communication 353
Referencing 358

Questions: Part 7 .... **362**

— Reports 362
— Letters 365
— Proposals 368
— Notices and circulars 369
— Instructions 369
— Press release 370
— Essays and articles 370
— Telegram and telex 371
— Advertisements 372
— Faxing and electronic mail 373

Electronic mail and its effects on communication in organizations 373
Effect of the personal computer and the Internet on communication 374

PART 8

18 Graphic Communication   377

Summary 377
Key points 378
What is graphic communication? 379

Questions: Part 8. . . . . **396**

PART 9

19 How to Approach a Case Study   401

Summary 401
What is a case study? 402

Questions: Part 9. . . . . **408**

PART 10

20 Writing a Summary and a Comprehension Test   415

Summary 415
Précis 419
Executive summary and synopsis 419
Abstract 420
Why would a reader need a summary? 420
The comprehension test. 427

Questions: Part 10. . . . . **429**

PART 11

21 Mass Communication and Organizations — 437

Summary 437
Key points 438
Introduction 439
Functions of the mass media 440

Questions: Part 11 . . . . **444**

PART 12

22 Grammar, Usage, Sentence Structure and Punctuation — 447

Summary 447
Introduction 449
Rules of number 449
Rules for case 452
Rules for participles 452
Gerunds, or verbal nouns. 453
Defining and non-defining relative clauses 453
Rules for 'and which' 454
Rules for 'shall' and 'will' 454
Rules for 'can' and 'may' 455
Rules for 'may' and 'might' 455
'May have'; 'might have' 456
Rules for 'its' and 'it's' 456
Rules for sequence of verbs 457
Position of 'only' and 'even' 457
The split infinitive. 458
Sentence structure 458
Rules for punctuation. 460
Internal punctuation 461
Writing clearly and concisely. 463

Questions: Part 12 . . . . **467**

PART 13

23 Intercultural Communication — 475

Summary 475

Key points 476
Important definitions in intercultural communication 476
A convergence model of communication as a tool to understanding intercultural communication 481
What can organizations do to improve intercultural communication? 482

Questions: Part 13. .... **486**

PART 14

Answers to Questions   **489**

PART 1 (Chapters 1–2) 491
PART 2 (Chapter 3) 495
PART 3 (Chapters 4–5) 499
PART 4 (Chapters 6–9) 504
PART 5 (Chapters 10–14) 511
PART 6 (Chapters 15–16) 524
PART 7 (Chapter 17) 537
— Reports.. 537
— Letters 545
— Proposals 556
— Notices and circulars................................... 559
— Instructions 563
— Press-release.. 565
— Essays and articles 567
— Telegram and telex..................................... 568
— Advertisements 571
— Faxing and electronic mail............................. 573
— Electronic mail and its effects on communication in organizations 574
— Effect of the personal computer and the Internet on communication... 577
PART 8 (Chapter 18) 579
PART 9 (Chapter 19) 589
PART 10 (Chapter 20) 591
PART 11 (Chapter 21) 596
PART 12 (Chapter 22) 599
PART 13 (Chapter 23) 603

Index   **609**

PART 1

*Introduction to the Study
of Communication in Organizations*

•

The Process of Communication

CHAPTER 1

Introduction to the Study of Communication in Organizations

Summary

This chapter introduces the major themes of the book. It stresses that effective communication is vital if an organization is to survive. Communication enables organizations to coordinate their activities.

This communication is achieved by upward, downward and lateral (also called sideways or horizontal) communication.

Communicating is defined as a transaction. People work together to create meaning by exchanging symbols. This book stresses that people have to take one another into account. They also have to work together according to a set of rules. People have to ensure they share the same meanings when they use words. The same word can have different meanings for different people. The symbols that people exchange take many forms. They may be words, non-verbal symbols or graphic symbols.

Communication in organizations occurs in one-to-one groups, small groups and large groups. All of these vary in the demands they place on people.

Organizations also have to communicate with customers, suppliers and the general public.

Key points

- Communication in organizations is essential for their survival.
- Communication is a transaction.
- Communication involves the creation of meaning.
- Communication involves the exchange of symbols.
- Communication in organizations moves upward, downward and sideways.

Introduction

All organizations regard effective communication as essential for survival. Without communication a business would not exist. Businesses are concerned with a wide range of communication activities. First of all, communication within the company has to be as effective as possible. This involves a wide range of communication activities to ensure good upward, downward and lateral or sideways communication. Companies also have to communicate with other companies and suppliers, since good relationships with them are essential. The most important activity of all is communicating with customers; without them no company would exist.

This book stresses the central role of communication in business. Through communication people are able to coordinate their activities. This coordination makes organized behaviour possible.

Communication is very complex. Indeed, communication experts have difficulty agreeing on one definition to cover every situation. For the purposes of this book we may define communication as follows:

'communication is a transaction whereby participants together create meaning through the exchange of symbols'.

This definition stresses four major points:

- Communication as a transaction.
- People working together.
- The creation of meaning.
- The exchange of symbols.

Communication as a transaction

A transaction involves two or more people who construct meaning together. They have to take one another into account, and have to work together according to a set of rules.

People working together

This definition stresses the importance of people working together. People have to pay attention to each other at the same time. They have to learn to develop mutual expectations. If mutual awareness exists then mutual influence becomes possible.

Creation of meaning

People need to ensure that others understand what they are saying. Words do not have meaning in themselves. People give meaning to words. The same words may therefore have different meanings for different people. Effective communication therefore demands that people work together to ensure that the meaning created is the same for all. There must be a sharing of meaning.

Exchange of symbols

Exchanging symbols enables people to create meanings. Symbols may take many forms:

- They may be *verbal*. Words are used when one speaks or writes to others in an organization.
- They may be *non-verbal*. These may take the form of gestures, facial expressions, the way people stand, and the use of voice in different ways.
- They may be *graphic*. Graphic communication takes the form of tables, line graphs, bar graphs and diagrams.

Contexts in organizations

Dyadic context

Communication in an organization takes place in a variety of contexts. A great deal of the communication takes place between two people. This is called a dyadic context. Examples of this context are one-to-one interviews, manager instructing subordinate or middle manager reporting to senior manager.

Small groups

Small groups are another example of a communication context. Groups may gather to share information, make decisions about company policy or decide on a sales strategy.

Large groups

Large groups in an organization are another context. They might meet for a departmental briefing or for a general discussion. The whole company might also gather for a special function.

External environment

Organizations function within the context of an external environment. This environment consists of customers, suppliers, the general public, government departments and the country as a whole. Companies will undertake advertising or public relations campaigns to communicate with these people. They will also arrange meetings and write letters. Companies in southern Africa are, for example, striving to survive in an atmosphere of high expectations of change. They have to survive in the face of strikes, threats and violence. Workers are no longer prepared to accept orders without query. They are demanding a say in the running of companies.

Managers have to move away from an attitude of 'I'm the boss. You do as I say'. They have to move towards a style of communication that regards it as a transaction, or a creation of meaning. Communication has to become two-way, rather than one-way.

Communication activities

All these contexts will demand a large number of communication activities. The following table summarizes these activities.

Table 1.1
Contexts in organizations, communication activities and types of messages

one to one	*Small group*	*Large group*	*External*
Contexts			
Manager to Manager Manager to subordinate Worker to worker	Group of managers Manager and staff	Department Whole company	Customers Potential customers General public Local pressure groups
Communication activities in these contexts			
Discussion Problem-solving Making policy Interviewing Instructing Briefing	Discussion Decision-making Problem-solving Resolving conflict Instructing Briefing Brainstorming	Union meetings Deciding on long-term strategies Briefing Managing Directors and all staff/shareholders' meetings	Advertising Public relations Briefing Analysing customers' needs
Types of messages			
Spoken			
Face-to-face exchange Telephone Oral report Briefing	Face-to-face exchange Short talk Oral report Briefing	Speech	Speech
Written			
Instruction Memorandum Report	Report Circular Memorandum	Policy manuals Company's annual report Memoranda Circulars Notices Newsletters	Press releases Letters Advertisements Leaflets Newsletters

The above table stresses the range of communication activities in an organization. It also stresses the range of messages needed to keep an organization running.

Major functions for communication

Effective communication in a company has three major functions:
- Ensuring that products and services are of the best.
- Helping staff generate new ideas and adapt to changes.
- Ensuring that staff work well together, understand the organization's objectives and work to achieve those objectives.

Downward, sideways (lateral) and upward communication

Within the major functions described above, are specific contexts of communication. These are:
- Downward communication
- Sideways communication
- Upward communication.

Downward communication

This communication involves managers communicating down the line to subordinates. Managers might send the following types of messages:
- Information about the missions and goals of the organization.
- Feedback to subordinates on their performance.
- Procedures to be followed.
- Instructions for specific tasks.

Sideways communication

Sideways communication (also called lateral or horizontal communication), or peer communication, takes place between departments in a company or between managers of equal rank.

This type of communication involves the following types of messages:
- Reports on the activities of departments to keep other departments informed.
- Information to managers on company policies and progress so that they are able to make informed decisions.

Upward communication

This type of communication is called subordinate/manager communication. It involves communication from the lowest positions in the company to the highest positions.

The following types of messages are involved:
- Reports about individual problems and performance.
- Reports on what needs to be done and how to do it.
- Memoranda about the practical results of company policies and practices.
- Messages in suggestion boxes about specific staff problems.

Effective upward communication places heavy demands on managers and subordinates alike. Managers have to be prepared to listen to criticism, or to new ideas that might seem threatening. They have to foster an atmosphere of openness and trust. They should also strive to be as objective as possible.

Subordinates have to be prepared to suggest new ideas, and criticize present practices. They, also, have to be as honest and open as possible, if upward communication is to succeed.

The subject of the book

This Introduction has given a brief overview of communication in organizations. The following chapters go into more detail about the practical approaches that management and staff can adopt to ensure that their communication is as effective as possible.

The following areas of communication will be discussed in detail:
- The process of communication with particular stress on two-way communication, and barriers to effective communication.
- Communication in organizations with stress on upward, horizontal and downward communication, as well as the 'grapevine'.
- Small-group communication in organizations, with particular stress on effective communication in groups, leadership and problem-solving
- The conduct of meetings.
- Interpersonal communication, with particular stress on self-awareness, assertiveness, perception, listening and non-verbal communication.
- Interviews.
- The principles of effective message creation with the stress on choice of vocabulary, style, jargon and readability.

- The principles of effective oral communication with the stress on preparing a talk or oral report, formats for talks and oral reports, and effective audio-visual aids.
- Telephone techniques with the stress on assertiveness, listening and effective message-taking.
- The principles of effective written messages with the stress on the formats of a range of messages.
- The principles of graphic communication with the stress on effective tables, bar graphs and line graphs.
- How to tackle a case study.
- How to summarize and answer a comprehension test.
- Mass communication and organizations.
- Grammar and usage.
- Intercultural communication.

CHAPTER 2

The Process of Communication

Summary

This chapter discusses two types of communication model:
- a linear model; and
- a convergence model.

These models are designed to help the reader understand the complex process of communication. The linear model, shown in four stages, shows the major components in the process. The convergence model stresses how important it is to work together to reach an understanding.

The linear model shows the following main elements in communication:
- Sender
- Receiver
- Message
- Noise
- Barriers
- Feedback.

The sender and receiver exchange messages and feedback. Noise refers to any interference with the sending of a message. People also set up barriers that stop messages.

The chapter discusses intercultural communication. People from different cultures may not see things in the same way. Effective communication therefore demands understanding and tolerance. People should guard against stereotyping and seeing things only from their cultural viewpoint. This is called ethnocentrism.

The chapter discusses the differences between one-way and two-way communication. It then goes on to describe the different levels of communication in organizations:
- *Organizational communication* describes the flow of messages in the organization.
- *Mass communication* covers advertising in particular.
- *Small group communication* covers all communication in committees and formal meetings.
- *Interpersonal communication* covers one-to-one communication.

- *Public communication* describes the giving of talks or making speeches.
- *Intrapersonal communication* covers communication to oneself.

The need for a supportive climate is stressed.

Key points

- A sender, a message, a receiver and feedback are involved in the communication process.
- Barriers to effective communication need to be studied and understood.
- People need to work towards a convergence of meaning so that they understand one another.
- Communication in companies takes place through different levels. Each one needs to be studied and understood.

Communication models

In the Introduction, communication was described as a transaction. This definition implies that people have to work together to create a meaning. One person does not hand over meaning to another, as though it were a parcel to be unwrapped. Communication is viewed, rather, as an ever-changing process and unending. This complex process is hard to analyse. Communication researchers have therefore devised models to help them analyse the major elements in the process. Two models will be used in this chapter:

- a linear model; and
- a convergence model.

Please keep in mind that models simplify what is a very complex process. Models cannot show all the complexities of a real situation. They are, nevertheless, helpful in the study of communication.

The linear model helps to analyse the major elements in the communication process. The convergence model stresses the view that communication is a transaction in which meaning is created by both sender and receiver working together. This model also stresses the idea of the meeting of minds. People need to share the same meanings for words, concepts and ideas if they are to communicate successfully.

The linear model

This model shows communication as a system. This system involves an interrelated and interdependent set of elements working together for a specific purpose.

There are seven elements in the model:

- a sender
- a receiver
- a message
- a channel
- feedback
- psychological and physical noise as potential barriers
- a result.

The model is presented in four stages.

Stage 1 (figure 2.1) shows the sender initiating a message. The sender has to decide on the purpose of the message, for example to inform, persuade or instruct. The message then has to be encoded in a form that the receiver can understand. It then has to be sent in a specific format via a channel.

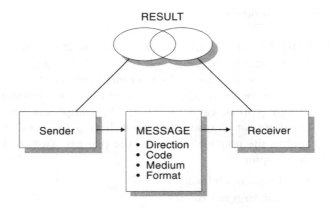

Figure 2.1
The elements of the communication process

Message

The model shows that the message must have a direction. Communication is not a random affair. The message should be directed at a specific receiver, with specific purposes in mind.

The sender has a range of codes to choose from. (S)he could, for example, use words or a non-verbal code.

A range of media may be used to send the message. The sender could, for example, use the written form for a message or the spoken form.

Finally, where appropriate, the message needs to be organized into a format such as a talk, oral report, written report or letter. Please keep in mind that not all messages will be organized into a specific format. Non-verbal messages do not, for example, have a format.

The receiver

The receiver decodes the message according to her or his knowledge of the subject, ability to use and interpret language and past experience. (S)he will generally make an immediate decision on how to react to the message.

The result

In Figure 2.1 the result has been shown as two shapes that overlap partially. This suggests that some communication has taken place. However, perfect congruence between the message sent and the message received has not been achieved.

In other words, the message sent is not identical to the message received. If the shapes did not touch at all, this would show that no communication had taken place, even though a message had been sent.

Ideally, in the most effective communication, the message sent should be the same as the message received. However, this rarely happens.

Figure 2.2 suggests why perfect congruence is seldom achieved.

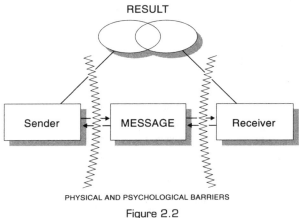

Figure 2.2
Barriers to effective communication

The stage above shows that both physical and psychological barriers can affect the result of communication. During a speech, for example, the noise created by machines nearby might drown out certain parts. The audience itself might be so noisy that the speech cannot be heard properly. The lighting or the air-conditioning might be faulty or the seating arrangements poor. In the case of a written message, the reproduction of a faxed message could be so poor that the message cannot be read. All these are examples of physical barriers to effective communication.

The receiver might not like the message being sent because it carries information that (s)he does not like. (S)he will then become defensive and not pay attention to the message. This is an example of a psychological barrier. The sender and receiver may come from different cultural backgrounds. These backgrounds may cause a psychological barrier to effective communication because each does not understand the other's values.

Major barriers to effective communication

There are many barriers to effective communication in organizations. The list below gives the major ones. You are encouraged to add your own from your experience.

- Failure to analyse the needs of the receiver.
- Poor listening, and lack of attention to feedback.
- Assuming that the receivers know more than they really do.
- Insensitive behaviour on the part of senders and receivers.
- Different cultural backgrounds.
- Too many people to pass on the message from the sender to the receiver.
- Poor feedback, with filtering, omissions and errors as messages are passed on.
- Insensitive or poor choice of language by sender or receiver.
- The sender's information may be insufficient or not clear enough.
- Poor encoding or decoding of a message, with errors, filling in of imagined gaps, and unjustified simplification.
- The wrong channel of communication may be used.
- Poor planning of information.
- Wrong emphasis in the information, so that the receiver does not know what the most important parts of the message are.
- Messages that are so packed with information that they are difficult to interpret and process.
- Messages in which the information is so thin that the reader becomes bored.
- Language that is too technical for the receiver, or technical language that is not in the receiver's field.
- Written messages that have been badly set out.
- Irritating mannerisms that stop people listening.
- An unsupportive or defensive climate in an organization that makes people unwilling to communicate openly.
- Different perceptions of situations and meanings of messages.

Sender and receiver

Figure 2.3 stresses the position of the sender and receiver in terms of their differing backgrounds and perceptions.

Cultural and work background

The sender(s) come(s) from a specific cultural and work background. This background means that the sender has a specific language, view of the world and views on situations. The sender's work background will give her or him certain experience and ideas of how to do things.

The receiver might not have the same culture, language or work background. Communication between the two will therefore be difficult

THE PROCESS OF COMMUNICATION

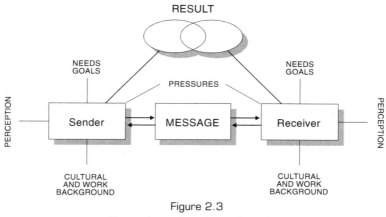

Figure 2.3
Perceptions of sender and receiver

unless each is sensitive to the other's needs. The attitudes of senders and receivers are crucial here. If attitudes are wrong very little communication will take place.

Perceptions

Both sender and receiver will see the world, the workplace and specific tasks differently. They therefore have to be sensitive to these perceptions to ensure that effective communication takes place.

Needs and goals

Senders and receivers have different needs and goals. If they understand this, they will become the more sensitive one towards the other. For example one may have a strong need for recognition, whereas another may have a need to get the job done as quickly as possible. Their goals would therefore differ and communication might, therefore, be difficult.

Pressures

Both sender and receiver could be working under different pressures. One might, for example, be a member of a union and under pressure to strike. At the same time (s)he knows the financial sacrifice that this will mean. The other, on the other hand, may be very worried about the company's finances and therefore desperate to get a job done. These pressures will make communication difficult.

Feedback

Figure 2.4 shows the importance of arranging for and receiving feedback.

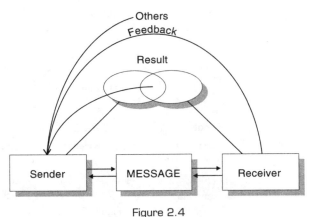

Figure 2.4
The nature of feedback

Senders and receivers should always arrange for feedback and be prepared to receive feedback, even if it is negative. Feedback tells the sender how the receiver has interpreted the message.

In *face-to-face* communication, feedback will be direct. Both sender and receiver will be giving constant feedback to each other as they exchange messages. If the sender is delivering a speech, (s)he needs to be sensitive to the audience's reactions and questions, as these are ways of receiving feedback.

Feedback on *written* communication is not often as direct. If the writer is lucky (s)he might receive immediate feedback. However, feedback is more likely to come from the result of the message. (S)he might also receive feedback from other people. This is called indirect feedback. The good communicator should always be sensitive to feedback, and should constantly adjust her or his message as a result of the feedback.

The convergence model

The previous models have stressed the various elements in the communication process. The model below stresses the transactional and continuing nature of communication. In this model the sender and receiver are shown to be constantly exchanging messages until they reach an understanding. The arrow shows that communication does not stop there. It continues for as long as the sender and receiver have anything to do with each other.

The convergence model shows the sender and receiver as both encoders and decoders of messages. As they send messages back and forth they are constantly changing roles. As they continue the transactions, they arrive at an understanding. However, the communication is still not perfect. This is shown in the model by the partially overlapping shapes.

THE PROCESS OF COMMUNICATION

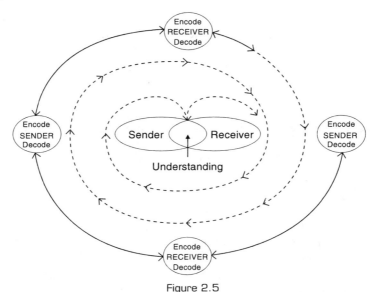

Figure 2.5
A convergence model of communication

The sender and receiver do not share all their experiences and meanings. If that particular transaction had been perfect, the shapes would have overlapped fully. Had the shapes not met at all, no communication would have taken place. The arrow then shows the transaction continuing.

Intercultural communication

The need for shared experiences and meanings for successful communication is particularly important in intercultural communication. People from different cultures will find it particularly difficult to communicate. They would need to take special care to establish common ground for communication. In particular, they would need to cultivate caring attitudes that would remove any suggestion of superiority or inferiority.

Cultural values would need to be acknowledged, and both groups would need to listen actively to ensure that they understand both the facts, opinions and the emotions communicated.

They should avoid negative generalizations about each other's culture. For example, a person from one cultural group should be careful not to take the attitude that everyone from the other group is dishonest or lazy. From this general statement, that person might then think that a particular person from that group is dishonest and lazy. This attitude is called cultural stereotyping.

Communicators should be careful not to see things only from their own cultural point of view. This is called ethnocentrism. Each group should strive to understand the cultural background of the other group. If this were achieved, they would understand why each communicated in a particular way.

Differences between one-way and two-way communication

The models in this chapter have stressed the need for two-way, rather than one-way communication.

Two-way communication stresses the great importance of feedback and constant interaction during communication. The negotiation of meaning is vitally important. People involved in interpersonal and small-group communication are in the best positions to give and receive feedback.

One-way communication is often characterized by lack of feedback, difficulty in obtaining feedback or delayed feedback. Advertisers, for example, spend a great deal of money on market research to establish their audience's needs and reactions. Feedback is, however, difficult to obtain.

In public communication, particularly with large audiences, feedback is a problem. Speakers therefore have to be especially sensitive to their audience's reactions.

In large organizations, obtaining feedback is difficult unless special attention is paid to it. Managers need to be careful about simply issuing orders as these could be interpreted as one-way communication.

Levels of communication in organizations

The communication models in this chapter have shown some of the factors to be taken into account when analysing communication in organizations.

Communication is not simply a matter of face-to-face communication. In organizations people participate in a number of different levels of communication. These are briefly described below. Each will be described briefly here and in more detail at later stages in the book.

- Organizational communication
- Mass communication
- Small-group communication
- Interpersonal communication
- Public communication
- Intrapersonal communication

Organizational communication

This level of communication involves communication within an organization such as a school, a university, a business or a government department.

It would be particularly concerned with the flow of information — upward, downward and sideways. It would also be concerned with the effects of managerial styles, leadership and motivation on communication. Effective communication within a business helps to ensure efficiency for customers. This type of communication covers many types of spoken and written messages.

Mass communication

Companies that advertise in the newspaper, on the radio or television, or issue press releases are involved in mass communication. Mass communication is involved with large audiences, frequent reproduction of messages and rapid distribution of messages. Feedback in mass communication is the most delayed. The audiences are the most difficult of all the levels of communication to define.

Small-group communication

Small-group communication in organizations covers communication when three or more people are working together. These groups may be involved in a range of activities from simply chatting to devising policies for a company.

In the best groups every member is encouraged to communicate to her or his full potential. A positive atmosphere or climate is established so that people work well together.

Interpersonal communication

Interpersonal communication occurs between two people. A great deal of communication in organizations is interpersonal. This type of communication calls for good control of language, good listening, sensitivity to non-verbal communication, and tolerance. It involves a range of spoken and written messages.

Public communication

Public communication describes public speaking in organizations. One person gives a lecture, talk or oral report to a small or large group. The audience usually does not participate.

In this type of communication the speaker is concerned with effective analysis of the audience's needs, appearance, good preparation, an effective style of delivery, effective non-verbal communication and the audience's response to the speech.

Intrapersonal communication

This is the most basic level of communication. It concerns the messages that we 'send' to ourselves. We constantly 'talk' to ourselves without saying anything out loud. These messages can simply be reminders to do something, positive messages or negative messages.

If we give ourselves constant negative messages we are likely to develop a negative self-image. This will affect our interpersonal communication, as will a positive self-image. We will often show our self-images by our non-verbal behaviour. Other people will interpret this behaviour and then communicate with us accordingly.

Implications for communication

The models of communication and the brief descriptions of levels of communication presented in this chapter stress the following:

- Communication is a transaction or creation of meaning. People have to work together to create meaning.
- Meanings are created by people. Words themselves have no meaning.
- Communication takes two levels:
  - the content of the message
  - the way in which that content is expressed (relationship).
- People need to be aware of the barriers to effective communication.
- People need to be aware of the specific demands that cross-cultural communication will make of them.
- There is no opposite to communication in organizations. You cannot not communicate. If there were no communication in an organization, it would cease to exist.

Need for a supportive climate

Everyone in an organization needs to strive to create a supportive climate. This will allow open, honest and effective communication to take place.

People need to listen empathetically so that they pay attention to the content of messages as well as the emotions expressed.

People from differing cultural backgrounds need to take special care to cultivate an atmosphere of equality. They should try to avoid seeing the situation entirely from their own point of view.

THE PROCESS OF COMMUNICATION

Questions: Part 1

(Answers to these questions are given on pages 491–494.)

Points for discussion

Discuss the following questions using ideas from your experience.

1. What do you understand by the statement that communication is a transaction?
2. How do people create meaning together?
3. What are the main conditions for successful communication in organizations?
4. What are the main differences between two-way and one-way communication?
5. Is two-way communication better than one-way communication? Give reasons for your answer.
6. Explain the main differences between intrapersonal, interpersonal and small-group communication.
7. What do you understand by the term 'public' communication? What are the differences between public and mass communication?
8. Explain the terms 'sender', 'receiver', 'message', 'medium' and 'channel'.
9. What do you understand by the term 'barriers to effective communication'? Explain how breakdowns in communication occur. Give examples from your experience of breakdowns in communication.
10. How would you ensure the best possible communication between people of different cultures?

Exercises

1. Choose any group of which you have been a member. You may, for example, choose a sports team, a classroom group or your family. Analyse the communication in that group. Do you think that it is or was effective? Back up your answer with careful arguments. Give examples to illustrate your arguments.
2. Choose an interpersonal experience that you feel was unsuccessful. Using a communication model, describe the barriers to effective communication that you experienced.
3. Choose an example of interpersonal communication that you thought was successful. Using a model of communication, analyse what you think the reasons are for the success of the communication.
4. Think of an important message that you wish to convey to someone else. Using the following elements of the model from this chapter, analyse how you will communicate this message:
   - sender
   - receiver

- message
- code
- medium
- channel

5. Observe yourself as a communicator. Analyse your communication during one day and write notes about your performance. In particular, analyse your performance as a sender and receiver of messages. Did you create any barriers to effective communication? What were they? What was the quality of your feedback? What kinds of messages did you send out?

PART 2

Communication in Organizations

CHAPTER 3

Communication in Organizations

Summary

Effective communication is central to all organizations. Communication makes organizations possible, and well-motivated people who can work together are vital for any organization. The best electronic communication systems will fail if people do not work well together.

This chapter defines an organization as a collection of people working together to reach specific goals. Individuals could not reach these goals if they worked on their own.

Six differences between organizations and other groupings are described. The chapter then describes the differences between a tall structure and a flat structure.

The chapter goes on to describe recent theories of organizations. The most recent theories stress the importance of people in organizations. Messages in organizations have productive and social value. They have to be used to get the job done, but they also have a social value. This social value helps people to work together.

Theories of motivation are then discussed. Some of these theories stress that people have needs and that these needs drive them to work so that they can fulfil them. Other theories stress that people perceive a benefit in doing something. They will then work to achieve that benefit.

Management and employees need to work together to find out:
- what employees' goals are
- what management's expectations are.

Four major types of messages are used in organizations:
- messages to maintain good relationships
- messages describing tasks
- messages giving instructions
- messages about the goals and philosophy of the organization.

The major barriers to effective message flow are described. The concepts of overloading and underloading are also described. Solutions to these problems are proposed.

The chapter also discusses the differences between culture and climate in organizations. The culture of an organization is a set of assumptions, beliefs, values and attitudes that people build up over time. An organization's culture is hard to describe because it has become part of people without their being aware of it.

Climate, on the other hand, describes the present trend of opinions, attitudes or feelings in an organization. A climate changes quite quickly as the environment in an organization changes.

Flows of information are then described. The major flows are upwards, downwards and sideways. The types of messages in each flow are described. Major barriers to upwards, downwards and sideways communication are then given.

The grapevine or informed flow of messages is discussed. Contrary to general opinion, the grapevine can serve a positive role in an organization. It serves as an important message source, and helps staff understand what is going on. However, the grapevine at its worst can spread rumours. These rumours, if acted on, can be dangerous.

The chapter then goes on to describe communication with customers, suppliers and the general public. It then discusses intercultural communication in organizations. Suggestions for avoiding barriers to effective intercultural communication are made.

Key points

- Effective communication makes organizations possible.
- An organization is defined as people working together to achieve goals they could not reach on their own.
- The structure of an organization will affect the flow of information, and how people work together.
- Management and staff need to understand each other's motivation.
- Messages about the goals and philosophy of an organization are important.
- Organizations need to guard against overloading and underloading information.
- The culture of an organization is a belief system that grows slowly over time. It is hard to describe.
- The climate in an organization is a set of current attitudes. It may change fairly quickly.
- People in organizations need to be aware of the different types of messages that flow upward, downward and sideways.
- People also need to be aware of the major barriers to good upwards, downwards and sideways communication.
- The grapevine (or informed communication network) can be useful. However, if it carries rumours that are acted on, it can be harmful.
- Organizations need to be aware of the different approaches to communication by people of different cultures.

Communication makes organizations possible

This chapter has the following objectives:

- To stress the fundamental importance of communication in organizations.
- To describe what an organization is and to summarize some recent theoretical views on organizations.
- To describe some recent theories of motivation, and the implications for communication policies.
- To discuss the importance of information and information flow in organizations.
- To discuss formal and informal channels of communication in organizations.
- To discuss intercultural communication in organizations.
- To draw together the implications of all the above for effective communication in organizations.

This book takes the view that effective communication is central to all organizations. A great deal of this communication depends on the people in an organization. Companies, for example, may have the best electronic communication system available. However, if the people operating the system are inefficient or unmotivated, the system will fail.

Communication in this book is described as a transaction. People in companies create meanings together by exchanging words and non-verbal messages. By doing this, they develop mutual expectations and begin to work as teams.

This interaction creates information and messages. These messages, in turn, create the need for more information and messages.

As the organization grows, structures have to be set up to ensure the best possible flow of messages. Effective communication enables these structures to be set up, developed and maintained. These structures, in turn, restrict the ways in which information can flow upward, downward and sideways in an organization and outwards from an organization.

This chapter briefly examines ways in which organizations are created. It also examines message flows. The implications for communication are listed at each stage.

What is an organization?

An organization is made up of groups of people who work together to reach specific goals. These goals cannot be reached by individuals working on their own.

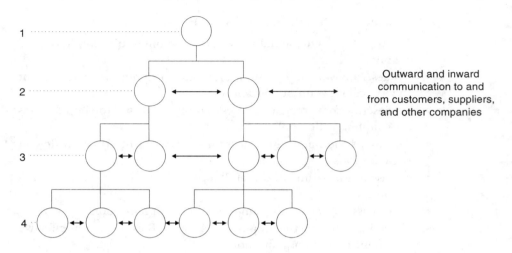

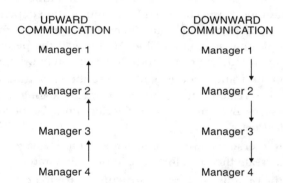

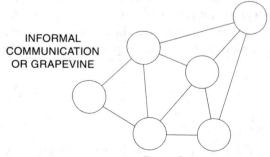

Figure 3.1
Flow of information in organizations

Six major characteristics make organizations different from other groupings:

- People do different jobs and have different responsibilities.
- There will be one or more places where power is held.
- Each post in an organization may be filled by a number of different people.
- Different sections of the organization depend on each other.
- Different sections of the organization work together to coordinate their activities.
- Different sections of the organization work together on a regular basis.

Implications for communication

- Communication systems have to be set up to ensure that the common goals can be reached.
- An atmosphere of trust has to be established to ensure that the best possible communication takes place.
- Members of the company have to be trained in the preparation and delivery of messages.

The flow of information in an organization

Figure 3.1 (opposite page) shows a typical organization. It also shows the various types of information flow that are studied in organizations.

All these types of communication will be discussed later in this Chapter.

Characteristics of organizations

The following characteristics of organizations will be described below:

- tall structure
- flat structure
- division into departments
- contracting lines of communication
- line and staff divisions.

Tall structures

Tall structures are organized to allow for a carefully controlled flow of messages up and down a hierarchy of managers and departments. Managers have tight control over their subordinates. They also control the flow of information. In tall structures the more levels there are in the hierarchy, the greater the risk of message distortion. In addition, there will be more and more rules to deal with the numbers and types of messages generated.

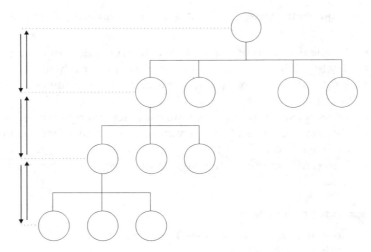

Figure 3.2
A tall structure designed for effective vertical communication

In this structure horizontal communication, or communication among managers at the same level in the hierarchy, is not encouraged, unless special arrangements have been made.

If managers did communicate horizontally this could be described as contracting lines of communication because the vertical flow of information has been bypassed. Contracting lines of communication might also refer, for example, to a junior manager who communicates directly with a senior manager, leaving out her or his immediate superior.

In general, 'contracting lines of communication' refers to any means of communication that bypasses the normal chain of command in an organization. A manager might, for example, send a direct message to a subordinate or group, and leave out people who would normally pass on such messages. Managers could do this by:

- inserting messages in pay packets
- addressing staff directly on the public address system
- calling a meeting
- sending out a notice.

If this occurs it could cause problems because those left out could be angry. It would also mean that not everyone has the same information. Managers who contract the normal lines of communication should, therefore, tell those left out what they have done.

Flat structures

In a 'flat' organization a senior manager might delegate a good deal to subordinates, and so have much less control. This type of structure, illustrated in figure 3.3, simplifies vertical communication by removing some levels in the hierarchy. Fewer distortions in messages would then result.

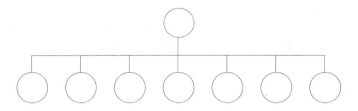

Figure 3.3
Example of flat structure

This type of organization requires a high level of communication skills in the field of conflict resolution because of the often conflicting tasks and outlooks of different sections. Communication skills in flat structures would need to be rather different from those in tall structures.

Creation of different departments

Organizations are generally divided into departments. These may be divided according to their function or according to the products they produce.

If people who do the same thing are grouped, we would, for example, find the following sections:

- personnel
- accounts
- computers
- sales.

Departments could also be divided according to product A, product B or product C. Functional departments have the advantage that they group specialists together. However, care has to be taken that departments do not defend their territories to such an extent that communication between departments becomes difficult.

Line and staff divisions

Organizations may also be described in terms of line and staff divisions. *Line* managers control the members of the company who work to achieve its goals. Line managers have expert *staff* to advise them on a range of special fields. Line managers can also delegate work to groups of staff specialists who work on specific tasks.

There are usually specialist staff in departments such as personnel, accounts, computers and research and development. All these special departments help the line managers achieve the goals of the organization.

This division between line managers and staff frequently leads to conflict. People in staff sections often feel they are treated as inferiors. On the other hand, line managers feel threatened by staff advice. They might also be put off by the over-use of technical terms used by staff sections.

Policies and procedures

Large organizations have to issue policy guidelines and procedures for regulating the flow of messages. These guidelines take the form of

- policy manuals describing the company's objectives and policies for achieving these objectives
- guidelines for departments, for example on how to write messages
- specific procedures to be followed to regulate the flow of messages
- detailed instructions for performing procedures.

Implications for communication

- An atmosphere of trust needs to be encouraged.
- Open and honest communication needs to be encouraged.
- Specialist staff need to avoid the use of obscure technical terms. They need to give their advice clearly and simply to avoid intimidating managers who are not expert in these fields.
- Line managers need to ensure that they listen and read carefully, and show that they value the advice given to them.

Theories about organizations — a brief overview

Studies of organizations in the early part of this century emphasized a rigid structure, order, and precise, scientific reasoning. They paid little attention to communication in organizations. Workers were considered to be little more than extensions of machines. Researchers assumed that a rigid and formal chain of command would be enough to get the job done.

People in organizations

Later theorizers began to stress the importance of human factors in organizations. They suggested that the existence of formal lines of communication within a formal structure was not enough to guarantee that a job would be done.

Staff members were regarded as people, rather than as machines. Theories took into account that their needs, interests, and viewpoints were important in the functioning of an organization.

These latter theorists have stressed participative styles of management that strive to generate an atmosphere of trust and confidence. If this type of atmosphere is generated, motivation will be high.

Need for open communication

If an atmosphere of participation is to be created, then there needs to be a great deal of open communication. This communication should take place in an atmosphere of trust. People also need to work together in an atmosphere of understanding. Teamwork needs to be encouraged and the goals should be set by the whole group, rather than imposed on them.

Managers need to coordinate activities and to encourage the flow of social and informative messages through the organization.

Social and productive value of messages

Organizations need to pay attention both to the social value of communication in organizations and to the productive value. The social messages in organizations are valuable for creating and maintaining relationships. The productive messages give the information that gets the job done. The social messages reflect the attitudes, beliefs and expectations of the people who run the organization. People are not predictable, and managers should understand that there is no simple way to deal with the variety of human problems found in their organization. It is important for them to be highly sensitive to people's needs.

No one best way to organize a company

Other theorists stressed that there is no one best way to organize the parts of an organization. In an unstable environment where a company has to adapt rapidly to changing demands, the best communication would be achieved if different sections were allowed to organize themselves according to their specific communication needs. For example, a research department developing new products over a long period could function very differently from a production section that had to produce goods immediately to meet immediate demands.

Sections have different needs

This differentiation causes difficulties in communication because each section has widely differing needs and perceptions. Both short-term and long-term attitudes need to be catered for in an organization. Managers need to integrate these two for the good of the company.

Managers need to have effective conflict-resolution skills in order to stop harmful interpersonal clashes. In addition, special care has to be taken to ensure that each section knows what the other section is doing and why. This places great demands on managers' and workers' interpersonal, oral and written communication skills.

On the other hand, an organization in a stable environment that does not demand rapid change, does not have to have widely differentiated communication systems. It can rely on a bureaucratic system, a rigid hierarchy of departments and standardization of communication systems.

Culture and climate in organizations

The culture and climate in an organization are very important. If the culture and climate are negative, for example, an organization will not be very successful. The differences between these two concepts will now be discussed before the flow of messages is described.

Culture

The culture in an organization refers to the pattern of basic assumptions, beliefs, attitudes and values that a group has built up. The group builds these up as it learns to cope with its problems of working as a group and adapting to the business environment. These assumptions, beliefs and values have worked well enough to be considered valid. People therefore feel that this is the correct way to perceive, think and feel in relation to their problems.

These assumptions, beliefs, attitudes and values evolve slowly over time. They have become so internalized by members that they are no longer aware of them. These assumptions, beliefs, attitudes and values become part of the collective mind of an organization.

People within a specific organizational culture will share a set of symbolic codes, for example, a language or non-verbal behaviour.

The culture becomes a conceptual framework within which an organization works.

A culture develops slowly over time. It is created by dominant founding members. As people join the organization they gradually learn the culture until it becomes part of them. Organizations tend to employ people who already hold some of the key beliefs.

Climate

A culture develops slowly and is hard to describe. The climate in an organization, on the other hand, changes quickly and is easier to describe. The climate describes the present trend of opinions, attitudes or feelings in an organization. A climate changes quite quickly as the environment changes.

Different parts of an organization may have different climates because they work under different conditions. The following will bring about changes in climate:

- Styles of management
- Pressure of work
- Available resources.

The climate in a group may change fairly rapidly from a supportive and positive one to a defensive and negative one. Managers and staff therefore need to be constantly sensitive to the climate in the group or section.

Culture and climate compared

The following table compares the key difference between culture and climate.

Culture	Climate
• Lasts a long time.	• May change quite quickly.
• Develops slowly.	• Develops quickly and changes quickly.
• Depends on a known past of some length of time.	• Does not depend on a known past.
• Operates on a higher level of unconscious assumptions.	• Operates at a level of attitudes and values.
• Collective, therefore individual variations are buried in the culture.	• Unique characteristics of members can be found.
• Not likely to be affected by short-term changes.	• Responds to short-term changes.
• Deeply buried in peoples' minds, therefore relatively invisible and hard to get at.	• Awareness more accessible and behaviour more visible.

Implications for communication

- Managers and staff need to cultivate an atmosphere of trust and open communication.
- Listening skills should be cultivated.
- People should be sensitive to each other's non-verbal communication.
- All managers and staff should become experts in the preparation and delivery of oral and written messages.

- Managers and staff should be experts in conflict resolution.

Theories of motivation in companies — a brief overview

This book argues that the hopes, feelings and aspirations of people are important. Managers therefore need to be concerned about what their staff do, how they do it and especially why they do it. Performance and motivation are linked.

Managers also need to study how and what to communicate to ensure that their staff are highly motivated. Effective communication can, for example, help someone to change her or his self-image so that (s)he looks at the world differently. Good communication combined with training can help change a worker's abilities and skills. People's goals and levels of aspiration can also be changed through effective communication.

Atmosphere of trust

At the personal level, managers need to encourage an atmosphere of . This atmosphere should reduce defensiveness. Listening skills are also very important in motivating staff.

An ideal communication style could be described as an *assertive style*. In this approach the individual is encouraged to stand up for her or his rights, but never at the expense of others. This style shows respect for oneself as well as respect for others. Individuals are encouraged to express their feelings, but without being aggressive.

Individuals should avoid a manipulative style in which they avoid threatening situations and use anger, hurt and guilt to manipulate other people's feelings.

Theories of motivation

There are many theories of motivation. They stress that people are motivated by a desire to satisfy many needs. Experts do not, however, agree on what these needs are and what their relative importance is.

This section will briefly summarize the following theories:

- Maslow's hierarchy of needs
- McClelland's theory of needs
- Hertzberg's two-factor theory
- Maccoby's managerial types
- Vroom's expectancy model.

The first two theorize that people do things in order to fill a need. Vroom's expectancy model, on the other hand, stresses that people do things because they expect to achieve what they perceive as a worthwhile goal.

Maslow's hierarchy of needs

Maslow[1] theorized that:

- People have needs and these needs form a hierarchy.
- Only when the basic need is satisfied, will people seek to satisfy the next need.
- Once a need is satisfied it no longer motivates. Only unsatisfied needs motivate.

Maslow's needs are listed in a hierarchy as shown in figure 3.4. The highest need is at the top.

Figure 3.4
Maslow's hierarchy of needs

McClelland's system of needs

McClelland[2] identified three major needs that suggest why people in organizations behave as they do:

- The need for achievement.
- The need for affiliation, or close interpersonal relationships.
- The need for power.

People with a high need for achievement are likely to seek tasks where they are fully responsible. They set goals for themselves and value competent colleagues.

People with a high need for affiliation strive to develop pleasant relationships with others. They like to work with people.

People with a high need for power are strongly involved with controlling others.

Hertzberg's two-factor theory

Hertzberg[3] developed a two-factor theory of motivation. He suggested that one group of factors, called *motivators*, was important in motivation. These factors related to the content of a job. Another group of factors, called *hygiene* factors, prevent dissatisfaction, but do not motivate. These have to do with the conditions under which the job is done.

The following are hygiene factors according to Hertzberg:

- Job security
- Working conditions
- Salary
- Company policy and administration.

If people are to be motivated they need challenging jobs that offer them personal growth, responsibility and recognition.

Managers often concentrate on hygiene factors and do not stress job enrichment.

Maccoby's management types

Maccoby[4] argued that the character and attitudes of managers are important when we are trying to understand why they do things. If top management's plans conflict with other managers' attitudes very little will be achieved.

Maccoby described four major types of character:

- *The craftsman.* Such a person is motivated by the work ethic. This person values respect for people, and is concerned about quality. He or she is a practical perfectionist, and seeks interesting work.
- *The jungle fighter.* These people are motivated by power. They see colleagues as potential partners or enemies. Subordinates will be used and then discarded.
- *The company person.* Such people are concerned for the people in an organization. They will strive to preserve the identity of an organization and derive a strong sense of identity from belonging to an organization.
- *The gamesperson.* Gamespersons like to be challenged. They thrive on competition, and like to be winners. They also enjoy taking risks and strive to motivate others. They are good team players and will be prepared to merge their goals with those of the company.

Vroom's expectancy model

Vroom[5] argues that motivation has to do with the choices people make in order to achieve their goals. People have a range of goals and therefore work differently.

Vroom uses three terms in his theory. He theorizes that major goals are not always directly achievable. They may, however, be achieved in stages.

- *Expectancy:* This describes people's estimate of the probability that their behaviour will help them to get what they want. This is described as a first-level goal.
- *Instrumentality:* This describes people's estimate of the probability that what they want will help them to reach a goal. This is described as a second-level goal.
- *Valence:* This concept describes the value of that particular goal to the individual, in comparison with other goals.

These concepts may be summed up as shown in the figure 3.5.

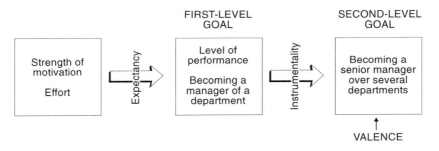

Figure 3.5
Vroom's expectancy model

This model may be explained as follows.

A person in a company has, for example, the goal of becoming a senior manager. This goal cannot, however, be achieved immediately. The person has, first of all, to work hard to become a departmental manager. Becoming a departmental manager would therefore become this person's *first-level goal*. If you have strong *expectations* that the first-level goal will be instrumental in helping you to achieve the second-level goal, then you will make a strong effort to achieve the first-level goal.

The valence of the first-level goal is determined by the degree of *instrumentality* that the person perceives between the first- and second-level goals.

If, for example, the above person feels that becoming a departmental head will have no influence on her or his chances of becoming a senior manager, (s)he may not be motivated to become a departmental head.

In other words, the individual's perceived probability of achieving the goal will motivate that person better than the goal itself.

This theory stresses that management needs to be very careful about setting goals for employees. Management may consider that these goals can be easily achieved. Employees, on the other hand, may consider that no matter how hard they work, they will not be able to reach the set goals. They will therefore not work towards those goals.

Management and employees need to communicate effectively to find out what:

- employees' goals are
- management's expectations are.

Summary of implications for communication

The above theories of motivation stress the need for managers and employees to work together to understand each other's motivations. They need to understand why people behave as they do.

They need to strive towards two-way, rather than one-way communication. Communication should be regarded as a transaction in which participants create meaning together in an atmosphere of trust. Effective listening skills need to be cultivated, as well as the ability to write clear messages.

Messages in organizations

This section discusses five major areas:

- The need for information in organizations.
- The need to structure an organization so that messages flow effectively.
- Types of messages in organizations.
- Message overload.
- Message underload.

Once these have been discussed, the chapter describes the flow of messages in organizations. This section covers vertical, horizontal and outward flows of messages.

The need to ensure good information flow

Organizations cannot exist without effective communication. This means that they need to be structured to achieve the best possible flow of information.

This structure does, however, place certain restrictions on how information flows, and the content of messages. In addition, members of an organization have different needs, perceptions and expectations. These mean that communication will not always be perfect.

For example, superiors might wish to get certain information from subordinates. The subordinates might not wish to give this information. On the other hand, subordinates might feel that they are entitled to certain information. However, superiors might feel that this information is confidential, and therefore refuse to give it to them.

Messages in organizations cover more than factual information. They also cover information about people's feelings and attitudes. When people have to work together they need to:

- find out what work needs to be done;
- tell each other about this work;
- control each other as the work progresses.

Organizations therefore have to design their communication systems to control

- the direction of messages
- the amount of information sent out to people under what conditions.

They also have to ensure that adequate feedback is received.

Types of messages in organizations

Four types of messages are found in organizations:

- Messages used to maintain good relationships.
- Messages containing information about tasks.
- Messages instructing people to do things.
- Messages about the goals, philosophy and ethics of the company.

Good relationships

These messages are not intended to give information or orders. They take the form of small talk such as:

- greetings
- comments about how people feel
- enquiries about people's health or families
- expressions of goodwill or sympathy.

All these messages are designed to keep communication going and to pave the way for future communication. They flow in all directions in a company.

Information

These messages contain information to enable the business to be run. This information needs to be as precise as possible so that people can base their decisions on accurate facts.

These messages flow in all directions in a company.

Instructions

These messages are the orders or guidelines given in a company to ensure that jobs are done. They may also include standard procedures to be followed when routine tasks are undertaken.

These messages generally flow from the top down.

Goals, philosophy and ethics

These messages contain certain guidelines to staff on the company's goals and philosophy. They also stress the ethical approach of the company to guide staff in their dealings with customers, suppliers and the general public.

These messages generally flow from the top down.

Major barriers to effective communication of messages

All those sending, receiving or passing on messages need to ensure that the message is:

- accurately heard or read and understood
- believed
- acted on.

However, even when people communicate with the greatest goodwill, messages can be distorted because of ambiguity or lack of understanding of the meaning.

The following are some of the major barriers to effective message flow:

- The number of stages through which a message has to go.
- The amount of time allowed for the message to move through the organization.
- Lack of understanding of what the message means.
- Shortening of messages because people cannot be bothered to share full information with others.
- Filtering of messages at each stage. (Each person judges what the next person should receive.)
- Deliberate distortion. (People send only what they want others to receive. They leave out information that they perceive as damaging to themselves.)
- Too much information is received at any one time. This is called overloading of information.
- Not enough information is received at any one time. This is called underloading of information.

Implications for communication

Companies need to establish the best possible conditions for distortion-free messages.

Some of these conditions are:
- Messages should be as accurate and clear as possible.
- Messages should give all the information essential to decision-makers at each stage.
- The right medium should be chosen for each type of message on each occasion. Messages could, for example, be spoken, written or graphic.
- The procedures for the giving and receiving of messages should be very clear. These should be rigidly kept to.
- There should be a clear system of authority and accountability.
- Conditions should allow for rapid transmission of messages and feedback.
- Organizations need to test the flow of information regularly. This testing will ensure that messages go where they are needed.

Overloading of information

If a person or department receives more information than (s)he or it can handle at any one time, this is called *overloading*. Overloading refers both to too much information and too complex information. If overloading happens, then messages pile up and mistakes are made in sending messages on. People also give inadequate answers or stock answers.

Some solutions to the problem of overloading

Organizations can take a number of steps to avoid overloading. They can:
- run courses to improve the ability of people to handle messages;
- encourage lower sections of the company to reduce the amount of information they send upward;
- add more communication channels;
- train staff to put messages in order of priority.

Underloading of messages

If a staff member or department does not receive enough information to do the job, this is called *underloading*. If underloading happens, the results are:
- mistakes because of inadequate information;
- boredom because people do not have enough responsibility;
- drying up of information in some channels.

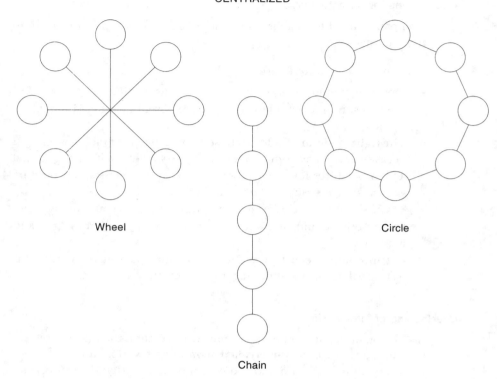
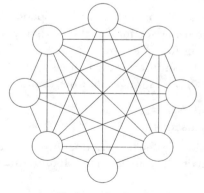

Figure 3.6
Communication networks

Some solutions to the problem of underloading

In order to prevent underloading companies can:

- ensure that all information channels are properly designed and properly used;
- ensure that each section of the company receives all the information necessary for it to operate successfully;
- ensure that staff members who work quickly and efficiently receive the right amount of information.

Flow of messages in an organization

This section discusses the flow of messages in organizations under the following headings:

- Networks
- Upward and downward flow of messages (vertical flow)
- Sideways flow of messages (horizontal flow)
- Informal channels of communication (the grapevine).

The communication in an organization has a purpose. Messages do not float around randomly. They are prepared with specific purposes in mind, have specific audiences and a specific content.

Networks

Networks in a company ensure that messages do not flow randomly. Networks are the interconnecting lines of communication used to pass information from one person or one section to another.

Networks may be classified as *centralized* or *decentralized*.

Centralized networks generally depend on one person at the centre. They are successful for simple tasks. Decentralized systems, on the other hand, do not depend on one person at the centre. Everybody communicates freely with everyone else without having to go through a central person. These networks are more successful when complex problems have to be solved.

Figure 3.6 illustrate types of networks

The *wheel structure* allows messages to be sent from the centre to each person on the outside. Each person communicates with the centre, but is unable to communicate with the other people. The chain is similar to the wheel, except that the people at the ends can communicate with only one other person. The circle allows messages to be sent to the left or right but not to other members of the circle.

The *all-channels network* allows all members to send messages to, and receive messages from, all other members.

The type of network chosen will determine the flow of messages and type of interaction.

Roles in networks

Individuals often do specific things in networks. Their tasks or roles are as follows:
- Isolate
- Liaison
- Gatekeeper
- Star
- Outside link (also called cosmopolite).

The *isolate* is a person who works on her or his own. That person may have been given a task to do that separates her or him from the group. Isolates need to ensure that they are not starved of information and contact with the rest of the network. They run the risk of not being able to work properly.

Liaison people form links between various work groups in an organization. They are critical for the effective working of an organization. Liaisons receive more feedback and have more opportunities to deal with others in their jobs.

Gatekeepers regulate the flow of information. They are able to decide what information will be sent on to other members of the network. Gatekeeping has positive and negative effects in an organization. On the positive side, a gatekeeper can prevent information overload by filtering and screening messages. On the negative side, a gatekeeper can screen out important messages. The gatekeeper's power lies in the control of access to messages.

Stars are the focus of most of the communication within the group. They have many relationships with other members. In an organization, stars tend to have a great deal of on-the-job influence with most group members. Sometimes their role is labelled as *opinion leader*. Opinion leaders are powerful and respected, and they are followed without having any formal leadership role.

An *outside link* or *cosmopolite* has a high degree of communication with the group's and the organization's environment. They give information to surrounding groups or to other businesses. They also bring information back into the group. By reporting outside information to the network they keep it going. Through contacts outside the system the cosmopolite brings vital information into the network about the activities of the environment within which the organization works.

Upward and downward flow of information

The vertical flow of information is crucial for the running of a company. This network allows for the giving of instructions and the receiving of feedback.

Downward communication

Messages sent from managers to subordinates generally have eight basic purposes:

- to describe the company's goals, philosophy and mission;
- to describe the company's ethical standpoint;
- to describe general company policies and procedures;
- to describe employees' relationships with the company;
- to instruct people on how to do a job;
- to give information on how one job is related to others being performed in a company;
- to give people feedback on how successful previous jobs have been;
- to give departments and individuals feedback on their general performance.

Types of messages in downward communication

Managers use the following types of messages when they communicate downward:

- oral and written instructions
- policy manuals
- memoranda
- reports
- notices
- in-house magazines or newspapers
- specifications
- inserts in pay packets.

Possible topics in downward communication

Management should handle topics such as:

- benefit programmes for employees
- a list of the company's products and how they are used
- careful descriptions of the types of relationships that management wishes to have with employees
- analyses of strikes
- records of union–management negotiations
- information on the company's dependence on customers
- existing rumours
- the company's viewpoint on issues
- social news
- instructions for performing tasks
- safety programmes
- contemplated changes in staff and production.

Barriers to effective downward communication

The following are the major barriers to effective downward communication:

- Managers are not sure what types of messages to pass down downward.
- Managers are not sure how much information to pass downward.
- Organizations have problems with the functional literacy of their staff.
- Information passed downward is not always relevant.
- Too much information is sent downward.

Functional literacy

'Functional literacy' refers to a person's ability to read and prepare the messages necessary *for a specific job*. These messages enable a manager, for example, to function as a manager. This manager has to be more than literate. (S)he must, for example, be able to:

- Read a long complex financial report containing graphics.
- Prepare a monthly report.
- Prepare letters and memoranda in the right style and tone.
- Prepare and deliver short, persuasive talks to customers.
- Talk on the telephone.

In some organizations up to 10 % of managers could be functionally illiterate.

Upward communication

Managers need to encourage a two-way flow of information so that they can judge how well their messages have been received.

The main purposes of *upward* communication are:

- to receive feedback on how well their messages have been received
- to receive feedback on the progress of tasks
- to receive feedback on employees' attitudes, motivation and perceptions
- to receive suggestions from staff
- to check on individual performance
- to receive proposals from staff.

Types of messages in upward communication

The following are the main types of messages involved in upward communication:

- oral and written reports
- memoranda
- proposals
- spoken and written suggestions.

Barriers to effective upward communication

The following are the most serious barriers to effective upward communication:

- Senders of messages fear that they will be seen as incompetent.
- Senders fear the response of 'you raised the problem, you solve it'.
- Messages are distorted as they move up the hierarchy. People leave out parts of messages that they think will harm them. They then send the rest of the message upward. People also accept parts of messages that please them, and ignore the rest.
- Managers are more likely to use and pass on messages that are positive, are appropriate to the situation and support present policy. They also accept and pass on messages that they feel are right.
- Employees keep quiet and do not pass on messages because they fear for their jobs.

Lateral or sideways communication

When two managers or departments at the same level in a company communicate, this is called *lateral communication.*

Lateral communication implies communication between equals such as department heads, or between similar departments.

If lateral communication is encouraged, management needs to decide:

- who is to be informed of which department's activities
- the amount of detail to be reported
- the medium to be used for this type of communication.

Much of this communication will take place through face-to-face discussions. In addition, reports and memoranda are used.

In some organizations it is difficult to communicate horizontally without sending messages upward to let people know what is going on. This might lead to overloading higher up.

Lateral communication can lead to problems. Different departments have a wide variety of tasks. These tasks give each one a different set of perceptions and a different point of view.

These differences could lead to rivalry and a reluctance to communicate. Departments use specialist vocabularies. These could make communication difficult. All these differences could also lead to conflict.

Managers therefore need to be sensitive in their choice of a technical vocabulary when they communicate laterally. In addition, they need to have a knowledge of conflict-resolution skills.

Barriers to effective sideways communication

The following are the major barriers to effective sideways communication:

- Rivalry between departments means that they withhold information from each other.
- Departments can become very specialized (for example, a computer department). People from other departments cannot understand their technical terms.
- Departments become isolated and are not motivated to communicate with other departments. Staff are not rewarded for good sideways communication
- Departments build their own small empires. They are reluctant to share their knowledge and resources with other departments.

Informal communication or grapevine

Sometimes staff in an organization find that the prescribed patterns of communication do not give them the information that they want. They will then establish their own informal communication system. This informal system, or *grapevine*, is particularly common when people work closely together.

The grapevine conveys information about people and their attitudes and relationships. It also carries interpretations of events, predictions about company moves, people's values and needs.

The grapevine fills an information void. It gives meaning to activities within an organization. It has three major functions:

- It serves as a barometer regarding the organization. It gives vital feedback to management regarding the organization.
- It serves as an important message source. The grapevine is most active when there are great changes in an organization. It is also active when information is new and when face-to-face communication is easy.
- It helps members of an organization to make sense of what is going on. As messages travel through the grapevine, management's messages are translated into words that make sense to workers.

A superficial view of the grapevine, then, is that it follows no set pattern of content or direction. Many managers assume that the information moving along the grapevine does not reflect credit on the company, is often inaccurate and causes problems.

Laboratory and company research suggest, however, that the grapevine need not be a meandering, uncertain and unreliable channel of communication; it can be fast and predictable in its direction and membership. It can also be more accurate than superficial observation might suggest.

There are three specific attributes of the grapevine that make it important and useful:

- It is fast.
- It is accurate: 75–90 % accuracy for non-controversial information.
- It carries a great deal of information. For example, it allows people to send messages that do not fit into the formal channels of communication. It also carries messages that develop relationships and create a sense of belonging.

Managers can, therefore, tell a great deal about the mood of their staff if they pay attention to the grapevine. At its best the grapevine allows people to blow off steam. It can also boost morale by uniting staff. The grapevine is very important when staff are interested in new policies or procedures. This is particularly so when there is some information available on the above changes.

Biases and judgements can then be removed as the information passes along the grapevine.

However, the grapevine at its worst can spread rumours. Rumours often convey prejudices, emotions and half-truths. They are often biased towards the rumour spreaders. Rumours are based on unverified information with very little supporting evidence. The greater the stress in an organization, the greater the likelihood of rumours.

Rumours can take on a life of their own. They can threaten an organization if they are taken as true and acted on.

Outward communication

Business organizations have to serve customers to survive. In addition, they have to communicate with the general public and with suppliers. All these activities could be termed *outward communication*.

Much of this communication takes the following forms:

- face-to-face discussion
- telephone calls
- meetings
- formal written reports
- formal written proposals
- letters
- press releases
- advertisements.

Companies have to ensure that they analyse the needs of their audience. In particular, their style of communication should stress the great importance of customers.

Members of organizations involved in face-to-face work, meetings or telephone calls, need to cultivate effective speech and non-verbal behaviour. Letters should stress service to the customer and should be written in a friendly or neutral tone.

A great deal of attention should be paid to the organization of messages.

Intercultural communication in organizations

The issues of intercultural communication are becoming more important as more and more people from different cultures work together in businesses. In addition, companies are increasingly involved in international trade. People's cultural backgrounds strongly influence their values at work and their communication styles.

Indeed culture is probably more important than people's professions, and roles in business.

Businesses can therefore no longer afford to regard a single cultural approach as the dominant one. The traditional western linear communication model, as discussed in Chapter 1, is not able to show all the complexities of intercultural communication. Other models will have to be developed.

This section discusses the following issues in intercultural communication:

- a definition of a culture;
- problems that affect communication when people from different cultures work together;
- different cultural approaches to:
  - time
  - rhetorical styles
  - media selection
  - management;
- what companies can do to encourage effective intercultural communication.

A definition of culture

A culture may be defined as a system of beliefs, assumptions and values shared by a group of people. These people will also share a set of symbolic codes, for example a language.

This group of people will also share a view of themselves and of the world.

Intercultural communication in a company takes place when a person from one culture communicates, or tries to communicate, with a person from another culture.

Problems with different cultures working together

If a company has one cultural approach as the dominant one, then troubles could arise. These troubles are not simply ones of language. Intercultural communication covers a wide variety of attitudes, perceptions and values. Even when people of different cultural backgrounds speak the same language they may not be able to communicate very well.

These difficulties could become so serious that people in a company become disunited. They then do not work together to achieve the company's goals.

Ethnocentrism is an approach that sees everything from one cultural viewpoint. Ethnocentrism can lead to the following reactions:

- People may feel uncomfortable working with others from different cultures.
- People regard their culture as superior.
- People may then become patronizing towards others from cultures that they feel are inferior to their own.
- People become insensitive to what other cultures regard as relevant and valuable.
- People misinterpret the actions of people from other cultures and may break valued rules of behaviour.

People also tend to judge a culture by the behaviour of individuals from that culture. This is called *stereotyping*.

Stereotyping can lead to rigid thinking about other cultures. This can lead to suspicion and breakdowns in communication.

Different approaches to communication

Cultures view time in different ways. Some cultures view time as a straight line, flowing like a river. This view stresses that time must be carefully planned and not wasted. Time is not viewed as renewable.

This view of time favours a style of communication which:

- values getting to the point quickly;
- values quick responses in discussion with very little introductory phrasing or politeness;
- divides tasks into units of time;
- favours direct bad-news letters.

Other cultures view time as renewable and flexible. It is not like a line, but more like a circle. It is not subject to waste, since there is no beginning or end.

This view of time favours a style of communication which:

- values an unhurried approach to negotiations;

- values an approach to priorities not governed totally by the passing of time;
- allows a more indirect approach to conversations or written messages;
- allows business talk to go off at a tangent so that all information can be seen in its proper perspective or context.

This cultural approach to time may view a direct approach as rude. It could also be regarded as unclear because it has not been developed fully.

Styles of communication

Cultures differ in what they see as clearly reasoned or logical.

One culture may value an approach that favours directness and confrontation. It may also value practical experience.

Another culture may favour a more indirect approach that favours agreement above confrontation. Decisions could be based more on feelings and intuitions. This approach favours the maintenance of group harmony.

One culture may favour the use of *electronic means* of communication. This approach would stress the use of written messages over face-to-face communication and spoken messages. Messages would be expected to be specific, exact and carefully argued. Specific rules and regulations for the running of a company are valued.

Another culture could rely more on *face-to-face* communication and spoken messages. This approach could mean that parts of messages are left unspecified. People would be expected to interpret more of what has been said. This approach might not emphasize the use of rules and regulations to the same extent.

One culture may value productivity, competition and monetary gain, whereas another may value quality of life, social welfare and cooperation.

One culture may stress the value of personal time and individual responsibility. Another culture may value a supportive work environment and group responsibilities.

Finally, one culture may value a rigid hierarchical structure where decisions are made from the top downward. Another culture, on the other hand, may value an egalitarian work environment with participative management.

What can companies do about the variety of cultural needs?

Those creating company policy need to ask two questions:

- How can people with different cultural backgrounds work together to create a company?
- How can the organization ensure that cultural values and approaches to communication are respected?

Companies could do the following:

- Strive to create an atmosphere of trust in which different approaches are respected.
- Stress that effective communication starts with individuals in face-to-face situations.
- Encourage free discussions on how different cultures view situations and approaches to communication.
- Draw up dictionaries of terms or concepts used in the organization. Show that definitions of these may differ.
- Stress that different approaches to communication are to be respected.
- Conduct regular discussions to try to reconcile different approaches to communication.
- Strive to accommodate different approaches to communication within the day-to-day running of the company.
- Encourage staff to be non-judgmental and empathetic listeners.
- Encourage staff to be sensitive to non-verbal behaviour.
- Encourage staff to strive for the best possible communication. They should be tolerant of mistakes and be prepared to ask for help when they know that the communication is not going well.
- Encourage, if possible, the learning of languages spoken by other cultural groups in the company.

Questions: Part 2

(Answers to these questions are given on pages 495–498.)

Points for discussion

1. How can companies organize themselves to ensure the best possible communication?
2. From your experience, what are the major barriers to effective communication in companies?
3. Explain the terms 'vertical' and 'horizontal' communication in companies.
4. What is meant by the term 'grapevine' as it applies to communication in companies? Is the 'grapevine' a good or bad means of communication? Justify your answer.
5. How do you think people are motivated to work hard? Is it possible to motivate people? Give examples to back up your answer.
6. What is meant by the term 'intercultural communication'? How can companies ensure the best possible intercultural communication?
7. Explain the terms 'overloading' and 'underloading' as they apply to information. How would you ensure that they do not take place?
8. What is meant by the term 'network' in a company? Give examples of networks.

Exercises

1. Examine an organization with which you are familiar. List all the positions in the organization. Then describe the communication networks, paying special attention to vertical and horizontal communication.
2. Find an organization where you are allowed to observe for two or three days. Try to establish the formal and informal communication networks. Decide whether the formal networks are effective or not. If they are ineffective, how would you improve them?
3. Examine the communication in a committee or team to which you belong. Decide how effective or ineffective it is. If it is ineffective how would you improve the channels of communication?
4. Examine your own cultural values. How do these affect your communication style and your approach to time? Ask someone from another cultural group what her or his communication needs are. If you were working together in a company, what would your communication policy be?
5. Visit a number of organizations. Ask people what they think the major barriers to communication are. What policy decisions would you take to eliminate these barriers?

References

1. Maslow, A: *Motivation and Personality.* New York: Harper and Row, 1954.
2. McClelland, D.C: *The Achieving Society.* New York: Van Nostrand Reinhold, 1964.
3. Hertzberg F., Mausner B., and Block Snyderman B.: *The Motivation to Work* 2nd ed. New York, John Wiley and Sons, 1959.
4. Maccoby, M: *The Gamesman* New York: Simon and Schuster, 1976.
5. Vroom, VH: *Work and Motivation.* New York: John Wiley and Sons Inc., 1964.

PART 3

Small-Group Communication

•

Formal Meetings

CHAPTER 4

Small-group Communication

Summary

A small group is defined as a number of people who have gathered together with a goal in mind. They may meet once only or over an extended period.

People in groups develop a set of values and norms that help them to work together. Groups at their best benefit a company because they allow people to work together to achieve the company's goals.

This chapter describes six types of groups:

- Informal groups:
  - conversational groups
  - tension-releasing groups
- Formal groups:
  - learning groups
  - policy-making groups
  - problem-solving groups
  - decision-making groups.

The characteristics of groups that work well are described. These are:

- a supportive climate
- effective interaction of members
- effective methods of getting the job done.

Stages in the development of groups are described.

The chapter then describes various theories of leadership. It goes on to describe four leadership styles. Effective leadership stresses the importance of the task and the interaction of members of the group.

After describing the characteristics of ineffective groups, the chapter describes conflict in groups. Conflict can have positive or negative results according to the ways in which it is approached. Conflict may be avoided or confronted. Three different approaches to conflict are then described:

- win–lose
- lose–lose
- win–win.

Key points

- Effective groups share a common goal. People in these groups interact well together to solve problems. They develop a set of norms and values that keep the group together.
- Groups at their best can benefit a company because people work together to achieve the company's goals.
- Groups, to work well, need:
  - a supportive climate
  - effective interaction of members
  - effective methods of getting the job done.
- Leaders may be appointed or may emerge in a group.
- Leaders may adopt various styles to get work done.
- Leaders should pay attention both to the task and to the needs of the people in the group.
- Conflict may be approached in a positive or negative way.
- The ideal resolution to conflict is a win–win solution, in which both sides reach their goals.

SMALL-GROUP COMMUNICATION

Introduction

Small groups are an essential part of any organization. They vary a great deal in size and structure. They may, for example, take the following forms:

- A formal meeting of the whole company with the Managing Director as chairperson.
- An Annual General Meeting of Shareholders with a chairperson and fixed agenda.
- A small group of seven managers who have gathered to solve a particular problem.
- A group of twenty staff members who have gathered for a one-day seminar to learn a new computer technique.

This section covers the following aspects of groups. It stresses the implications for communication at each stage.

- A definition of a group.
- The advantages of groups at their best.
- Types of groups.
- Characteristics of groups that work well.
- Phases in the development of groups.
- Leadership in groups.
- Conflict in groups and ways of managing conflict.
- Formal meetings.
- Methods of ensuring that meetings are effective.
- Duties of Chairperson, Secretary and Treasurer.
- Rules for the conduct of meetings.
- Notices of meetings, Agendas and Minutes.

Definition of a group

A group may be defined as a number of people who have gathered together with a goal in mind. These people may be together for a single meeting or may meet over an extended period. Such a group may or may not have an appointed leader.

The individuals in the group:

- share a common goal;
- interact together, sometimes over an extended period;
- develop a set of values and norms within the group;
- are prepared to take risks in the group;
- develop behaviour in the group that would not be seen outside the group.

This definition stresses that the group needs a purpose. It also stresses that the members interact to reach a decision. It therefore applies more to a smaller group than to a large Annual General Meeting that is run according to a set of procedural rules.

Styles of communication will also vary a great deal according to the size of the group. In a small group of five, for example, there will be a great deal more interaction than in a large meeting. For this reason, there is a separate section on meetings that are run according to a set of rules.

Advantages of groups

Managers use groups to get advice, to help them reach decisions and to apply these decisions. A wise manager knows that staff will be much better motivated if they are part of the decision-making process.

Groups at their best enable people to:
- get to know each other
- work well together
- exchange information, ideas, opinions and attitudes
- stimulate each other
- become involved in common tasks
- work together to achieve the company's goals.

Implications for communication

If groups are to work well, then managers and staff need to ensure that:
- effective listening takes place
- people are sensitive to each others' needs
- individuals are allowed to express themselves freely
- individuals hear each other out
- a supportive climate is developed
- people value each other
- people express themselves clearly and openly
- people acknowledge each others' contributions as valuable.

Types of groups

Six major kinds of groups occur in companies:
- *Informal groups*, for example
  - people engaging in small talk, or
  - tension-releasing groups.
- *Formal groups*, for example
  - learning groups
  - policy-making groups
  - problem-solving groups
  - decision-making groups.

A wide variety of communication styles will be found in these groups. Some groups, for example, will have a leader in charge. In other groups all members may have equal power. They will communicate to reach a consensus. Another group, such as a learning group, may need guidance from an instructor or seminar leader.

Managers and staff need to become aware of this variety of styles so that they are flexible.

Informal groups

These are *casual groups* without leaders. They gather informally, for example in a tea room or staff dining room. People simply get together for an informal chat and engage in small talk.

Informal lines of communication are developed. These then form part of the grapevine, which has already been discussed.

Informal groups are very important in a company. The informal contact made helps people get to know each other better. They also develop trust. These relationships will help them form better working groups in the future. These groups also help to draw in people who might otherwise become outsiders.

Tension-releasing groups

These groups are also informal. They have no leader. They gather together from time to time because of some event in the company that has caused tension.

These groups are important because they help people to discuss their anger and tension. In this way they serve as an outlet for tensions that could cause great problems if allowed to continue.

They are also important because people learn to understand each other better and to interact better.

Formal groups

Learning groups

These groups are more formal. They will usually have an appointed instructor or leader who guides the learning. Specific staff will be appointed to the group.

Learning groups are very important in companies because staff both increase their knowledge, and learn to:

- evaluate ideas
- define problems
- work together and stimulate each other
- cope with new information.

Policy-making groups

These are formal groups that work together to:
- decide on company policy
- create rules for the company
- plan for the future.

They will normally have an appointed leader and could follow an agenda. Members of such groups have to communicate responsibly. They have to be sensitive to each others' views and have to be highly skilled at evaluating information.

Such groups need to cultivate a supportive climate if they are to work well.

Problem-solving groups

These are formal groups set up to solve problems. They will normally have a leader who has an agenda.

These groups will be strongly oriented to the task. They have available a number of problem-solving procedures. Three of the main ones are described below. They will work best if they strive to reach consensus rather than having a decision forced on them by the leader.

Procedure 1
- Define the problem.
- Decide on the objectives of the department or company.
- Generate possible solutions to solve the problem.
- Evaluate each solution in terms of the objectives.
- Decide on the solution that best meets the objectives.
- Where possible, the group should evaluate the results.

Procedure 2

The leader may wish to avoid strong disagreement at the beginning of a problem-solving meeting. (S)he may then follow the Delphi Method:
- Everyone is asked to write down the main problems. No discussion is allowed at this stage.
- If the problem has already been decided on, people are asked to write down their solutions to the problem.
- All these problem statements or solutions are collected and listed.
- A list is given to each person.
- Each person rates the problems or solutions in order of importance.
- These rankings are put together for everyone.
- The group then discusses the rankings and strives to reach consensus on their relative importance. If possible, they avoid taking a vote.

Procedure 3

If the problem is more complex, group members could:
- analyse the problem.
- describe an ideal state in which the problem has been solved.
- analyse all the forces that are preventing their reaching the ideal state.
- analyse all the forces that could help them reach their ideal state.
- analyse how the helping forces could be used to overcome the negative forces.
- choose the best approach to reach the ideal situation.

A problem-solving group may, for example, meet to solve a problem of falling sales or high staff resignations.

Decision-making groups

These groups are formal. They will have a leader whose task is to see that policies are put into practice.

These groups could be working under pressure. Their decisions could well be unpopular. They will therefore focus strongly on the task, and will have long and serious discussions. They will have to make sure that they have the best information for making decisions.

A decision-making group may, for example, have to decide on whom to make redundant.

Characteristics of groups that work well

Informal and formal groups have one thing in common. If they are to work well together, members of the group need to interact effectively.

Effective communication is thus very important both for getting the task done and for ensuring that the people involved work well together.

If the group starts as leaderless, then each member of the group is responsible for seeing that he or she works well with the others. If a leader has been appointed, then that person is responsible.

Three conditions for effective groups

Groups need three conditions for effective decision-making:
- A supportive climate.
- Effective interaction of members. This interaction is called group maintenance or the process role of the group.
- Effective methods of getting the job done. These methods are called the task role of the leader or the group.

Supportive climate

If members wish to create a supportive climate in the group, they need to do the following:
- Strive to be non-judgmental of others' statements or ideas.

- Focus on the problem, rather than on personalities in the group.
- Strive to be honest and to respect the worth of others.
- Be willing to share responsibility with the rest of the group.
- Strive to explore issues rather than take sides.
- Strive to create a cohesive group.
- Work towards group, rather than individual goals.
- Strive to listen to others.
- Encourage questions with a great deal of give and take.

Effective interaction of members

Leaders need to pay a great deal of attention to maintaining good group interaction. In particular they should:
- encourage members to share ideas
- ensure, where possible, that hidden agendas are brought into the open (hidden agendas refer to individual motives that are not made clear to the group — a person with a hidden agenda may seek, for example, to manipulate a group)
- try to overcome differences when they occur
- ensure that everyone has a chance to be heard
- set the standards for the group
- stress the value of every contribution
- encourage good listening
- relieve tensions when they arise
- draw out quiet members of the group.

Getting the job done

If the group has to perform a task, then the leader and members should:
- suggest new ideas or approaches
- encourage the seeking and giving of information and opinions
- encourage the clarifying of ideas
- co-ordinate information
- define the progress of discussions
- summarize past discussions
- test to see if the group is ready to decide on the actions
- encourage consensus, rather than voting.

Implications for communication

Members of groups should ensure that they:
- listen as carefully as they can
- hear people out
- show that they value the ideas, opinions and values of others
- are sensitive to the non-verbal communication of others
- ensure good eye-contact

- speak clearly with a good choice of words
- use positive, supporting words, rather than critical words
- ensure that every person has a turn to speak
- record ideas accurately.

Stages of group development

Communication in groups will not always be perfect. Groups go through stages as they develop, and each stage will demand different styles of communication.

These stages may be described as follows:

- Stage 1: Members of the groups meet each other and start to break the ice. They start to create the rules for working together.
- Stage 2: This stage is marked by conflict. Group members are settling into their roles in the group. They may rush into problem solving before they have identified the problem properly. Some members may show frustration and even anger.
- Stage 3: If the group has worked out rules for interaction, they will now start negotiating seriously. They will start exploring ways to solve the problem, for example.
- Stage 4: If the communication in the group remains good, members will now work well together to find a solution to the problem.

Leaders in groups need to be able to handle these phases and steer the group to the most effective decisions. Members of groups also need to be aware of these phases so that they are prepared for them.

Leadership in groups

Some groups may get together without a leader. If the group has a serious task to perform, a leader may emerge. This leader is called an *emergent leader*. The group confers leadership status on this person. This person may not, however, remain the leader of this group in a different situation.

Other group meetings may be called by appointed leaders. These are called *designated leaders*. Problems can arise in groups with such leaders, if another person emerges as a leader. The two could clash if they do not understand what has happened.

Styles of leadership

Leaders do not act in the same way. They have a range of different styles, all of which will affect the ways in which they communicate.

The major styles of leadership may be described as follows:

- autocratic

- bureaucratic
- democratic
- laissez-faire.

The *autocratic* leader tends to give orders without much give and take in the group. Such leaders are strongly task-oriented and have strong views on how the task is to be accomplished. Conflict may arise in such groups if the members do not respect the leader.

The *bureaucratic* leader leads according to the rule-book. This approach is successful for most routine tasks, but can lead to stifling of original discussion if the task becomes complex. This style might also be adopted by an incompetent leader or by someone who lacks confidence.

Democratic leaders try to guide, rather than direct a group. They encourage full participation by all members of the group. They expect members of the group to reach decisions. Such groups are effective at solving complex problems because they are creative. However, they might not be all that efficient because of the time needed for all opinions to be heard and evaluated.

Laissez-faire leaders do not direct groups. Instead, they observe the group, and record what is going on. They give advice when it is needed. This approach to leadership is very effective for a group of highly motivated and creative people who are keen and able to get on with the job without being directed.

Theories of leadership

Researchers have tried to establish what makes a leader. If this is known, it would help a great deal in the selection of group leaders and the appointment of managers.

This section summarizes three theories of leadership and then outlines the implications for communication.

Trait theory

Early researchers in the field of communication theory tried to list a set of traits that they thought were important in leaders. They listed such traits as intelligence, self-assurance and empathy. They could not, however, agree on a suitable list.

The trait theory was not very helpful, since having a number of so-called leadership traits does not guarantee good leadership. Studies in leadership needed to approach the problem differently.

The functional approach

This approach examines and describes the *functions* that leaders would have to perform if they were to be good leaders.

These functions are divided into:

- task functions
- group maintenance functions
- functions that do not help the group.

The task and maintenance functions have already been discussed. Some of the unhelpful functions are listed below:[1]

- being aggressive
- interfering with the progress of the group
- competing with the rest of the group
- making personal statements that are irrelevant to the group
- seeking sympathy for one's situation
- withdrawing from the discussions
- joking inappropriately.

Blake and Mouton further refined this theory and produced a managerial grid which stressed that effective leadership demands equal attention to the task and the needs of the people in the group.[2]

The grid is shown in figure 4.1.

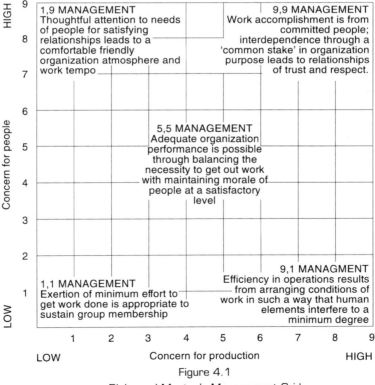

Figure 4.1
Blake and Mouton's Management Grid

This grid stresses that concern for people and concern for production should go together. Blake and Mouton recommended an ideal situation in which high production is achieved through people who are committed to the company.

The explanations in the other corners suggest that either an over zealous stress on production or on the interests of people will not be enough to achieve maximum productivity.

Implications for communication

This approach stresses the need for attention in a group to be paid both to the task and to the process functions.

The grid helps people to analyse the situation in a company. Steps can then be taken to adjust it.

The contingency approach

This approach stresses that approaches to leadership depend on three areas:

- the leader's style
- the needs of the group members
- the environment in which the group is working.

This approach suggests that approaches to leadership need to be flexible.

The leader. The leader has a particular level of intelligence, values, needs and goals. (S)he also has information.

The group. Members of the group also have needs, goals, values and attitudes. All these will affect the ways in which the group works.

The environment. The group works in an environment of company policy, norms and values. Members may have had little or a great deal of experience working together.

All these factors will affect the way in which a group works together.

Implications for communication

The contingency approach suggests that leaders need to be flexible in their approach. A group that is not experienced and does not have much information may need a leader to drive them to get the task done.

As the group becomes more experienced, the leader may pay much more attention to the relationships in the group. (S)he will also stress the need for the task to be done.

At a later stage, as tasks are completed, the leader will pay a great deal of attention to the relationships in the group.

SMALL-GROUP COMMUNICATION

Finally, as the group matures in experience and works well together, the leader may have to give only minimum attention to the task and the relationships in the group.

All these approaches will make different communication demands on the leader and members of the group.

Ineffective groups

Some groups do not work well. Two major aspects of groups affect the way in which they work:

- a destructive climate in the group
- a desire to maintain group cohesion at all costs.

Destructive climate

A destructive climate in a group will develop if members do not:

- value each others' contributions
- listen properly
- allow turn-taking.

Other characteristics of a destructive climate are:

- the passing of judgment on others' ideas and values instead of being non-judgmental
- manipulation of the proceedings for personal reasons that are kept hidden from the rest of the group (i.e. a hidden agenda)
- a superior attitude towards others in the group
- a dogmatic approach that rejects others' ideas as worthless
- a refusal to work with others on an equal basis.

Maintaining group cohesion at all costs

If a group decides to maintain its cohesion at all costs, then the group may become blind to its weaknesses.

This attitude may lead to:

- a refusal to accept any ideas that might change the group's present position
- an acceptance of only those ideas that support the group's views
- a refusal to think critically
- an illusion that the group's position can never be challenged
- reacting to others and their ideas as if they are the 'enemy'
- a denial of ethical responsibility
- an assumption that everyone else holds the same beliefs as they do.

Implications for communication

If a leader notes any of the above symptoms, then (s)he needs to:
- analyse the situation with the group
- encourage the development of a supportive climate
- encourage all members to state their points of view, even if these might not agree with the group's current thinking.

Conflict in groups

Conflict is inevitable when people work together. People may have strong views on how a project should be managed, for example. They may also have different leadership styles, different values and different needs. All these will lead to conflict.

Conflict may be approached from two points of view:
- *Negative approach to conflict*
  Conflict is always destructive and should be avoided because it is a sign of incompetence in a company.
- *Positive approach to conflict*
  Conflict may be used in a constructive way to stimulate better interaction and new approaches to solving problems.

The negative approach to conflict in companies leads to an attitude that conflict is caused by a few undesirable people. No conflict in a company is considered to be a sign of competence. Conflict is linked to the undesirable characteristics of anger, aggression and violence.

The positive approach views conflict as natural in an organization. Some degree of conflict can be helpful, provided that it is properly handled. Conflict can lead to better participation, higher motivation and greater creativity.

Proper handling of conflict can lead to the development of procedures for improved management of conflict in the future.

This view also recognizes that conflict can be harmful if people become so involved that they cannot concentrate on their work. Conflict can also lead to fear of being different. People then support what they regard as the safe position. If conflict is allowed to continue, then people will:
- withhold information
- stay away
- leave the company.

Types of conflict

People in organizations need to recognize that there are different types of conflict. Conflict may be described from two points of view:

- the people involved
- the type of conflict.

The people involved

If conflict is described from the first point of view, then it may be divided as follows:

- *Personal conflict.* This conflict is within people. They have conflicting needs, for example, and may not be able to meet all of these at once.
- *Interpersonal conflict.* This conflict is caused by differences in attitudes and experience in a company. People may be competing for scarce resources. They may also have to work with other people whom they do not like or who try to dominate them. This type of conflict can be destructive if people attack each other.
- *Organizational conflict.* As organizations become larger and more complex, conflict caused by people's different roles and functions cannot be avoided. People become cut off from others, and find it difficult to see things from their point of view.

The type of conflict

Conflict can also be described according to its type. It may, for example, be described as:

- value conflict
- content conflict.

Value conflict can be destructive, because people regard their values as fundamental to their existence. These are basic beliefs that people are very reluctant to change. In this type of conflict people may have to accept that it cannot be resolved easily. They need to work to find other areas of agreement.

Content conflict describes a conflict over what people view as facts or opinions. This type of conflict can be more easily resolved, provided personalities are not attacked.

Approaches to managing conflict

People may approach the management of conflict in two different ways:

- avoiding the conflict
- confronting the conflict.

Avoiding conflict

People avoid the conflict because they feel that they cannot handle it. They smooth over the differences and hope that the conflict will go away.

People may also try to postpone resolution of the conflict until the anger has disappeared.

This approach may help in a small way, but it does not allow people to settle the most important issues.

Confronting conflict

If people decide to confront the problem they could take three major approaches. They could:

- try to win, without considering the other side (win–lose)
- attempt a compromise solution (lose–lose)
- approach the conflict with the view that both sides can win (win–win).

Win–lose approach. This approach is based on power. One side or person uses authority to defeat the other side or person. This approach is only short-term, and can cause a great deal of anger.

Lose–lose. This approach is sometimes called a compromise approach. Each side makes some concessions, but nobody is completely satisfied. This approach is useful in the short term, but can lead to a great deal of dissatisfaction in the long run.

Win–win. This approach stresses that all parties can win if the conflict is handled carefully. The ideal approach here is that all parties sit on one side of the table solving the common problem. All sides focus on the problem, rather than proving who is right or wrong. They strive to work towards a common goal that will satisfy everybody. An atmosphere of trust is created.

Implications for communication

Those involved in conflict need to:

- analyse the type of conflict
- try to create an atmosphere of trust
- strive towards a win–win approach
- encourage all-channels networks in the group
- encourage effective listening
- acknowledge the values and interests of others
- encourage a clear statement of the problems
- strive to use language that is neutral rather than disparaging
- show verbally and non-verbally that they are concerned about others.

References

1. *Adult Leadership.* 1953: 18, pp. 17–18.
2. Blake, RR and Mouton, JS. "Managerial Facades". *Advanced Management Journal.* July 1966, p. 31.

CHAPTER 5

Formal Meetings

Summary

This chapter starts by describing the differences between a formal meeting and a small group. Formal meetings are called by means of a 'Notice of Meeting'. They work according to an Agenda. Formal Minutes are taken as a record of the proceedings. Formal meetings are run according to a constitution and a set of rules.

The duties of the Chairperson, Secretary and Treasurer are described, both before, during and after the meeting.

Rules for the conduct of meetings are described.

The chapter also shows examples of:

- a Notice of Meeting
- an Agenda
- the Minutes of a Meeting.

Key points

- Formal meetings are similar in some ways to small groups. However, they differ in that formal rules and a constitution govern their conduct.
- The Chairperson, Secretary and Treasurer have specific duties to perform before, during and after meetings.
- Formal meetings are called by a Notice of Meeting. They are run by means of an Agenda. A formal record or set of minutes is kept of the proceedings at the meeting.
- Formal meetings are run according to a set of rules.

Differences between formal meetings and small groups

This chapter makes a difference between small policy-making or decision-making groups and formal meetings for the following reasons:

Formal meetings:

- vary in size from seven people to an Annual General Meeting attended by hundreds of people
- are called by means of a Notice of Meeting
- have an Agenda
- have their proceedings recorded in Minutes
- are run by a designated Chairperson, who is helped by a Secretary and a Treasurer
- are governed by a set of formal rules
- may have a formal constitution that governs, for example, how often they meet.

Small groups may have some of these characteristics, but not all.

Aspects of formal meetings

This section covers the following aspects of formal meetings:
- Duties of the Chairperson, Secretary and Treasurer.
- Rules for the conduct of meetings.
- The writing of Notices of Meetings, Agendas and Minutes.

Duties of chairperson

The Chairperson should plan for the meeting well in advance. (S)he should do the following:

Before the meeting
- If the meeting is optional, ask if it is necessary.
- Ensure that the time and place are appropriate.
- See that an Agenda has been prepared and sent off in good time. This timing is especially important if a constitution lays down the period of notice for a meeting.
- Give people advance warning if they have to prepare topics for the meeting.
- Ensure that all proposals have been correctly worded and are properly seconded. People should get advance notice of these proposals on the Agenda.
- Check the venue to ensure that it is comfortable and has the right seating arrangements.
- Check that a microphone is available, as well as appropriate audio-visual aids and lighting.

- Check that the minutes of the previous meeting are sent out in advance, with the Notice of Meeting.
- See that sub-committees have met and that their reports are ready for the meeting.
- Prepare a Chairperson's report and send this out in advance.
- Prepare thoroughly for the meeting.
- If necessary allocate a time-limit for the discussion of each item. Example:
  12. Allocation of parking places for computer staff (ten minutes)
- Appoint someone to record the proceedings.

During the meeting

- Ensure that the meeting starts on time.
- Make sure that everyone has the Agenda, and understands it.
- Move the business of the meeting along.
- Keep to the agenda.
- Discourage distracting behaviour such as:
  - not listening
  - people talking off the point on their favourite subject
  - people talking past each other
  - apathy.
- Keep to the formal rules of debate where necessary.
- Allocate an order for speakers.
- See that everyone has a fair chance to speak.
- Summarize the discussion if necessary.
- Tie up loose ends.
- Identify any action that has to be taken and by whom.
- See that the Secretary records the exact wording of any decisions taken. The names of proposers and seconders should be recorded.
- See that the Secretary records financial transactions correctly.
- Where necessary, delegate responsibilities and have these recorded.
- Act impartially throughout the meeting.
- Strive to be fair when decisions are made.
- Exercise a casting vote only when no other way can be found of resolving a matter.
- See that motions have been correctly put and seconded.
- See that votes have been correctly counted and recorded.
- Summarize all decisions at the end of the meeting and ensure that people know what they have to do next.

Duties of secretary

The Secretary is normally responsible for:
- Keeping the records of the meetings in a Minutes book.

- Ensuring that the Chairperson is kept up to date with all the factors affecting the meeting.
- Keeping a correspondence file.
- Keeping an attendance register.

Before a meeting

The Secretary should ensure that:

- A notice of the meeting has been prepared and sent out within the time period prescribed in the constitution.
- The agenda has been properly set out with the correct wording. This should also be sent out in advance.
- All minutes are up to date, and that correspondence has been correctly filed so that it can be presented at the meeting.
- The venue has been booked and that the correct tables, chairs, microphone and audio-visual aids have been booked. (S)he should also ensure that the venue is ready for the meeting.

During a meeting

The Secretary should:

- Ensure that everyone signs the attendance register.
- Check that there is a quorum present, according to the constitution.
- Report to the Chairperson on the numbers present.
- Read out the minutes of the previous meeting if the minutes have not been sent out in advance.
- Record the proceedings, ensuring that exact wording, figures and names have been recorded.
- Ensure that all motions, with proposers and seconders, have been accurately recorded.
- Record the numbers who voted.
- Record the names of those who have to take further action, and deadline dates for this action, where relevant.
- Collect copies of the Chairman's and committee reports for filing.

After the meeting

After the meeting, the Secretary should:

- Write up the minutes of the meeting within seven days, and send them to the Chairperson for checking.
- Once the minutes have been checked, file a copy and send copies to the Chairperson and Executive Committee where appropriate.
- Write all letters as directed by the Chairperson.
- Brief the Chairperson on matters that have to be followed up.

- Brief sub-committees and individuals if they undertook to do specific things, before the next meeting. (S)he should also remind them of deadline dates.
- Help the Chairperson prepare the agenda for the next meeting.
- Check that all rules in the constitution have been correctly followed.

Duties of treasurer

A Treasurer's duty is to keep accurate accounts of all financial transactions. (S)he also has to run the bank account and prepare the accounts for annual auditing.

Before a meeting

Before a meeting the Treasurer should:
- Prepare appropriate financial statements for the meeting.
- Ensure that the Chairperson and the Secretary receive copies. The Secretary should place such statements in the minute book.
- Ensure that all figures on the Agenda have been correctly recorded.

During the meeting

During the meeting the Treasurer should:
- Read out the financial statement if appropriate.
- Present the accounts for ratification.
- Present the cheque list since the last meeting for the group's information.
- Answer any financial queries.
- Record any financial transactions that have to be completed after the meeting.
- Advise the meeting on all financial matters.

After the meeting

After the meeting, the Treasurer should:
- Check with the Secretary that all financial transactions have been correctly recorded.
- Pay any accounts as directed by the meeting.
- Keep the Books of Account up to date.
- Report to the Chairperson that accounts have been paid.

Duties of any other officials

If the organization or constitution allows for any other officials, they should:
- Prepare any reports necessary.
- Ensure that they attend all meetings.

- Work closely with the Chairperson.
- Keep accurate records of all that they do.
- Ensure that they do their duties according to the constitution.

Notice of meeting, agenda and minutes

All formal meetings are called by means of a typed Notice of Meeting. This Notice is normally accompanied by a formal typed Agenda. The proceedings are recorded in formal Minutes.

This section describes the format and content of the above messages.

Notice of meeting and agenda

The following example shows the format for a combined Notice of Meeting and Agenda. Please note that a section headed 'Notes' has been left open on the right-hand side. Those attending the meeting can make notes in this column. (See example on page 87.)

If the meeting is less formal and is to be attended by a small number of people from one department, then the Notice of Meeting and Agenda could be set out as shown on page 88. Notice that the Agenda is much more specific

Minutes of meetings

Minutes are the official record of the proceedings of a meeting. They also record the exact wording of:

- resolutions taken
- decisions on finances
- appointments to posts and terms of office
- instructions
- contracts.

Minutes are important documents for four major reasons:

- They remind those who attended and those who did not about the business of the meeting.
- They form part of the historical records of a company.
- Once approved, they are the official legally binding records of a meeting.
- They may be used as evidence in court.

Minutes should, therefore, be very carefully and accurately written. They should be factual, unambiguous and to the point.

Essential elements of minutes

Minutes should contain some or all of the following elements:

- name of the organization

ABC COMPANY

NOTICE OF MEETING

Notice is hereby given that the third Annual General Meeting of Shareholders of the above Company will be held at the Company's registered office 25, First Street, Townsville on Wednesday 3 August 19.. at 10h00.

Agenda

Item	Notes
1. Notice convening the meeting	
2. Apologies	
3. Minutes of Second Annual General Meeting	
4. Matters arising from the Minutes	
5. Correspondence	
6. Directors' Report for the year	
7. Balance Sheet and Profit and Loss Account for year ending 30 June 19..	
8. Auditors' Report on the accounts for the year ending 30 June 19....	
9. Election of Directors to replace Mr C. Zulu and Mrs A. Smith. Both of these have retired by rotation, and are standing for re-election.	
10. Declaration of dividends of seven per cent of the Preference Share Capital, and ten per cent on the Ordinary Share Capital for the year ending 30 June 19..	
11. Fixing of payment to Auditors for the past year	
12. Any other business	
13. Closure	

By Order of the Board
Signed:

A.C. Mkizi
Secretary
Date: 1 July 19..

Registered office
25 First Street
Townsville

ABC COMPANY
Production Department
Notice of Meeting

Our next Production Planning Meeting will be held as follows:

Date: 18 June 19..
Time: 10h00 to 11h00
Venue: Committee Room 2

Those attending: Joe Fischer, Ike Zitha, Fikile Mahlangu

Agenda

OBJECTIVE OF MEETING: To decide whether to recommend a 10% increase in production in the Trimming Department

Agenda item	Purpose	Time	Presenter	Materials to be read in advance
1. Establish criteria for making decisions	Consensus	15 min	—	—
2. Review 3-year production figures	Information	10 min	J.F.	Attached figures
3. Consider short-term use of excess capacity in Trim Department	Decision	30 min	I.Z.	Attached estimates and proposal

- type of meeting
- place, date and time of meeting
- the chairperson's name
- the secretary's name
- a record of the names of those who attended
- apologies for absence
- notice of meeting
- opening and welcome
- minutes of previous meeting
- matters arising from the minutes
- correspondence
- financial report
- new business
- general
- closure

- chairperson's signature and date
- Distribution list
- 'Action' column on the right-hand side, with deadline dates where appropriate.

The following example illustrates extracts from a set of minutes. Note particularly the use of:

- headings
- a multiple decimal numbering system
- the 'action' column.

Note the initials in the action-column. These show who is to take action. If deadline dates have been given for this action, then these dates should be given.

ABC COMPANY
Minutes of the third Annual General Meeting of the ABC Company held at the Company's Registered Offices, 25 First Street, Townsville on Wednesday 3 August 19.. at 10h00.

	Action and deadlines
1. Present Mr A. Wentzel (in the chair) Mr A.C. Mkizi (secretary) Mr S. Stander Mr K. Zulu Mrs A. Smith Twenty shareholders (see attached list)	
2. Apologies Apologies were received from: Mr Z. Motau	
3. Notice of meeting The Secretary read the notice of the meeting. The Chairperson declared the meeting open and welcomed those present.	
4. Minutes of Second Annual General Meeting These minutes, having been circulated in advance, were taken as read. Proposer: Mr K. Zulu Seconder: Mrs A. Smith	
5. Matters arising The Chairperson reported on the following matters 5.1 . . . 5.2 . . .	C.Z. 30 Aug 19 . .

	Action and deadlines

6. Correspondence
The Secretary read the correspondence relevant to the Second Annual General Meeting.
. . .
 	
8. Election of directors
The following were elected for the period 3 August 19 .. to 2 August 19 ..:
• Mr C. Zulu (proposer . . ., seconder . . .)
• Mrs A. Smith (proposer . . ., seconder . . .)
. . .
 	
10. Payment to auditors
Mr Wentzel, seconded by Mr K. Stander, proposed as follows:
'That the auditors, Messrs J.K Pelle and Partners, be paid . . . for the year 1 July 19 .. to 30 June 19 ..'
The meeting so *resolved*.
. . .
 	
12. Closure
The meeting closed at 11h30 with a vote of thanks to the Board of Directors.
 	
Signed: . . . .
       (Chairperson)
 	
Date:
 	
Attached: List of all those who attended.
            Distribution list
	
	K.S.
	2 Sept 19 ..

Guidelines for the conduct of meetings

The following are a set of guidelines for a formal meeting. Other guidelines have already been set on the specific duties of Chairpersons, Secretaries and Treasurers.

Duties of chairperson during meeting

The Chairperson should:

- sign the minutes of the meeting once they have been approved
- insist that all speakers address the meeting through the Chair
- name speakers to indicate when they may speak

FORMAL MEETINGS 91

- ensure that speakers receive a fair chance to speak
- insist that speakers keep to the agenda
- control the amount of time that speakers have
- close the debate on a topic when (s)he considers necessary
- hand over the chair to the Vice-Chair when (s)he is reading the Chairperson's report
- read the exact wording of a motion to the meeting before inviting debate on it
- appoint people to count votes by secret ballot or to count hands
- use a casting vote when votes for or against a motion are equal
- accept amendments to motions provided that they have been seconded
- give rulings on points of order
- call for a vote if any of these rulings is challenged.

Guidelines for speakers

Speakers:
- should address the meeting through the Chair;
- may speak only once on a motion (they may, however, speak on an amendment);
- may exercise their right of reply if they have proposed a motion (after this no one else may speak — proposers of amendments have no right of reply);
- retain their right to speak on a motion if they ask a question to gain information on that motion;
- cannot propose an amendment to a motion once they have spoken on that motion and it remains the same;
- may interrupt other speakers on points of order;
- may then speak on their points of order while the original speaker remains silent.

Proposing of motions

Meetings should follow the following guidelines on motions:
- Motions must be proposed and seconded.
- A motion may be added to with the consent of the proposer.
- The proposer and seconder have a right to speak first on a motion.
- Motions, if not amended, are put to the vote. If they are carried they become resolutions.
- Motions may be amended by changing, removing or adding words. An amendment needs a proposer and seconder.
- The amendment is voted on. If the amendment is approved by the meeting, the amended motion, called the substantive motion, is put to the meeting.

- Two amendments cannot be accepted together.
- Each amendment needs to be voted on separately.
- A motion cannot be withdrawn unless the meeting, as well as the proposer and seconder, agree.
- A motion is recorded as 'carried unanimously' if everyone votes for it. If nobody votes against it, it can be recorded as nem.con. (no-one against). This could apply if some people abstain.
- A proposal that opposes a motion cannot be accepted as an amendment. This should be put as a counter-proposal. The meeting will then vote on whether to accept this proposal or not. If the counter-proposal is defeated, the meeting will then vote on the original proposal. If the counter-proposal is accepted, then the original proposal falls away.

Types of motions

The following are a selection of motions used to regulate meetings:

- If someone feels that the discussion has gone on long enough (s)he can propose that 'the question now be put'. This motion, if accepted, means that the meeting has to vote immediately on the motion.
- Someone may wish the meeting to move on to the next motion on the agenda. (S)he may then propose a motion 'to proceed to the next business'. If this is carried, the meeting leaves the motion under discussion without voting, and moves on to the next motion.
- If the meeting is discussing a confidential matter, it may move into committee. A motion 'to move into committee of the whole' is put. If this is carried, everyone has to stay in the room until the meeting moves out of committee. Once the meeting moves out of committee the matter may not be discussed.
- If a member needs more time to consider a proposal (s)he may propose a motion 'to postpone' debate to a new date.
- A member who wishes the meeting to reconsider a resolution made at the meeting may propose a motion 'to reconsider' the resolution.
- A member who feels uneasy about a resolution taken at a previous meeting may propose a motion at the next meeting 'to review and rescind' a motion.

Questions: Part 3

(Answers to these questions are given on pages 499–503.)

Points for discussion

1. What do you understand by the term 'Organization'? Give examples of three organizations with which you are involved.
2. Explain the differences between line and staff divisions in an organization.
3. How would you create an atmosphere of trust in an organization?
4. Explain Maslow's hierarchy of needs.
5. Describe four kinds of messages in organizations.
6. Describe six major barriers to message flow in an organization.
7. Explain the terms *overloading* and *underloading* of information.
8. Describe six kinds of groups found in organizations.
9. Describe four leadership styles. Which style do you prefer? Why?
10. What are groups like when they do not work well?
11. Describe the task and maintenance roles in a group.
12. What do you understand by the term conflict? Does conflict always harm a group? Justify your answer.
13. Explain the difference between *value conflict* and *content conflict*.
14. Explain the *win–win* approach to conflict resolution.
15. You have been appointed Chairperson of a group. You have to run an Annual General Meeting. What would your duties be? What would the duties of the Secretary and Treasurer be?

Exercises

1. Take any group to which you belong. Analyse the behaviour of the group during a discussion or problem-solving session. Was the group dominated by one person? Were all members encouraged to communicate with one another? Did people withdraw from the group? Once you have completed your analysis, decide how you would improve the communication in the group.
2. This exercise focuses on roles in a group, as well as on task and group maintenance behaviours. The exercise is designed to help you examine the relationship between your behaviours in the group and your roles. Your procedure is as follows:

   Form groups of six. Write each of the following task and maintenance behaviours on cards.

| BEHAVIOUR IN THE GROUP ||
Task	Maintenance
Act as gate keeper Clarify ideas Summarizing past discussion	Draw out quiet members Strive to overcome differences Encourage members to share ideas

Roles in the group
- Mr Reddy — You own and run a grocery store
- Mrs Reddy — Wife to Mr Reddy. You have three children
- Ms Tasker — Sales Manager ABC Company
- Father Mkize — Dedicated priest
- Dr Bond — Scientist and winner of prizes for research
- Dr Mary Cook — Medical Doctor with her own practice

Select a behaviour and a role. Form a group in which you have to act out your behaviour and your role. At this stage, do not tell the others what you are playing. You have the following problem to solve in 20 minutes:

> All of you suffer from a rare blood disease. A special blood treatment plasma is available, but there is only enough for two of you. Decide which two will receive the treatment. There is no guarantee that the rest of you will survive.

Analysis

At the end of the exercise read out your behaviours and roles. Did these go well together? Were you able to tell what roles and behaviours others were playing? What conclusions can you draw about the relationship between roles and behaviours in groups? What conclusions can you draw about the differences between task and maintenance roles?

3. This exercise covers different leadership styles. Form a small group and select a problem to solve. Select one person to play a democratic leader, another to play an autocratic leader, and the third to play a laissez-faire leader. Start the discussion with one type of leader. After five minutes, change to another type of leader, and then to the third type.

   Discuss the problem for fifteen minutes, and then:
   - Discuss the group's task and maintenance orientation under each type of leader.
   - Try to establish whether any particular type of leadership encouraged task or maintenance behaviours more strongly.
   - Ask yourselves which type of leadership style you prefer.
   - Ask yourselves under which conditions each style of leadership would be effective.

4. This exercise covers problem-solving in groups. Form a group of ten members.

Your task is to use the following six stages to solve a problem:
- Define the problem.
- Decide on your objectives by answering the question: 'What must we do to solve the problem?'
- Generate possible solutions to the problem by asking: 'How can we best meet the objectives?'
- Evaluate each solution in terms of the objectives.
- Decide on the solution that best meets your objectives.
- Evaluate your solution in terms of the action taken.

Select observers

Select three observers from your group. They will observe the group as it sets about its task. The three observers should take notes about the group, using the following questions:
- Did the group use all the stages of the problem-solving procedure?
- Was any stage left out or given too much time? Why?
- Did the group go through any stages, such as conflict, during the exercise?
- Did a leader emerge?
- At what stage did the group reach consensus?
- How well did the group work together?

The problem

You are employed by a company. The company has a limited amount of money. This money has to be distributed among six divisions, each with its own needs and priorities. The divisions are as follows:
- Personnel (This division urgently needs extra funds to recruit staff and train them.)
- Computers (New computer programs are needed to keep the company competitive).
- Sales (The economy is shrinking. Customers are becoming much more selective. Sales people need to be sent on specialist sales courses to keep the company competitive.)
- Manufacturing (This division urgently needs to replace obsolete machinery.)
- New Product Development (If new products are not developed, the company will not remain competitive.)
- Public Relations (The company has had some bad publicity recently. Money is needed to re-establish the company's good name.)

Decide on the amount of money that you have available. Allocate this money to divisions according to your assessment of their needs.

5. Form a group of up to twenty. From this group choose a Chairperson, Secretary and Treasurer. Their task is to organize the Annual General Meeting of a company. They are to prepare a Notice of Meeting and Agenda. The rest of the group will attend the meeting as Shareholders. The Secretary should take minutes at the meeting.

At the end of the meeting discuss the differences between an Annual General Meeting and a problem-solving group.

PART 4

Interpersonal Communication

•

Active Listening

•

Non-verbal Communication

•

The Interview

PART

4

Interpersonal Communication

Active Listening

Nonverbal Communication

The Interview

CHAPTER 6

Interpersonal Communication

Summary

This chapter stresses that the person-to-person communication is the basis of all effective communication. Good interpersonal communication starts with a positive self-image. This self-image is built up through effective intrapersonal communication. This is communicating with oneself.

We perceive, or make sense of reality, through our senses. However, how we perceive the world will be different from other people. Our needs, expectations and experiences are different. We therefore select what we take notice of.

People tend to judge others on illogical grounds and may, therefore, gain a false impression of what they are like.

Organizations can help to improve perception by:
- encouraging people to understand their perceptional biases
- creating friendly and supportive situations
- encouraging a willingness to work together
- encouraging people to understand the needs of other departments
- encouraging people to give full credit to the knowledge and abilities of others.

People joining organizations have to learn two sets of rules:
- the formal procedures by which departments and the organization are run
- the informal rules by which people work together.

The Johari Window is then described. This describes open, blind and hidden areas as they relate to people. The open area is what people and those working with them know about them. The blind area represents what people do not know about themselves, but others do. The hidden area is what people know about themselves, but choose to keep hidden from others.

People should be encouraged to be open to feedback and to reduce their blind areas. They should also be prepared to level with other people and to reduce their hidden area.

When people communicate, they take on roles, and work according to a set of rules.

The chapter ends by comparing assertiveness with aggression. People should state their views, ideas and feelings, but not at the expense of others.

Key points

- Good person-to-person communication is the basis for all effective communication.
- A positive self-image is very important for good communication.
- We need to give ourselves positive self-talk.
- We perceive the world from our own frame of reference, or point of view.
- Because of this frame of reference, we often misjudge others.
- Organizations need to create an atmosphere in which people perceive one another more accurately.
- People have to learn formal and informal rules for working together.
- We interact according to our roles and a set of rules. We need to be sensitive to both of these.
- People should strive to be open to feedback, and be prepared to level with others.
- Assertiveness, rather than aggression, is important in interpersonal communication.

The importance of effective interpersonal communication in organizations

This book has taken the view that successful communication is a transaction. Both sender and receiver have to work together to create meaning.

The previous chapter covered communication in small groups. This chapter describes the basis of all effective communication: person-to-person communication.

An organization may have the best communication systems with efficient networks. However, if individual people do not work well together, these systems will fail.

This chapter covers the following aspects of interpersonal communication:

- intrapersonal communication or communicating with oneself
- the processes of perception and how wrong perceptions affect organizations
- the transactional nature of interpersonal communication
- listening
- non-verbal communication
- interviews, with the stress on job interviews
- the writing of a letter of application for a job, as well as a Curriculum Vitae.

Intrapersonal communication and perception

Intrapersonal communication describes the ways in which we communicate with ourselves. The messages we give ourselves help us to form a view of ourselves, or a *self-image*. We also build up a self-image as we work with other people. They react to us and give us messages about ourselves. We also form a self-image through past experiences.

Our self-image may be positive or negative. If we perceive ourselves in a positive way, we are likely to work confidently with others. However, if we perceive ourselves in a negative way, we might perform below our actual ability. This is called a *self-fulfilling prophecy*. People might then form a poor impression of us. A negative self-image might also make people *defensive*. Communication with these people is likely to be difficult.

The process of intrapersonal communication

Our brains become aware of internal and external *stimuli* through our nerves and sense of sight, sound, smell, taste and touch. The brain cannot cope with all the stimuli that it receives, so a process of *selection*, or *selective perception* occurs.

We therefore pay attention to very few stimuli at any one time. We tend to pay attention to the most *intense* stimuli. These are processed at three levels:

- the cognitive level, or level of information
- the emotional level
- the physiological level, or level of bodily needs in order to stay alive.

We should constantly keep in mind that people do not perceive the world in the same way. We cannot, therefore, assume that people will see any situation in the same way as we do.

Our process of perceiving stimuli is our way of making sense of reality. It also helps us to give meaning to experience. Our perception does not simply register 'reality'. We select according to our:

- self-images
- past experiences
- emotions and needs
- interests
- attitudes and beliefs
- language
- knowledge.

We tend to distrust messages that do not agree with our view of the world. We also protect our self-images against what we perceive as attacks.

People build up a *frame of reference* through which they view the world. This is a system of attitudes and values. It gives them a standard against which they can compare others' actions, and ideas.

Implications for communication

- People in organizations need to understand that our past experiences and frames of reference affect the way in which we interpret communication. These will differ from person to person.
- We have a set of values, attitudes, beliefs, opinions and prejudices. These will vary widely from person to person. They will affect the way in which people communicate.
- People's personalities differ. Some personality traits will help communication. Others will be barriers.

We need to be aware of the following potential barriers:

- Dogmatism or laying down the law. Dogmatic people have closed minds and may refuse to accept new ideas and opinions.
- Manipulation. Manipulative people try to achieve their goals by controlling other people.
- Self-esteem. People's self-esteem will affect what they say and how they receive the messages of others.

Problems with perception in organizations

Because we often perceive on non-logical grounds we make false judgments. The following are examples of some of these false judgments:

- We might judge a person as honest simply because (s)he smiles.
- We tend to perceive as correct people that we like and respect. Their opinions have greater weight with us.
- Our advance expectations of others may help us to decide whether we trust people or not. We may, for example, assume that a person whom we are about to meet is honest. When we meet that person we readily believe that person.
- We tend to stereotype or make general judgments about groups of people such as managers or union members. When we deal with an individual from that group we apply our group-judgment to that person. This judgement could be wrong.
- We may judge people according to a *halo effect*. We form a general impression that is favourable or unfavourable. We then use this general impression to judge specific traits.
- We may, for example, judge punctuality as a favourable trait. We might then judge a punctual person as productive and producing work of good quality.
- We sometimes *project* our feelings onto other people. Our present emotional state affects how we perceive others. We may, for example, feel frightened. We then perceive others as frightening, whereas others might not.

What can organizations do to improve perception?

Members of organizations should strive to:

- understand their perceptional biases
- create friendly and supportive situations in which to work together
- develop a willingness to work together
- give more credit to people we do not know for having knowledge and special abilities
- understand needs and perceptions of departments other than their own.

Interpersonal communication

Effective interpersonal communication is vital in organizations. Many people change their jobs because of poor interpersonal communication. People therefore need to understand what is involved in effective person-to-person communication.

A great deal of interpersonal communication covers two people working together. This is called a *dyad*. These two people are equally responsible for the transaction. Each has to:

- send messages
- receive messages
- give feedback
- interpret non-verbal messages
- listen carefully both the to facts and to the feelings behind the facts.

The two have to construct meaning together. They develop roles in the dyad and communicate according to a set of rules. They are communicating at the level of self-image, feelings about themselves and attitudes towards their points of view.

People joining companies have to learn two sets of rules. The first set covers the formal written rules that regulate their work. The second set covers the unwritten rules that regulate people's interpersonal communication.

This section has been written to help the reader understand some of these unwritten rules. It covers the following:

- A description of the Johari Window. This shows the relationship between what we reveal about ourselves to others and what we choose to keep hidden.
- Roles and rules in dyads.
- Some interpersonal communication skills that are useful in dyads.
- Active listening.
- Non-verbal communication.

The Johari Window

The Johari Window was designed by Joseph Luft and Harrington Ingham.
It shows the relationship between what the individual chooses to reveal about himself or herself and what (s)he chooses to keep hidden.

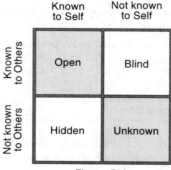

Figure 6.1
The Johari window

INTERPERSONAL COMMUNICATION

The *Open* section stresses that we know certain things about ourselves and are prepared to share them with others. The more we share with others about our hopes, fears and expectations, the easier they will find communicating with us.

The *Blind* section stresses that there are areas of ourselves that we do not know about. However, others know about these areas. These may, for example, be mannerisms that others find irritating.

The *Hidden* section stresses that we are aware of certain things about ourselves but choose not to reveal them to others. These could, for example, be hopes and fears that we do not wish to reveal to others.

The *Unknown* section represents information that we do not know about ourselves. Others do not have this information either.

Varying sizes of the sections

These sections have been shown as equal in size. However, they will vary in size according to the type of one-to-one communication that we are involved in. For example, when we communicate with a stranger our open area will be small and the hidden area large. As we get to know one another better, these areas will change in size.

Levelling and feedback

If we wish to reduce our hidden area then we deliberately tell people about our hopes, fears and specific knowledge that we have kept hidden. This is called *levelling* with others. We choose to level with others or not according to the value that we place on the communication.

If we are willing to receive *feedback*, then we are able to reduce our blind area. We learn from what others tell us about ourselves, and so improve our communication.

Open-receptive communication

In our one-to-one communication we should strive to have the open area as large as possible. The hidden area should be as small as possible and we should strive to reduce our blind area as much as we can.

Roles and rules in dyads

We take on different roles as our one-to-one communication changes from day to day. These roles will affect the ways in which we relate to others. They help us to interpret other people's behaviours and to negotiate meaning with them.

These roles have to be negotiated in terms of:
- the situation
- the other person's position

- your view of your position.

Roles are often linked to our or the other person's:
- professional status
- age
- gender
- level of seniority
- level of authority
- level of experience
- job position.

Once we have decided on our and the other person's roles, we will develop patterns of behaviour that we feel are appropriate for any situation.

As we work together in one-to-one situations, we develop sets of rules. These rules are not written down but are understood. For example, some rules could cover:
- turn-taking
- amount of eye-contact
- the distance we keep
- appropriate timing of meetings
- people's special likes and dislikes.

People in organizations should take special care to be sensitive about their roles and the rules for interpersonal communication.

Interpersonal skills in dyads

Effective one-to-one communication demands certain skills. This section briefly discusses the following skills:
- being assertive rather than aggressive
- clearly stating your feelings, perceptions and interpretations of what others have said and done
- clearly stating what you intend to do
- clearly stating the motives behind what you have said or plan to do
- giving and receiving feedback.

Assertiveness

If you are assertive you firmly express your wishes, feelings and perceptions without being rude to or dominating the other person. Your assertive statements should not be at the expense of the other person. In this way you show that you value yourself.

You would then ensure that the other person has a chance to assert her or his opinions.

If, however, you were aggressive, you would dominate the other person. You would not allow an exchange of feelings or views. This could lead to a great deal of tension and a breakdown in communication.

Clear statements of perceptions and feelings

Effective one-to-one communication also demands clear statements of how you:

- perceive a situation in terms of your senses
- understand a situation once you have perceived it
- feel about yourself and the other person in a particular situation.

It is very important that people in a dyad sense that they are understood in terms of the facts, and how they feel about those facts. Strength of feeling should be acknowledged.

Clear statements of fact, intentions and actions

Basic to all interpersonal communication is an ability to state facts or problems clearly. However, being able to state facts is not enough. You also have to be able to say what your motives are in stating those facts.

In the same way, if you have taken action, are doing something or plan to do something, tell the other person. Tell him or her what to expect of you. Stress that you are aware of what you are doing, and the effect your actions have on him or her.

Reference

1. Luft, J. *Of Human Interaction.* Palo Alto, California: National Press Books, 1969.

CHAPTER 7

Active Listening

Summary

Effective listening is essential in all face-to-face communication. This chapter distinguishes between hearing, which is a passive process, and active listening, in which the listener is deeply involved with the speaker's message.

Listening actively means that you strive to be in touch with facts, opinions and attitudes expressed by the speaker. You give feedback and ask prompting questions to show that you are listening.

Active listening is very important for five major reasons:
- People are more easily persuaded in face-to-face situations.
- People have less time to evaluate.
- People are less inclined to be critical in face-to-face situations.
- Poor listening stops the flow of conversation.
- Poor listening results in poor understanding.

The major barriers to effective communication are listed. These are:
- cultural differences
- the credibility and roles of the speaker
- insensitive use of language
- selective perception.

Poor listening habits are also listed. The major ones are:
- Jumping to conclusions.
- Trying to get all the facts instead of listening for key points.
- Not listening to your juniors or to people whom you perceive as inferior.

Listeners need to motivate themselves to listen. They need to decide exactly why they are listening. Listeners should also analyse their own biases. Finally, they should check that they share the same meanings of words with their partner.

Speakers should plan their messages well and should use the beginnings and ends of messages to achieve the greatest impact.

Key points

- Listening is different from hearing.
- Listening is an active process.
- Active listening means that the listener is deeply involved with what the speaker is saying.
- Effective listeners need to be aware of bad listening habits.
- Active listening involves the following:
    - motivating yourself as a listener
    - hearing the speaker out
    - not jumping to conclusions
    - checking that you share the same meanings of words
    - giving feedback
    - asking questions to show that you are listening.
- Speakers should organize their messages very carefully to ensure that they are properly listened to.

Active listening

Effective listening is essential in interpersonal communication. We spend a great deal of our time listening. We therefore need to understand:
- what stops good listening
- the techniques for active listening.

This section covers the following aspects of listening:
- the differences between hearing and active listening
- the barriers to effective listening
- techniques for effective listening.

The words 'hearing' and 'listening' are often used as though they had the same meaning. This section however, distinguishes between the two. *Hearing* is a passive process in which we receive the sounds in a conversation. *Active listening*, on the other hand, is a process whereby we are deeply involved with the speaker. We pay attention to both the facts and opinions expressed, as well as to the speaker's feelings. We remain alert and offer helpful feedback. This feedback takes the form of:
- summaries and paraphrases of what is being said
- statements about what we think the speaker feels
- questions to clarify what is being said
- non-verbal signs that we are listening.

Active listening is very important in interpersonal communication for five major reasons:
- People are more easily persuaded by spoken communication, than by written communication.
- In spoken communication we have less time to evaluate what is being said.
- We are less inclined to be critical of spoken communication.
- Poor listening stops the flow of conversation because speakers quickly become aware that they are not being listened to.
- Poor listening results in poor understanding both of the facts and of the speaker's attitudes and emotions.

Barriers to effective listening

The following barriers stop effective listening. Speakers and listeners should analyse their bad listening habits and eliminate them.

The following factors can cause poor listening unless people become aware of them:
- cultural differences
- the speakers' and listeners' roles in the organization
- the perceived credibility of the speaker or listener
- stereotyping

- manipulative behaviour
- insensitive use of language
- effects of non-verbal behaviour
- selective perception
- the place where listening occurs
- the emotions of the speaker and listener
- the type of technical language used.

In addition to the above, the following poor listening habits can destroy interaction:

- jumping to conclusions based on your own points of view before the speaker has finished
- pretending that you are paying attention and allowing your mind to wander
- trying to listen for all the facts, rather than concentrating on the key issues
- listening for the facts only, and ignoring the speaker's attitudes and emotions
- refusing to listen when you perceive the listening task to be too difficult or uninteresting
- refusing to listen to people whom you feel are inferior in status or knowledge
- mentally criticizing the speaker's delivery and appearance
- being easily distracted by the surroundings.

Techniques for effective listening

The following techniques should help you become an active listener:

- Decide exactly why you are listening. You might, for example, be listening to:
  - get the main ideas
  - draw proper inferences from the material
  - hear difficult material
  - evaluate and apply the new information
  - check whether the speaker is being logical
  - analyse the persuasive techniques used by the speaker
  - decide how the speaker feels about his or her ideas
  - follow directions.
- Motivate yourself to listen actively.
- Regard listening as a physical and mental process.
- Show that you are listening by leaning forward and giving verbal and non-verbal feedback.
- Listen until you have heard the full message. Then respond. Don't jump to conclusions before the full message is over.
- Ensure that you evaluate the whole message.

- Try to see the message from the speaker's point of view. This is called empathic listening.
- Check the meanings of words with the speaker to ensure that you share the same meanings.
- Be alert for the incorrect use of joining words such as 'because', 'since', 'for', 'as'.
- We can think faster than we can speak. Use this time to summarize the key points.
- Try to find out what the speaker's feelings are. Respect these feelings.
- Be aware of your own biases and prejudices. Try to overcome them as you listen.
- Ask questions to clarify points.
- Ask yourself whether the speaker's opinions are sound.
- Reflect the message back to the speaker to check that you have listened accurately.
- Provide clear and unambiguous feedback.
- Strive to analyse your listening errors and to correct them.

What can speakers do to ensure that they are listened to?

In two-way communication, both the sender and receiver are responsible for the negotiation. As speakers, you could do some of the following things to help the listener:

- Prepare the listener for your message.
- Time the message properly. Ask yourself how long the listener will take to absorb strange material.
- Use the beginnings and ends of messages effectively, because they have the greatest impact.
- Make the plan of your message clear.
- Always give the facts. Try not to be vague. Your listener should not be left to guess what your message is.
- Do not move through the message too quickly, or too slowly.
- Attract and re-attract the listener's attention.

CHAPTER 8

Non-verbal Communication

Summary

Good interpersonal communication depends both on active listening and on people's ability to interpret non-verbal communication. This chapter has two aims:

- to make you aware of how non-verbal cues work in interactions
- to make you aware of the range of non-verbal signals.

It is very important to be aware of non-verbal signals for five reasons:

- We rely on first impressions to judge people.
- First impressions are hard to change.
- We judge people in terms of our own beliefs about non-verbal behaviour.
- We judge people on facial expressions, eye-contact, mouth, voice, gestures, the way they stand and what they wear.
- We use non-verbal stereotypes to judge people.

Non-verbal communication is a continuous process. It is often more reliable than spoken communication. It is also a better way of showing emotions.

There are, however, three major problems with interpreting non-verbal communication:

- It is often ambiguous.
- Meanings of non-verbal communication have to be judged from the total context.
- People need to interpret non-verbal signals in clusters, rather than on their own.

The chapter goes on to describe a number of types of non-verbal communication:

- silence
- paralanguage (the way one says things)
- facial expression and eye-contact
- touching
- proxemics or distances between people
- clothing and accessories such as jewellery

- Objects and the environment within which one works
- Cultural views of time.

Key points

- Effective person-to-person communication depends on one's ability to interpret non-verbal signals.
- We often judge people on first impressions. These could be wrong.
- Our first impressions are hard to change.
- We judge people in terms of our own beliefs about non-verbal behaviour.
- We judge people on their facial expressions, voice, gestures and clothes.
- Non-verbal communication is often a more reliable way of judging people than is spoken communication.
- Non-verbal communication is often ambiguous. It should, therefore, be judged from its total context.
- Non-verbal communication is judged according to a range of types. Each type needs to be described and studied.

NON-VERBAL COMMUNICATION

Introduction

Non-verbal communication is the basis of all interpersonal communication. Successful communication at this level depends largely on our ability to understand our own and the other person's non-verbal communication.

Many people are, however, unaware of, or insensitive to, non-verbal messages. The aim of this section is, therefore, to make you aware of:

- the range of non-verbal signals
- how these signals work in interactions.

The need to be sensitive to non-verbal cues

We need to be as sensitive as possible to non-verbal cues for five major reasons:

- In new situations, people often rely on first impressions to make up their minds about strangers. They notice obvious things about them. From these superficial cues they make all kinds of judgments, often inaccurate. For example, we might judge a stranger with a high forehead and spectacles as very intelligent; we could be wrong in this judgment.
- When we meet strangers we judge them in terms of our own beliefs about appearance and non-verbal behaviour. Even though these beliefs may be inaccurate, we use them to fill in gaps about our knowledge of strangers.
- Our first impressions are often hard to change.
- We make up our minds about people from their facial expressions, eye-contact, mouth, voice, gestures, the way they stand and what they wear.
- We often use non-verbal stereotypes for judging people. We might, for example, decide that all short men are aggressive. When we meet a short man, we assume that he will be aggressive. We then start communicating with that stereotype in mind and cause unnecessary trouble.

Three major differences between non-verbal and verbal communication

Non-verbal communication differs in three major ways from verbal communication:

- In face-to-face communication it is a continuous process. Communication is going on even if you say nothing.
- Non-verbal communication is usually to be trusted above what people say. People have to be very skilled to lie both non-verbally and verbally.
- Non-verbal communication is a more effective way of showing emotions and attitudes than is spoken communication.

Problems with the interpretation of non-verbal communication

There are, however, three major problems with the interpretation of non-verbal communication:

- Like words, non-verbal communication can be ambiguous.
- The meaning of any non-verbal message needs to be established from the total context, rather than from the behaviour on its own.
- Non-verbal signs have to be interpreted in clusters, rather than individually. For example, someone with folded arms may not be setting up a barrier. (S)he may simply be trying to be comfortable.

The range of non-verbal communication

Each day people show their moods, attitudes and emotions through body language. However, non-verbal communication covers far more than simply body language.

This section describes the range of non-verbal communication. The following types are described:

- silence
- paralanguage
- kinesics or body movement
- facial expressions and eye-contact
- touching
- proxemics or distance, and territoriality
- clothing and accessories such as jewellery
- objects and the environment within which people work
- people's views of time.

Silence

Silence during interpersonal communication is important. When silence is well used it helps people to engage in genuine two-way communication. Silence encourages effective turn-taking, and can show that the other person is listening.

Silence in the form of pauses is also important in public speaking. It allows the audience time to absorb what people are saying, particularly if the information is strange.

People can, however, misinterpret others' silence. They decide why others are silent, without asking them. They then communicate with them on the basis of an incorrect judgement.

Silence has a range of meanings. It could, for example, show:

- contemplation
- fear
- shyness
- concentration

- boredom
- anger
- embarrassment
- respect.

People might, however, make a mistake and decide that shyness is actually rudeness or that fear is actually boredom. A person showing respect through silence might be misjudged as angry. All these mistakes could lead to breakdowns in communication.

If one person is often silent, the other person should try to find out why so that they can communicate with understanding.

Paralanguage

This word describes the ways in which we speak, rather than what we say. It covers the following aspects of our voices:

- the intonations, or rise and fall of the voice
- how fast or slowly we talk
- how loudly or softly we talk
- how resonant our voices are
- how harsh our voices are
- the level of tension in our voices.

It also covers clearing of throats, coughs and even crying.

As we listen to paralanguage we make up our minds about people's:

- age
- emotions
- feelings about themselves and their subject
- attitudes towards us
- intelligence
- level of sophistication.

These judgements could be quite wrong.
We should, therefore, take great care to cultivate lively voices that help listeners to judge accurately how we feel about ourselves and our subjects. We should also strive to understand other people's paralanguage.

Kinesics

This term describes our body movements as we interact with others. In particular, the study of kinesics covers:

- the way we walk
- how we stand in relation to others
- our arm and hand movements
- the ways in which we sit.

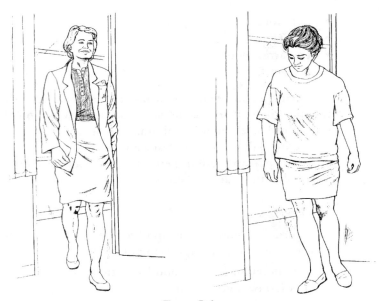

Figure 8.1
Walking into a room

All these movements and positions affect the ways in which we communicate. They also affect how people interpret us.

We might, for example, walk into a room with our eyes and head down and our backs bent. People could then assume that we have a problem and are not very interested in working with them. On the other hand, if we walk boldly into a room and look at people, they are more likely to communicate positively with us.

Body movements can, however, be more subtle than this. You might, for example, find yourself taking up the same body posture as someone that you like. This is called an *echo posture*. It helps to create harmony between two people. You might, for example, cross your knee towards a person who also has crossed legs.

When we stand to deliver a speech, it is very important that we do not:

- fold our arms
- twist our backs
- cross our legs.

All these could be taken as signs that we are setting up barriers, or that we are uneasy about what we are saying.

Our hand movements during conversations are very important for *regulating* the ways in which we take turns. Effective hand movements with open palms also help us to keep the attention of our audience. Open body positions with our arms spread help us to show our sincerity.

When we sit we could be tense or relaxed. We could also be leaning forward to listen or leaning back. These postures show our feelings towards the other person and the subject. Leaning forward to listen is an effective posture for active listening. Leaning back could show that we wish to withdraw from the conversation.

Figure 8.2
Echo posture

We tend to be more relaxed with people of equal or lower status. We are more tense with people of higher status.

All these postures will affect the way in which we communicate with others.

Facial expressions and eye-contact

We constantly judge other people by their facial expressions. We look at their hair, eyes, foreheads, mouths, chins and the state of their skin. However, people have learnt to adjust their facial expressions to ones that they judge to be socially acceptable.

We therefore need to observe people's faces very carefully, particularly their eyes, if we are to gain a true idea of their feelings.

Eye-contact is significant when we work with other people. It is used to *regulate* conversation in the same way as hand-movements. Good eye-contact signals that the communication channels are open. From a western point of view we tend to suspect people who do not look at us. We have greater confidence in people who look at us while we are speaking. They also give us a feeling of worth and authority. People show by the amount of eye-contact whether they are dominant or submissive. People who are dominant and confident tend to have greater eye-contact, than do people who are not very confident.

During speeches, speakers should keep up good eye-contact with an audience, even if it is a large one. They should try to look at individuals in the audience, rather than sweeping their eyes over the audience.

We should, however, note that some cultures value looking down as a sign of respect. If, therefore, we are working with people from different cultures, we should try to find out and respect their attitudes to eye-contact.

Touching

Cultures vary a great deal in their attitudes to touching. People involved in intercultural communication need to be aware of this. Some Western cultures are, for example, classified as non-touch or non-contact cultures. People from other cultures, however, may value touching during conversations, particularly to gain attention or to interrupt. If people from these two cultures work together there may be problems, if they are not aware of these different customs.

Figure 8.3
Touching

Even in 'non-touch' cultures, however, a touch to the elbow or shoulder can be reassuring, since it is seen as non-threatening. Such touching is also effective for gaining a person's attention. Touching may also encourage people to disclose more information than they would normally have. Touches to the cheeks and head are strong signals of affection.

Proxemics, or distance and territoriality

We all carry with us a 'space bubble' or comfort zone. If people invade this zone we feel very uncomfortable. These space bubbles vary a great deal from culture to culture.

The study of proxemics covers people's use of space and how they react to the space around them. It also covers people's territoriality or desire to maintain their own space. Territoriality includes a study of table seating and table shapes.

From a Western point of view, we like to keep a distance of at least one-and-a-half metres when we meet people for the first time. We also use this distance when we conduct business at an interpersonal level.

People from other cultures might for example, wish to conduct business within a much smaller space. This desire could cause tension for people who need more space. Adjustments would then have to made on both sides.

When people have to be very close together, as in a lift or train, their *intimate zone* (actual contact to about 25 centimetres) is being invaded. They cope with this tension by silence, eyes turned away and a rigid seating or standing position that avoids contact if possible.

People who know each other tend to stand closer together when they are talking. They might, for example, use a *personal distance* ranging from 50 cm to one-and-a-half metres.

People in organizations need, therefore, to study each others' spatial needs and respect them in interpersonal communication.

Territoriality

Our 'space bubble' or comfort zone is very important to us. This space bubble often expands to the size of our motor cars. We start to feel tense if people persistently drive on our bumpers.

We express our attitudes towards territory by saying:

- 'My office'
- 'My desk'
- 'My house'

We try to expand our territories by putting our hands on our hips. We also expand our territories by surrounding ourselves with books, bags or

Friendly

Aggressive

Figure 8.4
Proxemics

briefcases. More space is often given to senior managers in organizations. They have larger offices and larger desks. These desks give managers more space. However, they can also become *barriers* to good communication because they can be used to dominate people by keeping them from the manager.

Senior staff may also cause tension if they 'invade' junior staffs' space. They could, for example, walk into a junior's office unannounced, go up to him or her, remain standing and demand instant attention. Junior staff could also cause problems if they invade senior staffs' space. People in organizations need, therefore, to be sensitive to other peoples' territories.

Seating

Seating arrangements affect the ways in which people communicate. A round table at a staff seminar would be effective, because it encourages eye-contact. A lecture, on the other hand, where less interaction is needed, could be given to people in rows of seats.

Seating arrangements at an oblong table will affect the ways in which people interact. Figure 8.5 illustrates what could happen.

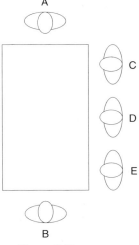

Figure 8.5
Table seating arrangement

People who sit at A or B are given the status of leaders. People seated at D are likely to be very involved with the meeting. However, people seated at C and E run the risk of being ignored, particularly by people at the ends of the table. People at C and E need to ensure that they are given a chance to participate. In addition, people at the ends of the table need to ensure that they pay attention to the people on their immediate left and right.

If people have to use a desk for interpersonal communication they should consider talking across the corner of the desk. This reduces the distance between them, and the corner of the desk is less of a barrier. If they are working on a task where they need desk space, they should consider working side-by-side or across the width of the desk. They should encourage good eye-contact and the reduction of barriers.

Clothing and accessories

Clothing and accessories such as ties, belts and jewellery satisfy our desire for attention. They also satisfy our need to be accepted as members of groups and for self-esteem.

However, clothing and accessories are important for other reasons. They are very much part of communication in organizations.

How we dress at work is an important part of the impression that we make on other people. People build up impressions of what we think about ourselves, our status, our interests and our personalities. What we wear can influence our success at work.

People in organizations should, therefore take great care over what they wear.

Objects and the environment

Objects such as office furniture, curtains, carpets and pictures on the wall affect us positively or negatively. All these objects help to provide a good or bad working environment. We react better in a good working environment that we do in a bad one. In one experiment, for example, people were asked to describe the attractiveness of a series of photographs of faces.[1] The raters were placed in three different rooms. One room was an unattractive storeroom, another was furnished simply as an average office, and the third room was furnished as attractively as possible with curtains, a carpet and good furniture. The raters in the attractive room described the faces in more positive terms than did the raters in the other two rooms.

Raters in the attractive room recorded feelings of pleasure and enjoyment. Those in the storeroom recorded feelings of irritability and hostility.

Organizations should, therefore, pay a great deal of attention to the working environment because it affects peoples' reactions and the ways in which they work.

NON-VERBAL COMMUNICATION

Looking uninterested

Leaning forward to listen

Figure 8.6
Listening

Time

People from different cultures view time differently. Many western organizations view time like a river flowing. Once time has gone past, it cannot be recovered. This view stresses that time is precious and should not be wasted.

Time is also viewed as an object that should not be lost. This view of time values punctuality. Lateness, particularly where people of higher status are involved, is regarded as a negative message.

Other cultures may view time in a different way. They may, for example, view time as renewable or circular. This view might not regard lateness as an insult, because time has not been wasted. Business might then be conducted in a different way.

People in organizations should be sensitive to different views of time and should be prepared to discuss them. In the end, however, organizations will have to decide on their time values, because different views of time in one organization could result in tension. They could also cause difficulties if organizations are competing with others with different time values.

Reference

1. Maslow, AH and Mintz, WL. "Effects of esthetic surroundings: 1. Initial effects of three esthetic conditions upon perceiving 'energy' and 'well-being' in faces" *Journal of Psychology* 1956, 41: pp. 247–54.

CHAPTER 9

The Interview

Summary

The interview is a special type of one-to-one communication. Here the interviewer or group of interviewers control the meeting. They ask prepared questions and expect answers.

An interview is defined as a planned conversation during which questions are asked and answered. This conversation is designed to exchange information and attitudes about a specific subject. A job interview is aimed specifically at forming an impression of the interviewee. This impression will help the interviewer decide on the interviewee's suitability for the job.

Interviews differ from ordinary unplanned conversations for three main reasons:
- They need specialist knowledge.
- They occur in controlled settings.
- They need formal, prepared questions if they are to be successful.

Four types of interviews are described:
- Information-seeking
- Appraisal
- Exit
- Job

A plan of preparation for the interviewer and interviewee is described.

The chapter also gives examples of open and closed questions. It describes the main advantages and disadvantages of each type.

A panel interview is then discussed. This differs from a one-to-one interview, in that a group of people have to be co-ordinated. Each person is responsible for questioning.

The chapter ends with an example of a letter of application and a curriculum vitae.

Key points

- An interview is a special type of interpersonal communication.
- An interview is a planned conversation during which questions are asked and answered in a fixed setting.
- Interviewers need specialist knowledge if they are to be successful.
- Interviewers and interviewees have to plan for interviews.
- Effective interviewers have to use a range of open and closed questions.
- Interviews have to be planned so that they are properly structured.
- Panel interviews need to be very well organized because a group has to be co-ordinated. Each person should be responsible for a set of questions.
- An effective letter of application and curriculum vitae are very important if people wish to be interviewed.

THE INTERVIEW

Introduction

The interview is a special type of interpersonal communication. Interviews may be conducted by one interviewer or by a panel of several interviewers. The interviewer controls the interviewee by asking a set of prepared questions. The interviewee is expected to answer these questions.

At its best the interview should be a controlled conversation, rather than a random flow of information.

This section covers the following aspects of interviews:

- A definition of an interview.
- A discussion of the special nature of interviews.
- Types of interviews.
- Factors relevant to all interviews.
- The interviewer's preparation.
- The interviewee's preparation.
- A discussion of the interview and the phases through which it should go.
- Major problems in interviews.
- Letters of application for a job.
- The curriculum vitae or facts about the applicant.

Definition of interviews

This section describes four types of interviews. The first definition covers all these types. The second definition is more detailed. It covers the job interview, which is regarded as the most important type of interview.

General definition

An interview is a planned conversation between two parties, during which questions are asked and answered. This conversation is designed to exchange information and attitudes about a specific subject.

Definition of a job interview

A job interview is a planned conversation about a specific job. During this conversation the interviewer(s) ask questions, which the interviewee answers. These questions are designed to exchange facts and opinions. They are also designed to help both parties form an impression of the other.

These definitions are relevant to a one-to-one interview and a panel interview. They stress:

- a conversation, rather than an interrogation
- a planned, rather than a random flow of information

- properly designed questions
- the need to exchange facts and opinions
- the need to form impressions on both sides.

Interviews may be *structured* or *unstructured*. Structured interviews are carefully prepared in advance, with questions written out. Such interviews are designed for very specific purposes.

Unstructured interviews are more flexible. The interviewer may depart from her or his specific plan. The interviewee is allowed scope to answer questions in detail even if these details are not fully relevant to the plan. The interviewer will, however, try to keep to a general plan.

The special nature of interviews

Interviews differ from ordinary conversations for a number of reasons:
- they demand specialist knowledge if they are to be successful
- they take place in a controlled setting
- they are two-sided and are conducted in a predictable way
- the roles of interviewer and interviewee are prescribed
- they are conducted with specific purposes in mind
- they rely on effective verbal and non-verbal communication for their success
- they rely on active listening
- they are based on formal questions and answers.

Types of interviews

Interviews may be divided into four major categories:
- the information-seeking interview
- the appraisal interview
- the exit interview
- the job interview.

The information-seeking interview

This type of interview takes two major forms:
- *The market survey*, where the interviewer chooses individuals from a target group. These interviewees are then questioned to gain information about opinions on and attitudes towards certain products.
- An interview in which a staff member in an organization has a *grievance*. A personnel officer might then interview that person to gain information.

The first type will be structured with carefully worded questions and a clear purpose. The interviewer will have to:
- select the person from the target group

- obtain that person's co-operation
- use specific questions using tactics to obtain the best response
- evaluate the results.

The second type will be non-structured to allow the complainant to express her or his grievance. The interviewer will have to use prompting or probing questions. He or she will have to listen with great care. Both the interviewer and the interviewee will have to work together to define specific problems.

The appraisal interview

This type of interview is designed to tell people how they are doing in an organization. It is also designed to improve people's performance on the job and to help them work towards specific goals.

The interviewer will start by giving the interviewee information on his or her performance. This opening should then develop into a conversation in which the two work together to plan work goals. The interviewer should be very careful:

- to stress the person's performance, rather than criticize the person
- to be very specific about strengths and weaknesses
- to help the interviewee decide on specific reasons for weak performance
- to help the person plan specific future performance to reach specific goals.

Although the interviewer is very much in control here, (s)he should strive to make the interview a two-way process.

The exit interview

This type of interview is designed to find out why people have resigned from an organization. Since there might be some ill feeling here, the interviewer should try to establish a pleasant and trusting atmosphere.

The interviewer should plan specific questions to encourage the interviewee to give honest answers. The interviewer should practise active listening. (S)he should use prompting questions to encourage a free flow of information, opinions and feelings.

The job interview

Since the job interview is so important for an organization, this section goes into more detail. It covers:

- the factors relevant to the job interview
- the differences between a one-to-one interview and a panel interview
- the interviewer's preparation
- the interviewee's preparation

- the phases of a typical interview
- the panel interview
- characteristics of a good interview.

Factors relevant to a job interview

A job interview is a transaction. The interviewer and interviewee work together to establish whether the interviewee is suitable for the job. The interviewer may also try to find the right job for a person.

Figure 9.1 summarizes the various factors that are important in a job interview. This figure stresses some of the most important factors in a job interview. Each is briefly discussed below.

- *The interview setting:* The interviewer needs to set up the interview so that the transaction is as favourable as possible. An interview across a desk makes the interview very formal. The interviewer should therefore consider using easy chairs and a low table. The room should be as pleasant as possible.

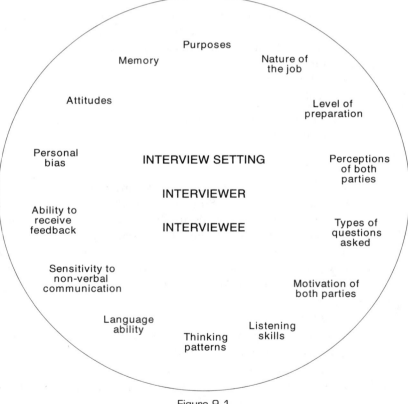

Figure 9.1
Important factors in a job interview

- *The interviewer:* (S)he should be very well prepared with clear purposes, a good plan and well constructed questions.
- *The interviewee:* (S)he should have studied the job specifications and read as much as possible about the company. (S)he should also have prepared possible answers to a range of questions.
- *Purposes:* A successful interview should be organized round a clear set of purposes. The interviewer should decide exactly what (s)he wants to gain from the interview. (S)he should make these purposes known to the interviewee, who should come with a clear set of purposes. These purposes should become clear during the interview.
- *Nature of the job:* The interviewer needs to have a detailed description of the job. This description will help him or her to plan the questions.
- *Level of preparation:* Interviewing needs special skills and careful preparation. Interviewers need to be well prepared to make the interview a successful transaction. They need to understand other people's motivation. In addition, they need to understand:
  - how to plan an interview
  - how to prepare effective questions.

  Interviewees need to understand exactly what job they are applying for. They should also study the company and anticipate the questions that are likely to be asked.
- *Perceptions:* Both parties will arrive at the interview with different perceptions. They should strive to understand these perceptions by careful questions and answers.
- *Types of questions:* A good interview should be conducted by means of carefully prepared open questions in specific areas. These questions enable the interviewee to talk freely. Closed questions, demanding exact answers, should be used only to fill in details.
- *Motivation of both parties:* Both parties need to be motivated to give of their best. Lack of motivation from one side will soon become obvious and could destroy the interview.
- *Listening skills:* Both parties need to practise *active listening*. They should listen both for the facts and the attitudes and motivations behind these facts. The interviewer should hear the interviewee out and not jump to conclusions. The interviewee should listen carefully to questions. (S)he should strive to answer exactly what was asked.
- *Thinking patterns:* These may be different for each party. Each should, therefore, strive to understand the thinking patterns of the other. A good understanding will lead to a better transaction.
- *Language ability:* Ability to use language clearly and accurately is extremely important. If the interviewer is uncertain about his or her language ability, then (s)he should write out each question. The interviewee should practise answering questions beforehand so that (s)he has an exact word-stock to draw from. Both parties should keep

in mind that meanings are in people. They should, therefore, ensure that they give the same meanings to words.
- *Sensitivity to non-verbal communication:* Each party should strive to be sensitive to the other's non-verbal communication. They should show that they are listening actively and should regulate their turn-taking. Interviewers should analyse their non-verbal biases and stereotypes. This analysis should help them to judge people more fairly.
- *Ability to receive feedback:* This is especially important for interviewees. They should be sensitive to responses from the interviewer so that they can adjust their answers.
- *Personal bias and attitudes:* Both sides should be aware of their own biases and attitudes. This general awareness will help them to be more sensitive both to the types of questions asked and to the replies.
- *Memory:* Both parties should strive to remember exactly what the other has said. Accurate remembering will help the interviewer to guide the interviewee. (S)he will also be able to return to key points for clarification. The interviewee will be able to remember difficult questions. (S)he will also be able to refer to earlier points to strengthen present answers.

Differences between a one-to-one interview and a panel

In a one-to-one interview the interviewer is fully responsible for planning and running the interview. A panel, on the other hand, shares the responsibility. A panel generally has a Chairperson and a number of members. The Chairperson will divide out the responsibilities. Each person will normally be responsible for certain groups of questions. At the end, the panel will decide jointly whom to appoint.

The interviewer's preparation

Interviewers should go through the following procedure:
- Prepare a job description.
- Read the applications and summarize key points about each applicant.
- Define the objectives of the interviews and prepare a plan.
- Prepare a range of general and specific questions suitable for each candidate.
- Make sure that the interview room has been well prepared.
- Prepare a checklist of desired characteristics. This will help quick note-taking during the interview. These ticked-off points can then be used for detailed note-taking after the interview.
- Prepare a score sheet so that each candidate can be rated out of ten on a set of characteristics. This will help the interviewer make quick comparisons.

Example

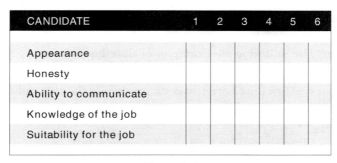

Figure 9.2
Candidate scoring grid

Open and closed questions

The interviewer should plan a range of questions for each stage of the interview. *Open questions* require general information. They enable interviewees to expand on a topic, express opinions, and to give the reasoning behind opinions. *Closed questions*, on the other hand, demand specific answers, even 'yes' or 'no'. They restrict the interviewees' choices.

Examples of open questions

The following are examples of open questions:

- What is your reaction to the recent changes in tax laws?
- In what ways do you think that you could increase sales?
- How would you evaluate the success of our new job policy?

Advantages of open questions

The major advantages of open questions are as follows:

- They help to show the interviewee's ways of thinking and priorities.
- They give an interviewee freedom to construct an answer.
- They show how much an interviewee knows.
- They show how articulate the interviewee is.
- They help to build up a good relationship because the questions do not imply a judgement.
- They can be less threatening if the interview becomes tense.

Disadvantages of open questions

The major disadvantages of open questions are as follows:

- They take time and energy to ask and answer.
- They need expert preparation.
- They make it more difficult to control the interview.

- Recording the answers during the interview is more difficult.
- Answers may be interpreted differently if there is a panel.

Examples of closed questions

The following are examples of closed questions:

- When did these problems start?
- How long have you been producing the new radios?

Advantages of closed questions

Closed questions have the following advantages:

- They save time.
- They allow the interviewer to control the flow of information.
- They enable the interviewer to obtain exact information.
- They enable the interviewer to fill in gaps in the interviewee's replies.
- They help a shy interviewee to start talking.
- They enable interviewers to ask a number of questions in a short time.

The disadvantages of closed questions

The main disadvantages of closed questions are as follows:

- They limit the replies.
- They can turn an interview into an interrogation.
- The interviewee could become defensive if too many closed questions are asked.
- They can restrict the interviewee's choices of answer and need to explain.

Preparing a range of questions

Interviewers should prepare a range of open and closed questions under the following headings:

- Home background
- Work history
- Education and training
- Career plan
- Reasons for applying for job
- Leadership
- Initiative
- Flexibility
- Independence
- Ability to get on with others
- Motivation
- Communication skills.

The interviewee's preparation

The interviewee should prepare as follows:

- Gain as much knowledge as possible about the company.
- Study the job specification closely.
- Analyse his or her strengths and weaknesses.
- Prepare to sell himself or herself by stressing what (s)he can do for the company.
- Think carefully about his or her career objectives.
- Draw up a list of questions that could be asked, and plan how to reply to them.
- Draw up a list of questions that (s)he would like to ask.

Phases of a typical interview

Most interviews go through a set of phases. Interviewers should prepare different approaches and questions for each phase.

The first phase is the introduction. The interviewer will put the candidate at ease. (S)he will explain the purpose of the interview and will explain the broad categories of questions to be asked.

The next phase enables the interviewer to move into the interview properly. (S)he will now start obtaining facts, opinions and attitudes from the candidate.

The next phase entails detailed negotiation. Some early replies will be followed up. Detailed questions about the job will be asked. The candidate will be encouraged by open and closed questions to give detailed and specific answers.

The final phase enables the interviewer to sum up. (S)he will also tell the candidate:

- what will be done with the responses
- what will happen next.

The candidate is encouraged to ask questions at this stage. The interview is then concluded on a friendly note.

The panel interview

A panel is normally controlled by a Chairperson, who allocates duties. There may even be a Secretary who records the proceedings. A panel has the following advantages:

- Each person can be responsible for a specific set of questions.
- The other members can concentrate on the candidates' answers and take notes.
- Each member can use his or her special knowledge to help the panel choose the best candidate.

There are, however, some major disadvantages of a panel:
- Panels need a great deal of time to prepare.
- Members may not be well prepared and questioning may be poor as a result.
- Members may not agree on candidates. They then make compromises and do not necessarily choose the best candidate.

If panels are to work well, they need to get together well in advance. They can then discuss the best ways of tackling the interview. Duties can be allocated in advance so that questions can be prepared.

Characteristics of a good interviewer

A good interviewer should ensure that (s)he:
- is well prepared
- does more listening than talking
- does not jump to conclusions
- leads the candidate on
- does not guide the candidate into giving the 'correct' answer
- uses an effective range of open and closed questions
- strives to translate the facts and opinions from the interview into accurate predictions of how the candidate will perform on the job.

The job application

The *letter of application* and *curriculum vitae* are crucial in any job search. Their quality and content will make someone decide whether to interview you or not.

The letter of application

Your letter of application should be short and to the point. The letter should be clearly written and very well set out. It should have the following content:
- A clear subject-line stating the post applied for.
- An opening paragraph giving more detail about the post, with a reference to an advertisement.
- A statement of the applicant's reasons for seeking the job.
- A statement of the applicant's objectives in the job. Here the applicant should stress what (s)he can do for the organization.
- A statement of the applicant's career objectives.
- An indication that the applicant knows something about the organization.
- A reference to an attached curriculum vitae.
- Contact telephone numbers.

585 Globe Mansions
16th Street
SIMONSVILLE
3685

24 August 19—

Mr J. Xhaba
Personnel Officer
XYZ Company
Cross Street
JOHANNESBURG
2001

Dear Mr Xhaba

APPLICATION FOR POST OF ASSISTANT ACCOUNTANT

I wish to apply for the post of Assistant Accountant, as advertised in the ABC Newspaper on 20 August 1992.

The post of Assistant Accountant in your company would be of great interest to me, as I wish to pursue a career in cost accounting.

I believe that I can make an effective contribution to your company for the following reasons:
- my B.Com. degree
- my previous experience in accounting
- my knowledge of management
- my ability to get on with people.

I wish to pursue my studies in cost accounting part-time, and plan to become a Chartered Accountant in three years' time. I believe that these plans will fit in with your company's proven record of sound financial planning.

I attach a curriculum vitae containing the names of three referees. These people may be contacted in confidence.

I am available for an interview at any time. My telephone numbers are:
- Work (021) 8723456
- Home (021) 6282434

Yours sincerely

A.J. MATTHEWS
Encl. Curriculum vitae

Example

An example of a letter of application is shown on page 141. Please note that this is not a model answer. It should not be copied slavishly, as each applicant may wish to stress different aspects in the application. Note that a full-block style has been used.

The curriculum vitae

This is a record of your personal details and the important facts about your life. It should also be a document in which you sell yourself. The curriculum vitae should contain the following sections:

- Personal details
- School record
- Record of post-school studies (if relevant)
- Career to date
- Job objectives
- Career plans
- Awards and scholarships
- Membership of professional organizations, and offices held
- Willingness to be transferred
- Developed abilities

The following example illustrates a possible curriculum vitae. Note that it has been set out to be highly readable.

```
                    CURRICULUM VITAE

1. PERSONAL DETAILS
   Full name: Andrew John Matthews
   Age: 25
   Gender: Male
   Marital Status: Single
   Place and date of birth: Simonsville, 1967-08-15
   Nationality: South African
   Home Language: English
   Other Languages: Xhosa
   Military service: Two-year compulsory service
      completed, 1985-1986
   Health: Excellent
   Present Occupation: Junior Accountant
   Address:      585 Globe Mansions
                 16th Street
                 SIMONSVILLE
                 3685
```

Telephone Numbers: Work (021) 8723456
                   Home (021) 6282434

2. ACADEMIC DETAILS
   2.1 Matriculation: Simonsville High School
       Year: 1984
       Certificate: Transvaal Senior Certificate
       Subjects and symbols:
          English B   Mathematics C,
          Science C   Afrikaans B
          History C   Xhosa C
   2.2 Senior School Achievements
       Prize for English, Std. 10
       Prefect
       Chairman, Accounting Society
       First team hockey 1984

       Developed Abilities at School:
       My experience as a prefect and a Chairman of
       the Accounting Society helped me to develop
       my ability to:
       - run an organization
       - get on with people
       - organize the accounts of a small group.

   2.3 Tertiary Education
       University: University of the South,
       1987-1989
       Degree: B.Com.
       Subjects: Accounts I(2-), II(2+), III(2+)
       Auditing I(2+), II(2+)
       Environment of Business I(2-), II(2-)
       Mathematics I(a) (2-), 1(b) (2-)
       Industrial Relations I(2-), II(2-), III(2-)

   2.4 University Activities and Achievements
       Sport: First team hockey 1988-1989, Captain
       1989
       Society: Member of Committee, Accounting
                Society 1988, 1989

       Developed Abilities
       During my career at University I developed
       the following abilities:
       - To discipline myself to long hours of study
       - To schedule my time accurately

- To lead a group
- To get on with a wide range of people.

I was also able to develop my theoretical and practical knowledge of accountancy.

3. EMPLOYMENT EXPERIENCE

1987-1989: Vacation work at XYZ Supermarket as an accounts clerk

1990-present: Assistant Accountant at ABC company, Simonsville

Developed Abilities
My working experience has enabled me to:
- adapt to the working environment of a large organization
- get on with a wide variety of people
- improve my theoretical and practical knowledge of management
- improve my theoretical and practical knowledge of accounting.

4. CAREER PLAN

I plan to pursue a career in Accounting, with Cost Accounting as my special interest. I am, at present, studying part-time, and plan to sit the C.A. Board Examinations in three years' time.

5. OTHER ACTIVITIES AND INTERESTS

Hiking: I belong to a hiking club and go on regular hikes.
Sailing: I belong to XYZ Yacht Club, and sail regularly.

6. SUMMARY OF DEVELOPED ABILITIES

My career to date has enabled me to:
- build up my practical and theoretical knowledge of accounting and management
- work effectively with a wide range of people

```
            - work effectively in small groups, especially
              committees.

            7. REFEREES
            The following have agreed to act as my referees:
            Mr J. Bloggs
            Chief Accountant
            XYZ Supermarket
            SIMONSVILLE
            3685

            Professor A. Smith
            Department of Accounting
            University of the South
            SOUTHVILLE
            3797

            Mrs I. Jenkins
            Accountant
            ABC Company
            SIMONSVILLE
            3685
```

Implications for communication in organizations

Effective interpersonal communication in organizations demands that:
- People cultivate positive self-images by giving themselves positive messages.
- People strive to gain an accurate idea of others.
- People strive to avoid stereotyping others and to get to know them as individuals.
- People strive to avoid being dogmatic.
- People strive to be open to feedback and to level with others so that they reduce their hidden and blind areas.
- People strive to be assertive rather than aggressive.
- People strive to listen actively and to motivate themselves as listeners.
- People strive to understand and be sensitive to others' body language, particularly the personal space bubble, attitude to time and eye-contact.
- People strive to organize their messages effectively so that they are properly listened to.
- People in charge of interviews prepare effectively to get the best candidate for the job.

Questions: Part 4

(Answers to these questions are given on pages 504–510.)

Points for discussion

1. Discuss and define the following terms. Give examples to illustrate your definitions.
   - Intrapersonal communication
   - Selective perception
   - Frame of reference
   - Stereotyping
   - Dyadic communication
   - Assertiveness
2. Discuss the effect that your positive or negative self-image has on the way you communicate.
3. Discuss the concept of defensiveness. In what ways are people defensive? How does defensiveness affect communication?
4. Discuss the following terms as they relate to the Johari Window:
   - Open area
   - Hidden area
   - Blind area
   - Feedback
   - Levelling

   Use the above terms to explain your communication with others.
5. Discuss the term 'non-verbal communication'. What part does non-verbal communication play in interpersonal communication? Discuss the approaches of different cultures to:
   - distance between people
   - eye-contact
   - time
   - touching.

   How could different approaches in the above areas affect communication in organizations?
6. Discus the term 'active listening'. What steps can you take to ensure that:
   - you listen actively
   - you are effectively listened to?
7. Discuss what is necessary to ensure a good interview. Discuss the interview from the point of view of the interviewer and the interviewee.
8. Give examples of open and closed questions. What are the advantages and disadvantages of each type?
9. What should a good letter of application contain?

10. What details should be put into a curriculum vitae? How should it be set out?

Exercises

1. This exercise is designed to help you explore your perceptions of yourself. Work with a partner. Each person should ask the other: 'How do you see yourself?' Each person should be given five minutes to answer this question. Once you have each had five minutes, each partner should tell the other how (s)he sees him or her. You should then compare your self-concept and your partner's view of you. Are the views different? Do you have a false view of how others see you? Does your view of yourself affect the way in which you communicate with others? Do you give yourself positive or negative feedback? How does this feedback affect your self-image?

2. Analyse your perceptual biases. Try to find out why you like some people and not others. Do you judge people in terms of a set of stereotypes or fixed ideas about people? Can you describe these fixed ideas?

3. Try to analyse your own frame of reference. From what basis do you judge what you see? For this exercise you will need to analyse:
   - your background
   - your values or basic beliefs
   - your attitudes
   - your prejudices.

   Once you have done this exercise, compare notes with a partner. Try to understand how your views of the world differ. Discuss how your views affect the ways in which you communicate.

4. Work with a partner on the Johari Window. Discuss what you understand by the following terms:
   - hidden area
   - blind area
   - open area
   - feedback
   - levelling.

   Each partner should write down three positive things about the other. Discuss whether this feedback has changed your blind areas. Discuss with your partner how you could reduce your hidden area and increase your open area by levelling with your partner, You could, for example, tell your partner about any hopes and fears you have about a course that you are about to start.

   Discuss with your partner how you would use the Johari Window to describe a trusting relationship and a relationship that has just started. Change the size of each square to show the relationships.

5. Work in a group of three for this exercise on listening. Each person is *A*, *B* or *C*. Choose a subject about which you have strong feelings, such as abortion or abuse of drugs. *A* should discuss this topic with *B* for five minutes. *B* should then reflect back to *A* what (s)he has said. *C* should act as a check to see that *B* has listened carefully. The three should then discuss the quality of the listening that has taken place.

   Each person should take it in turn to be a speaker, listener or referee. Once the exercise is over, the group should discuss the meaning of:
   - active listening, and
   - empathic listening.

   They should then discuss barriers to effective listening and ways of overcoming them.

6. Form a group of three. Decide on a suitable post in a company, and prepare for an interview for that post.

   Choose an interviewer, interviewee and an observer. The interviewer and interviewee should take up to twenty minutes to prepare the interview. Once they are ready the interview should take place with the observer taking notes.

   The observer should use the following questions as guidelines:
   - How was the seating arranged?
   - How did the interviewer greet the interviewee?
   - Did the interviewer set the interviewee at ease at the beginning of the interview?
   - Was the interview taken through a set of stages?
   - Did the interviewer explain the purposes of the interview?
   - Did the interviewer give the interviewee some idea of the range of questions to be asked?
   - Did the interviewer do more listening then talking?
   - What types of questions were asked? Were there open questions to get the interviewee talking? How were closed questions used?
   - What was the quality of the listening?
   - Was each person sensitive to non-verbal communication?
   - How did the interview end?

   Allow up to twenty minutes for the interview. The observer should then give feedback. This should be followed, by a general discussion on how to make interviews successful.

7. Evaluate the letter of application on page 149. Rewrite it to improve it.

THE INTERVIEW

The Recruiting Officer
XYZ Company
CAPE TOWN
8000

Dear Sir

I believe that you have the right job for me. The job of sales clerk that you advertised will give me the opening that I have been looking for. It is close to my home and offers me an ideal opportunity to get myself started on a career in sales.

I hear that you offer a very good financial deal and excellent training. I could benefit a great deal from these.

I look forward to hearing from you.

Yours sincerely

P. Smith

PART 5

The Rhetorical Situation

•

Planning and Organizing Messages

•

Choosing an Effective Vocabulary

•

Style, Tone and Jargon

•

Elements of Readability

CHAPTER 10

The Rhetorical Situation:
Deciding on your purposes and analysing your audience

Summary

This chapter covers the first stages of preparing a good message:
- deciding on one's purposes
- analysing the needs of one's audience.

Writers and speakers should strive to turn vague information into messages that communicate. Such messages are prepared in a specific format, such as a report, with clear purposes and a specific audience in mind.

The communicator has to ask a number of questions about the message. These questions are called the *Rhetorical Situation*. Apart from purposes and audience, senders of messages should ask:

- How should I plan my message?
- In what order should I present my ideas?
- How can I present a coherent message?
- How can I achieve a unified message with the right emphasis?
- What should my style be like?
- How can I set out a written message so that it is highly readable?
- How can I ensure that my vocabulary is appropriate and correct?
- How can I avoid jargon?

The chapter suggests a range of purposes for messages. It also suggests ways of analysing the needs of the audience.

Key points

- Senders need to turn vague information into messages that communicate.
- Senders are preparing messages in an age when people's reading ability is going down.
- A number of questions have to be asked in order to prepare messages that communicate. These questions cover format, planning, organiz-

ing, writing in an appropriate style, using the right technical vocabulary and achieving high readability.
- Senders have a wide range of purposes to choose from.
- An audience has to be described in broad terms first of all. The specific audience should then be described.

The rhetorical situation

Chapters ten to fourteen describe the principles of preparing, organizing and presenting a range of messages in organizations. These principles are then applied to oral and written messages in Parts Six and Seven.

In particular, the following aspects of messages are described:
- what a message is
- analysis of one's audience
- analysis of one's purposes
- planning and organizing messages
- choosing an appropriate style
- choosing an appropriate vocabulary
- avoiding jargon
- presenting a written message in a highly readable way
- writing at the correct level of formality.

Two major questions

The following questions are asked:
- What are the conditions under which organizations communicate today?
- How may we turn vague information into precise messages that communicate?

What is a message?

A message is any information that is passed from one person to another. This information will normally be organized with specific purposes and a specific audience in mind. Messages may vary from a one-to-one conversation to a formal talk, oral or written report or business letter.

Conditions under which organizations communicate today

Today organizations are communicating in an age when:
- people are bombarded with a large number of messages.
- messages have to be very effective to gain and hold people's attention.
- people's ability to read effectively is decreasing.
- electronic media have greatly increased the speed with which messages are created and sent.
- English, if it is the medium of business communication, may not be the home language of the increasing numbers of people from various cultures who are joining businesses.

How does one turn information into communication?

Given the above conditions, how may we turn information into effective communication?

First of all, creators of messages should keep in mind that:
- The message is the message received, rather than the one sent out.
- All information is a puzzle for others.
- Both oral and written communication should be seen in terms of negotiation of meaning.

The rhetorical situation described

The rhetorical situation describes the major choices that have to be made when people create formal, structured messages. These choices will turn unstructured information into effective communication.

What are these major choices?

Keeping a specific message form such as a letter or report in mind, people should:
- analyse their audience
- decide on their purposes
- plan and organize their messages in a coherent way
- select words to suit the audience and purposes
- select the right technical terms
- select the right level of formality
- decide on the most effective layout to achieve good readability
- select the most effective message type from the range below:
    - report
    - letter
    - memorandum
    - in-house journal article
    - proposal
    - notice for board
    - circular
    - instructions
    - procedures
    - press release.

Figure 10.1 summarizes the main features of the rhetorical situation. It shows that the final message is built up stage-by-stage. Knowledge of the theory and careful preparation will result in a much more effective message.

The following chapters will discuss each stage in preparing a message. Examples are given where relevant. This chapter concentrates on *audience* and *purposes*.

THE RHETORICAL SITUATION

Figure 10.1
The rhetorical situation

Analysing the needs of your audience

Audiences may be divided into four broad categories:
- *A lay audience:* This audience is not expert in your field. The person or people may, however, be expert in other fields. Do not assume that a lay audience is a stupid audience.
  You would need to explain technical terms for this audience. You would also have to give more background detail.
- *An expert audience:* This audience is an expert in your field. You do not have to explain technical terms or give much background information.
- *A technical audience:* This audience comprises technicians. They might or might not be experts in your special field. They have detailed technical knowledge, and are interested in the practical results of your message.

- *A mixed audience:* This audience consists of experts and non-experts. They could, for example, be a board of directors who are going to decide on a proposal that you have written.

  This audience is difficult to communicate with because you have to cater for so many needs. It is better to use fewer technical terms here and to explain the terms that you have used.

Specific questions about the audience

Once you have chosen your broad category of audience, then describe your actual audience in detail. Ask the following questions:

- What is the size of my audience?
- What age is my audience?
- What is the gender of my audience?
- What is the level of education of my audience?
- What is the cultural background of my audience?
- What is the intelligence level of my audience?
- What language does my audience speak?
- What is the occupation of my audience?
- What is the position of my audience in the company?
- What is the income of my audience?
- What is the status of my audience in business and the community?

The answers to these questions will affect the way in which you prepare your message.

Once you have answered the questions above, ask yourself the following questions:

- Will my message be listened to or read by a number of people or by one person?
- What does my audience already know about my subject?
- What are the audience's attitudes to my subject and message?
- What are the audience's attitudes to me and my objectives?
- Under what conditions does my audience work? Do they, for example, work under unpleasant conditions? Are they under great pressure?
- What will my audience's objectives be when they receive my message?

All these questions stress that one should always be very sensitive to the needs of one's audience.

Deciding on your purposes

You could choose from a range of purposes such as:

- to *describe* a process
- to *explain* how something works

- to *instruct* a group
- to *record* the results of an investigation
- to *evaluate* results and to *recommend* action
- to *generate goodwill* for your company
- to *persuade* someone
- to *propose* that money be spent
- to *sell* a product
- to *apologize* to an angry customer
- to *inform* someone
- to *reject* a proposal.

You could combine two or three of the above purposes in one message. You could, for example, write a report with the following purposes:

- to *record* results
- to *evaluate* the results
- to *recommend* action.

A business letter could be written with the purposes of *persuading* someone, and *generating goodwill* at the same time.

CHAPTER 11

Planning and Organizing Messages

Summary

Well-organized messages are essential. This chapter sets out a range of techniques for achieving messages that are easy to listen to or read.

Any audience needs to know two things at once about a message:
- What are its purposes?
- What is it about?

A well-organized message starts with good research and effective use of sources. The details of every work consulted should be recorded on a bibliography card. Notes and records of interviews should also be recorded on cards.

Once the research has been done, information has to be organized. This chapter recommends an approach in two stages:
- Brainstorm ideas by creating a mind-map or creative pattern.
- Then organize the ideas by means of a topic outline.

The topic outline, either down or across a page, helps the sender to ensure *unity, coherence* and *emphasis*. A unified message is one that has one major theme flowing through it. A coherent message is one in which each stage flows into the next with good transitions. A message with the right emphasis is one in which the most important idea is very clear to the audience.

This chapter stresses the importance of using the beginnings and ends of messages because these are the points of major impact.

Messages should be organized so that they follow a specific plan. This could be a time-plan, general to particular, particular to general or largest to smallest.

Messages should be given a 'shape' such as a diamond, pyramid or inverted pyramid. This shape will guide the flow of information for the best impact.

Key points

- Plan messages very carefully.
- Research information and use bibliography and note cards.
- Use a creative pattern to generate ideas.
- Once you have generated ideas, use a topic outline to achieve unity, coherence and emphasis.
- Use the beginnings and ends of messages to achieve the greatest impact.
- Take great care to make the middle sections of messages as effective as possible. The middle sections are the weakest sections.
- Use a diamond shape for a business letter.
- Use a pyramid shape for a report.
- Use an inverted pyramid for a press release or for newspaper writing.
- Use specific orders of information for the best impact.

PLANNING AND ORGANIZING MESSAGES 163

Introduction

Well-planned and well-organized messages have a great impact on an audience. The best messages are easy to follow. They will be remembered better than badly organized messages.

Any audience needs to know two things immediately about a message:
- What are its purposes?
- What is it about?

This chapter discusses the following techniques for achieving well planned and well-organized messages.
- Building up a set of bibliography cards for researching a topic in depth.
- Writing notes on note cards.
- Use of creative patterns or mind-maps to start organizing information.
- Use of a vertical or horizontal plan to organize information.
- Ways of organizing information.
- Using an outline to achieve unity, coherence and emphasis.
- Using the diamond and pyramid shapes to help one organize information.
- Using the beginnings and ends of messages to achieve the greatest impact.
- Preparing coherent spoken and written messages.

Using bibliography cards

If you are asked to write an article for your in-house magazine, for example, you will have to research your topic in some detail. You could also be asked to write an investigative report that needs research.

These tasks mean that you will have to:
- Make up a list of written sources such as books, journal articles and reports.
- Gather information from books, journal articles and other written sources.
- Record your notes on cards.
- Interview people and record the key points.
- Search the Internet for relevant information.

When you start your research, record the authors and titles of the sources that you propose to use.

Consider the following sources:
- *Reports.* Many organizations keep a library of past reports. These could give you information on what has happened in the past in your field.

- *Journal and magazine articles.* These will give you up-to-date information.
- *Encyclopaedias.* They will give you general information on your topic.
- *The Internet.* This will give you access to a vast amount of up-to-date information.

If you need to do further research, then the following *sources in libraries* will help you:

- *Bibliographies.* These list the details of publications on specific subjects. You could also consult the bibliographies at the ends of books and journal articles. These could give you ideas for further reading.
- *Indexes of Abstracts.* These briefly summarize the content of journal articles. They could give you valuable pointers for further reading.

Interviews. If you organize these carefully they will give you specific ideas and expert opinions on topics that you would not easily gain from other sources.

Develop and evaluate your bibliography

Once you have gathered a number of sources, you should write out a bibliography card for each source. You should also record each interview on a card. Figure 11.1 illustrates a bibliography card.

Once you have built up your set of cards, decide on the value of each source. Ask yourself the following questions.
- What is the authority of the writer?
- What is the value of this information to my theme?

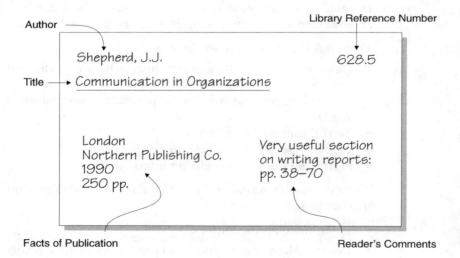

Figure 11.1
Example of a Bibliography Card

PLANNING AND ORGANIZING MESSAGES

- Am I dealing with vague or definite statements?
- Is the writer making careful judgements or are the arguments weak?

Record interviews

When you interview people, record each interview on a card as follows:

```
Name of Interviewee: _____. Position: _____
Company: _____
Date: _____ Time: _____ Length of interview: _____
Place of interview: _____
Nature of interview —  structured: _____
                       unstructured: _____
Main points discussed: _____
_____
_____
Interviewer's comments: _____
_____
```

Figure 11.2
Example of an interview record card

Using note cards

If you have to take down a large number of notes, then write your notes on a set of cards. These cards are much better than loose sheets of paper because:

- They can be organized and sorted easily.
- They can be carried round.
- They are compact.
- They force you to concentrate on essentials.

The example in figure 11.3 illustrates a note card. Note the comments. The card should be about 20 × 15 cm in size.

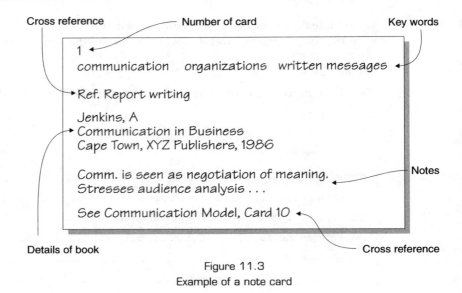

Figure 11.3
Example of a note card

Planning information

Once you have gathered your information, you need to organize it. Do not arrange your information into straight lines immediately. Rather organize your information in two stages:

- *Stage one*: A pattern of inter-connected ideas radiating from a central idea.
- *Stage two*: A topic outline with a thesis statement and numbered headings.

This approach will ensure that you use all your key ideas.

Figure 11.4 illustrates a creative pattern, or mind-map. Note that each idea is connected. Continue this process until you have reflected the content of your notes. Then check that each group of ideas fits together. Move ideas into other groups by using arrows as shown.

Topic outline

Once you are satisfied with your pattern, select major items and supporting points and arrange them in an outline. This could be either a *vertical* or a *horizontal* outline. At the top of the outline write in one or two sentences what the information is about. This is your *thesis statement* or key idea. A good thesis statement will help you to achieve a *unified* message. A unified message has one central theme running through it. A good outline will ensure that you do not jump from one idea to another and back again. Your audience should then be able to follow your argument.

PLANNING AND ORGANIZING MESSAGES

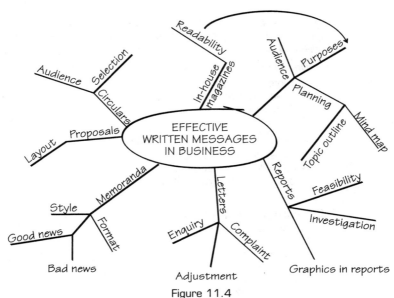

Figure 11.4
Example of a creative pattern or mind-map

Example of vertical plan

Make a preliminary vertical plan. Then move information round until you are satisfied. Then prepare a final plan. Figure 11.5 illustrates part of a final vertical plan. Note the multiple decimal numbering system and the indenting.

A horizontal plan

A vertical plan moves down a page. A horizontal plan, on the other hand, moves across a page. This enables you to see the whole plan more easily. Turn an A4 page onto its side for a horizontal plan.

Figure 11.6 illustrates a horizontal plan. Please note that it is incomplete.

When you have drawn up your outline, check that:
- your major headings are in the right order
- your information under each heading is in the right order.

When you are satisfied, then prepare an *introduction* and a *conclusion* where appropriate.

> *Thesis statement:* This article discusses the techniques for writing effective messages in companies. It stresses purposes, audience, the correct format, style and readability.
>
> 1. *Decide on your purposes*
>   1.1 Inform
>   1.2 Generate goodwill
>   1.3 Persuade
>   1.4 . . .
>
> 2. *Analyse the needs of your audience*
>   2.1 Knowledge of subject
>   2.2 Readiness to receive the message
>   2.3 Status in the organization
>   2.4 . . .
>
> 3. *Decide on the correct format*
>   3.1 Written message
>   3.1.1 Report
>   3.1.2 Proposal
>   3.1.3 Letter
>   3.2 Spoken message
>   3.2.1 Talk
>   3.2.2 Oral report
>
> 4. *Plan the message*
>   4.1 Research the topic
>   4.2 Create a pattern
>   4.3 Draw an outline
>
> 5. *Choose effective style and readability*
>   5.1 Select an appropriate style
>   5.2 Ensure good readability

Figure 11.5
Example of a Vertical Topic Outline

> *Thesis statement:* This article discusses the techniques for writing effective messages in companies. It stresses purposes, audience, the correct format, style and readability.
>
> | 1. Decide on purposes | 2. Audience's needs | 3. Format | 4. Planning | 5. Style and Readability |
> |---|---|---|---|---|
> | 1.1 Inform
1.2 Generate goodwill
1.3 Persuade | 2.1 Knowledge of . . .
2.2 Readiness to . . .
2.3 Status in organization | . . . | . . . | . . . |

Figure 11.6
Example of an Horizontal Topic Outline

Choosing an appropriate style: ensuring unity, coherence and the right emphasis

This chapter has already stressed the great importance of a unified message.

All messages should also be *coherent*, or properly linked together. This means that in a talk every idea should flow logically into the next. In addition, every section should flow into the next.

In a written message, this means that every sentence should flow logically into the next. In addition, every paragraph should flow into the next.

Listeners and readers should be given plenty of *signposts* to direct them. The following are examples of signpost words:

- Conjunctions, such as 'because', 'if', 'but', 'however'.
- Reference words such as the pronouns 'it', 'this', 'these', 'those'.
- Key nouns that are repeated at various stages in the message.
- Key pronouns such as 'he', 'she', 'they' and 'that', which refer back to nouns.
- Numbering words, such as 'firstly', 'secondly', 'lastly'.
- Sentences or groups of words linking paragraphs, such as 'The paragraph above showed that . . . ', or 'These, however, were not the only reasons why . . . ' . Paragraph links can point downward to the next paragraph or upward to the paragraph above.

The following examples illustrate the techniques of *signposting* to achieve coherence. Speakers and writers should provide good transitions between sections.

Example from a speech

> 'I'm going to describe the process in *three* stages. *First* I want to . . .
> The *second* stage covers . . . *As a result* we found that . . .
> *However, these findings* did not . . .
> *In addition*, the mistake of . . .
> *Finally*, I'd like to describe the *third stage* . . .

Note that joining words, phrases and sentences are in italics.

Example from writing

> Good face-to-face communication depends largely on good *listening*. In this article I plan to cover the *key points* about *active listening*. I will cover these *key points* in the following order:
> - motivating yourself as a *listener*
> - becoming aware of your *bad listening habits*

> - the techniques of *active listening*.
>
> I will conclude with a summary of the key points that I have made.
>
> How do you motivate yourselves as listeners? . . .
>
> *However*, being motivated as listeners does not take you far enough. You need to know what your *bad listening habits* are.
>
> Research suggests that the following are among the *worst listening habits*. Are you guilty of any of *them*?
>
> . . .
>
> Now that you have analysed your *bad listening habits*, I wish to *move on to* the techniques of *active listening*.
>
> *Active listening* . . .
>
> *In conclusion* . . .

Different messages demand different techniques for achieving a coherent discourse. *An essay or article* in continuous writing depends on:

- good links between sentences
- good transitions between paragraphs.

A report, on the other hand, depends on:

- good headings
- an effective numbering system
- good transitions between paragraphs
- good links between sentences.

These different approaches are illustrated as follows:

Coherence in an essay or article

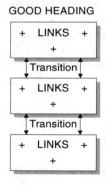

Figure 11.7
Achieving coherence in continuous writing

Coherence in a report or proposal

Figure 11.8
Achieving coherence in a report

Achieving effective emphasis

Achieving the right *emphasis* means that your audience recognizes your most important points straight away.

Effective emphasis can be achieved by:

- Using the beginnings and ends of messages to state and summarize your key points
- Using the topic or key sentences of paragraphs to state your main ideas
- Devoting more space or time to key points
- Repeating key ideas and points
- Ensuring that you do not bring in irrelevant points to break your unifying thread.

Points of major impact in a message

The *beginnings and ends* of messages have the greatest impact. Pay special attention to the *beginnings* of your messages. Strive to create a *good first impression* because this is likely to last throughout the message. Use this point of major impact to summarize your key points. Your readers should know at once what the message is about.

A bad first impression could destroy your message.

What people hear or read *last* they are likely to remember best. This applies especially to short messages and to articles. However, research suggests that very few people read the appendices at the end of reports.

Use the *ends* of messages to summarize and to urge action. Use the ends of business letters to generate goodwill for your organization.

Middle sections of messages are the weakest

The *middle sections* of messages are the weakest parts of the message. For talks and oral reports make sure that you use non-verbal communication and a good message structure to carry your message.

Make sure that the layout and organization of your written messages are very good in the middle. People tend to skim the information. You should, therefore, try to attract and re-attract their attention.

Different ways of organizing information

When you organize your information consider some of the orders below. If you have studied these in advance, you should be able to prepare better outlines and write more effective messages.

- *Time order:* You could move from past to present or from present to past.
- *Size order:* You could begin with the largest item and move to the smallest, or you could go the other way round.
- *Familiar to unfamiliar:* Here you could start with an idea that your audience understands. You could then move to what is unfamiliar in easy stages.
- *Simple to complex:* You could start with a number of simple ideas. You could then combine them into a more complex idea.
- *Cause to result:* You could describe a number of causes and then give their results.
- *General to particular:* You could start with a general statement and then move to particular arguments to illustrate your general statement.
- *Particular to general:* You could give a number of specific examples and then put them together to make a general statement.
- *Comparison* You could compare two ideas by showing how they are similar and how they differ.
- *Problem to solution:* You could state a problem and then show, step-by-step, how to solve it.

Shaping information

All messages should have a particular 'shape' or format. This section suggests three major shapes describing:

- business letters
- reports
- press releases

Diamond shape for business letters

Think of a business letter as a diamond, as illustrated below.

PLANNING AND ORGANIZING MESSAGES

Figure 11.9
A diamond shape for a letter

The letter starts with a sharp point at the subject-line. It then has an overview of the key points. After that it moves to more detailed information before closing with another sharp point.

Pyramid shape for reports

A report, on the other hand, may be seen as a pyramid resting on a broad base of detail in the appendices. This is illustrated in figure 11.10.

Figure 11.10
A pyramid shape for a report

Note that the *Conclusions* and *Recommendations* have been placed before the *Body*. They are there because the evidence is that very few people read the body of the report or the appendices. People do, however, read the Conclusions and Recommendations because they are needed for decision-making. The above order is strongly recommended.

Note that each major section of the report is written with a different audience in mind. The summary is written for the widest possible audience. It is non-technical for a *lay audience*.

The *Introduction, Conclusion* and *Recommendation* are written for a *mixed audience*. They are the decision-makers. They could be a committee or a Board of Directors comprising experts and non-experts. This section is therefore partly technical to cater for experts and non-experts.

The *Body of the Report* and the *Appendices* are fully technical. They are written for an *expert audience*.

This approach to audience in the writing of reports in organizations is strongly recommended.

The inverted pyramid for press releases and newspaper writing

When you are designing a message such as a press release or an article for an in-house magazine, consider using the *inverted pyramid*. This shape puts *all* the most important information at the beginning. The information then becomes less and less important. This enables an editor to remove information from the bottom up without losing key points.

An inverted pyramid is illustrated below:

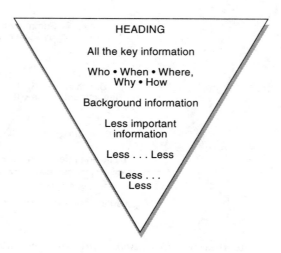

Figure 11.11
Inverted pyramid for a press release

Checklist for well-organized messages

Use the following checklist to ensure that your messages have a really good impact.

Have I
- Stated my purposes clearly?
- Analysed the needs of my audience?
- Selected the right format?
- Brainstormed my ideas in the form of a creative pattern?
- Selected main and supporting points and put them into an effective topic outline?
- Organized my information effectively?
- Used the beginnings and ends of my messages for the best impact?
- Checked for unity, coherence and emphasis?
- Shaped my message correctly?

CHAPTER 12

Choosing an Effective Vocabulary

Summary

It is very important to choose a vocabulary to suit your purposes and your audience. This chapter sets out a framework to help you choose an effective vocabulary for professional messages.

This chapter covers the following key aspects of vocabulary:

- words and meanings
- differences between fact and opinion
- functions of words
- guidelines for choosing a vocabulary for professional messages.

Words are not containers of meaning. They gain their meanings through use and agreement. These meanings are recorded in dictionaries. However, words are ambiguous, and senders of messages have to find out if they and the receivers of messages share the same meanings.

Words have a core of meaning, which is called a *denotation*. In addition, many words have suggestive qualities called *connotations*. Words with strong connotations can convey powerful positive or negative messages. They should therefore be used with care.

People need to distinguish between fact and opinion. Factual messages rely on words with strong denotations. Such writing or speaking is described as *a referential style*. If people express opinions they will use words with strong connotations. This approach is called an *emotive style*.

Words have specific functions in communication. They can be used to:

- give facts
- express emotions
- persuade
- acknowledge people's presence.

The chapter gives a set of guidelines for choosing a professional vocabulary. These are summarized as follows:

- Select the right technical terms and define them.
- Choose familiar, rather than unfamiliar words.
- Choose carefully between referential and emotive words.
- Choose between generic and specific words.

- Choose words at the right level of abstraction.
- Choose concrete, rather than relative or abstract words.
- Avoid words that pre-judge a situation.
- Choose formal, rather than informal words.

Key points

- Always check that you share the same meanings with receivers of your messages.
- Define technical terms.
- Do not be tempted to choose long, difficult words to impress others. Rather choose simple words.
- Give facts where you can. Avoid sending messages at too high a level of abstraction.
- Distinguish between fact and opinion.
- Avoid words that pre-judge a situation.
- Select your vocabulary according to a set of rules. Make sure that you choose every word because you want it to be there. Do not select words at random.

CHOOSING AN EFFECTIVE VOCABULARY

Introduction

Once you have planned the message, the next stage is to start writing it. The correct choice of vocabulary to suit your purposes and your audience is very important.

This chapter has been designed to help you choose the most effective vocabulary for messages in organizations. The following points are covered:

- words and meanings
- properties of words
- ensuring that people share the same meanings of words
- differences between fact and opinion
- functions of words
- guidelines for choosing a vocabulary for messages in organizations.

Words and meanings

Words on their own have no meaning. They take on meaning as people use them. Others then agree on these meanings, and dictionaries record them. Meanings of words do, however, change over time, and dictionaries have to be kept up to date. Take the words 'disinterested' and 'advise'. A dictionary might suggest that 'disinterested' means 'impartial'. However, it is also being used with the same meaning as 'uninterested'. Users of this word therefore need to be quite clear that they share the same meaning.

'Advise' means 'to give advice'. However, in business letters it is often used to mean 'inform', as in 'We wish to advise you that your order has arrived'. Which is the 'correct' meaning? Are both correct?

Meanings are in people. Words are symbols. They mean what they stand for or refer to in the opinion of users. Users therefore assign meanings to words. There is no guarantee that all users have assigned the same meanings to those words.

Words are often ambiguous. The best definitions should, therefore, quote examples of how words are used. Words take on meaning when used in *contexts*. Take the word 'knot' for example. It is meaningless on its own.

- Does it refer to a ship's speed?
- Is it something tied into a piece of string?
- Is it a mark on a piece of sawn wood that shows where a branch was?
- Is it a group of people?

The word 'message' is used in this book. What does it mean on its own?

- Is it spoken?
- Is it written on a scrap of paper?

- Is it a long, factual report?
- Is it a highly emotional love-letter?
- Is it a business letter declaring someone redundant?

People make two major mistakes with words:

- They assume that the word is the thing that it represents. The word 'company', for example, is not the group of people that it refers to.
- They assume that one word can refer to all of something. The word 'organization' is general. It cannot refer exactly to every kind of organization. Further definition is necessary.

This failure to distinguish between 'all' and 'one' or 'some', leads to poor thinking and poor communication. It leads to dangerous generalizations such as 'All X's are dishonest'. Some, or one may be dishonest, but not all.

Denotations and connotations of words

The word *denotation* refers to the *core of meaning* that is reflected in a dictionary. *Connotations*, on the other hand, are the suggestive qualities that words take on. These connotations are difficult to record in a dictionary. Nevertheless, they convey strong positive and negative messages.

Many scientific and technical words are strictly denotative. They carry virtually no suggestive qualities, and can be used precisely. Words such as 'thermostat' or 'oxygen' refer to specific concepts.

Most other words are not nearly as precise. The word 'information', for example, can refer to a wide range of messages. It could refer to:

- a textbook
- a notice
- a report
- a talk
- a circular
- an article in an in-house journal.

Words with strong connotations are important in communication. However, people need to use them very carefully in messages. They convey attitudes, both positive and negative, and can leave lasting impressions. They are very effective for generating goodwill for an organization if chosen with care.

The following examples show the kinds of messages that connotations can convey:

- We wish to select from your *colourful* range of materials. (Positive)
- Your range is too *gaudy* for our *superior* clientele. (Negative and condescending)

- I found your behaviour at the last meeting to be *childish*. (Negative)
- These paintings show a *childlike* simplicity. (Neutral to positive)
- It has been drawn to the attention of the undersigned that you continue to *materialize* at work late. (Negative, stiff and condescending).
- I *notice* that you have arrived at 08h30 twice this week. (Neutral and factual)

Synonyms

Because of their wide range of denotations and connotations, words can seldom be interchanged. People need to be very sensitive to shades of meaning when they choose words. The important point about working with closely related words such as 'big' *and* 'large' is to know how they differ.

For example, are 'small', 'tiny' and 'minute' the same? How do 'large' and 'huge' differ? Do they differ only in degree? Are 'enough' and 'sufficient' synonyms? Is 'sufficient' a more formal word than 'enough'?

Functions of words

Words perform a range of functions in messages. Their major functions are to:

- convey facts
- convey opinions
- persuade
- help people communicate in social settings.

Conveying facts

If a sender's purpose is to convey facts then (s)he should use words with strong denotations. Checkable facts should be given.

The following example from a report illustrates factual language. This is also called *referential* language.

> The building contains fifteen columns of reinforced concrete. Each column is 5 m high, and measures 30 cm × 30 cm. These columns have been placed 10 m apart.

Conveying emotions

Words that carry emotions have a range of connotations. These connotations suggest opinions, rather than facts.

The following example shows a mixture of fact and opinion. The opinion is dominant. The words expressing opinions are also called *emotive* language.

> This is a fine building of its kind. The soaring and graceful columns support a brilliantly designed upper storey that houses a suite of elegant offices.

The words 'fine', 'soaring', 'graceful', 'brilliantly' and 'elegant' convey opinions. They also have strong connotations of approval.

Differences between fact and opinion

People sending and receiving messages should take great care to distinguish between fact and opinion.

Compare: 'You are the best salesperson in the team'. (opinion)
With: 'You sold ten motor cars in the last month, compared with Peter's five'. (fact)

Compare: 'You are a thief'. (opinion)
With: 'The missing purse was found in your bag'. (fact)

Using words to persuade

People could attempt to persuade others either by using factual language or by using emotive language, or they could use a mixture of the two.

The following example illustrates an attempt to persuade by means of facts. The writer has avoided strong connotations.

> Buy the XYZ pump for the following reasons:
> - It has a phosphor bronze impeller guaranteed for five years.
> - It can pump 200 litres of sludge a minute.
> - It has a head of 8 m.
> - All parts are locally made.
> - The supply of parts is guaranteed until 1998.

The next example tries to persuade people by emotive means:

> Buy the tried and trusted XYZ pump. You won't find a better one anywhere. It can pump a greater volume than most other pumps. It's more reliable and does the job where you want it.

Most of the language above is pure opinion. The only fact is that the pump exists.

CHOOSING AN EFFECTIVE VOCABULARY 183

Using words for social reasons

People use standard words when they meet and part. These standard words are used to acknowledge other people. They can be used without thinking, and often do not carry the meanings that on the surface they should.

A greeting such as 'How are you?', will often be responded to with 'I'm fine thank you'. The speaker would not expect a long description of someone's health. These social formulas help to oil the wheels of conversation. They are therefore very important to help people in organizations, especially strangers, to work together.

Figure 12.1 summarizes the main functions of words.

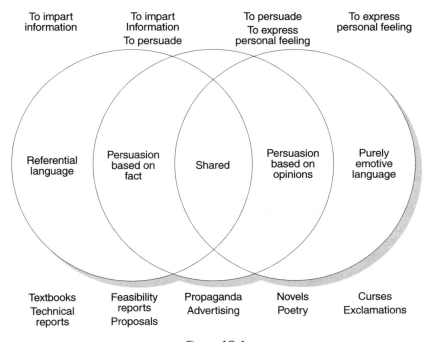

Figure 12.1
The main functions of words

Choosing a vocabulary for professional messages

This section gives a range of choices to help you select an appropriate vocabulary for professional messages. It covers the following:

- How to deal with technical terms.
- Choosing between familiar and unfamiliar words.
- Using appropriate referential and emotive words.
- Choosing the right generic and specific words.

- Choosing words at the right level of abstraction.
- Dealing with concrete, relative and abstract words.
- Avoiding words that pre-judge a situation.
- Selecting formal and informal words.

Dealing with technical terms

Technical terms are essential for the right audience. However, where possible they should be avoided for a mixed or non-technical audience. However, even a technical or expert audience may not understand all your terms.

You therefore have a range of choices:

- You could define all technical terms in a glossary or special dictionary for that message. This would be a successful approach for a technical report.
- You could leave out all technical terms.
- You could, in a talk, start by defining your key terms. You could write these on flip chart paper or on an overhead transparency.
- You could explain terms as you come to them in your message.

Many people are tempted to choose difficult technical words because they appear impressive. However, messages crowded with these terms do not communicate effectively. You are strongly advised to keep your messages simple.

Choosing between familiar and unfamiliar words

Choose familiar, often-used words, rather than seldom-used ones. Unfamiliar words make messages more difficult. They often increase the number of syllables per word as well. This makes messages hard to read and listen to.

Compare the following:

Less familiar	*More familiar*
to take cognizance of	to note
to terminate	to stop or end
to proliferate	to increase
disbursements	payments
emoluments	income

Using appropriate referential or factual words and emotive words

Referential words are factual, whereas emotive words suggest an attitude. Referential words are more appropriate in reports. A mixture of referential and emotive words would be better in business letters.

Compare the following.

Referential (factual)   *Emotive*

The XYZ motor car used 10 *l* per 100 km in city driving   The motor car is fuel efficient

His mass is 40 kg   He is skeletal

Choosing the right generic and specific words

Generic words are general words. They refer to classes or groups of words. Specific words, on the other hand, refer to individuals, objects or events.

The generic word 'message' could, for example, refer to the specific 'technical report', 'proposal', 'letter of adjustment'. The division is not, however, as clear-cut as this. Some words are more specific than others. Compare the following:

Generic	*Less Generic*	*More specific*	*Very specific*
Letter	Business letter	Letter of adjustment	Letter of adjustment to Mrs X who complained about a faulty article. The letter tells her that the article will be replaced.

Reports should be as specific as possible. Other messages will contain words that are more or less specific according to the sender's choice.

Choosing words at the right level of abstraction

The above examples, moving from generic to very specific are part of a *ladder of abstraction*. This is a very useful tool for helping you to choose the most effective vocabulary. The more specific your vocabulary, the less your audience will have to guess what you mean.

Figure 12.2 illustrates a short ladder of abstraction. The more steps in the ladder the greater the choice of words. The more carefully words are chosen, the more accurate the message.

Senders of messages should make sure that they choose the right level of abstraction for their messages. Each level gives vague or specific information. Make sure that you choose through knowledge rather than at random.

Compare the following examples:

> We are concerned about the precipitous decrease in profits in the recent past. A downward adjustment in prices should be considered.
> (Highly abstract)

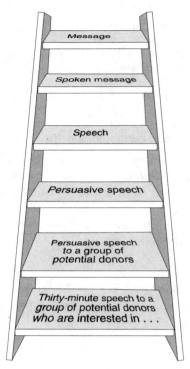

Figure 12.2
Ladder of abstraction.

> We are concerned about the 50% drop in profits in 1991. We should consider reducing our prices by 30% in 1993.
> (More concrete)

Dealing with concrete, relative and abstract words

Words may be divided into the following categories:

- concrete
- relative
- abstract.

These are convenient categories to describe the type of information that words give.

Concrete words

Words are not, of course, concrete. This category is, however, useful for describing words that refer to concrete referents that we can see, touch or smell. Such words are lower on the ladder of abstraction. Examples are 'office desk', 'word processor' or 'envelope'.

Relative words

These words are generally classified as adjectives or adverbs. They mean different things to different people, and generally reflect the user's opinion. Words such as 'huge', 'excellent', 'rich', 'poor' and 'very' are relative words. They should be avoided in messages such as reports where the stress is normally on facts.

Abstract words

Abstract words are high on the ladder of abstraction. They refer to general concepts and have no specific referents against which they can be checked.

Words such as 'organization', 'management', 'labour' and 'cost' are difficult to define. Examples to illustrate each word are essential if people are to understand their exact meaning. They are very hard to define without examples.

You should, therefore, be very careful when you use abstract words. Always give examples at a low level of abstraction so that the audience knows how you are using the abstract word.

Avoiding words that pre-judge a situation

Senders should be careful about using words that pre-judge a situation. Such words have positive or negative connotations that make clear communication difficult.

Compare:

- Why are you *idling* here when you should be preparing the report? (Negative connotation)
- Why are you relaxing here when you could be outside? (Neutral to positive)
- Who is that *man* with Estelle? (Neutral)
- Who is that *slob* with Estelle? (Negative)

Selecting formal and informal words

Senders should choose words that are appropriate for the level of formality of their message. A formal report or business letter needs a different vocabulary from an informal talk.

Compare the following levels of formality:

- The writer wishes to tender his apologies in this matter. (very formal)
- I wish to apologize for the mistake. (formal)
- I'm terribly sorry about this. (informal)

Informal words such as 'nice' and 'terribly' do not have precise meanings.

Compare the following examples:

Informal	*Formal*
Fantastic	Enjoyable
Guy	Man
Quote (noun)	Quotation

Organizations should use a vocabulary that is formal, rather than informal.

Checklist for choosing the right word

- Have I chosen words with *exact* meanings?
- Have I *defined* technical terms?
- Have I checked that I and my audience *share* the same meanings?
- Have I chosen words with the right *connotations*?
- Have I chosen *referential* words where appropriate?
- Have I used words that *pre-judge* a situation?
- Have I chosen words at the right *level of abstraction*?
- Have I chosen words at the right *level of formality*?
- Have I avoided *relative* words in factual messages?
- Have I given examples to help my audience understand any *abstract* words that I have used?

CHAPTER 13

Style, Tone and Jargon

Summary

This chapter sets out a framework to help you choose an effective spoken and written style. Style is defined as a way of speaking or writing. Words are selected and put together for a range of purposes and audiences.

Style may be defined in terms of its level of formality. It may also be described in terms of whether it is:

- personal or impersonal
- active or passive
- concise or wordy
- clear or ambiguous
- concrete or abstract.

Examples are given to illustrate all of these.

The chapter describes five levels of formality:

- high formal or frozen
- formal
- consultative
- casual
- intimate.

All these styles are illustrated.

Following the discussion of style, the chapter describes tone. It defines tone as the attitude of the sender towards the receiver, as reflected in the message. Tone is described by using such relative words as 'friendly', 'unfriendly', 'stiff' or 'relaxed'.

The characteristics of jargon are then defined. *Jargon* is any language that is hard to understand because it has:

- Technical words unsuited to the audience
- Large numbers of long, unfamiliar words
- Long, complex sentences
- Long paragraphs.

Key points

- Choose the right level of formality.
- Do not be too formal.
- If possible, write in a personal style.
- If you have to use an impersonal style try to make it impersonal active, rather than impersonal passive.
- Use the active form in preference to the passive form.
- Be as concise as you can.
- Avoid ambiguity by checking that your pronouns refer back to specific nouns. Check your punctuation and the meanings of words.
- Give facts and figures where you can. Do not present messages at too high a level of abstraction.
- Make your tone friendly or neutral. Avoid an unfriendly tone.
- Write clearly and simply. Avoid the elements of jargon.

STYLE, TONE AND JARGON

Introduction

Once you have chosen the right vocabulary, you need to put the words together in a style to suit your purposes, the audience and the message.

This chapter covers the following aspects of style:

- a definition of style
- levels of formality
- differences between a personal and an impersonal style
- techniques for writing clearly and simply, with the stress on
    - an active, compared with a passive style
    - a concise, compared with a wordy style
    - a clear, compared with an ambiguous style
    - a concrete, compared with an abstract style
    - a simple, compared with a complex style
- tone in communication
- the elements of jargon, or what makes messages hard to understand.

The chapters on vocabulary and style should be read together, as the principles in each are linked.

Style and tone defined

Style may be defined as a way of selecting and putting words together for a range of purposes and a range of audiences. It refers to a way of writing or speaking.

Style and tone are closely linked. *Tone* is defined as the sender's attitude towards the receiver and the material being communicated. Tone is reflected mainly in the choice of vocabulary.

A style may be defined in terms of:

- how formal it is
- whether it is personal or impersonal
- whether it is active or passive
- whether it is concise or wordy
- whether it is clear or ambiguous
- whether it is concrete or abstract.

This chapter will describe each of these aspects with examples.

Levels of formality

A written or spoken style may be described in terms of five different levels of formality. Figure 13.1 illustrates these five levels. Each of these styles is illustrated with comments.

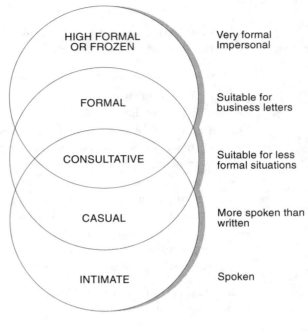

Figure 13.1
Levels of formality

High formal or frozen style

This style is often impersonal. It is characterized by:

- a very formal vocabulary comprising long, unfamiliar words
- long, involved sentences
- long paragraphs.

The subject matter is often complex. Very little attention is paid to the relationship between the writer and the reader.

Example 1

```
As a result of this experiment on durability, it
can be hypothesized that the original substance
was of a dense nature, of great durability and lon-
gevity with the ability to withstand sustained
high degrees of pressure.
```

Note the very formal vocabulary and long sentence.

Example 2

The following example is an extract from a memorandum.

> It has been noted by the Personnel Department that the need for a course in telephone techniques should be regarded as of high priority by our organization in the immediate future. This belief has been strengthened by an in-depth investigation of a large number of telephone conversations undertaken by a team of investigators under the supervision of this Department.

Note the use of the impersonal 'it' and the passive forms such as 'has been noted' and 'should be regarded'.

People in organizations should avoid this style. It is hard to read and very difficult to listen to.

Formal style

This style is less formal than the high formal style. It is an effective style for all types of oral and written messages.

The following example illustrates this style.

> The Personnel Department has noted the need for a course in telephone techniques. This course should be a high priority.
>
> A team of experts strengthened our belief when they investigated a large number of telephone conversations.

Note the active style, the short sentences and the short paragraphs.

A formal style should have:
- formal and complete sentences
- short sentences
- short paragraphs
- a simple but formal vocabulary
- no slang

- no short forms such as 'you're' and 'I'm'.

Consultative style

This style is less formal than the formal style. It is suitable for spoken and written messages in organizations. It is particularly suitable for memoranda and talks or oral reports within a company.

The following example illustrates a consultative style.

> We in the Personnel Department feel that there's a great need for a course in telephone techniques.
>
> We've become even more sure of this need now that we've gone through a report from some experts. They analysed a large number of telephone conversations and came up with some surprising answers.

Note the following aspects of the above style:
- It uses the personal pronoun 'we'.
- It uses the short form 'we've'
- The vocabulary has been simplified.
- The vocabulary is more casual. Note, for example, 'came up with'.
- The sentences have been kept short but complete.

This style is used when writers or speakers wish to establish and maintain a close relationship with their readers or listeners.

Casual style

This style is more suited to speaking than writing. The language is conversational, and the sentences may be incomplete. Abbreviations are used.

The following memorandum was written in a casual style:

> My Department feels that we're in need of some training in telephone work. We've had some experts in. They've been analysing what's been going on telephonewise. What a shock! Our telephonists haven't a clue!

STYLE, TONE AND JARGON

Note the short forms and casual vocabulary such as 'haven't a clue'. Note, also, that the sentences are short.

Intimate style

This style is used among people who know each other very well. It uses short forms, informal words and incomplete sentences.

The following example illustrates this style:

```
Hi there! We dropped in to see you. Alas! No-one
in. See you Saturday. Cheers!
```

This style is not suitable for organizations.

Personal and impersonal styles

A personal style uses personal pronouns. It is generally less formal than an impersonal style. An impersonal style uses the impersonal pronoun 'it'. It also uses more passive structures and is more formal. The following examples illustrate each style:

Personal style

```
Dear Mrs Jones

SEWING MACHINE ORDER

I am pleased to let you know that your machine has
arrived. We shall be testing it over the next two
days. Once we are satisfied we will deliver it to
your home.
```

Impersonal style

```
The writer was instructed to report on the major
problems in the distribution of XYZ products. It
has been found that delivery routes have been
badly planned and that the company's agents have
not been planning properly.
```

This style is suitable for reports where the stress is on the content, rather than on the writer. Note, particularly, the use of:

- 'the writer'
- the passive forms
- the impersonal 'it'.

Active and passive styles

English uses two voices: active and passive. The following examples show the difference:

Active	The Director (Actor)	dictated (Action)	the memorandum (Acted on)
Passive	The Memorandum (Acted on)	was dictated (Action)	by the Director (Actor)

The active form is called 'actor-action order'. This is a more vigorous style. Where possible, writers and speakers should use it. A passive style makes writing less direct. It can lead to long-windedness if writers are not careful.

The passive style is however acceptable:

- When a report has to be written impersonally. An impersonal style and the passive often go together, as in: 'It is recorded by X and Y that temperatures . . . '.
- When a writer wishes to emphasize a point, as in: 'The regulations have been broken once again'. This stresses the regulations. It is more effective than 'someone has broken the regulations once again'.
- When you wish to remain neutral in a potentially difficult situation, as in: 'The form was returned unsigned' rather than: 'You did not sign the form'.

Note

The ideal style for a report is an *impersonal, active* style, as in: 'Smith and Jones note that . . . ' or 'The writer examined all the cases reported . . . ' rather than:

'It was noted by Smith and Jones that . . . ' or 'All the cases reported were examined by the writer'.

A concise, rather than a wordy style

A long-winded style wastes everyone's time. Using ten words when five would do costs organizations a great deal of money. Messages are much longer than necessary and take longer to prepare.

A long-winded or wordy style has the following characteristics:

- too many words to express what could be expressed simply
- long, involved sentences.

STYLE, TONE AND JARGON

The following examples illustrate a wordy style and a re-written version.

```
Taking all these factors into consideration at
this point in time it can be safely assumed that
the accident was not of a serious nature and that
we need to take cognizance of the warnings issued
in the recent past.
```

This could be re-written as follows:

```
All these factors suggest that the accident was
not serious. However, we should note the recent
warnings that we have had.
```

Concise messages are those in which every word counts. There is no need, however, to make every sentence so reduced that it becomes meaningless.

A clear, rather than an ambiguous style

A clear style helps the reader or listener to understand the meaning straight away. There should be no doubt about this meaning.

Ambiguous messages, or messages with more than one meaning, are caused by:

- vague references of pronouns such as 'it' or 'they'
- poor word order
- words that have more than one meaning in the sentence
- poor punctuation.

Compare the following examples:

'What he said at the meeting he did not know'
(Do the two 'hes' refer to the same person?)

This sentence could be corrected as follows:

'Mr Jackson said that he did not know what Mr Solomons had said at the meeting.'

'We may choose three approaches here. When we discuss *it* we ... '
(What does 'it' refer to?)

We should rather say:

'We may choose three approaches here. When we discuss *these three approaches* we ... '.

A concrete, rather than a vague style

A concrete style gives facts and figures. A vague style gives vague information that is difficult to use.

Compare the following examples:

> 'Many people consider that the drastic drop in sales was caused by . . . '

> 'The Sales Director and her staff consider that the 50% drop in the sales of XYZ soap in January 1992 was caused by . . . '

Where possible, messages should be concrete, rather than vague.

Tone in messages

Tone, the attitude of sender to receiver, is very important in spoken and written messages.

Tone in spoken messages is conveyed by your voice, facial expressions, the way you stand and the words you use. Tone in written messages is conveyed by the words and the ways in which they combine.

Tone is described by relative words such as:

- friendly — unfriendly
- relaxed — stiff or pompous
- formal — informal

Where possible, the tone of a speech should be friendly or neutral, rather than aggressive. The tone of a report should be neutral. The tone of a business letter should be friendly or neutral.

Compare the tone of the following:

```
Receipt of your letter is acknowledged. Please be
advised that your interest will be deposited by
the undersigned in the designated account.
```

The above is pompous and unfriendly. It could be re-written as follows:

```
Thank you for your letter of 20 January. I am
pleased to let you know that I shall be depositing
your interest in your account. (Friendly and yet
formal)
```

STYLE, TONE AND JARGON

Jargon

The term 'jargon' describes any language that is hard to understand for the following reasons:

- It contains many technical words that the audience cannot understand.
- It contains a large number of long, unfamiliar words.
- It contains many unnecessary words. This is called *circumlocution* or talking and writing round the point. These unnecessary words are called *redundant* words.
- It contains long, complicated sentences.
- It contains stock phrases.

Business letters, in addition to the above characteristics, may contain stock phrases or sentences. These are classified as business jargon. Some examples are:

- Please find enclosed . . .
- We are in receipt of . . .
- Your letter of 29 January refers . . .
- Your goodselves
- We are pleased to advise that . . .

Writers should replace these phrases and sentences with clear, simple writing.

The following example illustrates some of the elements of jargon:

```
Your letter of the 25th inst. refers. Please be ad-
vised that the undersigned has taken cognizance of
your complaint about the company's negligence in
the matter of the abovenamed contract, and we un-
dertake to leave no stone unturned to ensure that
all problems are rectified by us.
```

Note the stock words and phrases:
- inst.
- refers
- please be advised
- taken cognizance
- abovenamed
- leave no stone unturned.

In addition, note the long sentence and high number of syllables per word.

Checklist for an effective style
- Have I selected the right level of formality?
- Have I selected the right personal or impersonal style?
- Have I used an active rather than a passive style?
- If I have used passive forms, are they suited to the message?
- Have I been as concise as possible?
- Have I been clear?
- Have I avoided ambiguity?
- Have I been concrete, rather than abstract?
- Have I used the right tone?
- Have I avoided elements of jargon?
- Have I kept the number of syllables per word as low as possible?

CHAPTER 14

The Elements of Readability

Summary

Readability is defined as the success that readers have in interpreting a written message. Readability refers to all the elements in a text that help readers to cope with that text.

This chapter stresses that we are now in a visual age. Written messages have to look attractive to compete with the many attractive pictures that people look at.

Readability depends on the writer and the reader. Readers need to gain information and be treated in a friendly way. They also vary in their ability to read efficiently.

Writers have to cater for these needs. What techniques can writers use to make their messages readable? Their major techniques are:

- have very clear purposes.
- describe the needs of the audience very carefully.
- select the right vocabulary.
- write short sentences and paragraphs.
- use a numbering system and headings.
- set out the message with plenty of white space.
- use correctly expressed lists.

The chapter goes on to show how to calculate a fog index. This index shows the school reading age for which a message has been written.

Key points

- Write messages so that they attract and re-attract the reader.
- Make written messages visually attractive.
- Use a range of techniques to keep people reading your work.
- Keep the number of syllables per word as low as you can.
- Adjust your sentence length and vocabulary to cater for your audience's reading age.

Introduction

The term *readability* refers to all the elements in a written message that make it attractive and help people to read it easily.

This chapter describes a range of techniques to make your written messages as readable as possible.

We are now in a visual age. Written messages have to compete with a vast range of attractive pictures. Writers therefore have to understand how to make their written messages as attractive as possible.

Writer and reader

The readability of a message depends on the writer and the reader. For that reason, writers should be as sensitive as possible to the reader's abilities and needs.

The writer has to cater for:

- The reader's emotional needs. These needs are to be treated in a friendly way. Readers do not like to feel that they are being treated like machines.
- The reader's need to gain information from a message. The message therefore needs to be clear and easy to follow.

In addition, the writer relies on the reader's ability to:

- read efficiently
- understand the message.

What can writers do to cater for readers' needs?

Writers have a range of techniques that they can use to cater for the reader's needs. They are:

- putting summaries at the beginning
- presenting messages that are well-organized, unified, coherent and with the right emphasis
- providing good linking words in paragraphs
- providing good transitions between paragraphs
- writing in a clear, simple style
- choosing a simple vocabulary suited to the audience
- explaining difficult ideas by giving examples
- keeping the number of syllables per word as low as possible
- writing at a low level of abstraction
- writing short sentences
- using punctuation to help readers understand
- writing short paragraphs
- using lists where appropriate

THE ELEMENTS OF READABILITY

- underlining where appropriate
- using headings as signposts
- using a multiple decimal numbering system
- indenting sub-sections
- choosing an effective typeface
- using white space
- reducing the eye-span by presenting the message in columns or by increasing the size of the margins
- using colour to attract the reader
- choosing paper of appropriate quality.

For longer messages such as reports, writers should ensure that:

- The cover is attractive.
- The Title Page is well set out.
- The Table of Contents is well set out.
- Graphics are properly integrated into the report. They should be in the report where their content is being discussed. They should be introduced and then analysed so that the reader knows how to interpret them. Key points in any graphic should be highlighted.

All the above techniques stress that writing is both a verbal and a non-verbal activity.

Many of the above issues have already been discussed. This chapter will therefore cover a selection of the other techniques, with examples.

The following techniques will be discussed:

- Using a multiple decimal numbering system
- Using headings
- Using lists
- Writing short sentences
- Underlining key points where appropriate.

Using a multiple decimal numbering system

A multiple decimal numbering system is very useful if the information is complex. This system shows the reader:

- what the most important points are
- the order of these points
- how the sub-points relate to these points.

The following example illustrates a multiple decimal outline with underlined headings.

Example 1

PROCEDURE FOR LETTER WRITING IN BUSINESS

1. Decide on purposes of letter
   1.1 To give facts
   1.2 To record
   1.3 To generate goodwill
2. Decide on type of letter
   2.1 Letter of enquiry
   2.2 Response to enquiry
      2.2.1 Good news
      2.2.2 Bad news
   2.3 Letter of complaint
   2.4 Letter of adjustment
      2.4.1 Good news for reader
      2.4.2 Bad news for reader
3. Select appropriate style
   3.1 Formal style for formal occasions
   3.2 Consultative style for less formal occasions
4. Select techniques for achieving good readability
   4.1 Subject-line to prepare reader
   4.2 Headings as signposts

Note that headings should be as complete as possible. Avoid one-word headings. Underline the main headings to make them stand out. Indent sub-headings.

Using lists

Lists are very effective. However, writers should present them carefully.

- All lists should be introduced.
- Every item in the list should follow logically and grammatically from the introduction.
- Every item in the list should follow the same grammatical structure.

The following examples illustrate techniques of listing:

Example 2

```
The Personnel Department should ensure that all
new staff are:
- given an induction course
- introduced to their colleagues in their
  Departments.
```

The following list is wrong.

Example 3

```
  The Personnel Department should ensure that:
  - all new staff are given an induction course
✗ - to introduce all new staff to their colleagues in
    their new Departments.
```

The item marked with a cross does not follow from the introduction. In addition, the items are not the same grammatically.

The following paragraph illustrates the potential for a list:

Example 4

```
All new staff should be inducted in three phases.
In the first phase they are introduced into the
company. The second phase is the introduction to
the Department. The third phase is specific train-
ing for their jobs.
```

This passage could be rewritten as follows:

```
All new staff should be inducted in three phases:
 - Phase one is the introduction to the company.
 - Phase two is the introduction to the Department.
 - Phase three is specific training for their jobs.
```

A list improves the readability of the passage.

Example 5

The following long sentence could be re-written in short sentences:

```
When the auditor addresses his report, he ad-
dresses it to the members of the company, and he
must therefore know that his duty is to these mem-
bers who should be able to use his statements to
base investment decisions on.
```

> An auditor must address his report to <u>the members</u> of the company. His duty is to these members. They should be able to use his statements to base their <u>investment decisions</u> on.

Three sentences instead of one make the second passage more readable. Note that *members* and *investment decisions* have been underlined for emphasis.

Calculating a fog index

The Gunning Fog Index is a useful way of calculating the fogginess of a passage of continuous writing. This index is based on:
- The average number of words per sentence.
- The percentage of words of three syllables or more. These are classified as long words

The Fog Index gives the reading level of a passage related to the American grade system.

The procedure for calculating a Fog Index is as follows:
1. Take a passage of not less than 100 words to the nearest sentence.
2. Count the number of words. Remember that all numbers should be written out as words. For example, 1992 counts as three words.
3. Count the number of sentences. Remember that a colon (:) counts as a full-stop.
4. Work out the average word-length of sentences by dividing the number of words by the number of sentences.
5. Count the number of words with three or more syllables. Do not count:
   - proper nouns — these are, for example, the names of cities and the titles of posts such as *Director*
   - long words ending with 'es' or 'ed'.
6. Work out the percentage of long words.
7. To calculate the Fog Index, add the answers from 4 and 6 and multiply by 0,4. This factor gives the reading level of the passage.

Fog index applied to an example

The Fog Index of the following passage is calculated:

> Communication[1] in small groups is very important[2] in all organizations[3]. Many decisions[4] are made in small groups, rather than by individuals[5]. To be effective[6], small groups need practice. People in these groups also need to

THE ELEMENTS OF READABILITY 207

> understand[7] how to work in groups. They need, in particular[8], to understand[9] that equal attention[10] should be paid to the task and to the ways in which people work together[11]. This second aspect is called the process role of groups. People need to listen to each other. They should also be very sensitive[12] to each others' non-verbal behaviour[13]. If they do not work well together[14], they are not likely to solve problems very well.

- This passage has 110 words.
- There are nine sentences.
- The average number of words per sentence is $\frac{110}{9}$, which is 12,2 words per sentence.
- There are 14 long words.
- The percentage of long words is, therefore, $\frac{14}{110} \times 100$. This is 12,72 %.
- Calculate the fog index as follows.
  (1) Add the average number of words per sentence to the percentage of long words. The calculation is: 12,2 + 12,72, which is 24,92.
  (2) Multiply this total by 0,4. The calculation is 24,92 × 0,4, which is 9,96. This is the fog index of the above passage. This falls within the easy reading range shown in the table below.

The following table should then be used to calculate the level of education at which this passage is aimed:

17	VERY DIFFICULT
16	
15	MORE DIFFICULT
14	
13	
	─────DANGER LINE─────
12	DIFFICULT
11	
	───── EASY READING RANGE ─────
10	
9	
8	STANDARD
7	
6	FAIRLY EASY

The danger-line shows the school-leaving level of 12. This means that a passage with a fog index of 12 should be readable for a group of school-leavers. A passage with an index of 13 and above has been written for students at colleges or universities.

Senders should target their messages to the lowest level of potential reader. The lower the fog index, the easier the message should be to read.

Note. Do not rely on the index as the only guide to readability. Make sure that you understand your audience's needs. Then use a range of readability techniques.

Practical suggestions for writing

In business, aim at:

- an average of fifteen words per sentence
- no more than 10 % long words.

This combination gives a fog index of 10, which falls into the easy reading range.

If you have to write technical messages, then you will have to use more technical words. In technical writing, aim at:

- an average of fifteen words per sentence
- no more than 15 % long words.

This combination gives a fog index of 12, which is safe.

Checklist for readability

- Have I put a summary at the beginning of my message?
- Have I planned my message properly?
- Is my message coherent?
- Have I provided good transitions between paragraphs?
- Have I written in a clear, simple style?
- Have I kept the number of syllables per word as low as possible?
- Have I written short sentences and paragraphs?
- Have I used lists correctly?
- Have I used an effective numbering system?
- Have I used headings?
- Have I provided enough white space?
- Have I reduced the reader's eye-span by using columns or wide margins?
- Have I written at an appropriate fog index?

THE ELEMENTS OF READABILITY

Questions: Part 5

(Answers to these questions are given on pages 511–523.)

Points for discussion

1. Explain the 'Rhetorical Situation'. What are the key factors that affect a message?
2. What is meant by the terms 'unity', 'coherence' and emphasis'? Give examples to illustrate your answers.
3. Give three examples of good links between paragraphs.
4. Explain what a mind-map is.
5. What is the procedure for preparing a topic outline?
6. Explain what is meant by vertical and horizontal plans.
7. How would you define the term 'message'?
8. Explain how you would analyse the needs of an audience for a letter or report.
9. What are the points of major impact of a message?
10. Explain why a business letter is organized in a diamond shape.
11. Why is a report shaped in the form of a pyramid?
12. Why are newspaper articles and press releases written in the form of an inverted pyramid?
13. Give six different ways of organizing information.
14. Explain how words get their meanings.
15. Explain the terms 'denotation' and 'connotation'. Give examples to illustrate your answer.
16. What are the four major functions of words in messages? Give an example of each function.
17. Explain the differences between 'referential' and 'emotive' language. Give an example of each kind of language.
18. What is the difference between 'generic' and 'specific' words? Give examples to illustrate each kind.
19. Explain what is meant by 'the ladder of abstraction'. Give examples to illustrate your answer.
20. What is the difference between 'concrete', 'relative' and 'abstract' words? Give an example of each type of word.
21. What is meant by words that 'pre-judge' a situation? Give examples of such words.
22. Explain the differences between formal and informal words. Give examples to illustrate your answer.
23. What is meant by the following terms referring to style:
    - high formal
    - formal
    - consultative
    - casual

— intimate?

Give an example of each kind.

24. Explain the main differences between a personal and an impersonal style. Give an example of each style.
25. Explain the differences between an active style and a passive style. Give examples of each style.
26. What is meant by 'tone' in messages? Give examples of different tones.
27. Give four elements of jargon. Give examples to illustrate each element.
28. What is meant by the term 'readability'? Give eight techniques for presenting a message in a highly readable way.

Exercises

1. Evaluate the organization of the following letter report. Pay special attention to the beginning and end of the message. Are they effective? Rewrite this message so that it is well organized. Write in a clear, simple style and use techniques for making it more readable.

    Dear Mr Buthelezi

    On the 28th and 29th July the undermentioned attended the eighth ABDS (Active Budgeting Directive System) training course at Head Office. It was conducted by Michael Jimba and Godfrey Sampson of Computer Dept. The course lasted one and a half days, and was composed of several short lectures and tests. The tests consisted in analysing elementary budgeting problems and writing ABDS models to solve these problems. (A model is simply a program written in ABDS). The models were then entered into the computer by the programmer via the VDU terminal and run, and an output obtained on the printer.

    Six people attended the course, three of whom were from our branch in the YXZ Buildings. The other branch members were Adrian Sisulu and Ken van Zyl.

    A comprehensive ABDS user manual was handed out to each person attending the course.

    In conclusion, ABDS is an easy language to use, is very English-like in quality and is very useful for handling a range of specific problems.

    It can be used not only for financial and accounting or investment work, but in other fields as well.

THE ELEMENTS OF READABILITY

It is the writer's opinion that ABDS would be useful in the Accounts Dept. for solving Budgeting problems as part of Expenditure Request justifications, payouts and profit after taxes. It is ideally suited to this type of problem. In fact, a model has been compiled by Mr J. Snyders for this very purpose and can be made available for use.

2. The ten items below are in random order. Rewrite them so that they make a coherent paragraph. Ensure that each sentence flows logically into the next.
   (*a*) concluded that the earth is a planet
   (*b*) the development of scientific thought has often led
   (*c*) in an effort to suppress Galileo's ideas
   (*d*) this conflicted with the current belief
   (*e*) to conflict between the proponents of a new idea
   (*f*) the church had him imprisoned
   (*g*) for example Galileo after studying the movement of the moons of Jupiter
   (*h*) and those who follow the established belief
   (*i*) rotating round the sun
   (*j*) that the earth was the centre of the universe

3. Is the following passage coherent? Does one sentence flow logically into the next? Rewrite the passage to improve it.

   'Storage is potentially the most important source of hydrocarbon emissions in the petroleum refinery industry. Floating roofs normally are a sealing element between the roof and the tank wall. The floating section is usually 3 cm smaller in diameter than that of the tank. The space is usually sealed by vertical metal plates connecting the braces to the floating roof. The plates are fixed with a fabric seal extending from the top of the plates to the inner surface of the tank.'

4. Does the following passage have one unifying theme flowing through it? If it does not, what sentences should be removed?

   'We owe some of the scientific ideas on which radar was based to our knowledge of bats. Most people fear bats because they are night creatures and seem ugly and unattractive. They have also heard stories of blood-sucking vampire bats. Bats are considered to be not much more than flying mice. Zoologists noticed that bats did not collide with objects, even though they are blind and fly at night. They found that bats send out noises inaudible to man and that they use the echoes of these noises to find objects. This principle of echo-location was used in radar.'

5. Replace the following words with simple everyday words. Try to use words with as few syllables as possible.
   - detrimental
   - sufficient
   - possesses
   - numerous
   - remuneration
   - endeavour (verb)
   - facilitate
   - ascertain
   - utilize
   - indicate

6. Rewrite the following sentences to improve them:
   - It is believed by this author that the company policy may be incorrect.
   - These reports are prepared by the Salespeople every Monday.
   - The success of this project is the responsibility of the Personnel Department.
   - A committee performs the function of determining the leave dates.
   - Reduction of the inventory was effected by the staff.
   - These reports are in agreement with other evidence.

7. The following passage is written at a high level of abstraction. It also has some examples of jargon in it. Rewrite it simply and at a lower level of abstraction. Where possible, replace the general statements with factual statements.

> 'It is imperative that the firm practise extreme conservatism in operating expenditure during the coming two years. The firm's past operating performance has failed to reach its financial targets for the reason that a preponderance of administrative assignments have been delegated to personnel who were ill-equipped to perform in these capacities. Recently instituted administrative changes stressing experience in operating economies have rectified this condition.'

8. Rewrite the following extract from a letter to get rid of the jargon.

> 'Your esteemed favour of the 12th inst. refers; in reply to which the undersigned stresses that no stone will be left unturned until our salesperson's alleged discourtesy to you is investigated.
>
> In the meanwhile, enclosed please find a gift token as an indication of our concern and the esteem in which we hold your goodself.'

9. Describe the tone of this extract from a letter. Is it suitable? Rewrite the extract to improve it.

> Dear Mr X
>
> We find it extremely difficult to believe your complaint of January 1st regarding the failure of your Zing portable radio to pick up stations 40 km away.
>
> All of our other customers report excellent reception from stations much further away. We want you to know that our engineering staff have put the best materials and knowledge into the design of the Zing. Your complaint therefore seems incredible.

10. Work out the fog index of the passage below. Rewrite it to a fog index as close to 9 as possible.

> 'Early last week the Minister called a meeting of the private sector to discuss with the Department of Commerce the continuing problems presently concerning the Government brought about by the situation in Iran, and generally to discuss with the private sector what can be effected to bring about savings in the consumption of fuel, with particular emphasis on the middle distillates. It

appears that there is an imbalance in the
consumption of the various fuels. When crude oil is
refined a proportion goes to petrol, a second
proportion goes to the middle distillates, i.e.
diesel and paraffin for jet aircraft, and finally,
heavy furnace oil.'

PART

6

Oral Messages

•

Using the Telephone Effectively

CHAPTER 15

Oral Messages

Summary

This chapter describes the formats for talks and oral reports. A talk has a Beginning, Middle and End. An oral report, on the other hand, has a more rigid format. Its main sections are:

- Terms of Reference
- Summary of Report
- Findings
- Conclusions
- Recommendations.

The chapter goes on to suggest a procedure for preparing a talk or oral report. This procedure involves:

- a careful analysis of one's purposes and audience
- preparing a mind-map
- selecting key and supporting ideas and organizing them in a horizontal topic outline
- the preparation of postcard-size cue-cards.

Giving a persuasive talk needs a special approach. The speaker could use the following appeals to persuade:

- a logical appeal
  This appeal uses facts as its basis.
- a psychological appeal
  This appeal is based on an analysis of the audience's needs, desires and motives. It should always stress the benefits to the audience.
- a personal appeal
  This is based on the speaker's reputation or credibility.

Presenting the talk or report demands the speaker's special attention to:

- non-verbal communication, especially voice, eye-contact and hand movements
- dress and general appearance
- audio-visual aids.

The speaker's credibility is very important. This chapter stresses that speakers do not have credibility. It is given to them by the audience. Speakers need to pay attention to:

- the beginning and end of their message
- using facts to back up general statements
- establishing common ground with the audience
- their delivery.

The advantages and disadvantages of the following audio-visual aids are then discussed:

- the overhead projector
- the flip chart
- chalk and white boards
- posters
- models
- slide projectors
- video machines
- tape recorders.

The chapter concludes with a number of suggestions for handling questions.

Key points

- Make sure that you know the formats for a talk and oral report.
- Know your purposes and your audience very well.
- Use a horizontal topic outline for your plan.
- If you are aiming to persuade your audience, use logical, psychological and personal appeals.
- When you present your talk or report, use a personal style. Pay attention to your non-verbal communication and your appearance.
- Make sure that you come across as enthusiastic about your audience and your topic.
- Do your utmost to achieve credibility. Remember that your audience gives you credibility.
- Always back up your key points with audio-visual aids.
- Prepare for questions.

… ORAL MESSAGES 219

Introduction

People in organizations spend a great deal of their time speaking. Much of this is, however, impromptu. People have to respond immediately to many requests, questions and statements. Impromptu, or unprepared speaking, is the most common form of public speaking that we do.

This chapter, however, covers the *prepared talk* and *oral report*. The chapter covers the following:

- formats for a talk and oral report
- preparing a talk or oral report
- preparing a persuasive talk
- presenting a talk or oral report
- the credibility of the speaker
- using a range of visual aids
- answering questions.

Focus of this chapter

Many of the principles that apply in this chapter have already been discussed in Part Five of this book (Chapters 10–14). They will therefore be referred to only briefly here.

This chapter will therefore focus on:

- the formats of talks and oral reports
- preparing talks and oral reports
- presenting talks and oral reports
- the range of available audio visual aids and their advantages and disadvantages.
- audience response and questions.

Formats for a talk and a report

Each of these oral messages has a specific format.

Format for a talk

A talk has a simple structure:

- a beginning
- a middle
- an end

Beginning of talk

The beginning of the talk is very important. Listeners make up their minds very quickly about the speaker's:

- attitude towards them and towards his or her subject

- knowledge of the subject.

Speakers should strive to create a very good first impression. They should tell the audience:

- why they are listening
- what they will gain from listening.

Speakers should use one or more of the techniques below to gain the audience's attention:

- Ask a question.
- Refer to current or recent events that link with the topic and give it added interest.
- Begin with an unusual statement or statistic that attracts interest.
- Refer to a specific problem that makes the audience think about their topic.
- Show a diagram, picture or object to attract interest.
- State the main points of their talk.

Middle of talk

The middle is often the weakest part of the talk. Speakers should, therefore, ensure that they:

- Attract and re-attract the audience's attention with good non-verbal communication.
- Organize their talks very well.
- Ensure that they present the material coherently, with good transitions.
- Use audio-visual aids to back up their key points.

End of talk

Speakers should ensure that they end on a high note. The end of the talk should leave a lasting impression. Speakers should not allow the talk to fade out. They could select from the techniques below to achieve the impact they need:

- Summarize the main points.
- End with an appeal for action.
- Ask a challenging question.
- Use a quotation, statistics or vivid illustration to sum up the main idea.
- Remind the audience why the key points are important to them.

Speakers should not introduce new material at the end. This will confuse the audience.

Format for an oral report

An oral report is normally based on a written report. It will therefore follow the format for a written report.

People normally present reports because they have been instructed to:
- Investigate a problem.
- Report on the feasibility of a project.
- Report on a situation.

An oral report therefore has a more rigid format than a talk. The format is as follows:

Introduction

- A brief statement of the Terms of Reference or instructions given to the speaker. (These are also called a Brief.) The Instructions should include:
    - the name of the person who gave the instructions
    - the date of the instructions
    - the main instructions given.
- An overview or summary of the report. This summary should include:
    - a statement of why the audience needs to listen to the report
    - a statement of what the audience will gain from listening
    - a brief description of the background to the report
    - a brief statement of the purposes of the report
    - a brief summary of the key findings
    - the main conclusions
    - the main recommendations.

Body of Report

- A brief statement of the procedure used to gather the information. (This could, for example, cover interviews, site inspections, reading of articles or the use of special equipment.)
- The main findings, backed up with visual aids such as overhead projector transparencies or flip-chart paper.

Conclusions

- These are the insights gained from the facts, and the implications of the facts. (Note that no new information is given at this stage.)

Recommendations

- These are the proposed actions to be taken as a result of the findings and conclusions.

Preparing a talk or oral report

A good oral presentation results from careful preparation. The following procedure is strongly recommended. Please note that chapter 10 gives detailed guidance on these procedures.

- Decide on your purposes. These could, for example, be
  - to inform
  - to persuade
  - to entertain.

  Chapter 10 gives more information on purposes.
- Analyse the needs of your audience.
- Decide what your audience needs to know or do at the end of your presentation. This decision will help to give you focus.
- Prepare a mind-map of your ideas.
- Prepare a horizontal topic outline of your selected key and supporting ideas. This will give you the body of your talk or report.
- Add the Introduction and Conclusion to your plan.
- Once you are satisfied with your plan, prepare postcard-size cue cards as your notes. Ensure that you
  - number each card
  - write key points only with large letters for easy reading
  - write on one side only
  - tie the cards together so that you can work your way through them without dropping them.

The following examples of horizontal plans illustrate

- the body of a talk
- the complete talk.

Horizontal outline for body of talk

This outline shows three main points, numbered 1–3, with supporting ideas.

- Purposes
  The purposes of this talk are to
  - inform the audience of the procedure for writing a bad-news letter of adjustment
  - persuade the audience that this procedure is effective
- Audience
  The audience is a group of experts in marketing. They are attending a workshop on letter-writing as they wish to keep up to date on the latest techniques.

Introduction	1st main point **Planning letter**	2nd main point **Organizing letter**	3rd main point **Writing letter**	Conclusion

• Importance of well-planned letters of adjustment
• Handling bad news in letters
• TRANSPARENCY
• Overview of talk
	• Purposes
	  – Inform
	  – Give bad news
	  – Maintain goodwill
	• Audience needs
	• Attitude of audience
		• Indirect approach
		  – Thanks
		  – Explanation
		  – Bad news
		  – Goodwill
		• Beginning of letter
		• Middle of letter
		• End of letter
			• Subject-line
			• Neutral opening
			  – Establish goodwill
			• Clear, simple style
			• Neutral to friendly tone
			• Good readability
			• Jargon-free
				• Sum up key points
				• TRANSPARENCY
				• Set the audience a task of writing a bad-news letter of adjustment

(3 minutes)	(5 minutes)	(5 minutes)	(5 minutes)	(3 minutes)

1 Planning letter	2 Organizing letter	3 Writing letter
Purposes Inform Give bad news Maintain goodwill Audience needs Attitude	Indirect approach Thanks Explanation Bad news Goodwill Beginning of letter	Subject line Style Tone Readability Jargon free

Complete horizontal outline for talk

Note that the speaker has added the following to the plan (see page 223):

- an Introduction
- a Conclusion
- visual aids
- rough timing for each section.

Note that the same approach applies to an oral report.

Use this final outline to help you prepare the details of your talk or oral report.

Preparing a persuasive talk

A persuasive talk needs a special approach. People would find it easier if they could base all persuasion purely on facts. However, this is not often possible. In reality, they have to use a combination of facts and personal appeal based on the audience's needs and goals.

Persuasion may be defined as follows:

> 'An attempt by a person or group to change the attitudes, beliefs or behaviour of another person or group.'

This definition stresses that persuaders have to take into account the beliefs, attitudes, needs and goals of others. Persuaders should also find out if the audience is likely, at the start, to be positive or negative towards them and their ideas.

Approaches to persuasion

Persuaders could use

- a logical appeal
- a psychological appeal
- a personal appeal.

Logical appeal

This appeal uses facts as a basis. The persuader could use an inductive or deductive approach.

The *inductive* approach uses specific examples as a basis for making a general statement. This approach is useful if your audience starts off against your view.

If you were a salesperson, you could, for example, show specific results of tests to move towards a general statement of your product.

The *deductive* approach starts with a general statement and moves to specific statements to back it up. This approach is effective if you feel that your audience is likely to accept your general statement as long as you support it with specific examples.

Note:

- Use both sides of an argument to persuade people. Do not simply argue from one point of view.
- If you feel that your audience is hostile, start with points with which they can agree. Then move to your point of view.

Psychological appeal

This approach is based on an analysis of the audience's needs, desires and motives. It should stress the benefits to the audience.

Personal appeal

This is based on the speaker's reputation or credibility.

Note:

Persuaders need to show their knowledge of the facts. They also need to persuade through their own attitudes and enthusiasm.

Plan for a persuasive message

The following outline plan for a persuasive talk is suggested below

Introduction
- Gain the audience's attention
- Establish common ground with the audience
- Work on points of agreement with the audience
- Stress the advantages for the audience

The Middle
- Develop the argument in terms of its advantages and disadvantages
- Work from the problem to the solution
- Keep stressing the advantages to the audience

The End
- Stress the desired action in terms of what the audience can gain.

Presenting the talk or report

Once you have prepared your talk or report, you should rehearse it in front of an audience. Encourage your audience to discuss problems with you. Check your timing. Ensure that you can use your audio-visual aids effectively. Check the balance of your presentation so that you allocate the correct time to each stage.

When you present your talk or oral report pay special attention to your:
- Non-verbal communication, particularly your voice, eye-contact, your hand-movements and the way you stand
- Your dress and general appearance
- Your level of enthusiasm
- Your style
- The quality of your audio-visual aids, and the way in which you use them.

Show genuine concern for your audience. Make immediate eye-contact with your audience, and try not to read too much from your cards.

Make sure that you dress appropriately. When you start, stand evenly on both feet. Do not cross your arms and legs or twist your back. Use gestures to emphasize points and to keep contact with the audience.

Make sure that you:
- Speak with a lively voice, using a personal style
- Speak clearly
- Speak at a speed that allows your audience to tune in to your voice
- Vary your speed
- Use your voice to emphasize key points
- Use pauses for impact.

The speaker's credibility

A speaker's credibility is vital. The audience must believe in the speaker if his or her message is to have any impact.

Credibility may be defined as 'an attitude towards a sender held at any given time by a receiver'. This definition stresses that credibility is conferred on a sender by the receiver. A sender has no credibility. It also stresses that credibility is dynamic. It changes all the time, and may change from the beginning of a talk to the end.

In presentations, three kinds of credibility are recognized:
- Initial
- Derived
- Terminal.

Initial credibility is conferred on the speaker before (s)he starts. This is based on what the audience believes about the speaker.

Derived credibility is conferred on a speaker during the presentation. It is based on:

- the way the speaker puts across the message
- the impact of the message
- the quality of the speaker's delivery.

Terminal credibility is conferred on a speaker at the end of the presentation.

Credibility may, therefore, change during a presentation. Speakers should, therefore, pay attention to every stage of a presentation.

Credibility may be described as a combination of the audience's assessment of the speaker's

- level of authority
- trustworthiness
- intentions towards the audience.

Achieving credibility

Speakers can make themselves credible by:

- paying very careful attention to the beginning of the message
- ensuring that they are introduced by someone respected by the audience
- paying close attention to their appearance
- selecting their ideas carefully and supporting what the audience likes
- using facts to back up general statements
- making sure that their delivery is excellent
- establishing common ground with the audience
- appearing open-minded and sincere
- ending on a powerful note.

Using audio-visual aids

Audio-visual aids are essential if you wish people to remember points. These aids have the following advantages:

- They create an immediate impact.
- They make ideas more concrete.
- They emphasize and reinforce key points.
- They give variety to a presentation.
- They help to convey ideas if time is limited.
- They create an aura of professional competence if well presented.
- They guide the speaker and the audience.
- They help to keep the attention of the audience.

Audio-visual aids should support the talk or report. They should never replace it. Keep in mind the following points about audio-visual aids:

- They should not be over-used, because they could destroy the balance of the talk or report.
- They should be audible, visible, simple and immediately understandable.
- They should be well-planned.
- They should be kept on long enough for the audience to listen, look at and absorb the material.
- They should work efficiently.

The following audio-visual aids will be briefly discussed. Their advantages and disadvantages will be given.

- The overhead projector
- The flip chart
- Chalk and White boards
- Posters
- Models
- Slide projectors
- Video machines
- Tape recorders

The overhead projector

The main advantages are:

- The speaker can remain facing the audience.
- The speaker can plan in advance, or write on transparencies in front of the audience.
- It can be used with the lights on.
- It is suitable for large or small venues.
- Transparencies can be stored and re-used.

The main disadvantages are:

- They may be subjected to power failures and broken bulbs
- They need a good screen at the correct angle for the best image.

When you prepare transparencies, ensure that:

- they are simple
- letter size is about 9 mm high, and lines are about 1,5 mm thick.

Do not obscure the image on the screen. Use a pointer. Switch off the projector when you are not using it.

The flip chart

The main advantages of the flip chart are that:

- It is easily portable.

- It does not need power, and so can be used inside and outdoors.
- The speaker can prepare in advance or write during the presentation.

The main disadvantage is that it is not suitable for a large audience.

When you use the flip chart, make sure that:

- you write boldly using colours that stand out
- you keep the letters about 5 cm high
- you keep each sheet simple.

Keep in mind that you can write notes in pencil on each page if you prepare in advance. These notes will guide you during the presentation.

Chalk and white board

Each board is used in the same way. The main advantages are that:

- they are easy to use
- they allow the speaker to create a message and build it up during the presentation
- they allow the speaker to control the pace at which the visual image is built up
- they can be used in a large or small venue.

Their main disadvantages are that:

- a white board can take on a glare if the lighting is wrong
- poor handwriting and drawing can destroy the visual impact.

When using a board, make sure that you:

- write boldly and carefully
- stop talking while you write. Then turn to talk to the audience
- use a pointer and stand aside so that people can see
- use strong colours
- practise in advance what you plan to write.

Posters

Posters differ from flip chart paper in that:

- They are designed to stand on their own.
- They are prepared in advance.
- They are professional in appearance.

Their main advantage is that they can be prepared in advance and re-used. They can also be left on permanent display for added impact.

Their main disadvantages are that they need specialist knowledge to prepare. They are also costly. There is no guarantee that viewers will understand the full impact of the message without explanation.

When designing a poster, ensure that:

- the poster can stand on its own
- the lettering is clear and legible
- all diagrams are properly annotated.

Models

These are generally scaled-down models of large objects. However, they may also be scaled-up models of small objects.

Their main advantage is that they can make available to an audience a large or small object that would not normally be available. Their main disadvantage is that they are accessible to a small audience only.

When using models, ensure that you:

- tell the audience what their scale is
- display the model prominently during your presentation.

Do not hand a model round during your presentation as it will distract the audience.

35 mm slide projector

The main advantage of a slide projector is that the pictures are very attractive and can hold an audience's attention. Their main disadvantage is that you may lose contact with your audience when you switch off the lights. They are also subject to power, bulb and mechanical failures.

When you use a slide projector make sure that you:

- do not include too many slides
- allow the audience time to absorb each slide
- use a light pointer to show people where to look.

Video

The advantage of a video is that it illustrates vividly the spoken and visual together. It may be shown with the lights up so that the speaker can maintain contact with the audience.

The main disadvantages are that expensive equipment has to be used. It is subject to more frequent breakdowns than simpler equipment. It may also draw attention away from the speaker because of its strong attraction.

When using a video, make sure that you:

- test the equipment and the film at the venue
- have everything ready for immediate playing.

Tape recorder

A tape recorder is very useful for illustrating speech or other sound effects. However, unless it is of very good quality, it will not give good reproduction. This is a particular problem in a large venue. A tape recorder on its own is suitable for a small audience.

If you use a tape recorder, make sure that you try out the equipment and the cassette in the venue beforehand. Make sure that everything is ready for instant playing when you need it.

Audience response and questions

Talking to a sluggish audience

If your audience is likely to be sluggish, or you find it sluggish when you are talking, then try the following:

- Prepare some questions in advance and write them on an overhead transparency. Use these either to start or end your talk.
- Build questions into your talk. Your questions should develop your argument, stimulate the audience and encourage participation.

Handling questions

All your oral presentations give you the chance of involving your audience. The most useful involvement is through questions. The most effective technique is to set aside time for answering questions at the end. Keep in mind that if you have a very large audience you might have to write the questions on an overhead transparency.

Ensure that you control the situation so that your audience participation does justice to the audience, content of your speech or talk and the time-restrictions placed on your speech. Unreasonable numbers of questions and interruptions can ruin an otherwise good speech.

Guidelines for controlling questions

The following six guidelines will help you to control questions:

- Make sure that you know your audience, your purposes and your subject very well.
- Try to anticipate what areas of your subject are most open to questioning. Try to predict what questions your specific audiences will ask.
- Try to answer each question, or try to react to all questions.
- Carefully consider the rest of the audience. Try to satisfy the questioners and the rest of the audience.
- Do not feel or act as if you know everything or have to win every argument.

- Try to encourage good questions and audience participation. Speakers easily discourage questions with even a slightly overbearing attitude. Do not make people angry so that they decide to give you a bad time.

Difficult questions

This section has been designed to help you answer difficult questions. What would you do if:

1. The question actually contains two questions?

   Example

   Why do you make the goods like this, and what do you think of the method?

   Action

   Refer each part back to the questioner. Then answer each part separately. Some questions become very complex. Do your best to analyse each section and answer it separately.

2. The question has a false inference in it?

   Example

   How can you make your staff happier so that they can become more productive?

   Action

   This question implies that *happiness* and *productivity* go together. Point this implication out to the reader. Say that you cannot, therefore, give a fair answer.
   Ask the questioner to rephrase the question.

3. The question is a leading question?

   Example

   This job calls for a lot of work at night. You don't mind late work do you?

   Action

   Point out that this question forces you into answering 'yes' when you might not want to. Ask the questioner to rephrase the question.

4. The question is emotionally loaded?

   Example

   Would you be for or against sending our surplus fruit to the desperate people of . . . ?

Action

Point out that not everyone would agree that the people in question are 'desperate'. State politely that you would rather not answer the question as it has been phrased. Ask the questioner to rephrase the question.

5. The question is off the point?

Action

Either ask the questioner to rephrase the question or ask if you can delay an answer until after the presentation. Do not insult the questioner by pointing out that the question is off the point.

6. The question is naïve and obvious? It shows that the questioner has not been listening.

Action

Either ask if you can delay an answer until after your presentation, or answer simply and carefully, with no implied criticism of the questioner.

7. The question is used as an opportunity for the questioner to interrupt, take over and show off?

Action

Stop the speaker as firmly and as politely as you can. Say that there will be an opportunity to ask questions at the end.

8. You think that you know what the question is going to be before the questioner has finished speaking?

Action

Stop yourself from completing the question yourself. Hear the questioner out.

9. You do not know the answer?

Action

Do not be tempted to bluff your way through. Admit that you do not know. Ask if anyone in the audience can help you.

10. For some reason, you prefer *not* to answer the question?

Action

State honestly that you would rather not answer the question.

CHAPTER 16

Using the Telephone Effectively

Summary

The telephone is often the first point of contact with an organization. Organizations should, therefore, strive to create an image of themselves over the telephone that is:
- helpful
- efficient
- friendly.

A good telephone procedure is, therefore, very important. Organizations should encourage their staff to:
- Use their voices carefully. They should sound
  - friendly
  - interested
  - concerned.
- Follow four stages in answering calls:
  - Stage 1: Establish a good relationship
  - Stage 2: Record the message
  - Stage 3: Solve the caller's problem
  - Stage 4: End the call on a positive note.
- Listen for facts and emotions.
- Take notes.
- Choose words carefully.
- Show a positive attitude.
- Be assertive, rather than aggressive or submissive.
- Prepare for calls.
- Control calls.
- Prepare a suitable message pad.

Telephone users have the following rights:
- to know to whom they are talking
- to say if it is inconvenient to take the call at that moment
- to state their needs
- to have their needs properly listened to
- to be told what the other person expects of them
- to refuse a request without feeling guilty.

Telephone callers should plan their calls to make them as efficient as possible.

Key points

- Use your voice carefully over the telephone. People will judge you and your organization partly as a result of your voice. Come across as friendly, interested and efficient.
- Use active listening techniques.
- Establish a good relationship with the caller immediately.
- Record the message carefully.
- Show that you are listening.
- Solve the caller's problem.
- End on a positive note.
- Choose your words carefully.
- Be assertive, rather than aggressive or submissive.
- Control the call.
- Prepare for calls.
- Have a properly designed record pad.
- Be prepared to say if it is inconvenient to take a call at that moment.
- Be prepared to turn down a request without feeling guilty.
- Tell the caller what you expect him or her to do.

USING THE TELEPHONE EFFECTIVELY

Introduction

This chapter covers the following aspects of telephone communication:

- Establishing a good telephone procedure
- Four key stages in answering the telephone
- Being assertive, rather than aggressive
- Preparing for calls
- Controlling calls
- Handling difficult callers
- People's rights as telephone users
- Professional telephone behaviour.

Telephone as first point of contact

Often the telephone is the first point of contact with an organization. It may be the only contact for many callers. Organizations need, therefore, to create an image of themselves over the telephone that is:

- helpful
- efficient
- friendly.

Establishing a good telephone procedure

Organizations need to establish good telephone procedures. They also need to establish a consistent approach to the way the telephone is answered throughout the organization.

Bad telephone techniques can cause problems because:

- It is easier to be vague and rude over the telephone.
- The telephone may be seen as interrupting people. They then speak in an irritated way and make callers angry.

People's voices are crucial over the telephone. They may create or destroy a relationship with callers. People need, therefore, to cultivate voices that sound:

- friendly
- interested
- concerned
- efficient.

People also need to cultivate good listening habits. They stop listening for six major reasons:

- They make up their minds in advance about what the caller is going to say.
- Something draws their attention away from the call.

- The caller has an uninteresting voice.
- The caller has an accent that is hard to understand.
- They panic because they are inexperienced in handling difficult calls.
- The caller is angry.

Rules for effective telephone techniques

Four key stages in answering a call:

Stage 1

- Establish a good relationship with the caller.
- State the name of your organization clearly.
- Introduce yourself clearly.
- Establish whether or not it is convenient to carry on.

Stage 2

- Establish the reasons for the call.
- Record the message.
- Read the message back.
- Use open and closed questions to negotiate the message.
- Show that you are listening by making listening noises.

Stage 3

- Solve the caller's problem.
- If you cannot, say what you will do next.

Stage 4

- End the call on a positive note. Try always to establish and maintain goodwill.

Listen for total message

Listen for the facts and the speaker's attitudes and emotion. Try to get the total message, especially when the caller is angry.

Take notes

Help yourself to concentrate by taking notes from the beginning. Have a telephone pad and pen next to the telephone at all times. Read back the message to ensure that you have recorded it correctly.

Use your voice carefully

Speak slowly and carefully to give the caller the impression that you are interested in him or her, as well as in the problem.

Show that you are alert, calm, confident and enthusiastic.

Vary your voice and show that you are listening by saying 'I see' or 'Yes' or 'mmm'.

Choose your words carefully

Aim your language at your caller's level. Do not be tempted to use technical terms that are likely to confuse listeners.

Show a positive attitude

Be positive and helpful. Avoid negative words such as 'busy', 'don't know', 'I'll try to help you'.

Offer immediate help. If you cannot solve the problem immediately, take down the details. Say that you will deal with the matter as soon as you can.

Ensure that you follow up any complaint. Let the caller know when (s)he may expect help.

Be assertive, rather than aggressive or submissive

When a caller is angry, try not to be intimidated. Answer in a confident way. Ask the caller's name and use it. Control the call by asking open-ended questions such as 'What do you think the fault is?' Make it clear to the caller that you are writing down all the relevant points. State clearly what you will do next.

Do not

- Simply say 'hullo'.
- Assume that you will not be able to help.
- Ask weak and submissive questions such as 'I don't suppose I can be of any help?' This question risks an immediate 'no!'.
- Leave the details unrecorded.
- Simply offer to take a message.
- Respond angrily to the caller's anger.
- Let the call end with the caller dissatisfied.

Prepare for calls

Make sure that you have a very good knowledge of your organization and its recording procedures.

Have a properly designed record pad ready, as well as a pen.

Control calls

Answer promptly. If possible, allow the telephone to ring no more than three or four times.

Greet the caller as follows:

- 'Good morning / afternoon'
- 'Thank you for calling'
- The name of your organization
- Your name

- 'Can I help you?'

Ask the caller's name and use it. Use appropriate open and closed questions to keep control of the conversation.

If people are holding on, keep them informed of the situation.

Prepare a suitable message pad

Prepare a message pad with headings such as the following:

TELEPHONE MESSAGE

Caller's name:

Telephone number:

Company:

Call taken by:

Date: *Time:*

Details of call:

Level of priority:

Action to be taken:

A telephone user's rights

When people make or receive telephone calls, they have a right to:
- Know to whom they are talking.
- Say that it is inconvenient to take the call at that moment.
- State their needs.
- Have their needs properly listened to and responded to.
- Ask a range of questions to prompt the caller or to find out how to get information.
- Have their questions answered promptly, efficiently and courteously.
- Be told why their requests will not be met.
- Be told what the other person expects of them.

- Offer to help the other person.
- Refuse a request without feeling guilty.

Callers' techniques

People preparing to make a call should ensure that they have:
- thought about their call in advance
- prepared a plan, especially if the call is complex
- prepared an overview to guide the listener.

Callers should announce who they are and their position. They should then explain the purpose of the call.

Questions: Part 6

(Answers to these questions are given on pages 524–536.)

Points for discussion

1. Discuss the range of your purposes when you are giving a talk (*a*) to a small group, (*b*) to a large group. Link these purposes to a lay, expert and mixed audience.
2. Discuss the range of your purposes when you have to give an oral report to a small group of experts.
3. How would you prepare a talk or oral report? Discuss each stage in detail. Pay special attention to your planning methods.
4. Discuss the meaning and significance of the following terms. Give examples:
   - horizontal topic outline
   - initial credibility
   - derived credibility
   - terminal credibility.
5. Discuss a range of techniques that you would use to:
   - start a talk
   - start an oral report
   - end a talk
   - end an oral report
6. What techniques would you use to hold the attention of your audience in the middle of your presentation?
7. Explain the following approaches to persuasion. Give examples to illustrate each approach.
   - logical appeal
   - psychological appeal
   - personal appeal.
8. If you know that your audience is hostile to you, how would you organize your arguments?
9. You have prepared your talk, and now have to present it. What techniques would you use to gain and keep your audience's attention?
10. Discuss the advantages and disadvantages of the following audio-visual aids:
    - the overhead projector
    - the chalk or white board
    - the flip chart
    - the 35 mm slide projector
    - the tape recorder.
11. How would you handle the following types of questions?

USING THE TELEPHONE EFFECTIVELY

- A very complex question with three parts to it.
- A question that shows that the questioner has not been listening.
- A question that has a false inference in it.
- A question that is emotionally loaded.
- A question that is off the point.

12. What telephone techniques would you use if you had to handle a large number of incoming calls?

13. What techniques would you use if you wished to be assertive, rather than aggressive or submissive over the telephone?

14. What rights do you have as a telephone user?

Exercises

1. You have been asked to give an eight-minute talk on the presentation of persuasive messages. State your purposes, select an audience and prepare a horizontal topic outline.
   What aids would you use?

2. Analyse the following questions in terms of their difficulty. Explain how you would handle each one.
   - This post calls for long periods away from your family. You don't mind being away do you?
   - Our company's social upliftment programme is excellent. Would you be for or against spending 50 % of our budget to help the wretched people of . . . ?
   - Why do you follow these procedures for answering telephones, when will you consider changing them and what changes will you bring in?
   - How can you make your staff more contented so that they become more reliable?

3. You have been asked to investigate a problem in your company, draw conclusions and recommend action. Select a specific problem such as absenteeism or resignations. Then prepare the outline for your oral report.

4. Prepare an eight-minute persuasive talk aimed at your Board of Directors. You want them to change from a 40-hour working week to a 45-hour working week. What logical and psychological techniques would you use? How would you establish and maintain your credibility?

5. You have been asked to give a ten-minute talk on writing bad-news letters. Prepare three overhead transparencies to back up your talk. Show on your plan when you would use these transparencies.

6. You have been asked to prepare guidelines for good telephone techniques in your organization. Write out these guidelines, paying special attention to:
   - creating a good first impression
   - stages in handling a call
   - being assertive
   - managing calls
   - taking notes
   - ending on a positive note.
7. Write a circular for all staff in your organization, setting out the rights of telephone users.

PART 7

Written Messages in Organizations

CHAPTER 17

Written Messages in Organizations

Summary

Reports

Reports are fixed-format documents. They are written as a result of instructions given to someone to investigate and report on a problem. The major purposes of reports are to:

- inform
- record facts
- persuade
- help in decision-making
- recommend action.

Reports are written for a wide variety of audiences. The writer should therefore cater for a mixed audience as the most likely readers. Many reports are used by such readers for making decisions. There are three major types of reports:

- informative
- investigative
- feasibility.

The informative report stresses the facts. The investigative report gives the results of an investigation and recommends action. The feasibility report examines whether something can be done or not and recommends action.

This book recommends the following sections of reports in the order below:

Preliminaries

- Title Page
- Acknowledgements
- Terms of Reference (The Instructions given)
- Summary
- Table of Contents
- List of Illustrations

- Glossary (Special dictionary for the report) (You may also define difficult words at the bottom of each page.)
- List of Symbols.

Body of report

1. Introduction
2. Procedure for gathering information
3. Conclusions (Insights and implications)
4. Recommendations (The action to be taken)
5. Findings (The facts)
6. List of References
7. Bibliography
8. Appendices.

Reports should be written in a formal, impersonal and objective style. They should be set out in a highly readable way.

Letters and memoranda

This section discusses the formats and conventions for writing letters and memoranda.

Letters

Letters are often the only contact that people have with organizations. They should, therefore, be carefully written so that they act as ambassadors for the company. Letter writers need to know how to:

- plan letters
- write in a clear style
- write to achieve a friendly tone
- make their letters readable.

This chapter covers the preparation of letters. It also stresses that writers should know:

- The formats of letters
- How to write the following types of letters:
    - good-news, neutral and bad-news
    - letters of enquiry
    - responses to enquiries
    - letters of complaint
    - letters of adjustment
    - letters of invitation.

Examples of each type of letter are given.

Memoranda

In contrast to letters, memoranda are written inside companies. They have fixed formats that show the sender and the intended receiver.

Memoranda should have:

- a good subject-line
- a clear opening paragraph announcing the topic
- good readability
- a clear style
- a good, friendly tone.

Memoranda are written in a formal to consultative style.

Proposals

A proposal is a document written to get action. It uses facts, rather than highly emotive language, to get action.

Proposals should be:

- well organized
- well set out
- clearly written.

The recommended format for a proposal is as follows:

- a clear heading that states the proposed action
- a summary of the proposal, giving all the key points
- the background to the proposal
- the detailed proposal
- the justification for the proposal
- reinforcement of the proposed action.

Notices and circulars

Notices and circulars are written for a general audience. Notices are designed to be pinned on boards. They have to attract people walking past if they are to have any impact. Circulars are written for sending round a company or for sending to customers. Both are generally informative.

A notice should have:

- A good heading
- An introduction
- A main message in point-form.

A circular is often sent out as a memorandum inside a company. It should then conform with the standards already set out for memoranda. Circulars to customers are generally sent out as letters. They are both informative and persuasive.

Instructions

Instructions are directions, commands or guidelines. They are essential in organizations because they help to co-ordinate activities. They also promote safety because people are able to work within guidelines.

Instructions tell people:
- what to do
- what not to do
- how to do something.

They are normally formal and use imperative forms such as '*Open* the package . . . '.

Technical instructions should have the following format:
- Title
- Introduction
- Theory and Principles of Operation
- List of Equipment and Materials
- Description of the mechanism
- Instructions for assembly
- Performance instructions
- Precautions and warnings.

Graphics such as flow charts, logic trees and algorithms are used in instructions.

The press release

The press release is a form of advertising. An organization sends a press release to a newspaper or broadcasting station when it wishes to inform the public about its activities in certain fields.

A press release should be written in continuous writing like an essay. It should be organized in the form of an inverted pyramid. The key points should be contained in the first paragraph. After this paragraph, the writer should give some background information. After this the writer should give less and less important information.

Essays and articles

Essays and articles are written as continuous writing. They are often written after the writer has done research on a specific topic. Both of these rely for their readability on:
- a clear title
- a good opening paragraph to prepare the reader
- good links between paragraphs
- good links between sentences
- effective unity, coherence and emphasis

- a good closing paragraph to sum up the key points.

The writer should go through five stages of preparation and writing:

- Stage 1 = Undertake research
- Stage 2 = Plan and Organize the Material
- Stage 3 = Write the first draft
- Stage 4 = Edit the draft
- Stage 5 = Write the essay or article

In-house journal articles are written to inform or entertain. They are often designed to make the staff feel like a team. These articles should be organized like a press release.

They are often written in a less formal style than are essays. The writer may use headings to enhance readability. Headings are not normally used in essays.

Telegrams and telexes

Both of these are being superseded by the fax machine. However, they are still being used by some organizations, especially when fax machines are not yet available.

A telegram is written in a cryptic style. Only key words are used. These should:

- give facts
- state actions
- name people.

A telex is a cross between a letter and a telegram. It is printed in capital letters. A telex should be set out like a letter with good readability. Headings and a numbering system should be used. The style should be clear and simple.

Advertisements

Most advertisements are written by specialist firms. This chapter therefore covers only the Classified Advertisement and the advertisement for a vacant post. A classified advertisement stresses the facts. It is not set out in any special way to attract the reader's attention. Classified advertisements are published at the backs of newspapers under headings.

An advertisement for a vacant post should give:

- the name of the company
- what the post is
- what qualifications are needed
- any age limits
- what the job entails

- an address for applications.

The electronic office

The electronic office is one where messages are transmitted electronically, rather than on paper. The electronic office offers many advantages to businesses:

- Messages can be transferred faster.
- Businesses can react faster to customers' needs.
- Many routine tasks can be taken over by the computer.

Computer-based work-stations exist in many companies. Each work-station includes a terminal connected to a main-frame computer, a word processor and a printer. This arrangement allows many people to have access to the same information.

Word processors are used to process work electronically, instead of by hand. This allows the sender to check the message before printing it.

Electronic mail networks allow people to send messages from one computer to another.

Companies now have a great deal of information to store. This must be stored so that it can be retrieved easily. Companies use:

- filing cabinets
- card files
- rotary files
- horizontal files
- magnetic or floppy discs
- microfilm or microfiche.

Electronic mail and its effects on communication in organizations

Summary

Electronic mail (or e-mail) is any form of message carried electronically from one computer to another. Many companies see e-mail as a very effective means of communication. This new technology enables them to communicate worldwide. It gives them a competitive advantage because it is:

- fast
- inexpensive
- readily available
- independent of the receiver's presence.

A number of problems have, however, arisen. Companies need to solve these problems if they are to use e-mail successfully.

People find that e-mail messages are harder to read than the same messages on paper. At the same time, e-mail messages are becoming more casual.

Organizations will have to decide how formal or informal to make their messages. In addition, e-mail messages contain emotional comments in the form of emoticons such as smiling faces. These emoticons are not normally used in business messages.

Other problems that organizations face are as follows:

- E-mail can blur hierarchies.
- E-mail can increase the volume of messages and therefore costs.
- E-mail increases the choice of media for conveying messages.
- E-mail changes the nature of message permanence and security.
- E-mail changes the rules about who owns the message and whether it is private or not.
- E-mail needs its own guidelines for good manners.

Anyone in an organization who has an e-mail address may communicate with anyone else. People need, however, to remember that e-mail messages are not private. Courts in the United States have ruled that an e-mail message is the property of the organization, not of the individual in the organization who sent or received it. Organizations may therefore monitor e-mail messages and use them as evidence against staff.

Because of the relative newness of e-mail, organizations need to draw up guidelines to help their staff to send e-mail messages that communicate effectively.

Key points

- Many companies see e-mail as a very effective form of communication.
- Companies may now communicate worldwide with great ease.
- E-mail messages are becoming more casual. However, they need to be prepared very carefully.
- E-mail will blur hierarchies in organizations because communication is now desk-to-desk, with nobody to check messages in between.
- E-mail will increase the volume of messages and could increase costs.
- E-mail messages are causing problems about the nature of message permanence and security.
- E-mail messages are not as secure as messages typed on paper.
- So far, courts in the United States have ruled that companies, rather than individuals, own the e-mail. Staff will therefore have to be careful about the content of their e-mail messages.
- Companies will have to draw up their own guidelines for good manners in e-mail.

Effect of the personal computer and the Internet on communication

Summary

Organizations find themselves in the midst of a computer revolution. They have to adapt rapidly to the explosion of computer technology. People now sit for long hours in front of computer screens. Organizations have therefore had to redefine and redesign their workplaces. In addition, people can now work from home as though it were an office.

The Internet has given people quick access to vast amounts of information. In addition, the personal computer gives average people the power to make complex calculations that they could not have done a few years ago.

People can now create and print a range of high-quality business messages, using personal computers. These personal computers have given ordinary staff members the knowledge and power to challenge management. The personal computer is a decentralizing force in organizations. This access to information has given rise to three main problems:

- Protection of information
- Effects on society when individuals have access to what was private information
- Possible attempts by organizations and governments to stop access to all this information.

At this stage the solutions to these problems are not clear.

Anyone with a personal computer, the right software and a modem can get access to the Internet. The Internet is an electronic system that connects millions of individual computers. Internet communication takes many forms:

- Worldwide Web pages
- Usenet groups discussing many topics
- E-mail messages
- People sending their CVs to get jobs
- Groups working together on projects.

Because the Internet is not controlled, Internet messages have to be checked with great care. The credibility of sources is not guaranteed.

The Internet is hard to classify because it is such a new medium. It is like a telephone on the one hand, and on the other it is like a broadcasting station. Internet audiences are hard to classify.

As the information highway is gradually developed, business messages will become more flexible. They will be less tied to paper and will be conveyed by many different media.

Personal computers inside and outside companies will be connected. As a result, businesses will become smaller and decentralized. People will be able to keep in touch electronically, instead of having to move about the country. People will be able to work from home instead of going to offices.

Key points

- We are in the midst of a computer revolution.
- Office space has had to be redefined and redesigned because people now use computers for long periods.
- People now have access to vast amounts of information. Because of this, they are able to confront and challenge management from a position of strength.
- The personal computer is a decentralizing force in organizations.
- People can now produce a range of first-class business messages using computers and printers.
- Information in networks needs to be protected because many people have access to it.
- People now have access to the Internet by means of their personal computers.
- The Internet is an electronic system that connects millions of individual computers.
- Internet messages do not have the same credibility as messages from the traditional mass media. This is because the Internet is not owned or controlled by one group.
- It is hard to classify the Internet as a medium of communication. It is like a telephone, but is also like a broadcasting station.
- As the information highway is gradually established, business messages will no longer be tied to paper. They will be conveyed by means of a range of codes and media.

Referencing

Writers sometimes have to use other people's ideas. These ideas have to be acknowledged. Two methods are described in this chapter:

- the numbered system
- the Harvard system

The numbered system uses a list of References and a Bibliography. The Harvard System uses brief references in brackets in the text, and a Reference Appendix.

Many people are now getting information from the Internet. This has to be correctly referenced. The concept of Uniform Resource Locations (URLs) enables business writers to give specific locations for their sources.

A URL has four parts: protocol, site, path, file. This chapter gives examples of how to reference:

- a Worldwide Web home page
- a book, online
- an encyclopedia article, online
- a Newsgroup article, online
- personal e-mail.

Reports

Introduction

Reports are widely used in organizations for making decisions. They should, therefore, be:

- based on careful research
- clearly and logically written in an objective, impersonal style
- constructed with the appropriate sections
- well presented with high readability
- written with a specific audience in mind.

This section covers the following essential aspects of report writing:

- What a report is
- The purposes of reports
- The audience for reports
- Kinds of reports in organizations
- Formats for reports
- The content of each section of a report
- Format for letters of transmittal
- Letter reports
- Summary reports
- Logic in reports
- Style and readability in reports.

What is a report?

Note: Please read Part Five (chapters 10–14) in conjunction with this Part. Part Five gives a set of general principles that apply to all written messages.

A report is an informative, fixed-format document. It is normally written because someone has been instructed to investigate a problem, draw conclusions and recommend action.

Reports have the following characteristics:

- They have clearly defined sections.
- They are based on facts.
- They are used for making decisions.
- They often give detailed technical information.
- They should be set out in a highly readable way. (See chapter 14.)
- They should be written in a formal, impersonal style. (See chapter 13.)
- They are often accompanied by a Letter of Transmittal. This letter records that the work has been done.

The purposes of reports

Reports are written with a range of purposes in mind. The main purposes are to:

- help people make decisions
- inform
- recommend action
- persuade
- record facts.

Reports are especially useful in large organizations. Managers ask subordinates to write reports to keep them informed of a wide variety of problems in all areas of the organization.

These reports then become a permanent record. They can be sent round to a large number of people, who are then kept informed about what is going on in the company.

The audience for reports

A wide variety of people will read reports. The writer should, therefore cater for experts and non-experts. Reports are often used by groups of people for making decisions. Writers should, therefore, be prepared to write for a *mixed audience* whose needs will differ. Some will need detailed technical information, whereas others will need only the Conclusions and Recommendations.

Writers should, therefore, be prepared to *select* information and to set it out in clearly defined sections.

Kinds of reports in organizations

Many kinds of reports are written in organizations:

- Committee Reports
- Reports on sales
- Interim project reports
- Reports to Boards of Directors
- Reports to large conferences.
  All these reports may be divided into three major kinds:
- Informative reports
- Investigation reports
- Feasibility reports

Informative reports give the facts of a situation. The writer will also stress the *procedure* that (s)he followed to get these facts. The writer might, for example, be asked to inform management of the damage caused by a factory fire.

Investigation reports are written because the writer has been instructed to investigate a problem, draw conclusions from the facts and recommend action. The writer has, for example, been asked to investigate the causes of a factory fire, draw conclusions on the causes and recommend action.

Feasibility reports are related to investigation reports. They are written because someone has been instructed to investigate whether something can or should be done or not.

The writer, might, for example, have been instructed to report on the feasibility of repairing a factory building after a fire. (S)he would be expected to draw conclusions about whether the building can be rebuilt. (S)he would then be expected to recommend whether to rebuild the factory or not.

Evaluative reports. Investigation and Feasibility Reports *evaluate* the facts. This evaluation is written as a set of *conclusions*. These are the *insights* gained from the findings, or the *implications*.

Technical reports. Technical reports contain a large amount of technical information. This information is often set out in the form of tables and graphs of various kinds. They may be Informative, Investigation or Feasibility reports.

Interim reports. These reports are written to inform managers of the progress of a project. A number of these reports could be written before the final report is written.

Formats for reports

Reports contain a number of sections. Each of these sections has a specific content and a specific purpose.

Elements of reports in traditional order

A full professional report contains the following sections in the order below. Note that the report is divided into two major sections:

- Preliminaries (pages numbered with Roman numerals)
- Body of Report (pages and each section numbered with Arabic numerals).

Each major section starts on a new page.

Preliminaries

- Title Page
- Acknowledgements
- Terms of Reference (Brief)
- Summary
- Table of Contents

- List of Illustrations
- Glossary (Difficult words may also be defined at the bottom of each page.)
- List of Symbols

Body of report

1. Introduction
2. Procedure used to gather Information
3. Findings (The facts)
4. Conclusions
5. Recommendations
6. List of References (if other people's work has been used)
7. Bibliography
8. Appendices

Pyramid order of report sections

Chapter 11 recommends an order of presentation different from the traditional order. This pyramid order is as follows:

Preliminaries

The same as the traditional order.

Body of Report

1. Introduction
2. Procedure
3. Conclusions
4. Recommendations
5. Findings
6. List of References
7. Bibliography
8. Appendices

Note

This list records all the possible sections of reports. The writer should *select* the sections relevant to the report and the Terms of Reference.

An *Informative Report* would stress *Procedure* and *Findings*, for example.

Investigative and *Feasibility* reports would stress Procedure, Findings, Conclusions and Recommendations.

This pyramid order is based on more and more detail as the report progresses. The report rests on a base of very detailed information in the appendices.

This order is *strongly recommended*. It moves the conclusions and Recommendations closer to the beginning of the report. This is very helpful for decision-makers. They do not need to read all the details of the findings before they reach the Conclusions and Recommendations.

Content of each section of a report

Each section of a report has a specific content. The sections will now be discussed in detail, with examples.

Title page

A Title Page should contain the following:
- a clear, informative title
- for whom the Report has been prepared
- by whom the Report has been written
- the date of the Report.

This page should be well set out with good readability. It should give the reader a very good first impression of the report.

Example

```
          INVESTIGATION INTO THE FEASIBILITY OF REPAIRING
           THE XYZ FACTORY BUILDING DAMAGED BY FIRE
                        ON 20 SEPTEMBER 1992


         PREPARED FOR:    Mr J Joseph
                          Factory Manager
                          XYZ Pty Ltd
                           Durban

         PREPARED BY:     Ms F Nandi
                           Factory Supervisor
                          XYZ Pty Ltd

                          30 September 1992
```

Acknowledgements

This section is used to thank people who helped the writer. It is essential to acknowledge the help of others. It is an important section for generating and keeping up goodwill. Note the impersonal style.

Example

```
ACKNOWLEDGEMENTS

The writer wishes to thank the following for their
help during this investigation. Without their
help, this investigation would not have been possi-
ble.

- Mr A Zulu, XYZ Factory Overseer
- Mr Z Petrus, Local Fire Department
- Ms L Mathias, Construction Manager at A.B.C.
  Construction
- Mr A Smith, Ace Steel Company

The writer also wishes to record the invaluable
help of Mr J Joseph. He ensured that the investiga-
tion could take place quickly and efficiently.
```

Terms of reference (brief)

These are the instructions given to the investigator. They are called Terms of Reference because everything in the report refers back to these instructions. Without a clear set of instructions, no investigation or report is possible.

The Terms of Reference are sometimes called a Brief. A Brief is also a set of instructions.

Terms of Reference should contain the following details:
- Who instructed the writer
- When the instructions were given
- A detailed list of exactly what the investigator is supposed to do
- The date when the report has to be handed in.

Note

Anybody who has to write a report should *ensure* that (s)he has been carefully briefed. (S)he should be prepared to negotiate with the briefer until *both* agree on the exact instructions. Bad reports are often caused by bad briefing, rather than by bad investigations.

Example

```
TERMS OF REFERENCE

Mr J. Joseph, Factory Manager of XYZ Pty Ltd, com-
missioned this report on 21 September 1992. He was
anxious to resume production after a fire that had
damaged the XYZ Factory Building in Cross Street
Durban.

Mr Joseph's specific instructions were to:
- Investigate the extent of the structural damage
  to the XYZ Factory Building caused by the fire
  on 20 September 1992.
- Investigate the cause of the fire.
- Consult with Mr A. Smith, Ace Steel Company, to
  establish whether the factory framework should
  be replaced.
- Consult with the Safety Insurance Company to
  find out how much they will pay out.
- Draw conclusions from the findings as to whether
  the building can be repaired or not.
- Recommend specific action on repairs to the
  building, keeping in mind the amount available
  from the Insurance Company.
- Report by 30 September 1992.
```

Summary

The summary should be so well written that it replaces the report for the busy reader. It should be brief, but complete. It should be clearly written for a wide lay audience. A good summary should help the reader decide whether to read the main report or not.

Summaries vary considerably in length. Some companies ask for 300 words, or no more than one page. Other companies expect a longer summary. This book recommends a summary of between 5 % and 10 % of the length of the original.

A summary should contain the following in the order below:
- an opening sentence stating what the report is about
- a brief statement of the background to the report
- a statement of the main purposes of the report

- a brief statement of the procedure used to gather information
- the main conclusions reached
- the main recommendations
- the main findings.

Example

(Note that this summary reflects the pyramid shape of the report.)

SUMMARY

This report describes the results of an investigation into the feasibility of repairing the XYZ Factory Building, Cross Street, Durban, after a fire.

The writer was asked to investigate the possible repair of the XYZ Factory Building after a fire in the paint storage section. Management wished to have the building repaired rather than rebuilt so that production could be resumed as quickly as possible.

The purposes of this report are to:
- describe the main procedure for gathering information
- give the main conclusions
- give the main recommendations
- record the major findings.

The writer gathered her information by:
- Inspecting the factory on three occasions
- Interviewing a number of witnesses to the fire
- Interviewing two experts from Ace Steel Company
- Inspecting the plans of the building.

The main conclusions are that:
- the factory can be repaired
- the Insurance money will cover the cost of the repairs.

The writer recommends that:
- plans be drawn up immediately by ABC Architects for the repair of the Factory Building
- the repairs be put out to tender as soon as the plans have been drawn up.

> The above Conclusions and Recommendations are based on the following findings:
> - That the major columns as indicated in the plan in Appendix I have not been damaged.
> - That the main roof beams have remained unaffected by the fire.
> - That 500 asbestos sheets on the roof have been broken.
> - That six cross-beams, shown in red on the plan in Appendix I, are cracked.

Table of contents

This lists all the major and minor headings in the report. It shows the reader:
- how the information has been organized
- the pages where each section may be found.

Example

```
TABLE OF CONTENTS

Section                                                    Page

Acknowledgements                                              i
Terms of Reference                                           ii
Summary                                                     iii
List of Illustrations                                         v
Glossary                                                     vi
1. INTRODUCTION                                               1
2. PROCEDURE FOR GATHERING INFORMATION                        3
3. CONCLUSIONS                                                5
4. RECOMMENDATIONS                                            6
5. RESULTS OF INVESTIGATION INTO FIRE DAMAGE                  7
   5.1   Description of damage to main columns                7
   5.2   Description of damage to main roof beams             9
   5.3   Description of damage to cross beams                11
   5.4   Description of damage to asbestos roof              13
   5.5   Description of water, flame and smoke
         damage                                              15
         5.5.1 Water damage                                  15
         5.5.2 Flame damage                                  17
         5.5.3 Smoke damage                                  19
6. LIST OF REFERENCES                                        22
7. BIBLIOGRAPHY                                              23
8. APPENDIX 1: PLAN OF FACTORY BUILDING                      24
```

List of illustrations

A list of Illustrations gives the title and page-number of every illustration in the report. If there are Tables and other types of illustrations, then the List of Illustrations is divided as follows:
- List of tables
- List of figures

If there are only graphs, diagrams and other graphics, then the heading is LIST OF FIGURES.

Examples

```
LIST OF ILLUSTRATIONS

List of tables                                    Page
1. Numbers of asbestos sheets damaged              13
2. Water damage to machines                        15

List of figures
1. Layout of main columns                           7
2. Layout of Roof Beams                             9
3. Layout of Cross Beams                           11
```

Glossary

A glossary is a special dictionary for the report. All technical terms are listed in alphabetical order and defined. Writers may also define difficult words at the bottom of each page.

Example

```
GLOSSARY

Cross beam     This is a steel H-shaped beam spanning
               between the main beams
Main beam      This is a steel H-shaped beam support-
               ing the roof
Roof beam      This is a steel H-shaped beam used in
               the roof structure
Smoke damage   This is defined as damage caused by
               smoke such that the item can no longer
               be used.
```

List of symbols

In a technical report, the writer might use special symbols with specific meanings. These should be listed and defined.

Example

```
LIST OF SYMBOLS
Δ   Relative strength of roof beams
β   Measure of the brittleness of heated asbestos
    sheets
Σ   Measure of level of smoke damage
```

Introduction

The Introduction prepares the reader for the report. It sets the scene so that the reader:

- understands why the report is necessary
- is prepared for the report.

An effective Introduction contains the following sections:

- Background to the Investigation
  This tells the reader why the investigation was necessary. It gives the essential historical background to the problem investigated. It can also refer to previous research done in this field.
- Purposes of the Report
  This section tells the reader what the writer plans to achieve in the report.
- Scope and Limitations
  This section tells the reader about the depth to which the investigator has gone. It gives the reader an idea of the areas covered.

  The writer also notes the limitations of the report in terms of the instructions. The writer should, for example, record the fact that (s)he was unable to get all the information because of a limitation of time or money. (S)he may also have been unable to interview all the people that (s)he intended to.
- Procedure for Gathering Information
  If the procedure can be described very briefly, it may be put in the Introduction. If, however, the procedure is more detailed, then it should be put in a separate section following the Introduction.

- Plan of Development
  The writer uses this section to prepare the reader for the organization of the report. It tells the reader what the main sections are and their order in the report.

Example

---

1. INTRODUCTION

    1.1 Background to investigation

    This report gives the results of an investigation into a fire that damaged the XYZ Factory Building in Cross Street, Durban on 20 September 1992. The Factory was processing a R2 million export order at the time.

    Mr Joseph, the Factory Manager, was extremely concerned about the loss of production. He immediately ordered an investigation to establish whether or not the factory could be repaired. He did not want to have to rebuild the factory if this could be avoided. He felt that a six-week delay in shipping the order would not jeopardize the firm's good name.

    The writer therefore undertook this report immediately.

    1.2 Purposes of Report

    The purposes of this report are to:
    - Describe the procedure used to gather the information
    - Describe the damage to the main columns, roof beams and cross beams
    - Describe the damage to the asbestos roof
    - Draw conclusions from the findings
    - Recommend action.

    1.3 Scope and Limitations of Report

        1.3.1 Scope

        This report covers an in-depth study of smoke and flame damage to the steel frame and roof of the XYZ Factory Building.

> 1.3.2 Limitations
>
> > This investigation is limited to the XYZ building. Damage to other buildings was not investigated. Because of limitations on time the writer was able to interview only six key people out of a planned fifteen.
>
> 1.4 Plan of Development
>
> > This report has been divided into four main sections. The Introduction is followed by the Conclusions and Recommendations. These are followed by the Results of the Investigation.

Procedure for gathering information

Here the investigator records how (s)he gathered the information for the report.

Example

> 2. PROCEDURE USED FOR GATHERING INFORMATION
>
> > The writer gathered the information for this investigation by:
> > 2.1 Inspecting the damaged building on 22, 23 and 25 September.
> > 2.2 Consulting Messrs A. Smith and S. Zulu of the Ace Steel Company on 24 September.
> > 2.3 Interviewing six people who were working in the factory when the fire broke out.
> > 2.4 Checking the plans of the Building.
> > 2.5 Consulting with the local Fire Brigade Chief, Mr K. Prinsloo.

Conclusions

The conclusions are based on the facts gathered. They are the *implications* of the facts, or the *insights* that the reader has gained from the investigation.

Since the writer is expressing *opinions* here, (s)he may use some emotive language and relative words. (S)he should take care, however, not to be too emotive.

At this stage the writer should not introduce any new information. Please note the bridging sentence at the beginning of the example.

Example

```
3. CONCLUSIONS
   The writer has drawn the following conclusions
   from the findings.
   3.1 Damage to structure
       The damage to the structure of the building
       is extensive.
   3.2 Repairs to structure
       The main structure of the building, although
       damaged, can be repaired.
   3.3 Cause of fire
       The fire was caused by an electrical fault
       in the Paint Store.
   3.4 Damage to roof
       The roof has been so badly damaged that it
       will have to be replaced.
```

Recommendations

The recommendations are based on the conclusions. They are the actions that should be taken as a result of the findings and conclusions. Recommendations are expressed by means of action-verbs. If possible, the writer should give details here. Recommendations should be expressed at as low a level of abstraction as possible. Please note the bridging sentence at the beginning of the example.

Example

```
4. RECOMMENDATIONS
   As a result of the findings and conclusions, the
   writer recommends the following:
   4.1 Repairs to structure
       Replace the following roof beams as shown in
       the figure below:
       Beam No. 2
       Beam No. 3
       Beam No. 4
```

```
    4.2  Painting of beams
         Clean all beams and repaint them with two
         coats of rust-resistant Z-Paint. These coats
         should be followed by two coats of Battle-
         ship Grey IronGrip Paint.
    4.3  Replacing of roof
         Replace the asbestos roofing with new sheets
         of PGR Asbestos Sheeting.
    4.4  Replacing of all wiring
         Replace all wiring with fire-resistant DEF
         Wiring.
    4.5  Installation of smoke detectors
         Install fifteen smoke detectors as shown on
         the accompanying sketch.
```

Findings

These are the facts of the investigation. The writer should set out these facts in a logical and coherent way. The facts should also be set out in a readable way. The writer should use:

- a multiple decimal numbering system
- specific major and minor headings
- good coherence in paragraphs
- good links between paragraphs.

The writer should guide the reader step by step through each stage of the findings.

Example

Please note that this example has been shortened.

```
    5. RESULTS OF INVESTIGATION INTO THE FIRE
       5.1 Description of damage to main columns
           Twelve H-shaped columns support the roof.
           These twelve columns, although blackened,
           have not been affected by the fire. All the
```

rust-protective paint has been burnt off.[1]
Figure 1 below, illustrates the layout of the main columns.

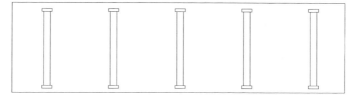

Figure 1: Layout of Main Columns

5.2 Description of Damage to Main Roof Beams

Six main roof beams support the roof. Three of these have twisted as a result of the heat. The sketch below shows the damaged beams.

Figure 2: Layout of Roof Beams

These beams are directly above the paint store where the fire started.[2]

Please see the detailed roof-plan in Appendix 1.

5.3 Description of damage to cross beams

. . .

5.4 Description of damage to asbestos roof

. . .

5.5 Description of water, flame and smoke damage

    5.5.1 Water damage

       . . .

    5.5.2 Flame damage

       . . .

    5.5.3 Smoke damage

       . . .

List of references

The writer should acknowledge any work written by others that (s)he has used. If (s)he uses a *superscript number system*, as can be seen in 5.1 and 5.2, then (s)he should use a List of References and a Bibliography. These are both illustrated here.

Note:

If the writer had used the Harvard Method a different approach would have been necessary. This approach is discussed at the end of this chapter.

The List of References is placed at the end of the major section or at the end of the report. They are set out in order of *appearance* in the text. The Bibliography based on the References is written in alphabetical order of the surnames of authors.

Example

---

6. LIST OF REFERENCES

   1. B.J. Koutsoudas, Fire Damage in Steel Buildings, London, ABC Press, 1985, pp 58-60.

   2. A. van Sand, 'A Study of Paint Fires', Journal of Paint Technology, Vol. 6, No. 2, April 1990, pp 3-12.

Bibliography

A Bibliography is used with a List of References if the writer uses a numbered citation style. The entries in the Bibliography appear in alphabetical order of surname of the authors. Page numbers of books are not given, but the first and last page of the article in a journal are given.

Example

---

7. BIBLIOGRAPHY

   Koutsoudas, B.J., Fire Damage in Steel Buildings, London, ABC Press, 1985.

   Van Sand, A., 'A Study of Paint Fires', Journal of Paint Technology, Vol. 6, No. 2, April 1990, pp 1-14.

Appendices

Material that is too detailed for the Body of the report is placed in the Appendices. The writer should refer to this material in the Body of the Report.

Appendices should contain the following:

- detailed tables
- detailed calculations
- computer printouts
- examples of questionnaires
- very detailed specifications
- transcriptions of conversations
- case histories.

Example

```
8. APPENDIX 1
   Detailed plan of steel structure of XYZ factory
   (The plan would appear here.)
```

Letter or memorandum of transmittal

The Letter or Memorandum of Transmittal introduces the report to the reader. The report is an impersonal and objective message. The letter or memorandum, in contrast, is personal and friendly. It is used to create goodwill between the writer and the reader.

The letter should be written to a client outside the firm. The memorandum should be used inside a company.

Each of these should:

- Introduce the report to the reader.
- State how successful or unsuccessful you think the investigation has been.
- State what limitations there were on the investigation.
- Refer briefly to your main findings.
- Refer briefly to your conclusions and recommendations.
- State what personal insights you gained through the investigation.

NOTE: The report illustrated in this section should be accompanied by a Memorandum of Transmittal.

Example

XYZ PTY LTD
Memorandum

To: Mr J. Joseph
               Factory Manager

From: Ms F. Nandi
               Factory Supervisor

Date: 30 September 1992

Subject: INVESTIGATION INTO FIRE DAMAGE AT XYZ FACTORY BUILDING

I have pleasure in attaching my report on the above fire damage. I believe that my investigation has been successful in spite of the severely limited time that I had.

I found that the main columns in the building were sound, even though all the paint had been burnt off. I concluded that these main columns do not have to be replaced. I did, however, find that three roof beams had been twisted. These will have to be replaced.

This investigation proved a stimulating and challenging task. I found all the factory staff to be very friendly and co-operative. I also found the Consultants from Ace Steel to be experts at their job and very helpful.

I believe that my conclusions and recommendations are realistic given our tight schedule.

Thank you for giving me this task.

F. NANDI

Example

The example below shows the format for a letter of transmittal.

XYZ CONSULTING COMPANY
365 First Street
Industria
Harare

Ref. PF/20/9

20 September 19..

Mr K. Sithole
46 Main Street
Harare

Dear Mr Sithole

REPORT ON FIRE IN ABC PAINT FACTORY, THIRD STREET, INDUSTRIA

We have pleasure in enclosing our report on the above fire. We have followed your instructions with care, and believe that our report reflects this care.

We found that the cause of the fire was an electrical fault in the paint store. The intense heat of the burning paint twisted three roof beams and cracked 30 % of the roof panels.

We have concluded that the frame of the building can be repaired, and recommend that these repairs start immediately.

Thank you for giving us this task. We found all your staff to be very co-operative. Should you wish us to explain anything in the report we shall be very happy to do so.

Yours sincerely

F. NANDI (MS)
SENIOR PARTNER

Encl. Report
F.N./jj

Letter reports

Some reports are written as letters. The letter would then start off in a formal, but emotive style. The factual report would then follow. This factual section is written impersonally with high readability.

The letter ends on a friendly note.

Example

Dear Ms Martins

REPORT ON CUSTOMERS' COMPLAINTS ABOUT WASHAWAY SOAP

We have investigated customers' complaints about Washaway Soap as you requested on 10 September —. We concentrated only on the Sharp Supermarket in Third Street because most of the complaints came from there.

Our results are as follows:

1. COMPLAINTS ABOUT PACKAGING

    1.1 Wrappers coming unstuck

       . . .

    1.2 Wrappers torn

       . . .

2. COMPLAINTS ABOUT POOR WASHING QUALITY

    2.1 . . .

We have concluded that 60 % of the customers had legitimate complaints. We therefore recommend that all customers who complain should be given their money back.

We have enjoyed working for you on this project. Thank you for your support.

If you wish to discuss this report further, please let us know.

Yours sincerely

M. NAIDOO
DIRECTOR

Summary reports

Summary reports are brief reports. They follow the same format as the long report illustrated in this section. However, they contain the main points only. They are set out in a highly readable way. The reader should be able to find the main information quickly.

A summary report should have the following sections. Each section should be brief and should have only the key points:

1. Title
2. Terms of reference
3. Brief introduction containing a short procedure section
4. Conclusions
5. Recommendations
6. Main findings only.

Example

The following example shows how the writer should present a summary report.

INVESTIGATION INTO FIRE DAMAGE AT XYZ FACTORY

1. TERMS OF REFERENCE

Mr J. Joseph, factory manager of XYZ (Pty) Ltd, commissioned this report on 21 September 1995. He was anxious to resume production after a fire that had damaged the XYZ factory building in Cross Street, Durban.

Mr Joseph's specific instructions were to:

- Investigate the extent of the structural damage to the XYZ factory building caused by the fire on 20 September 1995.
- Investigate the cause of the fire.
- Consult with Mr A. Smith, Ace Steel Company, on the best method of repairing the steel frame of the factory building.
- Consult with the Safety First Company on the best fire detection systems to install.
- Draw conclusions on the cause of the fire.
- Recommend specific actions to repair the building and to prevent similar accidents.
- Report by 30 September 1995.

2. CONCLUSIONS

The writer has drawn the following conclusions from the findings:

2.1 Cause of fire

The fire was caused by sparks from a welder's torch. Welders were repairing a section of the roof. A strong gust of wind blew the sparks onto bales of material, which caught alight.

2.2 Damage to structure

Damage to the steel structure is limited to six steel columns only. These will have to be replaced.

2.3 Damage to roof

Damage to the roof is not serious. It will take two days to repair.

2.4 Fire detection systems

The best fire detection system is the Firestop system installed by Safety First.

3. RECOMMENDATIONS

As a result of the findings and conclusions, the writer recommends the following:

3.1 Replace six steel columns

Appoint the Ace Steel Company to replace the six damaged steel columns.

3.2 Install fire detectors

Appoint Safety First to install a Firestop fire detection system.

3.3 Replace all wiring

Replace all electrical wiring. Appoint Electrical Installations CC to do this job.

3.4 Paint the internal structure

Paint the internal structure of the fracture with Fire Inhibitor, a special paint for preventing damage to metal.

> 4. RESULTS OF INVESTIGATION INTO THE FIRE DAMAGE
>
> 4.1 Cause of fire
>
> Welders were repairing a section of the roof. A strong gust of wind blew sparks onto flammable material. The fire was confined to one corner of the factory.
>
> 4.2 Damage to steel columns
>
> Six steel columns were damaged. They have twisted out of shape and are no longer safe. Repairs are covered by insurance.
>
> 4.3 Damage to material
>
> Twenty per cent of the material in the factory was damaged by water and smoke. This damage is covered by insurance.
>
> 4.4 Fire detection equipment
>
> Firestop detection systems are used by 80 % of all factories in the Durban area. They can be installed immediately.
>
> 4.5 Damage to wiring
>
> Sixty per cent of the wiring has been damaged. It will have to be replaced.
>
> F. Nandi
> Factory Supervisor
> 30 September 19—

Logic in reports

The body of every report should be developed logically. Writers should always ensure that they reach conclusions through a logical process.

Writers should ensure that they:

- have remained objective
- have concentrated on the facts
- have not confused fact and opinion
- have used referential language
- have accumulated enough evidence to reach a conclusion
- have used logical connections
- have not jumped to a conclusion.

Style and readability in reports

Reports should be written in a formal, objective, impersonal and referential style. They should be very well set out so that readers can get at the information quickly. All the techniques suggested in chapter 14 should be used.

Graphics should be:

- included in the text where they are needed
- properly numbered with good titles
- properly introduced
- properly analysed so that the reader knows what to look for.

Checklist for reports

- Have I gathered my information effectively?
- Have I written down the Terms of Reference accurately?
- Have I included all the relevant sections?
- Have I set out my Title Page attractively?
- Have I written my summary so well that it can replace my report for the busy reader?
- Have I included the right sections in my Introduction
    - Background
    - Purposes
    - Scope and Limitations
    - Procedure
    - Plan of Development?
- Have I set out my Findings in a factual way?
- Have I based my Conclusions on my Findings?
- Have I written out my Conclusions as Implications or Insights rather than as facts?
- Have I written my Recommendations in terms of exact action?
- Have I included very detailed material in my Appendices?
- Have I fitted my graphics into my text effectively?
- Have I used exact language throughout?
- Have I put my whole report together for maximum impact?

Letters

Introduction

Business letters are often the only communication that people have with organizations. The content of these letters, and the way in which they are expressed will therefore have a very important impact on people. Business letters also act as ambassadors for companies. They help to meet the organization's objectives by generating goodwill and helping customers.

Letter writers should, therefore, understand how to:

- prepare an effective letter
- write in a style suited to the reader's needs
- write in a tone that establishes a good relationship
- generate goodwill
- request and respond to requests
- complain and respond to complaints
- write good-news, neutral and bad-news letters.

This section therefore covers the following aspects of writing business letters that communicate:

- Planning letters
- Writing in an appropriate style
- Achieving the right tone
- Making letters readable
- Formats for letters
- Writing good-news, neutral and bad-news letters
- Writing special kinds of letters.

Planning letters

Anyone writing a business letter should go through all the stages of the Rhetorical Situation discussed in chapter 10.

Purposes of letters

Letters are written to:

- give facts
- ask for information
- persuade
- complain
- get action
- establish a rapport with the audience
- generate goodwill.

A business letter may have several different purposes. Writers therefore need to be skilled in planning and writing to achieve these purposes.

Audience

Writers should analyse the needs of their readers very carefully. The letter should cater for the reader's emotional need to be treated in a friendly way. It should also cater for the reader's needs for information and to get action.

The letter should also be clearly written in language that the reader can understand.

Planning letters

Chapter 11 discusses planning in detail. This section will therefore only touch on the main points.

A letter should be so well planned that the reader is able to follow the letter from beginning to end. The ideas should flow logically with good transitions between paragraphs. Sentences should flow evenly one into the next. Letters should be unified, coherent and have the right emphasis.

If a letter has to contain a number of topics, then the reader should be prepared for these. The example below shows how this could be done.

Note how the writer has used the subject-line, the opening paragraph and separate headings to guide the reader.

Example

Note that this letter has been shortened.

```
Dear Ms Magaba

SALE OF CLOTHING - COLOURS, PATTERNS, AND SIZES

Thank you for your letter of 20 July. We are very
happy to sell the clothes that you offered us.

We would, however, like to negotiate on three as-
pects of the sale:
- colours of dresses
- patterns available
- sizes available.

Colours of Dresses
. . .

Patterns Available
. . .

Sizes Available
. . .
```

Writing in an appropriate style

All business letters should be simple and clear. Many writers are, however, tempted to write in a complex style with long words. They think that this approach looks impressive and will impress others.
In reality, this style will simply confuse readers.
The following example illustrates this approach.

Example

```
The undersigned is of the opinion that no good
will eventuate from the aforesaid proposition. It
is therefore proposed that postponement of a deci-
sion be regarded as imperative.
```

This could be rewritten as follows:

```
I am not happy about your proposal. I therefore
urge you to delay a decision.
```

Letters should be written in a formal or consultative style depending how relaxed and friendly you wish to be. These styles are illustrated in chapter 13.

Achieving the right tone

Tone is defined as the attitude of the writer to the reader. An effective tone is very important in letters. Writers should strive to be neutral or friendly. They should avoid a stiff, pompous, unfriendly and tactless tone.

Tactless letters imply that the reader is wrong or inferior. A tactless tone stresses suspicion, obligation or compulsion.

The following suggestions will help you to write in a more appropriate tone:

NOT: Your letter of 23 April refers
BUT: Thank you for your letter of 23 April.

NOT: Please find enclosed
BUT: I have pleasure in enclosing . . .

NOT: Your company *claims* that
BUT: Your letter states that . . .

NOT: In response to your letter about the *alleged* loss of goods

BUT: We are concerned that you have not received the goods that we sent you.

NOT: Your clerk must have misunderstood our instructions
BUT: Our list of instructions stressed that . . .

NOT: You failed to sign the attached form
BUT: The attached form was sent to us unsigned. (Note the use of the passive here.)

Making letters readable

Use a range of techniques to make letters readable. The following techniques are effective:

- a clear subject-line
- an overview at the beginning
- headings, even in a one-page letter
- lists
- short sentences
  (an average of 15 words per sentence is recommended)
- short paragraphs
- one-sentence paragraphs to highlight important points
- a simple vocabulary
- a short summary of key points at the end
- action stressed at the end.

Formats for letters

Letters have a set form. The block-form is widely used to-day, and is the form shown below:

Example

This example illustrates the *block format*. Please note the comments in brackets.

```
(Heading)              ACE LEATHERWORKS (PTY) LTD
                       38 FIRST STREET, INDUSTRIA
                       P.O. BOX 35 INDUSTRIA
                       PH: (011) 537689
                       FAX (011) 537699

(Reference)            Ref. 2/3/93

(Date)                 25 August 19—
```

```
(Inside Address)        Mr J. Jephtas
                        28 Diagonal Street
                        CREDITVILLE
                        4569

(Salutation)            Dear Mr Jephtas

(Subject-line)          ORDER FOR FINE LEATHER
                        (ACE 25/6)

(Body of letter)        Thank you . . .
                           . . .
                        The leather . . .

(Complimentary close)   Yours sincerely

(Typed name)            M. NGOZA
(Position in Company)   SALES MANAGER
(Reference to items enclosed)    Encl.
(Initials of sender and typist) MN/ab
```

Each of the above sections will now be commented on.

Heading

Many companies use pre-printed stationery. The heading or letterhead would then include:

- The name of the company, with a Logo
- The type of business
- The address
- Telephone and fax numbers
- Names of company executives

If there is no pre-printed heading, then the writer's address should be typed on the left-hand side above the inside address.

Reference

This gives a code to enable the letter to be filed and easily retrieved. Both sender and receiver use this code to refer to all correspondence related to the topic. The reference is placed above the date.

Date

This is the date on which the letter was written. In the block style it is placed above the inside address.

Inside Address

This address identifies the receiver by name or firm. If possible, a person should be named in the address.

Salutation

This is the standard opening of the letter. The person named in the address should be named here. If a post is named, then use 'Dear Sir' or 'Dear Madam'. If a company is named, then use 'Dear Sirs'.

Subject-line

This is a heading that gives the subject of the letter. It is essential to have this heading. It should be typed in capitals and underlined. It could also be typed in bold capitals. The subject-line should always stand out from the letter. It is placed after the salutation.

Body of the Letter

This includes the following:

- The opening paragraph that gives the subject of the letter
- The middle paragraphs that develop the letter
- The closing paragraph that summarizes, stresses action and generates goodwill.

Complimentary Close

The complimentary close should be 'Yours sincerely' if someone has been named. However, if 'Dear Sir(s)', or 'Dear Madam' has been used, then the letter should end with 'Yours faithfully'.

Signature

The sender should sign her or his name above the typed name.

Typed Name

This gives the initials and name of the sender, followed by the sender's position in the company. If the sender does not show otherwise, the reader will assume that the sender is a man. It is very important that senders state how they wish to be addressed. For example, a woman might wish to be addressed as 'Ms', 'Miss' or 'Mrs'. Senders might have special titles such as 'Dr' or 'Prof.' These should be shown after the typed name.

WRITTEN MESSAGES IN ORGANIZATIONS 289

Reference to Item(s) Enclosed

The term 'Encl.' is used to show that another document is enclosed with the letter. This could also refer to several documents. It is useful as a record that other documents have been sent.

Initials of Sender and Typist

The initials of the sender normally appear first in capitals. The initials of the typist follow in small letters.

Presentation of Letter

Letters should be typed on good quality bond paper. The quality of the paper is very important for creating a good impression.

Attention-line

Some letters have an Attention-Line. These letters should be written as follows:

Example

```
XYZ (Pty) Ltd
Cross Street
ACEVILLE
1234


Attention: Mr J. Khan


Dear Sirs (Address the Company; not Mr Khan.)
```

An outline plan for a letter

The following outline plan for a letter shows the great importance of organizing a letter very carefully. Please note the comments.

- Address
  If possible, name someone.
- Salutation
  Use the person's name.
- Subject-Line
  Make this as full as possible.

Opening Paragraph

This paragraph should:

- tell the reader immediately what the letter is about
- summarize key points

- establish goodwill through its tone.

It should be written with short sentences and a simple vocabulary. This paragraph should be short. It should be written to give the reader a good first impression.

Middle Paragraphs

These paragraphs should:

- be short and written in a clear, simple style
- be very well set out using a range of techniques such as headings and lists to make them as readable as possible
- have short sentences.

They should develop the letter logically, giving the necessary facts.

Final Paragraph

This is a very important paragraph. It should:

- be written clearly and simply
- be written with an effective tone to generate goodwill
- state what the reader should do next
- state what the writer will do next
- leave a good final impression.

Example of letter

The following example shows a letter that has been written according to the principles described.

```
              STAR PUBLISHERS (PTY) LTD
                 11 Star Road Bookville
           Tel: (123) 596578   Fax: (123) 596579

Ref: 1/6/8
10 September 19—
Ms J. Turner
Super Research Company
P.O. Box 58
BOOKVILLE
5678

Dear Ms Turner

RESEARCH PROJECT 58: POTENTIAL MARKETS FOR ABC REC-
IPE BOOK

I am very pleased that you are willing to undertake
research into potential markets for our ABC Recipe
```

Book. Please start the research straight away.

It should be undertaken in three stages:
- Stage 1 Research into local demand
- Stage 2 Research into country-wide demand
- Stage 3 Research into specific recipe needs.

Stage 1: Research into local demand
Please start on this stage right away. We should be grateful for some figures by the end of October. These will help us formulate our immediate marketing strategy.

Stage 2: Research into country-wide demand
We should be very happy if you could let us have figures by the end of February next year. These figures will help us to plan the next phase of our marketing strategy.

Stage 3: Research into specific recipe needs
We need the results of this research only at the end of next year. At that stage we shall be planning a number of specialist recipe books. Your figures will be essential for our detailed planning.

Please take this letter as our permission for you to go ahead. We look forward to working with you.

Yours sincerely

K. BHAWA
MANAGING DIRECTOR
KB/gc

Writing bad-news letters

Writers of good-news and neutral letters announce the main points of their messages immediately. However, with bad-news messages they should cushion the blow of the bad news. Bad-news messages should be written with:

- a neutral subject-line
- at least one buffer paragraph.

Writers of bad-news letters should always try to keep the goodwill of the readers, even though these readers get bad news.

The following alternative plans are suggested for bad-news messages. Writers should select either a direct or indirect plan according to their purposes.

PLANS FOR BAD-NEWS MESSAGES

DIRECT PLAN	INDIRECT PLAN
Neutral Subject-line APPLICATION FOR POST . . .	Neutral Subject-line APPLICATION FOR POST . . .
THANKS Thank you for your application for this post. We appreciate your interest in joining our company.	THANKS Thank you for your application for this post. We appreciate your interest in joining our company.
REGRET We find your qualifications and experience most impressive. However, we regret that we do not have any vacant posts at the moment	REASON Our company has decided to promote internally for the next year . . .
REASON Our company has decided to promote internally for the next year . . .	REGRET We find your qualifications and experience most impressive. However, we regret that we do not have any vacant posts at the moment
THANKS Thank you for your interest in our company	THANKS Thank you for your interest in our company

Writing different kinds of letters

This section covers the writing of different kinds of letters. All of these demand special knowledge and a special approach. The types of letters covered are:

- letters of enquiry and request
- responses to enquiries
- letters of complaint
- letters of adjustment.

Letters of enquiry and request

These letters ask for information or ask someone to do something. They should be so well written that the reader is happy to reply. The task of replying should be made easy.

The plan for the letter should be as follows:

Subject-line

This clearly announces the subject.

First Paragraph

Start with a clear statement of why you have written the letter. State:
- what you want
- who wants it
- why it is wanted.

Do not apologize at the beginning.

Middle of Letter

This part should give exact details, preferably in a list.

Final Paragraph

Generate goodwill by thanking the reader and reinforcing the action asked for at the beginning.

Example

ACE CATERING COMPANY
28 Third Street
Townsville 4568
Tel: (031) 586312 Fax: (031) 586313

20 September 19—

Mrs J. Singh
The Sales Manager
Food Supplies Ltd
53 Eighth Street
JAMESTOWN
9983

Dear Mrs Singh

ENQUIRY ABOUT BULK SUPPLIES OF RICE

Thank you for your prompt reply to my telephone call today. I confirm that we are interested in buying bulk supplies of rice from you. However, before I start detailed negotiations, please give me the following specific information.

1. We need about 20 kg of rice a week. Can you guarantee such a supply of rice for the next year?

```
    2. How soon can you deliver after the date of our
       order?
    3. What type of packaging do you use?
    4. What discount will you offer for cash?

    Please let me have your answers in the next ten
    days so that we can start detailed negotiations.

    Yours sincerely

    J. SIMBA
    CATERING MANAGER
    JS/ab
```

Replies to Letters of Enquiry and Request

These replies should be specific. They should answer each item so that the reader can use the answers to make a decision. Writers should also try to generate goodwill because these letters could result in business for their company.

The plan for the letter should be as follows:

Subject-Line

This should clearly announce the subject.

First Paragraph

- Thank the enquirer for her/his letter.
- Restate the request to show that you have understood the inquiry.
- Use this paragraph to generate goodwill.

Middle of Letter

- Give exact answers, point-by-point.
- If you are enclosing price lists or any other messages, refer to them.
- If you cannot meet with any request, say so and express regret. Always try to be as helpful as possible. Say why you cannot give all the information.

Final Paragraph

- Invite the writer to respond for any help or information (s)he may need.
- Use this paragraph to generate goodwill.

Example

FOOD SUPPLIES LTD
53 Eighth Street, Jamestown 9983
Tel: (046) 21567   Fax: (046) 21568

25 September 19—

Mr J. Simba
Catering Manager
Ace Catering Company
28 Third Street
TOWNSVILLE
4568

Dear Mr Simba

ENQUIRY ABOUT BULK SUPPLIES OF RICE

Thank you for your letter of 20 September, enquiring about bulk supplies of our rice. We are very happy to meet your needs, and I should like to answer your questions as follows:

1. We can certainly supply 20 kg of rice a week. We guarantee our supplies for the next year. We keep large stocks in our warehouse and always order six months in advance.
2. All orders are sent off within 24 hours of receipt. We use the very efficient local road transport services.
3. We pack all our bulk rice in double-thickness sealed polythene bags. Each bag weighs 5 kg. These bags are packed into cardboard boxes.
4. We offer a 30 % discount for cash on delivery. We treat 90 days as cash.

I attach our latest brochure listing our range of products. If you have any further queries, I shall be very happy to answer them.

Yours sincerely

J. SINGH (MRS)
SALES MANAGER
Encl. Product brochure
JS/mb

Refusals to Requests

Sometimes a request has to be refused. Writers should treat this type of letter as a bad-news letter. It takes a good deal of care to refuse a request without losing the goodwill of the reader.

The plan for a refusal letter should be as follows:

Subject-line

This should be neutral. It should not give the bad news.

Opening paragraph

The inquirer should be made to feel welcome.

Middle paragraphs

- The situation should be reviewed.
- The request should be refused.

Final paragraph

- The writer should suggest other possible sources of information or getting service.
- The writer ends with a friendly close. This is usually an offer of service in other areas in the future.

Example

```
25 September 19—
Mr J. Simba
Catering Manager
Ace Catering Company
28 Third Street
TOWNSVILLE
4568


Dear Mr Simba

ENQUIRY ABOUT BULK SUPPLIES OF RICE

Thank you for your letter of 20 September, inquir-
ing about bulk supplies of our rice.

Since our telephone conversation on 20 September
the situation has changed. We have received a fax
```

> from our agents in Malaya stating that regular supplies of rice cannot be guaranteed for the next six months because of poor rains.
>
> We very much regret, therefore, that we cannot guarantee supplies of rice for the next year.
>
> We shall, however, do our utmost to send you the quantities of rice that you have ordered. We will continue to offer our very best service in the supply of dried foods, as we have in the past.
>
> Yours sincerely
>
> J. SINGH (MRS)
> SALES MANAGER
> JS/mb

Claims and complaints letters

These letters are written because people wish to get action. They have a problem that needs to be solved, or a complaint that they wish to express. They may be angry, but they should remember that their main purpose is to get action. They should, therefore, be tactful. They should avoid accusations, sarcasm or other highly emotive language.

The plan for a letter of complaint should be as follows:

Subject-line

This should state the facts of the complaint.

First paragraph

A friendly opening that establishes a good relationship.

Middle paragraphs

- A statement of the problem.
- Full details of the problem to help the reader take action.

Final paragraph

- A motivation to the reader to take the desired action.
- A statement of what the writer considers to be fair action.

Example

30 October 19—

Mrs J. Singh
The Sales Manager
Food Supplies Ltd
53 Eighth Street
JAMESTOWN
9983

Dear Mrs Singh

BROKEN 5 kg BAGS OF RICE: INVOICE 2568 25 OCTOBER

Thank you for your prompt delivery of our first two orders for brown rice. The rice was of very good quality. However, the third order arrived with three broken bags. As a result, we had to buy extra rice at nearly twice the price.

Details of order

The details of the order are as follows:
Date of order: 22 October
Date of delivery: 25 October
Invoice Number: 2568
Delivery Lorry: Number 3
Driver: Mr K. Bhana
Number of bags delivered: Five
Number of bags found broken: Three

The three broken bags seem to have been broken during packing or delivery. We take the greatest care when we unpack our food consignments, and our unpackers state that they found the bags broken.

Since we did not break the three bags, we should be grateful if you would replace them when you send our next order.

Yours sincerely

J. SIMBA
CATERING MANAGER
JS/ab

Letters of adjustment

These letters are replies to letters of complaint. These are either good-news or bad-news letters. They should be written to generate as much goodwill as possible.

The following is a plan for a good-news letter of adjustment:

Subject-line

This should refer exactly to the details of the complaint.

Opening paragraph

- This should thank the writer for calling attention to the problem.
- It should express concern for the problem.

Middle paragraphs

- The reader should be told exactly what steps will be taken to solve the problem.
- If the reader has to take certain steps as well, then these should be explained.

Final paragraph

- The writer should again express concern.
- The writer closes by expressing goodwill and a desire to continue offering a service.

Example

The following example illustrates a letter that grants an adjustment.

---

5 November 19—
Mr J Simba
Catering Manager
Ace Catering Company
28 Third Street
TOWNSVILLE
4568

Dear Mr Simba

BROKEN 5 kg BAGS OF RICE: INVOICE 2568 25 OCTOBER
Thank you for your letter of 30 October. I am most concerned that three of our bags of rice arrived broken. I am also concerned at the inconvenience and loss that you suffered.

> I am very pleased to offer you five 5-kg bags of brown rice free of charge. They will be delivered with our next order on 10 November.
>
> I should be most grateful if you would return the three broken bags so that we can find out why they broke.
>
> Once again, please accept my apologies at your inconvenience. We assure you that we will take the utmost care to pack our rice and to give you the best possible service.
>
> Yours sincerely
>
> J. SINGH (MRS)
> SALES MANAGER
> JS/mb

Sometimes writers feel that they must *refuse adjustments*. Such letters are bad-news letters.

The plan for such a letter is as follows.

Subject-line

- This should refer to the subject in a neutral way.

Opening paragraph

- The complainant is thanked for calling attention to the problem.
- The writer expresses concern for the problem.

Middle paragraphs

- The writer reviews the problem.
- The writer refuses or partly refuses the adjustment.

Final paragraph

- The writer expresses goodwill and tries to maintain a good relationship with the complainant.

WRITTEN MESSAGES IN ORGANIZATIONS

The following is an example of a letter refusing an adjustment.

Example

> 5 November 19—
> Mr J. Simba
> Catering Manager
> Ace Catering Company
> 28 Third Street
> TOWNSVILLE
> 4568
>
> Dear Mr Simba
>
> <u>BROKEN 5 kg BAGS OF RICE: INVOICE 2568 25 OCTOBER</u>
>
> Thank you for your letter of 30 October. I am most concerned that three of our bags of rice arrived broken. I am also concerned at the inconvenience and loss that you suffered.
>
> I have checked with our packers and quality control supervisor. They report that all the rice was very carefully packed in plastic bags and then into our special delivery boxes. Our plastic bags are extra thick to withstand all bumps during delivery.
>
> I can only assume that the bags were broken when they were unpacked.
>
> I therefore regret that I cannot meet your request for a replacement of the three broken bags. However, as a gesture of goodwill, I shall be sending you a 5 kg bag of our finest brown rice.
>
> We shall continue to offer you the very best products and packaging at the lowest prices.
>
> Yours sincerely
>
>
> J. SINGH (MRS)
> SALES MANAGER
> JS/mb

Note

Bad-news letters are difficult to write. Writers should keep their language neutral or positive, rather than negative. They should never suggest that the person complaining has been careless.

Writers should avoid such expressions as:
- You failed to read the instructions.
- You claim that we packed the goods badly.
- We fail to understand why you neglected to sign the form.
- You must sign the form immediately and send it to us.

All these expressions put the reader in the wrong.

Unsolicited sales letters

These letters advertise products or services. People do not expect them. They therefore have to be very attractive and well set out to gain attention.

The following is a suggested plan for an Unsolicited Sales Letter.

Subject-line
- This should state the name of the service or product. It should also give the main selling point.

Opening paragraph
- This should gain the reader's attention.
- The main selling points should be given.

Middle paragraphs
- These paragraphs should expand on details already given.
- They should be very well set out.
- The writer should use the following readability techniques to attract attention:
  - The product in CAPITAL LETTERS
  - Repetition of product name
  - Headings
  - Lists
  - Short sentences
  - Short paragraphs.

Final paragraph
- This should urge action by referring to a reply-paid card.
- It should also give a telephone number for easy contact.

The following is an example of an unsolicited sales letter.

Example

> **RUSTPROOFERS**
> **12 Cross Street Cape Town**
> **Tel: (012) 345678   Fax: (012) 345679**
>
> Dear Customer
>
> <u>RUSTPROOF: A PRODUCT THAT STOPS RUST IN ITS TRACKS</u>
>
> How many rusty cars have you seen round Cape Town? Is your car rusting away and losing value? RUSTPROOF will stop rust in its tracks - all for R100.
>
> WHAT WILL RUSTPROOF DO FOR YOU?
> - RUSTPROOF has been tested in the worst weather conditions. It cannot be beaten.
> - RUSTPROOF binds with the rust and stops it right there!
> - RUSTPROOF can be polished.
>
> Consider this:
> - No primer
> - No expensive spraying equipment
> - Paint on and leave to dry
> - Dries in 10 minutes
> - Duco finish
> - Thirty colours to choose from
>
> HOW CAN YOU GET RUSTPROOF?
>
> Fill in the attached card and post it to us. We'll do the rest.
>
> If you prefer, call us toll free on 080 3456. Our highly trained consultants will give you <u>free advice</u> on rust-proofing your car.
>
> Remember - RUSTPROOF.
>
> Yours Sincerely
>
> J. Davis
> MANAGER

Letters of invitation

When organizations hold functions to which guests are invited, they send out formal invitations.

These invitations state:
- Who is holding the function
- The place
- The date
- The time
- The dress (where relevant)
- An address and telephone number for responding.

The style is formal. The following example illustrates a formal invitation. Note that this has been set out in the form of a letter.

ACE CATERING COMPANY
28 Third Street, Townsville 4568
Tel: (031) 586312   Fax: (031) 586313

24 November 19—

Mr and Mrs J. Singh
53 Eighth Street
JAMESTOWN
9983

Dear Mr and Mrs Singh

INVITATION TO CATERING DISPLAY: 3 DECEMBER 19—

The Board of Directors of Ace Catering Company has pleasure in inviting you to a display of our latest catering facilities.

The details of the display are as follows:
- Date: 3 December 19—
- Time: 18h00
- Venue: The Company's Showrooms, 28 Third Street, Townsville

Please let us know by 1 December whether you are able to attend. Our telephone number is (031) 586312.

We look forward to meeting you.

Yours sincerely

J. SIMBA
CATERING MANAGER

This invitation could also be written as follows.

ACE CATERING COMPANY
28 Third Street, Townsville 4568
Tel: (031) 586312   Fax: (031) 586313

THE BOARD OF DIRECTORS OF ACE CATERING COMPANY
request the pleasure of your company
at a display of their new catering facilities

On
3 DECEMBER 19—

At
THE COMPANY'S SHOWROOMS,
28 Third Street Townsville

Time
18h00

R.S.V.P. by 1 December 19—
Ms. K. Bhawa
P.O. Box 85, Townsville 4568
Telephone: (031) 586312

Checklist for business letters

Have I
- Prepared a letter that helps to create a good company image?
- Set out the letter in an up-to-date format?
- Catered for my reader's needs?
- Addressed the reader by name?
- Given the reader a clear subject-line that states what the letter covers?
- Created a good first impression in the first paragraph?
- Told the reader what the letter is about in the first paragraph?
- Given the facts in a clear and logical order?
- Written the letter in a coherent way so that the reader can follow the arguments?
- Written an effective closing paragraph that generates goodwill and tells the reader what to do next?
- Set out my letter in a highly readable way?
- Written my letter in a clear, simple style?
- Chosen words for the right tone?
- Kept the number of syllables per word as low as possible?
- Punctuated my letter well?

Memoranda

Memoranda, often called memos, are messages written inside organizations. They are organized like letters, but vary a great deal in formality. They may also be set out as reports with numbered headings.

Memoranda are used as follows:
- To communicate the same information to a group of people who have to attend a meeting.
- To inform people about company policies.
- To confirm points made in a conversation or meeting.
- To confirm decisions or agreements.
- To keep people informed of events in the company.
- To contact staff who are difficult to reach by other means.

Format of a memorandum

The format of a memorandum is totally different from that of a letter. Many companies have standard printed memorandum forms. If staff do not have such forms they create their own forms.

The form below illustrates the format for a memorandum.

```
                    NAME OF COMPANY
                      MEMORANDUM
    TO:                                    DATE:

    COPIES TO:

    FROM:


    SUBJECT:
```

The conventions for memorandum writing are as follows:

To

The person addressed is normally given a courtesy title such as Mr or Mrs only if (s)he is of higher rank than the sender. The job-title, for example 'Sales Director' is included. This avoids confusion, especially in large companies.

Copies to

If the memorandum has to be addressed to a receiver and other people for information, then the 'Copies to' section is used.

From

The writer may give a courtesy title such as 'Mr' or 'Mrs' if (s)he feels that the readers might not know her or him. If the readers know the writer, then the writer's name is enough. The writer will give his or her job-title if the company is large or the reader does not know him or her.

Date

Give the date of the memorandum for reference. The following style for the date is recommended: 6 December 19—.

Subject

Write a clear subject-line above the first paragraph. This should announce the title of the memorandum.

Conventions of memorandum writing

Memoranda do not have Salutations or Complimentary Closes. The writer normally has his or her typed name at the end. (S)he could also end off with initials.

Memoranda are written in styles ranging from formal to consultative. (See chapter 13 for examples.)

Example of Memorandum

The following example illustrates a memorandum:

ACE CATERING COMPANY
MEMORANDUM

TO: All Catering Staff   DATE: 29 November 19–

FROM: James Simba

        Catering Manager

SUBJECT: CATERING DISPLAY 3 DECEMBER — STATEMENT OF
         NEEDS

Thank you for agreeing to work over weekends to get the display ready. So far we've had 60 responses to our invitations. I now need written statements of your specific needs for 3 December.

Please send me, by 1 December, a statement of your needs at the display stands. I need to know the following:
- The name of your stand
- How many tables you need

- The amount of floor space that you need
- The number of helpers that you need
- Any specific lighting needs
- Any special facilities that you need such as refrigeration space.

I look forward to the display. It should be excellent, judging from the amount of work you have been doing.

J. SIMBA

Checklist for memoranda

Have I:

- Set out the memorandum correctly?
- Provided a good subject-line?
- Set out the memorandum clearly so that I will get the right response?
- Written the memorandum in a clear and simple style?
- Written to achieve a good, friendly tone?

Proposals

What is a proposal?

A proposal is a persuasive message. It is written to get action. This type of persuasion is based on facts, rather than on highly emotive language. Proposals should be:

- Well organized so that the reader knows at once what the proposed action is.
- Well set out with clear sections, a numbering system and effective headings.
- Well written in a clear, formal and simple style.

Proposals should also give readers exact details of costs, timetables and dates. They should be persuasive. The facts should be so well set out that the reader is convinced that the proposed action should be taken.

Format for proposals

A proposal is set out like a report. It should be accompanied by a letter of transmittal if it is sent outside the organization. Inside an organization, it may be accompanied by a memorandum of transmittal.

There are two types of proposal:
- Requested proposal
- Non-requested proposal.

The *requested* proposal is one that a client asks for. For example, a client may ask you for a proposal on what action you would take to solve a problem and how much your action would cost.

A *non-requested proposal* is written because you wish to generate work for yourself. You see a problem and propose action to possible employers to solve the problem.

Requested proposal

A requested proposal should have the following sections:
- Title page or title
- Client's instructions or terms of reference
- Client's objectives
- Summary of proposal. This should replace the proposal for the busy reader. It should include all key actions, costs and timing.
- Background to the proposal. This should contain:
  - the need for the proposal
  - a statement of the problem to be solved
  - the need for a solution
  - purposes of the proposal

- procedure used to set up the proposal
    - plan of development of the proposal (how the proposal has been set out).
- The detailed proposal. This should contain:
    - the scope of the problem
    - the boundaries of the proposal and what has to be done within those boundaries
    - limitations of the proposal
    - methods to be used to put the proposal into action
    - breakdown of tasks to be done and their timing
    - time and work schedule
    - detailed costing of proposed action
    - cost and method of payment to proposer.
- Justification of proposal. This is persuasive, and contains:
    - benefits from the solution
    - feasibility of the solution
    - likelihood of success.
- Urge to action.
    - This short section restresses the proposed action.
- Appendices or attachments. These should contain some or all of the following:
    - detailed figures to show how any proposed expenditure has been calculated
    - detailed calculations to back up any technical proposals
    - detailed results of questionnaires or other surveys
    - the company's employment policies
    - the company's success with other projects
    - a description of the company's staff and their qualifications and experience
    - the company's financial statements.

Non-requested proposal

The non-requested proposal contains all of the above sections. However, the proposers have to sell *themselves* as well. In the Summary, writers should state briefly who they are. In the *background* to the proposal, the writers should state what they do, and include the following:

- A brief description of the organization
- A brief description of experience with projects
- A brief description of staff experience and qualifications
- A brief statement of the company's financial condition
- A brief statement of the company's employment practices.

In the appendices, the writers should include:

- References from previous clients

- References to an earlier association if relevant
- Previous experience with projects
- Descriptions of staff, their qualifications and experience
- The company's organization chart
- Statement of the financial condition of the company
- Description of employment practices
- Physical location of the company
- Statement of the company's environmental policy
- Descriptive and advertising literature.

Example

Please note that this has been shortened in places.

```
PROPOSAL TO SPEND R100 000 IN 19— AND 19— TO
REPLACE SIX WORN-OUT FLAVOUR MIX FOOD MIXERS AND
SEVEN WONDER MICROWAVE OVENS

SUMMARY
The proposal
The writer proposes that this company spend R100
000 in 19— and 19— to replace:

- six worn-out Flavour Mix food mixers with Ace
  food mixers
- seven worn-out Wonder microwave ovens with
  Zippy microwave ovens.

Background to proposal

The above machines are no longer working to their
full capacity. They are having to be repaired on
average once a week. These repairs are costing
R1 000 per week.

Justification of proposal

- These machines are essential if we wish to
  compete in a difficult market.
- Our competitors have bought new machines during
  the past six months.
- The catering division needs these new machines
  for its series of open-day displays planned for
  January 19—.
```

1. BACKGROUND TO PROPOSAL

    1.1 Age of machines

    1.1.1 Flavour Mix food mixers

    These machines are now five years old. They have been used daily, and are now breaking down.

    They are costing us R1 000 per week. Our budget for maintenance and repairs is R100 per week.

    1.1.2 Wonder microwave ovens

    These ovens are now six years old. Each machine is used for four hours a day. Their performance has now deteriorated to 50 % in terms of the company's standard performance rating.

    1.2 Safety of staff

    Three of the company's caterers have had accidents in the last week with food mixers. These accidents were caused by faulty switches.

    1.3 Poor quality of cooking

    The microwave ovens are no longer cooking food correctly. This means that our products are being spoilt.

    1.4 Purposes of this proposal

    The purposes of this proposal are to:
    - Recommend the purchase of six Ace food mixers.
    - Recommend the purchase of seven Zippy microwave ovens.
    - Justify the choice of the above products.

    1.5 Procedure used to set up this proposal

    The writer:
    - inspected the faulty machines and tested them according to the company's fixed procedure
    - examined a range of six food mixers and eight microwave ovens
    - obtained quotations on the costs of all the above machines

- compared the machines using the company's standard procedure.

1.6 <u>Plan of development of this proposal</u>

The proposal starts with a summary. After this, the background to the proposal is given. The proposal is then given in detail. Following this, the proposal is justified.

2. DETAILED PROPOSAL

2.1 <u>Purchase of Ace Mix food mixers</u>

. . .

2.2 <u>Purchase of Zippy microwave ovens</u>

. . .

2.3 <u>Cost of above products</u>

. . .

2.4 <u>Timing of purchases</u>

. . .

2.5 <u>Maintenance and spares</u>

. . .

3. JUSTIFICATION OF PROPOSAL

3.1 <u>Increased competition</u>

Three more catering companies have set up businesses in our area. Our company therefore needs to have the best machines to compete.

3.2 <u>Competitors replacing machines</u>

Our competitors have replaced all their food mixers and microwave ovens in the past six months. They are therefore able to prepare and cook food more efficiently than our company can.

3.3 <u>Benefits from proposed purchases</u>

We will be able to keep our competitive advantage because our management system is more efficient than that of our main rival.

3.4 <u>Feasibility of the solution</u>

The proposed solution is feasible because our payback period will be only three years.

>   We will then have a major competitive advantage over our rivals.
>
> 4. ACTION TO BE TAKEN
>   The writer urges the immediate allocation of R100 000. This will mean that orders for mixers and microwave ovens can be placed overseas in good time.

Checklist for proposals

Have I:
- Stated the proposal as clearly as possible in the title?
- Summarized the proposal to give the reader a quick overview of the whole proposal?
- Given the background to the proposal?
- Given the proposal in detail, including costs, all other figures and an exact timetable?
- Justified the proposal?
- Reinforced the action at the end?
- Set out the proposal so that it is highly readable?
- Written the proposal in a clear, simple style?
- Written the proposal at the right level of formality?
- Written the proposal impersonally or personally according to my audience?

Notices and circulars

The audience for notices and circulars

Notices and circulars are often written for a general audience. A notice on a board, for example, should be designed to attract the attention of all who pass it. A circular is designed either for sending round a company, or for sending to customers. Writers will, therefore, find it difficult to write for an exactly described audience.

Notices

Notices contain a range of information, from procedures to follow in the event of a fire, to information on the attitudes of the company to smoking. Notices should be:

- attractively set out
- simple
- immediately clear.

They are normally displayed on notice boards where they have to compete for attention with many other notices. Companies should divide their notice boards into sections, as follows:

TODAY	PROCEDURES	GENERAL
	(E.g. if there is a fire or bomb threat.)	

The above sections will vary from company to company. In addition, a very important notice should be made to stand out in some way. A large red arrow could, for example, be attached to such a notice.

Format for notices

The following format is suggested for Notices.

Heading

This should be very clear and well set out. It should tell the reader at once what the message is about.

- *Introduction*

This should state who should be reading the message. If necessary, it should expand on what the Heading states.

Main message

This should be kept simple. The writer should set out the key points as readably as possible. (S)he should use:

- A numbering system
- Plenty of headings
- Items in point-form, rather than large blocks of writing
- A contact name and number if readers need more information.

Example

PROCEDURE IN CASE OF FIRE

All Staff

THIS NOTICE TELLS YOU

- WHAT TO DO IF YOU SPOT A FIRE
- WHERE TO GO IF YOU NEED TO ESCAPE

What do you do?
1. Inform the chief fire warden in the building. His number is 2345
2. Inform all staff on that floor.
3. Close all windows and doors in the area.
4. Do not attempt to put out the fire.

Where do you go?
1. Move calmly to the green fire escape door and make your way out of the building.
2. DO NOT USE THE LIFTS.
3. Report to your FLOOR MANAGER once you are outside.

Enquiries
J. Retief, Tel: 2345

Circulars

Circulars take a wide variety of forms. They may be written as memoranda addressed 'To: All Staff'. They may also be sent out to customers or suppliers as letters. However, they differ from normal memoranda and letters because they contain general information. They are designed to give a wide variety of people the same message.

WRITTEN MESSAGES IN ORGANIZATIONS

The format for a circular should be as follows:

Salutation

Memorandum: To: ALL STAFF
Letter: Dear Customer
                Dear Supplier

Subject line

This should be very specific. It should announce the subject immediately.

Opening paragraph

This should give the reader an overview of the message.

Middle paragraphs

These should be very well set out with high readability. The facts should be highly organized.

Final paragraph

This should:

- summarize key points
- stress action
- express goodwill

Example

This example has been written as a letter to all customers. The company is moving to a new building. The writer's aims are to:

- inform the customers of the move
- persuade these customers to come to the new building
- maintain the goodwill of these customers.

```
Dear Customer
MOVE TO 1 THIRD STREET CASTLETOWN
We are moving! Out present shop is too small to
meet our customers' needs. We have therefore de-
cided to move to 1 Third Street on 1 December 19—.
This well-designed shop in a developing area will
enable us to meet all your needs. We will be offer-
ing you:
 - Plenty of parking
 - Twice the floor-space
 - A full display of all our goods
 - Complete customer service.
```

> Move with us to 1 Third Street. We offer the best service in town.
>
> Yours sincerely
>
> J. SIMBA
> MANAGING DIRECTOR

Writing instructions

What are instructions?

Instructions are directions, commands or guidelines for readers. They are not simply orders.

Instructions are essential in organizations for seven major reasons:

- They help people to work together to achieve the organization's goals.
- They help people to do things on their own, but within guidelines.
- They ensure that staff know what to do in specific circumstances.
- They ensure that all staff do the same jobs in the same way.
- They save time because staff have set procedures to follow.
- They promote safety, because they tell people what to do and what not to do.
- They help people to get the best use out of products.

What should instructions do?

Instructions should tell people:

- what to do
- what not to do
- how to do something
- where to do something
- how much has to be done
- what is dangerous about what they are doing.

If people are assembling or using a piece of machinery, they need to be told:

- who should be doing the job
- when they should be doing it
- what the machine does
- how the machine does it
- what to use
- what not to use.

The language of instructions

Instructions should be written in a formal style. Verbs in the imperative mood are used.

Examples of such verbs are:
- Open the package . . .
- Assemble the parts . . .
- Bolt Part A to Part B, using . . .
- Do not over-tighten . . .
- Test the assembled machine . . .
- Store the machine in a cool place . . .
- Install the machine in the following order.

Format for instructions

Instructions vary a great deal in their purposes and audience. The following list of sections covers most instructions. The reader should, therefore, select those sections that are relevant for specific instructions.

Title

This should clearly state the purpose of the Instructions.

Introduction

This should state:
- Whom the instructions are aimed at
- The purposes of the instructions.

Theory and principles of operation

This section tells the reader the theoretical basis of the design of a machine. It also gives the principles of operation.

List of equipment and materials needed for assembly

The reader is given a list of equipment and materials needed for assembling the machine.

Description of the mechanism

Here the reader is told how the mechanism works.

Instructions for assembling the machine

The reader is told, step-by-step, how to assemble the machine.

Operating instructions

Here the reader is told how to operate the machine. This section could also list a clear set of instructions of what to do in a range of situations.

These could cover, for example, the operation of a telephone answering machine or the evacuation of a building.

Precautions and a warning

This section lists the precautions to be taken. It also warns readers about possible dangers such as over-heating, electrical shocks or moving parts that could injure them. This section could be placed at the beginning of the Instructions as well.

Graphic aids

Complex instructions should be backed up with graphic aids such as:

- photographs
- diagrams
- flow charts
- logic trees
- algorithms

Examples of instructions

The following examples illustrate a general set of instructions for staff. These are followed by a specific set of instructions for using a telephone answering machine.

Example

Please note that this example has been shortened.

ACE CATERING COMPANY
Instructions for disposing of food after displays

1. Introduction

These instructions have been devised for all staff in the *Catering Section*. Please read these instructions carefully. We produce a large variety of dishes for display. Careless disposal of these dishes after displays could lead to:

- Criticism from the public
- Pollution of the surrounding areas
- Withdrawal of our licence.

These instructions have been written to ensure that:

- You dispose of food in a hygienic manner
- You do not cause pollution
- We receive favourable reports from Inspectors.

2. Disposal of meat

Please ensure that you follow these instructions *exactly*.

    2.1 Collect all meat that has been on open display at the end of each exhibition.

2.2 Wrap this meat in our special disposal bags, ensuring that each bag weighs no more than 1 kg when full.
2.3 Place all the bags in our meat disposal boxes.
2.4 Ensure that each box is sealed.
2.5 Ensure that each box is incinerated in our incinerator in Block B.

Warning: *Under no circumstances* is this meat to be taken out of our display room and sold. It could be contaminated.

3. Disposal of salads

Please ensure that you follow these instructions *exactly*.

3.1 Collect all . . .
3.2 Wrap the salads . . .
3.3 Place all the bags . . .
3.4 Ensure that . . .
3.5 Ensure that . . .

Warning: Under no circumstances are salads to be taken out of our display rooms and sold. They could be contaminated.

Example

This is a more technical example. Note that this example has been shortened.

ACE CATERING COMPANY
Instructions for installing ABC Telephone Answering Machines

1. WHO SHOULD READ THIS?

These instructions are for all staff who are planning to install an ABC Telephone Answering Machine at their desks.

2. INTRODUCTION

The company is willing to supply an ABC Telephone Answering Machine to any staff member wishing to attach one to his or her desk telephone.

2.1 What these instructions do
These instructions tell you:
– How to install your machine
– How to record a greeting
– How to check that a greeting has been recorded
– How to play messages
– How to turn the machine on from a remote source to listen to your messages.

2.2 What the ABC Machine offers you
This machine offers you:
– Recording of up to 30 calls
– Power failure recovery
– Tape-full indicator.

3. HOW TO INSTALL THE ABC MACHINE

3.1 Equipment needed
- ABC Telephone Answering Machine.
- Adaptor for plugging the answering machine into the power source.

3.2 Installing the machine

Step 1: Place the answering machine on a hard flat surface near a telephone jack and power point.
Warning: Leave at least 4 cm of space above, and 12 cm of space at the rear of the machine for ventilation.

Step 2: Connect the answering machine to the telephone line as follows:
(a) Unplug the telephone from the jack and plug it into the telephone jack at the back of the machine. (See diagram.)

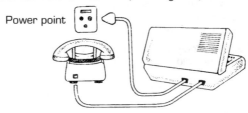

(b) Plug the telephone line from the machine into the telephone jack in the wall. (See diagram.)

Step 3: Connect the answering machine to power point as follows:
(a) Plug the adaptor provided into the power point. (See diagram.)
(b) Plug the other end of the adaptor into the answering machine. (See diagram.)
(c) Switch on the power so that the answering machine can begin a self-check and a telephone line check.

Warning: Always connect the adaptor *after* the telephone line has been connected so that the machine can test the telephone line signal.

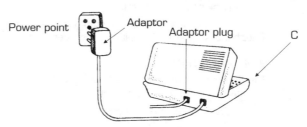

Step 4: Record a message as follows:
- Press and hold down the button marked A as shown.
- Start speaking when indicator light B starts flashing.
- Release button to stop the recording. Your greeting will be played back. Then the unit will re-set itself.

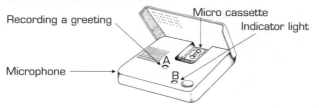

Recording a greeting

Use of graphics in instructions

Apart from photographs and diagrams, the following graphic devices are very helpful in showing the stages in a process:

- Logic trees (example below)
- Flow charts (example on page 324)
- Algorithms (example on page 325)

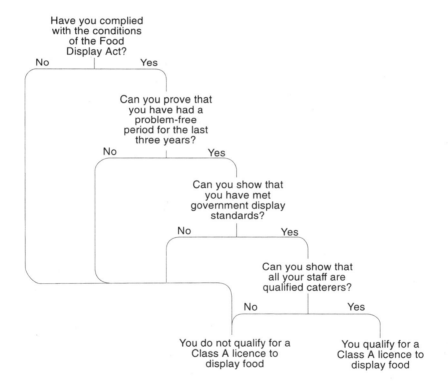

Figure 17.1
Example of a logic tree

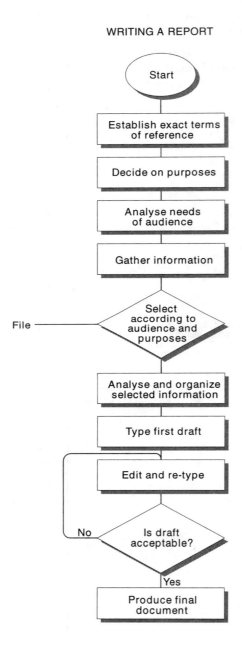

Figure 17.2
Example of a flow-chart

WRITTEN MESSAGES IN ORGANIZATIONS

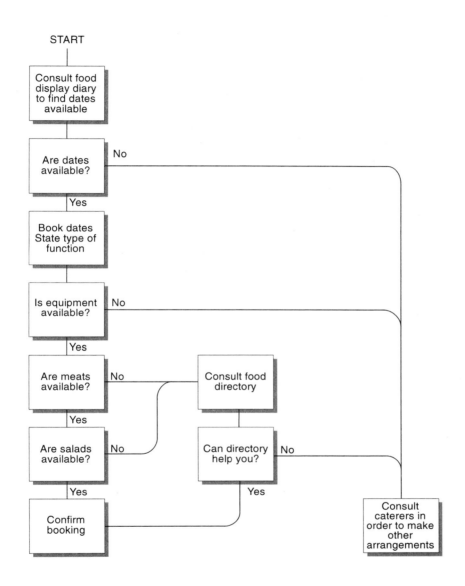

Figure 17.3
Example of an algorithm

Checklist for instructions

Have I:

- Made my purposes clear?
- Taken the needs of my audience into account?
- Arranged my instructions in the right order?
- Numbered each section correctly?
- Used headings and sub-headings?
- Kept my instructions short and to the point?
- Kept my sentences to an average of fifteen words each?
- Used exact words?
- Avoided ambiguous instructions?
- Stated exactly who should do specific things?
- Defined all technical terms?
- Stated warnings exactly so that all readers will understand them?
- Used the right instruction-words?
- Used graphics such as diagrams and photographs where relevant?

The press release

The press release, in-house journal article and essay

These three types of messages are related. They differ from reports because they are structured as continuous writing. Reports are structured as numbered sections with headings.

In addition, reports are factual and written in a referential style. Press releases, articles and essays, on the other hand, cover facts and opinions. They may be written in a referential or emotive style. They may also be written more informally than are reports.

Their subject-matter is also different from reports.

Characteristics of continuous writing

Continuous writing relies on:

- a very clear plan
- unity of ideas
- good coherence within paragraphs
- good links between paragraphs
- good emphasis of the most important ideas
- a good opening paragraph that prepares the reader
- a good closing paragraph, where relevant — this closing paragraph sums up the key ideas and leaves the reader with something to think about.

The press release

The press release is written like a newspaper article. It is a form of advertising. Companies send press releases to local newspapers or broadcasting stations. The press releases are designed to inform the public about company activities in the area of social responsibility, for example.

Charity organizations may wish to inform the public about projects to help poor people, the blind, or deaf people.

The press release is structured in the form of the inverted pyramid illustrated in chapter 11. This structure allows editors to:

- select key information from the opening paragraph
- cut the article from the end up so that it will fit into a newspaper.

The format of a press release is as follows:

- the statement 'NEWS RELEASE'
- a heading.
- an opening paragraph that gives the key facts, answering *who, what, where, when, why, how?*
- some background information.
- less and less important information.

- the sender's name, address, telephone and fax numbers, and e-mail address.
- a date for the release of the news if applicable.

The following example shows the construction of a press release. Please note that this example has been shortened.

Example

NEWS RELEASE

A boost for low-cost housing

The ACE Catering Company is to provide 25 low-cost houses for its hourly-paid staff. This scheme is part of the company's social responsibility programme. It has been developed in co-operation with the staff. They are being encouraged to buy these houses through a special home ownership scheme.

This scheme is the brain-child of Mr K. Singh, the Company's founder. He bought land for future development, but decided to use it for housing instead.

Each house, costing R25 000, has a family room, two bedrooms, bathroom and kitchen. Houses have been designed to allow building on. All services will be provided.

The ACE Catering Company has other Social Responsibility Schemes. Further plans include education bursaries, in-house training schemes and a transport scheme.

ISSUED BY
ACE Catering Company
28 Third Street
Townsville
4568

Telephone: (031) 586312
Fax: (031) 586313

Who writes press releases?

In a large organization such as an oil company, the press release will be written by a staff member in the corporate affairs or public relations department.

Medium-sized or small organizations that cannot afford to have special public relations departments will engage consultants to write press releases for them when they are needed. These consultants could be from a public relations company.

Checklist for an effective press release

Have I:

- Decided on the right newspaper to which to send the press release?
- Decided if my press release can be used on the radio?
- Analysed my audience?
- Selected an effective title?
- Placed all my key points at the beginning?
- Answered the questions *who, what, when, where, how, why*?
- Organized my writing so that the press release contains less and less important information?
- Written clearly and simply?
- Included the name, address and telephone number of the sender?
- Given a date for the release of the news, where relevant?

Essays and articles for in-house journals

The essay

Essays are written for a wide variety of audiences and for many purposes. This section will therefore concentrate on the following:

- preparing to write the essay
- the organization of the essay
- achieving unity, coherence and the right emphasis
- writing in a clear style.

The principles mentioned above have been discussed in chapters 10–14. This section will not, therefore, go into detail.

Preparing to write the essay

The writer should tackle the essay in five stages:

Stage 1: Undertake research
Stage 2: Plan and organize the material
Stage 3: Write the first draft
Stage 4: Edit the draft
Stage 5: Write the essay

Stage 1: undertake research

Essays require research. The writer should therefore consult appropriate books, journal and magazine articles, and reports. In addition, interviews may be necessary if the topic is a current one. The writer could also consult the Internet.

The writer should:

- build up a set of bibliography cards
- evaluate each source in terms of its relevance to the topic
- write notes on note cards
- record interviews on interview record cards.

Stage 2: plan and organize the material

At this stage the writer should:

- Decide on her or his purposes.
- Analyse the needs of the readers.
- Draw a mind-map of the key ideas. (See chapter 11)
- Using this mind-map, select the main and supporting ideas for the essay.
- Decide on an organization pattern, such as general to particular. (See chapter 11 for the range of choices.)

- Draw up a topic outline (see chapter 11). This outline should set out the main ideas in the chosen order. Each main idea should be supported by sub-ideas, also in the chosen order.
- Check that the topic outline enables him or her to write in a unified and coherent way. This outline should also help the writer to achieve the right emphasis.
- Plan good introductory and closing paragraphs. The Introduction should summarize the main points and prepare the reader for the main points of the essay. The conclusions should bring together the main points of the essay.

Stage 3: write the first draft

At this stage the writer should decide on the style of the essay. Should it be:

- formal or informal?
- impersonal or personal?

The writer should now write the essay ensuring that:

- every sentence flows into the next
- every paragraph flows into the next.

The reader should be able to follow the ideas stage-by-stage. The writer has to provide good signposting words, phrases and sentences. These guide the reader down each page. The writer should use:

- nouns that are repeated down the page to keep an idea flowing
- pronouns that refer back to previous ideas or forward to linked ideas
- joining words such as 'if', 'although', 'however', 'but' that show logical connections
- sentences that link paragraphs.

Stage 4: edit the first draft

The writer should now check the draft carefully, using the checklist below.

Checklist for essays

Have I:

- Selected the right facts and opinions?
- Chosen a good title that prepares the reader for the essay?
- Written a good, clear introduction that prepares the reader for the content?
- Organized my information so that it is clear to my reader?
- Kept to the organizational pattern that I have chosen?

- Provided signposts to my readers so that they are able to follow my argument?
- Ensured that I have a unifying theme running through my work?
- Ensured that I have good coherence and the right emphasis?
- Written my essay in a clear style?
- Written my essay at the right level of formality?
- Ensured that I have made a difference between fact and opinion?
- Chosen the right factual and emotive words to convey these facts and opinions?
- Written a good concluding paragraph to draw together my main ideas?
- Made my essay as readable as possible?

Stage 5: write the essay

The writer should now write the essay as carefully as possible checking all the time on:

- organization
- flow of ideas
- style
- readability

The following short example illustrates an essay. Note that the essay has been written in a formal, impersonal style.

Example

THREE ACTIVITIES THAT LEAD TO GOOD INTERPERSONAL COMMUNICATION IN COMPANIES

Good communication in companies starts with effective interpersonal communication. Management can devise the finest set of networks and organizational patterns. However, if the people do not work well together these networks will fail. This essay describes three aspects of interpersonal communication in companies. The first is good listening. The second is sensitivity to non-verbal behaviour, and the third is effective use of language. This essay will discuss each in turn.

Good listening, or active listening as it is sometimes called, is a physical process. It places demands on the listener's ability to concentrate on the full message. Good listeners should listen both for the facts and the emotions behind those facts.

> They should motivate themselves to listen, and should be as sensitive as possible to the speaker's non-verbal behaviour.
>
> A good understanding of non-verbal behaviour is essential for effective interpersonal communication. People should be particularly sensitive to the speaker's signs that (s)he wishes to join in the conversation. People should show that they are listening. They should ensure that they keep good eye-contact and should be aware of people's space-needs.
>
> The other side of good listening is good speaking. The effective use of language is the third topic of this essay. Speakers should always use language that is simple and geared to the listener's needs. They should not be tempted to use difficult words to impress. All that they will do is confuse the listener and destroy communication.
>
> In conclusion, this essay has stressed three key aspects of good interpersonal communication. Good listening, sensitivity to non-verbal communication and effective use of language will ensure that companies are good places in which to work.

The in-house journal article

In-house journal articles are normally written like press releases. They should be organized so that the reader gains a clear idea of the key points at the beginning. However, they differ from newspaper articles in that they:

- are written for a specific audience inside an organization
- are written to entertain, as well as inform
- have as their subjects domestic and personal issues relevant only to people inside the company.

In-house articles are usually written in a less formal style than are essays.

Writing an in-house journal article

The writer should follow all the stages described for the essay. They will not, therefore, be repeated here.

The example below suggests an approach to an in-house article. Notice that it is written in a less formal style. The writer is able to use headings to guide the reader. These headings would not normally be used in an essay.

Note: The same checklist may be used for essays and in-house journal articles.

Example

CAN YOU WRITE A LETTER THAT HELPS OUR BUSINESS?

By Sarah Brown

How many of us have sat down and analysed what we are doing when we write a letter? This company sends out over 100 letters a week. Have you ever considered the impact they have on readers? Letters are our ambassadors. Do we treat them as such?

Three questions about letters

In this short article I'd like to answer three questions:

- How do we cater for our readers?
- How do we organize letters for the greatest impact?
- How do we write in a clear style?

How do we cater for our readers?

Our top priority is to understand what our readers need. We need to find out what answers they want and what action to take. Our letters should be very well organized so that readers know exactly what they are about in the first paragraph.

How do we organize letters for the greatest impact?

The points of major impact in a letter are beginning and end. We should strive to create a good first impression. The first paragraph should establish goodwill. It should tell the reader what the letter is about.

The last paragraph is also very important. It should leave the reader with an impression of goodwill. We should make sure that we:

- tell the reader what we're going to do next
- tell the reader what (s)he should do next.

How do we write in a clear style?

We often write letters in a stodgy, boring style. We write long sentences packed with pompous words and stock phrases. Let's throw all of these out and choose a simple vocabulary and short sentences. Avoid stock phrases such as 'Enclosed please find'. Get to the point and don't waffle.

A final point

Remember that letters are our ambassadors. Make sure that they create a good impression and help us to do good business.

Telegrams and telexes

Telegrams and telexes are being rapidly replaced by fax machines and by e-mail. Nevertheless, some companies still use them. This section has, therefore, been kept short. It covers the following:

- principles of telegram writing
- principles of telex writing.

Examples of both are given.

Telegrams

Telegrams are written in a *cryptic style*. This style uses key words such as nouns and verbs only. The other words that help to create full sentences are left out.

A telegram should:

- give facts such as dates, times and places
- state actions
- name people.

The words used should create a clear message.
The example below illustrates a telegram:

```
CANCEL FLIGHT AB 357 TUESDAY 25 NOVEMBER PLEASE
BOOK FLIGHT WEDNESDAY 26 NOVEMBER TO ARRIVE NEW
YORK THURSDAY 27 NOVEMBER 20H00.
```

Telexes

Telexes are sent from one company to another via a telex machine. The telex has to be prepared by the sender and typed by an operator, who sends off the message. The message is received by a telex machine at the other end and printed out.

A telex is a cross between a letter and a telegram. Like a letter, it gives more detail than does a telegram. It can, however, be prepared in a cryptic style.

Telexes are printed in capital letters. Normally nothing is underlined.

Example

```
ATTENDANCE AT CONFERENCE ON NEGOTIATION 25 MARCH
1993

PLEASE CONFIRM THAT MESSRS SMITH AND ZULU ARE
ALLOWED TO ATTEND ABOVE CONFERENCE. PERMISSION
NEEDED TO
   - BOOK FLIGHTS THROUGH COMPANY'S AGENTS
   - CONFIRM CONFERENCE BOOKINGS
   - BOOK HOTELS
PLEASE ARRANGE LEAVE FOR ABOVE TWO FROM 20 - 30
MARCH 1993
CONFIRM ARRANGEMENTS WITH JOHN JACOBS TELEX 57856
BY DECEMBER 1992
```

Telexes should be set out as follows:

Plan for telex

Attention line

This should tell the receivers where the telex should be sent.

Subject line

This should clearly announce the subject of the telex. It should stand apart from the body of the telex.

Opening section

This should:

- Refer to previous messages
- State the purpose(s) of the telex
- Summarize the key points in the telex.
  It should be expressed in short sentences with a simple vocabulary.

Main sections

These should be presented in a highly readable way. The sender should use:

- headings
- short paragraphs
- short sentences
- a numbering system where appropriate
- a clear, simple style

Final section

The sender should:

- Re-emphasize the main points
- Say what (s)he will do next
- Tell the reader what to do next.

Checklist for telegram

Have I:

- Given all the important facts such as dates, times, flight numbers and hotel bookings?
- Named people?
- Used the right action-words?

Checklist for telex

Have I:

- Set out the telex with clear headings?
- Used a clear subject-line?
- Prepared the opening section so that the reader knows what the telex is about?
- Set out the middle sections in a readable way?
- Used the final section to summarize and state the action to be taken?
- Written in a clear, simple style?

Advertisements

Companies, in order to be competitive, have to advertise. Advertisements have to very skilfully prepared if they are to attract the attention of the public. Companies would therefore discuss their advertising needs and ideas with specialist advertising companies. Specialists would then prepare the advertisements.

For the above reasons, members of companies would not be expected to write their companies' advertisements. This section has therefore been written simply to give you an understanding of the elements of advertising. Members of companies might, however, be asked to prepare:

- Classified advertisements for newspapers or magazines
- Advertisements for vacant posts
- Unsolicited sales letters
- Circulars

Advertisements are designed to *attract attention*. Once the potential buyer has noticed the advertisement the company hopes to create an attitude that will persuade her or him to take the desired action, buy the product and keep buying the product. Advertisements are aimed at specific groups in the population. These groups are identified by means of market surveys. Their needs, dreams, hopes, desires, concerns and fears are then established. Once the advertising company has this information, it creates an advertisement aimed at the specific group. Such an advertisement would be designed both to *inform* and *persuade*. It should attract attention and set the mood for action.

The company will have to decide on the best medium to use. The radio is effective for advertisements that rely more on factual information. The visual impact is not important. Television, on the other hand, is very effective when the visual and the spoken word are important. The company would also consider using newspapers and magazines that rely on the visual impact of pictures and the written word.

The next section goes into more detail about the psychology of advertising.

The AIDA method in advertisements

Many advertisements are organized in four stages. These four stages are called the AIDA approach to constructing advertisements. These four stages are:

STAGE 1: Attention
STAGE 2: Interest
STAGE 3: Desire
STAGE 4: Action

Stage 1

The first stage is to attract the reader's, listener's or viewer's attention. This is called a *cognitive* stage. The audience starts *thinking* about the advertisement and its content.

Stage 2

At this stage the audience's *interest* is aroused. This is a more *emotional* approach to the advertisement.

Stage 3

The audience's *desire* is now aroused. This is also an *emotional* approach to the advertisement.

Stage 4

If the other three stages have been successful, then the audience is stimulated to *action*. This last stage is called an *action stage*.

Advertisers analyse people's needs, attitudes and desires. They try to 'teach' people what they want. They try to do this by:

- Selecting the media such as newspapers, magazines, radio and television.
- Aiming advertisements at carefully analysed segments of the population.
- Using pictures, words, colours and shapes.

Advertisers base their appeals on people's needs for:

- pleasure
- power
- security
- beauty
- a long life
- happiness
- health
- love
- social acceptance
- leisure.

Advertisers strive to communicate:

- the existence of products that will satisfy needs, wants and desires
- the qualities of products
- where products can be obtained.

More specifically, they strive to stimulate:

- the need for a category of product
- awareness of a specific brand
- an attitude towards a specific brand
- the intention to buy a specific brand

Once they have achieved the above, advertisers try to make buying as easy as possible.

Specific techniques used in advertising

The following is a brief list of some of the techniques used in advertising to gain and hold attention. These techniques are especially relevant to the writing of unsolicited sales letters.

- attractive photographs and sketches
- an effective *tone*
- questions
- imperatives such as '*buy* one now!'
- challenging statements
- quotations from famous people
- something unexpected
- appeals to people's desire for health, leisure, success, comfort, more money
- emphasis on the qualities of the product compared with rival products
- evidence from laboratory tests
- testimonials from authorities
- headings
- lists
- capital letters
- repetition of key ideas
- slogans
- offers of free samples
- an invitation to action by filling in a reply-paid card.

People in organizations might have to prepare advertisements for local newspapers. These would take the form of:

- classified advertisements
- public announcements
- notices of meetings
- vacant posts.

Classified advertisements are printed in newspaper columns under general headings such as 'Cars for Sale' or 'Businesses for Sale'. They have no special layout. They have to give the facts as briefly as possible.

The following is an example of a classified advertisement. It appears under the heading 'Business Premises to Let'.

JONESVILLE: Convenient premises on First Street comprising approx. 400 m^2 of Offices and Warehouse. Secure yard with loading bay and parking. Avail. Jan '93. Ph. Mr Said 384568 (ah).

The following illustrates an advertisement for vacant posts. Notice the stress on facts. The layout is simple and does not rely on any special advertising techniques to attract attention. It should, however, be well set out.

ACE CATERING COMPANY

We have vacancies for
SALES REPRESENTATIVES

Applicants should be between the ages of 21 and 40. They must have proven selling ability. A background knowledge of the catering industry would be an advantage.

We offer:
- Good salary and commission
- A company car
- On-the-job training.

These posts offer outstanding opportunities for men and women in a competitive and expanding field.

Written applications should be sent to:
The Personnel Manager
Ace Catering Company
28 Third Street
Townsville
4568

Checklist for classified advertisements and advertisements for posts

Have I:
- written a clear heading?
- given all the details so that readers know what they are buying or applying for?
- set out these details clearly so that readers can understand them?
- told readers where to telephone or write?

The electronic office

Many organizations today transmit messages electronically, instead of on paper. These may be classified as electronic offices. This section covers:

- The advantages of electronic offices
- Computer-based work stations
- Electronic mail
- Faxing
- Storage and retrieval of information

Advantages of electronic offices

The electronic office offers many advantages to businesses:

- faster transfer of messages
- faster access to information
- faster response to customers' needs
- faster response to what competitors are doing
- ability to analyse information more accurately
- elimination of many routine tasks that staff find boring
- freeing of staff to do more creative work.

Today the electronic office has fewer pieces of equipment. These pieces of equipment are largely related to the computer, word processor and the telephone line. These pieces of equipment can perform many of the functions that a range of special machines had to perform in the past.

Computer-based work stations

In many organizations computers have been installed on nearly every employee's desk. Each desk thus becomes a work station. This work station could include a terminal that is connected to a mainframe computer or smaller mini-computer. This arrangement allows many people to have access to the same information.

Some companies place a separate micro-computer at each work-station. This arrangement allows staff to work independently.

These work-stations are used to process data and to do work electronically instead of by hand. In word processing, documents are typed directly onto a screen. This allows the sender to edit the message and then to print it fault-free. People who have to process data at work-stations enter raw numbers such as sales, costs, inventories and other statistics into the company's data base. These numbers may then be manipulated and analysed. They can then be turned into information that the organization can use to improve its performance, for example in production and marketing.

Computers are extremely versatile because of the many *software programs* that are now available. These programs allow staff to perform sophisticated activities that only experts could do a few years ago.

Computers now enable companies to publish documents that are professional in layout and appearance. This is called *desktop publishing*. Software programs make possible a combination of word processing and graphics. Companies are thus able to produce a range of excellent newsletters, catalogues and reports. A few years ago these documents would have had to be sent to printers. The computer screen allows the sender to lay out blocks of text, headlines and diagrams so that (s)he can see exactly what will be printed.

Laser printers produce pages that are professional in appearance.

Electronic networks

Computers are very versatile when linked together within a building. Computer terminals and micro-computers at work stations can be linked to other micro-computers and to the mainframe computer. They can also be linked to printers. Such networks are called local-area networks or LANS.

These computer links give employees:

- access to computing power, data and a wide variety of equipment
- another channel for communicating.

Such links, because they use telephone lines, enable companies to communicate nationally and internationally. They are able to gain access to national and international data bases.

Electronic mail

A popular use of computer links is called electronic mail. This is called the electronic bulletin board if it is confined to one organization. An electronic mail system allows people to send messages via their computers to other people whose electronic address they know. Such messages are stored in the receivers' computers until they are read.

Studies have shown that electronic mail significantly reduces the amount of inter-office mail, photocopying and time on the telephone.

Small laptop or portable computers are now available. They allow people to process information out in the field. They also allow people to tap into the database at the head office. If this database is not big enough, then subscribers can consult central information banks.

Teleconferencing and video conferencing also use telephone lines. These types of conferencing allow people far apart to have a meeting using voice links alone, or visual links as well.

These telecommunication links will allow many people to work from home using links with their companies to keep contact with fellow employees and customers. A new word 'telecommuting' has been invented to describe working for a company while one stays at home.

Storage and retrieval of information

Organizations generate large numbers of messages. Many of these have to be saved for later reference. Efficient storage systems are therefore essential. They have to be so well organized that messages may be retrieved at any time.

This section briefly covers the following methods of storing messages:
- Filing cabinets
- Visible card files
- Rotary files
- Horizontal files
- Magnetic discs or floppy discs
- Microfilm and microfiche

Information in filing cabinets may be stored in many different ways:
- alphabetical order of subject
- date order
- alphabetical order of companies

Each filing drawer should have:
- clearly marked files
- an index page at the front of the drawer
- a card on the outside.

Other devices used to categorize information so that it can be easily found are:
- Visible card files in drawers:
  Each card summarizes information that directs the searcher to documents stored elsewhere.
- Rotary files:
  These files are similar to card files. The cards are stored on a rotating holder for easy access. These cards guide people to documents stored elsewhere.
- Horizontal files:
  These take the form of many shallow drawers in a cabinet. They are useful for storing plans and other large documents.

Computers and word processors have meant that new methods of storing information have had to be devised. The floppy disc has become a major source of information storage and retrieval in offices. The information on them has to be stored systematically. Directories have to be provided to show users how to find specific material. Floppy discs then have to be stored in special boxes in categories.

It is also possible to store audio and video cassette recordings. These cassettes are, however, sensitive to heat, dust and magnetism. They should, therefore be stored in a dust-free area and away from magnets.

Organizations that have very large files of information use micrographic equipment to reproduce document pages in miniature either on a roll of film or on microfiche. This is a single sheet of film.

This film can be read on a microfilm reader. A printer attached to the reader will print out what is needed. Microfilm and magnetic discs take up far less space than paper would.

Faxing

The fax or facsimile (Latin: 'make the same') machine is fast replacing the telex machine in most organizations. The fax machine, using a telephone connection, is able to transmit typed or hand-written messages to another fax machine immediately.

The advantage of the fax machine is that the sender does not rely on an operator. The sender simply dials the receiver's fax number and the machine sends the message.

Faxed messages should be:
- highly readable
- very clearly written with a dark ink.

If the message is to be filed, it should be photocopied because faxed messages sometimes fade. Poor handwriting should be avoided because reproduction in fax paper is not always perfect.

Faxed messages should be sent with a cover page. This should state:
- the receiver's name and company with a fax number
- the sender's name and company with a fax number
- how many pages are being sent.

The sender should also type 'Page 1 of 5', 'Page 2 of 5', etc. at the top of each page. Receivers can then check that they have received the whole message.

Checklist for faxing

Have I:

- Prepared the message clearly so that it will be easily read at the other end?
- Ensured that I have written very clearly so that the receiver will be able to read my message?

- Included a cover-page giving my fax number and stating how many pages there are?
- Typed or written 'Page 1 of 5' etc. at the top of each page?
- Dialled the correct number?

What is e-mail?

Electronic mail (e-mail), also called the electronic bulletin board, is any form of message that is conveyed electronically from one computer to another. Electronic communication means that we can communicate easily and instantly from offices, homes, schools and most forms of transport. If we own a computer, a fax machine and a modem we can communicate globally with anyone who has the same technology.

Electronic mail as an effective form of communication

Many organizations have accepted electronic mail (e-mail) as the best way of communicating electronically. Many organizations believe that e-mail gives them a competitive advantage because it is:

- fast
- inexpensive
- readily available
- independent of the receiver's presence.

Organizations are increasingly using e-mail for a range of business activities:

- product development
- training staff
- giving and receiving work assignments
- testing ideas and products
- staff administration
- solving problems
- sending out circulars (electronic bulletin board)
- marketing themselves and their products
- sending personal messages.

How should electronic messages be constructed?

Electronic messages are the same as the range of messages already described. Readers have to read a message on a screen, in the same way as they would read a letter, memorandum or report typed on paper. These messages have to be very well set out and highly readable if they are to attract attention. Messages on screens are harder to read than the same messages on paper.

Many e-mail messages in the form of memoranda and even letters are becoming informal. Their tone and structure are becoming more relaxed and less formal. This is because many users perceive e-mail to be a less permanent and less formal way of communicating. Casual exchange of e-mail messages is now called 'e-chat' because it is so informal.

Many receivers of e-mail are happy to accept these informal messages. However, readers are urged to make their messages more formal because the great advantage of e-mail could be lost if messages become too informal, badly organized, and hard to follow.

Characteristics of e-mail messages

Many e-mail messages now contain the following examples of a casual style:

- Sentences that are not complete
- Shortened words
- Acronyms (groups of first letters of words)
- Symbols (such as a smiling face) used to create emoticons
- Parts of messages out of order because readers reply by using the same message. They simply keep some sections of the original and delete others.

The above devices are normally not accepted in formal business writing. Should they be accepted in e-mail? Users of e-mail have not yet decided on the answer.

Business people do not normally feel the need to show strong emotion in their business messages. However, creators of e-mail messages often show emotions in their less formal messages. The examples below show some common short forms and emoticons found in e-mail:

BTW	by the way
FAQ	frequently asked question
FYI	for your information
PLS	please
TTYL	talk to you later
(:-)	sender is happy (or message is positive)
(:-(	sender is sad (or message is negative)

In spite of this more casual approach, writers should make sure that all their e-mail messages are easy to follow. They should have good headings and sub-headings. Their opening paragraphs should be very clear. They should express action at the end, and should express goodwill as well.

The effect of e-mail on organizations

This section covers six aspects of e-mail:

- e-mail can blur hierarchies in organizations
- e-mail can increase the volume of messages and increase costs
- e-mail increases the choice of media for conveying messages
- e-mail changes the nature of message permanence and message security

- e-mail changes the rules about who owns the message and whether it is private or not
- e-mail needs its own guidelines for good manners.

Blurring of hierarchies

Until recently, most organizations have been organized in some form of pattern. This pattern tells people the line of command. It also tells people about the formal lines of communication.

However, e-mail can cause major changes in the above communication process. Senders can now avoid the traditional communication hierarchies.

A secretary would normally screen all telephone and written messages. However, with e-mail, every person has an e-mail address. (S)he may therefore receive messages directly. This lack of screening means that anyone can communicate with someone several levels higher on the organizational chart. With e-mail, ordinary members of staff have a better chance that senior staff will read their messages.

This could mean that the hierarchy in the organization does not exist for e-mail, and that all users are equal. However, people in organizations have different amounts of power and status. They would like to keep these, and need some isolation if they wish to do so.

Only time will tell how people in organizations deal with this problem.

Increasing volume of messages and increasing costs

Experts in commerce and industry are predicting that the volume of electronic mail is likely to increase astronomically. At this stage, readers are reluctant to ignore e-mail, even when it could be classified as 'junk mail'.

For example, one business writer reported that she had 275 e-mail messages waiting on her computer one Monday morning. A world-famous software developer is reported as having received 5000 e-mail messages soon after his e-mail address was published. Clearly, these people have little hope of reading all their messages in detail. Organizations will have to work out ways of reducing the number of messages.

In addition, these messages could remain in electronic storage indefinitely if storage systems are not checked.

Any member of staff can now send the same message to all employees with one keystroke. Using wide area networks such as the Internet, users can find e-mail addresses for anyone who has access to e-mail. Companies can now use banks of computers to search for likely customers. They can send these customers a variety of messages all over the world.

Organizations will now have to set out their policies governing the use of e-mail. Any e-mail message sent out must support the organization's goals and mission. Unnecessary messages will tie down computer resources. These messages also cost the organizations a great deal in transmission and storage fees.

Increased media choices

E-mail has given companies a wider choice of media for sending and receiving messages. They may now use:

- telephones
- e-mail
- typed messages in the form of letters, memoranda, reports and proposals.

The choice of communication medium affects the ways in which employees project themselves and their organization. Organizations will have to develop guidelines to help senders choose the best medium and channel.

For example, an organization should not discuss an employee by means of e-mail. Such a message needs to be formal, secure and permanent.

The following table gives an idea of some of the characteristics of telephone, e-mail, and typed messages that are posted.

Table 1
Comparison of some characteristics of telephone,
e-mail and typed messages

Characteristic of message	Telephone	E-mail	Typed and posted messages
Formality of message	Varies	Usually informal	Varies, but more formal
Accountability of sender or receiver	Generally low	Moderate	High
Ease of distribution to a very large audience	Low	High	Moderate
Need for security of message	Moderate	Low	High, especially if confidential
Need for permanence of message	Low	Varies	High
Prescribed format	Low	Low	High
Ability to cross the hierarchy in an organization	Low	High	Low

Note that the above characteristics vary a great deal. E-mail differs a great deal from formal typed and posted messages. Staff therefore need guidelines on how and when to use these media.

Security and permanence of e-mail messages

Organizations face two major problems with e-mail:
- lack of message permanence on the one hand, and
- too much message permanence on the other.

A major advantage of using e-mail is that it should reduce the amount of paper used and filed in an organization. However, the long-term effects of using and storing e-mail have not yet been examined in detail.

Computer systems administrators estimate that an e-mail message could stay in a computer system for up to five years. All these messages could clog up a system and make communication difficult.

Staff will have to be taught to take much more care over storing important messages and deleting others. Organizations will also have to appoint people to supervise the storing of electronic messages.

Message ownership and privacy

E-mail messages are now causing legal problems about who owns the message. Does the individual own the electronic message, or does the organization own it? Laws already cover an organization's right to open mail and to monitor telephone calls. However, effective laws governing e-mail still need to be drawn up.

The following legal questions arise with e-mail:
- Are e-mail messages unofficial or official exchanges? They are perceived to be less formal and less permanent. Does this mean that they are less important?
- Are organizations allowed to monitor e-mail?

Recent rulings in the United States have allowed organizations to monitor e-mail messages and use them against staff in disciplinary hearings. Courts in the United States have ruled in favour of employers when there has been a dispute between the employee's right to privacy and the employer's right of ownership of the e-mail message.

Organizations are legally responsible for electronic messages sent by employees. Employees therefore need to be very careful about the messages that they send by e-mail.

E-mail manners

Many organizations do not yet have policies governing the format, content or use of e-mail. Users of e-mail therefore need to take care over their messages. They also need to show good manners.

The following guidelines should help people when they create e-mail messages:

Good manners on e-mail

- Be considerate. Do not give too much information in each message. Screens are harder to read than words on paper.
- Make your messages highly readable. Do not type the whole message in upper-case letters. Use headings, short paragraphs and sentences and lists.
- Focus your messages. If you start a new topic, use a new subject heading.
- Have really good subject lines. Make these unique. Good subject lines help readers to file, cross-reference and retrieve messages.
- Do not send junk mail such as chain letters. They overload systems.
- Check your distribution list before you send any mail that you have received. Receivers may already have copies of that item.
- Assume that the messages you send and receive are permanent. Do not say anything in e-mail that you might not want to be made public or sent on to others.
- Do not send on confidential mail without first getting permission.
- Be aware that e-mail might not be as private as you wish. If you wish to send a private message, then use another method of communication.
- Plan your messages carefully. Use text editors and spelling checkers to make sure that your message is accurate.
- Explain all technical terms if your readers have varying levels of knowledge.
- Do not add too many attachments to your e-mail. Large bulky messages clog the network and are hard to read.

Checklist for electronic mail

Have I:

- Named the receiver correctly?
- Set out a good heading?
- Presented my message in a well organized way?
- Stated my key points at the beginning?
- Stated exactly what I want?
- Stated exactly what the reader should do?
- Paid close attention to good readability?
- Given my electronic mail address?

Effect of the personal computer and the Internet on communication

Introduction

We are in the midst of a computer revolution. All organizations are affected by the explosion of computer technology and the pace of change. Many laws and regulations about the communication of information now have to be revised because of these changes.

The availability of computers and their links with the Internet have meant that people now sit for long periods in front of a computer screen. As a result, people have had to redefine and redesign their workplaces. In addition, people can now work from home as though it were an office.

Thanks to the Internet we now have quick access to vast amounts of information. This information would have taken us years to gather only two or three years ago.

The power of the personal computer

A personal computer, for example, now gives the average person the power to make calculations in one week that all the mathematicians who have ever lived until 30 years ago could not have carried out in all that time. Many of these complex calculations can now be done in a few minutes.

A personal-computer user can also:

- publish and distribute a magazine of very good quality using desktop publishing
- create a sophisticated three-dimensional drawing
- send a letter to a large number of customers
- create a wide range of effective business messages using a high-quality printer.

Organizations and increased individual knowledge and empowerment

Personal computers will certainly change organizations. For many years computers were thought to be a centralizing force. Using a mainframe computer, senior managers could have access to up-to-date files on all members of staff and on customers.

However, the personal computer has taken away this central power. Using personal computers and the Internet, ordinary staff members now have access to large amounts of information. This information was, until recently, available to senior management only. Ordinary staff members can now get a detailed and high-level picture of their company's operations. Any staff member can also send an electronic message to the chief executive, and expect a reply. Personal computers are therefore a decentralizing force.

As a result, those who hold power in organizations will have to make sure that every member of staff receives the benefits of the new technology. At the same time, senior management will try to keep their positions in the hierarchy. They may, however, find that their organization charts are no longer valid.

Problems arising from access to networks

Many people now have access to what were private networks and banks of data. Three questions arise as a result:
- How can the information in data banks be protected?
- What will happen to society if individuals have free access to what was once private information?
- What will happen if organizations and even governments attempt to stop access to all this information?

Organizations are now having to use encryption techniques to protect their information. They are also having to use passwords to stop people from gaining access to certain information.

At the moment, anyone who has access to the Internet can send a message to large numbers of others. That person can also receive messages from many sources. Organizations will have great difficulty in preventing their staff from gaining access to this information. Well-informed staff will be able to confront management and negotiate from a position of greater power.

Organizations could come under threat if others gain access to their confidential information.

The only way that organizations and even governments can gain control over the content of a network is to cripple the whole system. They will, however, be reluctant to do this.

The result of this access to information is that ordinary staff have much more power. Senior management will have to negotiate with staff with great care.

Personal computers and the Internet

Anyone with a personal computer, the right software and a modem can get access to the Internet. The Internet is an electronic system that connects millions of individual computers. This global network now connects between 30 and 40 million people. At the time of writing there are over 50 000 Internet discussion groups or news groups. Internet communication takes many forms:
- Worldwide Web pages operated by major news organizations. This is an information retrieval service based on hypertext.
- Usenet groups discussing a wide variety of topics. This system consists of a collection of electronic bulletin boards. At the time of writing

about 40 000 articles are posted every day to different newsgroups. Usenet groups have no central authority to moderate messages. However, many groups now have volunteers who monitor messages and decide which ones are appropriate.
- E-mail messages.
- People sending their CVs (resumés) to get jobs.
- Groups working together on projects.

Credibility of Internet messages

Internet users manage the Internet. No individual or organization actually owns it. Because of this unrestricted flow of information, leaders and managers are now asking: "should electronic messages be regarded more harshly than printed messages?"

This concern about computer-based messages has arisen because some messages are being sent by computer-generated personages. Traditional mass media have editors and fact-checkers to ensure that messages are accurate. The Internet, on the other hand, does not have this control. The credibility of sources does, however, vary on the Internet. Commercial sites carry relatively more credibility, and unknown sources carry less.

A much greater burden will therefore be placed on the user to determine how much faith to place in any given source.

In addition to the above problem, there is a more serious one. As more and more commercial and political information is made available, who will decide on which messages are allowed and which are not allowed? The answer is not yet clear

The nature of the Internet

The Internet is such a new medium of communication that it is hard to classify. It is like a telephone on the one hand, and like a broadcasting system on the other. In fact, the individual is now in control of a small broadcasting station. The Internet also allows person-to-person communication like a telephone.

The Internet may be viewed as a mass medium. Senders and receivers may be grouped into four categories:
- One-to-one communication with the senders and receivers not present at the same time. An example of this would be e-mail. (This is called asynchronous communication because sender and receiver are not present at the same time).
- Many-to-many asynchronous communication examples are Usenet, electronic bulletin boards and list servers that require the receiver to sign up for a service or to log on to a programme to access messages around a particular topic or topics.

- Synchronous communication that can be one-to-one or one-to-many. This means that sender and receiver are present at the same time. This type of communication can be organized around a topic, the construction of an object or role playing.
- Asynchronous communication is generally characterized by the receiver's need to seek out a site to access information. This type of communication may be many-to-one, one-to-one or one-to-many sender-receiver relationships.

The Internet is also used for entertainment as well as information. Is the Internet therefore the same as other entertainment media such as films or television?

Because of the wide variety of audiences and different functions of the Internet, it is hard to classify it exactly. Only time will tell how the Internet is classified.

The information highway

As the information highway is gradually established and developed, business messages will become much more flexible. They will be less tied to paper and will be conveyed by many different media. For example, a typed message on a screen could be accompanied by a video film clip and recorded voices commenting. It could also include a wide variety of diagrams.

People will be able to work together to create messages. These people do not have to be in the same office.

Personal computers inside and outside companies will be connected. Because of this, businesses will become smaller and decentralized. They will rely much more on consultants who communicate by means of computers. Advanced computer systems and software will allow companies to save money on the way they work. New networks and electronic tools will help companies to save money on business planning, sales analysis and product development.

Sales people in the field will be able to keep in touch with the head office. They will be able to check facts and find out what orders have come in.

People can now keep in touch electronically, instead of having to move about the country. Company reports will be available on the Internet. Readers will be able to manipulate the figures easily.

As computer software improves, e-mail will replace paper messages. In addition, networking will ensure that every user is connected to everyone else. These people will be able to exchange more complex messages containing high-quality three-dimensional graphics.

Portable computers will allow people to move about, and yet still be able to receive and send e-mail messages.

Finally, people will be able to work from home using the Internet to consult and access information. In 1994 in the United States, for example, there were more than seven million people who did not travel to offices. They used fax machines, telephones and the Internet.

The same trends are likely to develop in other countries.

Referencing

If you are writing long reports, essays or articles you might have to use other people's ideas. You would then have to acknowledge these ideas and give details of the books, articles and other documents that you have read.

This section briefly describes:

- What information to record
- How to reference the information using two methods, the numbered system and the Harvard system.
- Referencing material from the Internet.

What information to record

If you wish to record details of a book, then you should record the following on your bibliography card:

- author(s) (initial(s) and then surname)
- editor or translator (if relevant)
- title of the book (underlined or in italics)
- name of the series in which the book appears (underlined) and volume number in the series
- number of volumes (if relevant)
- number of the edition (if it is not the first)
- the facts of publication
  - place of publication
  - name of publisher
  - year published
- page number(s) to show where the information came from.

Record details of a journal article as follows:

- author(s) (initial(s) and then surname)
- title of article (in inverted commas)
- name of journal (underlined or in italics)
- volume and number of the journal
- date of the volume or issue
- page numbers of the relevant pages in the article
- page numbers of the first and last pages of the article.

Using the numbered system

If you use this system, then you should:

- number each reference in the message
- have a list of references at the end of the chapter or at the end of the document
- have a bibliography.

Example

A reference in a document would be written as follows. Note the numbers 1 and 2 in the text.

```
Smith and Jones refer to the following communica-
tion problems in organizations.¹ However, Anderson
describes the same problems in different terms.²
```

These numbers must be referred to in two ways:

- in a list of references (order of appearance)
- in a bibliography. (alphabetical order of surname)

```
List of References
1. J. Smith and L. Jones, Communication in
   Organizations, New York, ABC Publishers, 1985,
   p.6.
2. P. Anderson, "Classifying Communication Problems
   in Organizations", Journal of Business, Vol. 3,
   No. 2, June 1990, p.50.
Bibliography
1. Anderson, P., "Classifying Communication Problems
   in Organizations", Journal of Business, Vol. 3,
   No. 2, June 1990, pp 48-56.
2. Smith, J. and L. Jones, Communication in
   Organizations, New York, A.B.C. Publishers, 1985.
```

Harvard style

This style uses shortened references in brackets in the text. A List of References is *not* necessary. All the works referred to are listed in a Reference Appendix at the end. These entries are in alphabetical order of surname.

Example

```
Smith and Jones refer to the following communica-
tion problems in organizations (Smith and Jones,
1985, 6). However, Anderson describes the same
problems in different terms (Anderson, 1990, 50).
```

> Reference Appendix
>
> Anderson, P. (1990) "Classifying Communication in Organizations", <u>Journal of Business, Vol. 3, No. 2, June 1990, pp 48-56.</u>
>
> Smith, J., L. Jones (1985) <u>Communication in Organizations</u>, New York, ABC Publishers.

Citation of electronic sources in business writing

People are now searching the Internet for information. This information needs to be properly referenced to make these references credible. The following examples show how referencing from the Internet should be done. These examples cover:

- Worldwide Web home page
- Book, online
- Encyclopedia article, online
- Newsgroup article, online
- Personal electronic communication (e-mail).

General principles

The concept of Uniform Resource Locators (URLs) enables businesses to give specific locations of their sources. A URL has four parts:

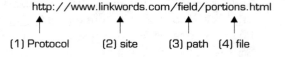

The following protocols are now in use:
- http
- gopher
- ftp
- telnet
- news.

Examples of citations

- Worldwide Web, home page
  Put items in the following order:
  Author/editor (if known). 'Title of page'. Revision or copyright date (if available). Publication medium (online). Page Publisher. Available: URL (Protocol: Site/Path/File). Access date.

  Example:
  'Sundstrom Personal View New York.' Online. Sundstrom, Inc.

Available: htpp://www.spvny. com. 14 Sept. 1996.

- Book, online
  Put items in the following order:
  Author. *Title*. Publication information for printed source (if available). Publication medium (online). Name of repository of the electronic text (if known). Available: URL (protocol: site/path/file). Access date.

  Example:

  Jackson, Willliam. *The Elements of Good Speech*. Buffalo, NY: W.A. Smith Press, 1990. Online. Columbia University.
  Available: http://www.columbia.edu/acis/smithson/strunk/strunk.html #11. 5 January 1997.

- Encyclopedia article, online
  Put items in the following order:
  Author (if given). 'Title of Material Accessed.' Date of material (if given). *Title of Encyclopedia*. Publication medium (online). Name of computer service or information provider (if available). Available: URL (Protocol: Site/Path/File) ['search term', if available for retrieval]. Access date.

  Example:

  'Market collapse of 1931.' *Knowledge Online*. Online.
  Available: http://www.ko.com
  ['market trends']. 5 April 1997.

- Newsgroup article, online
  Put items in the following order:
  Author (if given). 'Article Title.' Date. Newsgroup focus. Available: URL (Protocol: Topic.Subtopic(s)). Access date.

  Example:

  'Korea Sends Double Message on Ship Dispute.' 3 July 1997. World, Asia and Korea business. Available: news: clari.world.asia.korea.biz. 5 July 1997.

- Personal electronic communication (e-mail)
  Put the items in the following order:
  Sender (sender's e-mail address). 'Subject of Message'. E-mail to recipient (Recipient's e-mail address). Message date.

  Example:

  Jones, Bill (bjones@abc.com). 'First-Class Notes on Writing CVs'. E-mail to Mary Smith (msmith@cape.org). 15 July 1997.

QUESTIONS: PART 7

(Answers to these questions are given on pages 537–578.)

Reports

Points for discussion

1. What is meant by the following terms:
   - Terms of reference
   - Conclusions
   - Recommendations
   - Findings ?
2. What is meant by the pyramid approach to the setting out of reports?
3. Explain the following types of reports:
   - Informative reports
   - Investigative reports
   - Feasibility reports
   - Interim reports
   - Summary reports.
4. How would you set out the facts in a report?
5. What language would you use in the Conclusions and Recommendations of a report?
6. What style would you use when writing a report?
7. What techniques would you use to make your report as readable as possible?

Exercises

1. You have been asked to investigate customers' complaints about a certain product in a local supermarket. Your specific Terms of Reference are:
   - Investigate customers' complaints about XYZ tinned products.
   - Record these complaints and analyse them.
   - Draw conclusions about whether the complaints are justified or not.
   - Recommend specific action.

   Write the following sections of the report:
   - Terms of Reference
   - Summary
   - Table of Contents
   - Introduction
   - Conclusions
   - Recommendations
   - Findings

   Invent appropriate details.

2. Evaluate the following Conclusions and Recommendations. They have been written as one long paragraph. Are they easy to read?

   Rewrite them in two separate sections, one containing conclusions and the other recommendations. Use a multiple decimal numbering system. Write in a formal and impersonal style.

   Conclusions and Recommendations

   I came to the conclusion that the fire had been caused by an electrical fault in the paint store. We need to get the wiring straightened out in there so that paint can be safely stored. Another recommendation is that we install smoke detectors so that any potential fire is quickly detected. We'll also have to make sure that nobody smokes in the building. I've also come to the conclusion that the main pillars, although the paint has been burnt off, won't need to be replaced. They're basically sound. Another conclusion is that the asbestos roof will have to be replaced because many of the sheets have been cracked. My recommendation is that we replace these sheets with new asbestos sheets. They're better than corrugated iron. I've concluded that three of the main roof beams will have to be replaced because they're twisted. They should be replaced with the same type of steel.

3. Evaluate the findings section of a report below. Rewrite it using better headings and a multiple decimal numbering system.

   ADMINISTRATION

   Staff:
   28 % of the staff have resigned and of those remaining several are looking for alternative employment.

   No Trade Union matters were discussed and the payroll was successfully completed.

   Safety:
   Total number of Incident Reports submitted to Regional Office during March was fifteen.

   MAINTENANCE

   Mechanical:

Soap making section:

Soap making machine No. 1 repaired by ABC Company on 20.7.92. Now running well.

Soap making machine No. 2 will be repaired by ABC Company in the near future.

Protective plates have been made and are being fitted to the soap wrapping machine to protect workers.

Soap washing machine 1 sent to XYZ Company for changes to water pipes. Will be returned by end of October.
Soap washing machine 2 has been damaged irreparably.

Soap washing machine 3 will be kept running until machine 1 is returned.

4. Evaluate the following summary report. Rewrite it to improve it. Pay special attention to the content of each section and to the readability of each section. Write in a formal, objective and impersonal style. Invent extra details where necessary.

TERMS OF REFERENCE

We were asked to examine Stayfast Fabric Dye to find out why dyed materials do not keep their colour.

SYNOPSIS

We examined a range of fabrics and tested their ability to hold the dye in question. This dye has been specially made to withstand frequent washing. We therefore concluded that the material must be faulty.

We recommend that the materials be subjected to extensive tests before the dyeing process begins. Our findings were that four types of materials are used in the dyeing process:
- Pure wool
- An equal mixture of wool and cotton
- A mixture of cottons
- Artificial fibres

INTRODUCTION

Customers have been complaining that the dye is running when they wash clothes made with the range of materials dyed using Stayfast Fabric Dye. This report aims to give the findings of the investigation together with conclusions and recommendations.

The four types of materials were examined and tested for their ability to hold dye.

This report covers the results, conclusions and recommendations of the study.

CONCLUSIONS

All the materials tested have been made in such a way that they cannot hold dye when they are washed in clothes washing machines. The method of manufacturing is faulty and will have to be changed. The dyes will also have to be carefully tested and the formula changed if necessary.

RECOMMENDATIONS

Test a selection of materials for faulty manufacture. In addition, test the Stayfast dyes to check that the original formula has been followed.

Letters

Points for discussion

1. In what ways may letters be used as ambassadors for an organization?
2. What are the major barriers to effective letter and memorandum writing?
3. What techniques should be used to make letters as readable as possible?
4. What are the characteristics of a good letter-writing style?
5. What styles should be used for writing memoranda?
6. How do the formats for letters and memoranda differ?
7. Give examples of the following:
   - A salutation
   - A subject-line
   - A complimentary close.
8. Explain the block style in letter writing.
9. Explain how to write:
   - A letter of complaint
   - A letter of adjustment
   - A letter of enquiry

- A letter responding to an enquiry.
10. Explain how good-news and bad-news letters differ.

Exercises

1. Write a letter to a firm of booksellers. Ask them (*a*) if they are able to send you three books that you name, (*b*) if they are able to recommend books in the field of communication in business.
2. You are the credit controller in a company. Write to a company that has not paid its account for the past two months. Keep in mind that you wish to keep a good relationship with the company.
3. You are the Manager of your company. Write a letter to your local Town Clerk complaining about poor Municipal Services, particularly rubbish collection and street sweeping. Keep in mind that you wish to get action. Your style and tone should be appropriate.
4. You are in the Marketing and Sales Division of your company. You have received a letter of complaint about deliveries of certain goods.

   The writer has complained that:
   - She ordered the goods on 6 January and they were delivered only ten days later. This delay has caused her great inconvenience.
   - The goods delivered were not exactly what was ordered.
   - Some of the goods were damaged.

   Write a suitable letter of adjustment. It is very important that you keep this customer's goodwill.
5. You have already used up your leave for the year. However, an urgent matter of family business has come up. You need to be away for another three days to attend to this business. Write a memorandum to the Personnel Manager asking for an extra three days' paid leave. Justify your request in as persuasive a way as you can.
6. Write a letter to a company asking if there are any vacancies. Give suitable details about yourself.
7. Your company has just launched a new type of household cleaner. Write an unsolicited sales letter setting out the merits of this product.
8. Comment on the tone of the following extract from a letter. Rewrite the extract so that it has a neutral tone.
   Note: The word 'ultimo' refers to last month.

   ```
   Dear Sirs

   ABC (PTY) LIMITED

   We are in receipt of your letter of the 5th ultimo.

   Your second paragraph states that we 'allege' cer-
   tain items are 'unproved'. We don't 'allege' this.
   They are unproven in terms of our contract with
   ```

you. It is therefore incumbent upon *you* not us to get written permission therefor.

We are in terms of our appointment and in terms of the abovementioned Contract *only* the Consultants and *not* the Architects, Clerks or General Dogsbodies!!

Your second paragraph is completely absurd as:
(a) You state that you 'are unable to accept any account drawn up'.
(b) You state that the items were 'accepted by (you) in . . . without close (??) examination'.
(c) You will like 'it back so as to re-examine it'. Which of these do you actually intend?

9. Analyse the content, organization and language of the following letter of transmittal. Rewrite it to improve it.
Note that 'instant' refers to the present month.

Dear Mr Fish

PARKING GARAGE

Your letter of the 21st instant refers. I have finalized the design for the proposed parking garage. Please find attached the relevant design. The garage will be able to hold 283 cars and 25 motor-cycles. The gross cost is R1 296 000. Please accept the apologies of the undersigned over the fact that the price was underestimated in the letter dated 19—04-10. This means that the gross cost of housing each vehicle will be R6 488. The undersigned has stuck to the proposals set out in the last letter. The ramp joining the two decks has a very gradual incline (1:15) and houses 40 parking places. Adequate pedestrian walkways and stairways are included as well as emergency exits. Angle parking is used where pos sible and 90 degree parking only where it proved more convenient for traffic flow. Public toilets have also been included. The whole concept is geared for easy manoeuvrability.

Please let the undersigned know if anything is not clear and do not hesitate to contact me if anything is not to your liking.

10. You are marketing manager of your company. You have noticed that one of your best customers has not ordered from you for the past three months. This customer has, over the past three years, ordered large amounts of goods. You have a large stock of goods and wish to sell this stock as soon as possible. Write a letter and try to persuade this customer to place an order with you. Stress the advantages to the customer.

11. Write a short letter that will be sent out with the diaries that your company intends to distribute as presents. Try to generate as much goodwill as possible.

Proposals

Points for discussion

1. What is a proposal?
2. How should a proposal be organized?
3. What techniques should be used to make proposals highly readable?
4. What information should go into the *Background* to a proposal?
5. What information should go into the *Justification* section of a proposal?
6. What style should be used for a proposal?

Exercises

1. You are working in a department of an organization that needs to expand. You have been given the task of writing a proposal to persuade the Board of Directors to allocate R250 000 to your Department. This money will be spent on new equipment.
Write the proposal. Pay attention to your organization and readability.

2. Criticize the following extract from the beginning of a Proposal. Pay attention to the vague heading and the long Introduction before the writer gets to the point. Rewrite the opening to improve it.

PROPOSAL TO REPLACE MACHINES

1. Introduction

This department has, for the past five years, been doing good business with a wide range of customers. We have managed to expand in spite of the recession and loss of key staff. We are now in a position to break into new markets. These markets should help us to survive until the economy improves. Many machines in our catering division are taking heavy punishment and are now wearing out. We need to replace them. In particular, we need to replace our

WRITTEN MESSAGES IN ORGANIZATIONS

```
     microwave ovens and bulk food mixers. They will not
     be able to survive much longer.
     The approximate cost will be R100 000 spread over
     two years.
     2.Justification
          . . .
```

Notices and circulars

Points for discussion

1. How should a notice or a circular be organized?
2. When would you use a notice?
3. When would you use a circular?
4. What are the differences between a notice and a circular?
5. What methods should be used to attract readers' attention to recent notices?
6. What readability techniques should be used to make notices and circulars more effective?

Exercises

1. Write a notice for all staff informing them about the new arrangements for flexitime. Invent suitable details.
2. The staff of your company have reached an agreement about non-smoking areas in your building. Write a notice for all staff informing them of the details of the agreement. Inform staff where they may smoke and where they may not smoke.
3. Your branch of the business has been transferred to a new building. Write a circular to your customers telling them of the move. Take care to keep their goodwill. Encourage them to come to your new building.
4. Your company has recently imported a new range of car polishes. Write a circular to all your customers telling them about the range. Stress the advantages of the polishes and encourage your customers to buy them.

Instructions

Points for discussion

1. What are the purposes of instructions?
2. Are instructions simply orders? Justify your answer.
3. Discuss the sections of a good set of instructions.
4. What style would you use for instructions? Give an example.
5. Discuss the uses of the following in a set of instructions:

- A flow chart
- A logic tree
- An algorithm

Exercises

1. Your company has decided to recycle all waste paper. Write a set of instructions for all staff telling them how to save paper. Tell them how to bundle it for collection.
2. Your company has decided to do all it can to save water and electricity in your building. Write a set of instructions to all staff instructing them on what to do.

Press release

Points for discussion

1. For what reasons should a press release be sent out by an organization?
2. How should a press release be organized?
3. What are the reasons for this special type of organization?
4. What style should be used for a press release?
5. What techniques should be used to make a press release as readable as possible?

Exercises

1. You work for the Public Relations Department of your company. Write a press release to tell the public what company's social responsibility programmes are.
2. You work for an organization that cares for blind people. Write a press release to tell the public about your organization's plan for a National Week for the Blind.

Essays and articles

Points for discussion

1. What are the differences between the format for an essay and a report?
2. What techniques should be used to make essays and articles as readable as possible?
3. What styles should be used for essays and articles?
4. What are the purposes of essays and articles?
5. What is a bibliography card; a note card?

Exercises

1. Plan and write an essay on one of the following topics:

- Barriers to effective communication in organizations and ways of overcoming the barriers.
- An effective communication policy in an organization.
- Ways of encouraging good intercultural communication in organizations.
- Ways of creating an atmosphere of trust in an organization so that effective communication can take place.
- Effective training programmes to help people communicate better at the interpersonal level in organizations.
- Ways of achieving effective small-group communication in organizations.
- Letters as ambassadors for an organization.
- Effective report writing for decision-making.
- Using an in-house journal or magazine to create a sense of belonging and a good team-spirit.
- Understanding the process of communication by using a communication model.
- A policy for encouraging a good downward, upward and sideways flow of messages.

For each essay:
- Decide on your purposes.
- Decide on your audience.
- Write an effective title.
- Decide on your level of formality.
- Decide whether you wish to write in a personal or impersonal style.
- Decide whether you wish to write in a referential or emotive style or whether you wish to mix the styles.

2. Plan and write an in-house journal article choosing from the above topics, or from the list below. Go through the same stages listed above.
   - Write an article on sporting achievements of the company's staff over the last six months.
   - Write an article on a special achievement of a member of staff in the field of education. (S)he could, for example, have achieved a degree or diploma after six years of studying part-time.
   - Write an article on the company's successful family day.

Telegram and telex

Points for discussion
1. When should a telegram be used?
2. What is meant by a cryptic style in a telegram?
3. What key information should be put into a telegram?

4. What is a telex?
5. How is a telex sent from one company to another?
6. How should a telex be set out?
7. What techniques should be used to make a telex as readable as possible?

Exercises

1. You have arranged to attend a conference in London. Send a telegram asking a friend of yours to pick you up at Heathrow Airport. Give all the necessary details.
2. You have to go on a business trip to another city. Send a telegram to the Branch Manager in that city. Ask her to make all the necessary hotel bookings and to arrange interviews with branch staff. Tell her how and when you are arriving. Invent suitable details.
3. Prepare a telex in which you request the permission of Head Office to run a Sales Conference. You need a budget, secretarial help, transport and suitable rooms. In addition you need to ask permission to invite certain people from Head Office. Invent suitable details.

Advertisements

Points for discussion

1. What is meant by a classified advertisement?
2. When would an organization use a classified advertisement?
3. How should a classified advertisement be set out?
4. When advertising a vacant post, what information should an organization include?
5. Explain the AIDA approach to constructing advertisements.
6. Discuss six techniques, for example slogans, that advertisers use to attract the audience's attention.
7. Discuss six psychological appeals, for example the need for love, that advertisers use to stimulate an audience's desire leading to action.

Exercises

1. You have been asked to prepare a classified advertisement to sell two of your company's motor cars. Write the text of this advertisement for your local newspaper.
2. You work in the personnel section of your company. Prepare an advertisement for your local newspaper advertising vacant posts for Sales Assistants to work in the company's retail shop. Provide the necessary details of conditions of service.

Faxing and electronic mail

Points for discussion

1. What precautions would you take to ensure that your fax message is received and read at the other end?
2. If your fax message is hand-written, how would you ensure that it is readable at the other end?
3. What is electronic mail?
4. How does electronic mail differ from inter-office memoranda on paper?
5. What techniques would you use to ensure that your electronic mail is highly readable?

Electronic mail and its effects on communication in organizations

Points for discussion

1. What is the best way to present an e-mail message so that it may be read easily?
2. How formal should e-mail messages be? Should they all be at the level of e-chat or should they be kept formal?
3. What is a reasonable length for an e-mail message? Should there be attachments?
4. What policy should be adopted for storing important e-mail messages and deleting others that are not important?
5. How should organizations help staff to cope with the great increase in electronic messages?

Exercises

1. You have been asked to draw up and send an e-mail message to all staff on planned overtime. Prepare this message. Give the exact details of dates and times. Motivate your readers to accept this overtime.
2. Draw up a set of guidelines for e-mail good manners for your organization.
3. Draw up a set of legal guidelines for e-mail for your organization. These guidelines should explain to staff the legal problems that could arise when they use e-mail.
4. List the methods that you could use to make your e-mail messages easy to read.
5. Draw up a set of guidelines to staff on what e-mail messages to delete and what messages to store.

Effect of the personal computer and the Internet on communication

Points for discussion

1. Discuss how the use of personal computers has affected you and your organization. Pay particular attention to:
   - Individuals' access to information and how this affects their communication with senior management

   Direct communication with all managers and the effect this has on management's attitudes to staff
   - Time spent in front of computer screens and the effect this has on staff morale.
2. Discuss the use of the Internet and the ways in which it has affected you and your organization.
3. Discuss the use of the Internet in enabling people to work from home. How will this arrangement affect organizations?

Exercises

1. In your organization, speak to three members of staff who use computers. Ask them:
   - What types of messages they send out
   - What types of messages they receive
   - What problems they have with the above messages in terms of composing them on the screen and reading messages on the screen.

   What have you learnt from the exercise?

   Note: If you do not work in an organization, visit an organization of your choice.

2. Select a topic from the general theme of communication. An example could be 'readability indexes'. Find out what you can about your topic on the Internet.

   What have you learnt from this exercise?

3. In your organization, speak to three members of staff. Find out whether they use the Internet. Ask them what type of information they look for and why. Ask them whether they had any difficulty finding the information.

   Write a report on your findings. Then write a short report on what information you would look for on the Internet.

PART

8

Graphic Communication

CHAPTER 18

Graphic Communication

Summary

Graphic communication is communication using devices such as tables, bar graphs and line graphs. These graphic devices combine numbers, words, lines and shapes.

Graphic devices are very useful for showing relationships that would take a great deal of writing to explain. They give a quick visual impression and help readers to compare amounts easily.

These devices include elements that writers cannot use. These elements include use of space, colours and lines and dimensions such as length, breadth and depth.

Good visuals have a greater impact than just the written or spoken word on its own. Graphic devices should be properly integrated into a text. Each graphic should be placed into the text where it is needed. It should be introduced, and should then be analysed below, once the reader has had an opportunity to examine it.

This chapter describes the following graphic devices:

- Tables
- Area Graphs (circle graphs, pie charts)
- Bar Graphs
- Histograms
- Gantt Charts
- Line graphs
- Diagrams
- Pictograms
- Maps
- Hierarchical flow charts
- Flow charts
- Cartoons

Each type is discussed in terms of its suitability for a specific audience.

The chapter briefly discusses design techniques for graphics and bias in the presentation of graphics.

Key points

- Choose a graphic device that is suited to your purposes, audience and the material.
- Design a graphic so that it is clear and unbiased.
- Integrate all graphics into written messages.
- Number each graphic.
- Provide a clear title for each graphic.
- Write all labels horizontally.
- Provide a key.
- Write labels at the ends of line-graphs, rather than underneath the lines.
- Draw dark lines round bar graphs so that each bar stands out.
- Provide good contrasts between sections by means of effective shading.
- Choose a scale that does not mislead the viewer.
- Make sure that each graphic is as accurate as possible.

GRAPHIC COMMUNICATION

What is graphic communication?

Graphic communication is communication using devices such as tables, bar graphs, line graphs, cartoons, pictures and pictograms. These graphic devices often combine numbers, shapes and words. They are sometimes called non-verbal communication. However, this book defines them as graphics and graphic communication because words are often included. The term non-verbal communication should be reserved for the type of communication called body language.

This chapter covers the following aspects of graphic communication:

- The purposes of graphic devices.
- Types of graphic devices and their suitability for various audiences.
- Using graphic devices.
- Bias in designing graphics.

The purposes of graphic devices

Graphic devices help senders to communicate more effectively. They:

- Show groups of numbers that would be very difficult to show in a written message.
- Show relationships that would take many sentences to explain.
- Give a quick visual impression that enables a reader to compare amounts quickly.

These devices include elements that a writer cannot use. These elements include:

- The use of *space* as in tables.
- The use of *shapes*, as in bar graphs, illustrations, or pictograms.
- The use of *colours* to make points stand out.
- The use of *lines*, as in line graphs and algorithms to show relationships, and stage-by-stage procedures.
- The use of more than one *dimension* such as length, breadth and even depth.

Graphic devices have the great advantage that the audience can see all the components and relationships at once. In a written message, on the other hand, the reader has to follow the information in a fixed sequence.

Good visuals have a greater impact than just the spoken or written word. A combination of the spoken and visual can be up to twice as powerful as the spoken message on its own. In the same way graphic devices add visual appeal to a written message. They also help to explain difficult ideas, show *relationships*, *simplify* and *summarize*.

Types of graphic devices

The following graphic devices will be described and illustrated:

- Tables
- Area graphs (Pie-Charts)
- Bar graphs
- Histograms
- The Gantt Chart
- Line graphs
- Diagrams
- Pictograms
- Maps
- Hierarchical flow charts
- Flow charts
- Cartoons

Tables

A table is any grouping of numbers and other information in rows and columns. They are very effective for presenting large amounts of information in a small space.

A table should have the following sections:

STUB HEADING	COLUMN HEADING	
	Sub-heading	Sub-heading

TABLE NUMBER AND TITLE

Table Number:

Every table should be numbered above the table. Tables can be numbered from the beginning to the end of a whole report. They can also be numbered within each chapter.

Title of Table:

Every table should have a clear title telling the reader exactly what the table is about. This title appears *above* the table.

Stub Heading:

This heading is at the top of the left-hand column. The items in the column refer to information across the table.

Column Heading:

This heading is a general heading that describes the data in the columns.

Sub-Headings:

Each sub-heading describes the data in that column.

Note: If the Table has been taken from another source, then a proper reference should be given below the Table.

Example

Table 1
Machine Breakdowns by Machine at XYZ Factory

MONTHS	MACHINE BREAKDOWNS		
	Machine One	Machine Two	Machine Three
January	2	5	6
February	1	4	9
March	5	7	8
April	7	8	5
May	6	6	3
June	8	4	5

Note: The reader's eye is guided *downward* in the above table, If it is important to guide the reader's eye *across*, then lines should be ruled horizontally, rather than vertically. The following table illustrates lines drawn across.

Example

Table 2
Machine Breakdowns by Month at XYZ Factory

MONTHS	MACHINE BREAKDOWNS		
	Machine One	Machine Two	Machine Three
January	2	5	6
February	1	4	9
March	5	7	8
April	7	8	5
May	6	6	3
June	8	4	5

The first table stresses the machines. The second table stresses the months.

If a fully ruled table is used, then it is a good technique to highlight key numbers. The following example illustates this technique. Note that the table is not complete.

Example

Table 3
Machine Breakdowns by Month at XYZ Factory

MONTHS	MACHINE BREAKDOWNS		
	Machine One	Machine Two	Machine Three
January	2	5	6
February	1	4	**9**

Note: In the above table, the 9 has been highlighted because it is significant.

Audience for Tables

Tables are suited to a variety of audiences from lay to expert according to their complexity. Very detailed tables are difficult for a lay audience.

Area Graphs

These graphs, also called circle graphs and pie-charts, show how a total or area is divided up.

Area graphs are simple, and well suited to a lay audience. They give a general impression and are not suitable for showing exact amounts. It is difficult to guess proportions accurately.

The following example illustrates an area graph. Note that the largest proportion is given first. The graph should be viewed clockwise. Area graphs should be divided into a maximum of five or six sectors to have the best impact.

Note: All graphic devices, other than Tables, are called Figures. The title is normally put *below* the figure.

Example

Figure 18.1 shows an example of a pie chart. Note that it is helpful to put figures in to guide the audience.

Bar Graphs

Bar graphs are easy to read. They can be accurately interpreted if horizontal reference lines are provided.

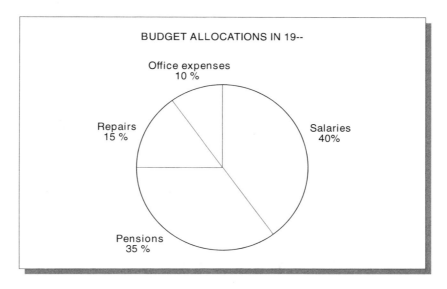

Figure 18.1
Budget allocations by percentage

Bar graphs are of various types. The types most often used are:
- Single bar
- Multiple bar
- Cumulative bar

Bar graphs are very good for:
- showing discrete information
- comparing amounts.

Bar graphs may be presented horizontally or vertically. Most bar graphs are presented vertically. However if a sender wishes to show stopping times for motor cars, for example, then horizontal bars would be effective.

Bar graphs are suitable for a lay audience.

Figures 18.2 to 18.6 illustrate various types of bar graphs.

In figure 18.2 three amounts are compared.

Note the *reference lines* in the figure 18.2. They are useful if the sender wishes to help the receiver read off exact amounts. An exact amount could also be written at the top of each column if this is important.

Multiple bar charts are very useful for comparison. Note the use of a key. There should always be a space between the clusters.

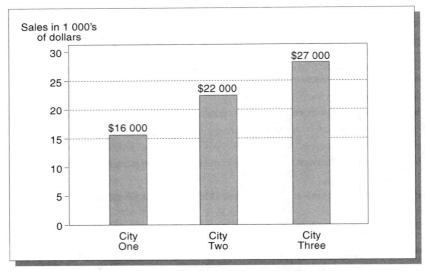

Figure 18.2
Example of a single bar chart: comparison of book sales by city

This type of bar shows how a total can be broken into component parts. Each bar in this illustration, is divided into three components. Each component shows the proportion of a total.

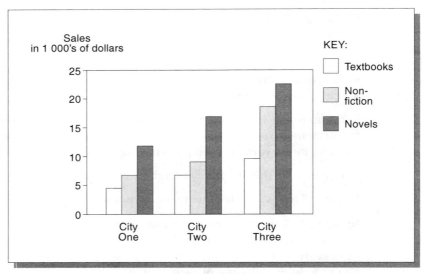

Figure 18.3
Comparison of sales of three types of book in three cities

Figure 18.3 could be presented in two other ways:
- As a set of three cumulative bars each bar showing a total. (See figure 18.4.)

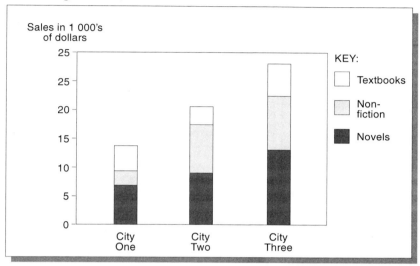

Figure 18.4
Cumulative bars showing the amounts spent on three types of books in three cities

- As a set of three bars showing proportions out of 100 %. (See figure 18.5.)

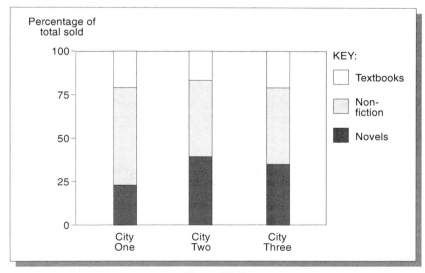

Figure 18.5
Cumulative bars showing the percentage of three types of books sold in three cities

Example of a horizontal bar graph

The graph in figure 18.6 has been arranged horizontally because stopping distance is important.

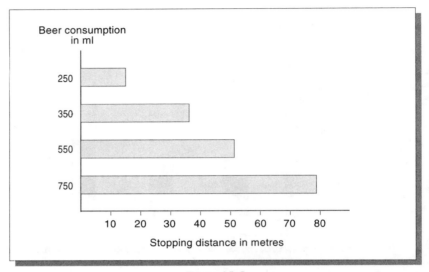

Figure 18.6
Stopping distances after drinking beer

Histograms

Histograms are like bar-graphs, but they have a continuous base. They show the distribution of something such as rainfall in terms of amounts or frequencies. These amounts or frequencies are shown over equal intervals such as months, weeks or days. Histograms are used when these intervals are discrete, rather than continuous. The area contained within the lines gives definite information. (See figure 18.7.)

Histograms are aimed at an expert or technical audience.

Gantt chart

Gantt charts are a type of bar chart. They are used in project planning to show when each stage in the process starts and finishes. (See figure 18.8.)

Gantt charts are used by specialists. Each bar shows the exact starting and finishing date for the job.

Line-graphs

Line-graphs are used to show a continuous relationship between two variables. The independent variable is shown on the horizontal axis. The dependent variable is shown on the vertical axis.

GRAPHIC COMMUNICATION

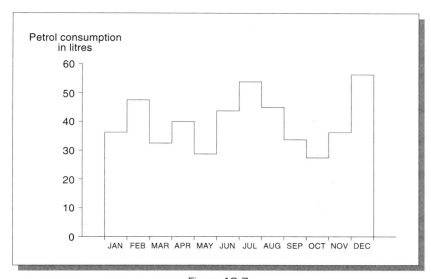

Figure 18.7
Histogram showing monthly consumption of petrol

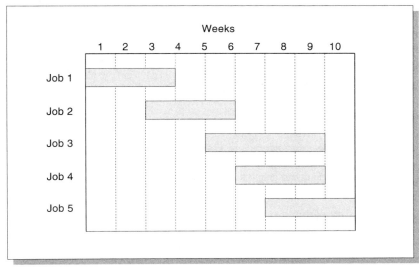

Figure 18.8
Gantt chart to show job planning over ten weeks

Line graphs are used by expert audiences. They are useful for showing trends. If senders want amounts to be read off, they should provide a grid.

Line-graphs are divided into three types:
- Jagged line
- Curves
- Cumulative jagged-line graph

Each type is illustrated here.

Jagged-line graph

This type of graph is useful for showing trends. The information could also be presented in the form of a bar graph. The jagged-line graph is used when the relationship between the two variables is suggested, rather than defined exactly.

Curve

This curve shows a relationship between two variables when the relationship between the two can be defined. (See figure 18.10.)

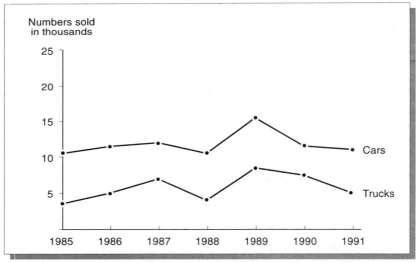

Figure 18.9
Jagged-line graph to compare sales of trucks and cars from 1985 to 1991

Cumulative jagged-line graph

This type of graph is related to the cumulative bar graph. It shows subdivisions in the dependent variable. The dependent variable could for example, be total profits. The subdivisions could show that these profits come from three sources — wines, brandy and beer for example. (See figure 18.11.)

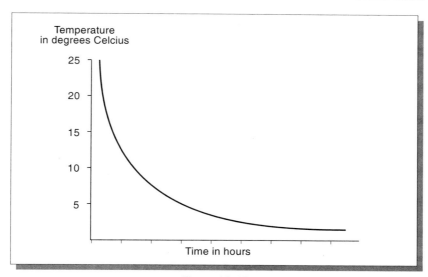

Figure 18.10
Curve to show the relationship between time and temperature

This type of graph is useful in company reports.

Note: In the graph below the total profit for each year is shown by the top line. The shaded sections between the lines show the amount of profit contributed by each category.

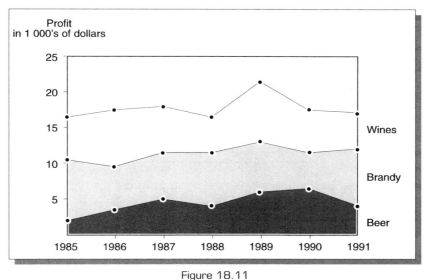

Figure 18.11
Example of a cumulative jagged-line graph to show profits made from beer, brandy and wines from 1985 to 1991

Diagrams and illustrations

Diagrams and illustrations give information in a wide variety of messages. They are very useful for simplifying complex material and ideas. They can also show views that a camera could not show. They are useful for a wide audience.

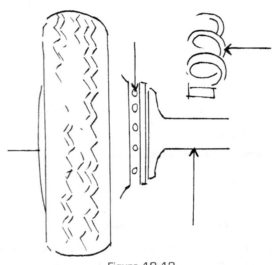

Figure 18.12
Illustration showing motor car suspension system

Figure 18.12 simplifies a complex assembly. Arrows are used to point to specific parts.

A diagram is more abstract than an illustration. The following diagram illustrates the communication process.

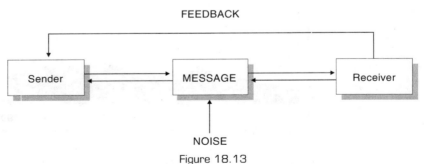

Figure 18.13
Diagram to show the communication process

Note: Photographs are often used to illustrate general and specific points in messages. If you use a photograph for a specific point, use an arrow to show the reader where to look. Do not let readers guess what the photograph illustrates.

Pictograms

These use outline figures to show statistical and other information. They give general information only, and are informal. They are very useful for a lay audience, particularly if people speak different languages.

Examples of pictograms

The information given is often elementary. The pictograms below, for example, give a very rough idea of the growth in the number of women employed over three years.

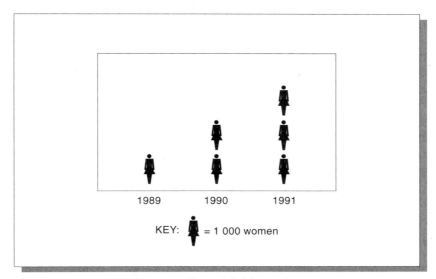

Figure 18.14
Pictograms to illustrate the growth in the number of women employed from 1989 to 1991

Maps

These vary from the very simple to the highly technical. They appeal to a wide audience.

A key should always be provided.

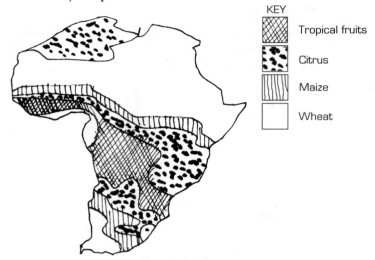

Figure 18.15
Map to show distribution of crops in Africa

Hierarchical flow chart

These are very useful to show how groups of people work together in an organization. They show relationships in a hierarchy.

This is sometimes called an organizational chart or organigram.

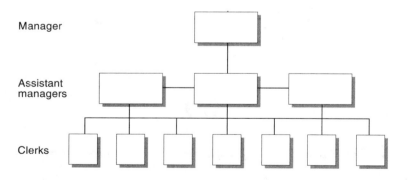

Figure 18.16
Hierarchical flow chart to show how managers and clerks are organized

Flow charts

These help readers to understand each step in a process. Lines are used to show flows of information, goods or instructions. Readers are able to follow a path and to decide what information is relevant to them.

Flow charts are aimed at educated lay audiences and also at specialists. The simple chart in figure 18.17 illustrates a set of stages in decision-making.

Note: Chapter 17 includes illustrations of a flow chart, a logic tree and an algorithm.

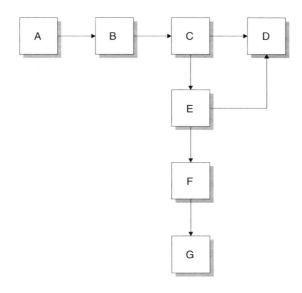

Figure 18.17
Example of flow-chart to show decision-making process

Cartoons

These are generally used for a lay or non-specialist audience. They are often used as a pictorial narrative instead of writing. They are used to entertain, to educate, to advertise and to make social comment. (See figure 18.18.)

Figure 18.18
A cartoon to illustrate the dangers of sunbathing

Integration of graphics into a written message

Graphics should be placed in the text where they are referred to. They will have the greatest impact in these positions. The most effective way of integrating a graphic is to:

- Refer to the graphic above the graphic.
- Place the graphic after the introduction.
- Analyse the graphic once the reader has been able to examine it.

The writer should *never* assume that a reader will understand exactly what the graphic illustrates.

Example

The example below illustrates the technique.

The table below illustrates the motor car sales figures for 1990 and 1991. The sales figures for car one and car two are compared.		
NUMBERS SOLD BY YEAR	**TYPES OF MOTOR CAR**	
	Car One	Car Two
1990	15 000	10 000
1991	10 000	6 000
The figures above show that there has been a decline in sales for both types of motor car. Please note the severe drop in sales of car two in 1991. The figure of 6 000 is a severe blow to the retail trade.		

Designing graphics

Make sure that you establish why you are presenting a graphic. Then analyse your audience.

Once you have establish your purposes and analysed your audience, then design a suitable graphic.

Pay special attention to:

- the size of the graphic
- the amount of material to be included
- the title of the graphic
- the wording of the captions
- the clarity of the graphic for the audience
- the accuracy of the graphic
- the integration of the graphic into your message.

Once you have the final product, check that you have:

- Provided good contrasts between adjacent sections by means of effective shading.
- Used dark lines round bars to make each bar stand out.
- Used shading to emphasize shapes and volumes.
- Written horizontal labels.
- Provided a key.
- Written labels at the ends of lines rather than underneath them.
- Provided a clear title.

Bias in graphic devices

When you design a graphic device try to avoid bias. If you are interpreting someone else's graphic, try to decide whether it is biased or not.

Bias may be introduced into graphics by:

- Choosing a deceptive scale.
- Omitting the zero on a scale and starting with a higher number.
- Labelling ambiguously.
- Selecting data that are favourable and leaving out other data.
- Drawing deceptive pictograms that give a distorted view of trends or numbers.
- Presenting diagrams or illustrations with the wrong perspective.

Questions: Part 8

(Answers to these questions are given on pages 579–588.)

Points for discussion

1. What is a graphic device?
2. How are graphic devices used in oral and written messages?
3. What are the differences between graphic devices and non-verbal communication?
4. What is a table? Explain the terms 'Stub Heading' and 'Column Heading'. How would you encourage a viewer to read across a table rather than down? For what audience would you use a table?
5. What is an area-graph? Give an example. For what audience is this suitable?
6. Explain what each of the following is. Give an example for each.
   - Bar graph
   - Histogram
   - Gantt chart
7. What is the difference between a jagged-line graph and a bar graph?
8. Give an example of a curve.
9. What is a pictogram? How are pictograms used?
10. What is a hierarchical flow chart? Give an example.
11. What is meant by integrating a graphic into a text?
12. Discuss six techniques that you would use in designing a graphic device.
13. Explain how bias may be introduced into a graphic.

Exercises

1. The following Table gives the average monthly water consumption in litres for a city. This consumption has been divided into use by businesses, schools and private homes.

    Convert these figures into a suitable graphic to be presented to ratepayers. This graphic should clearly show the monthly amounts of water used by each group.

    Assume that this graphic is part of a report. Integrate the graphic into the report.

CITY
Average monthly water consumption in litres

MONTH	CATEGORIES OF USERS		
	Business	Schools	Private Homes
January	20 568 000	10 531 000	35 458 000
February	20 431 000	8 658 000	30 561 000
March	20 608 000	8 700 000	27 428 000

MONTH	CATEGORIES OF USERS		
	Business	Schools	Private Homes
April	20 127 000	6 758 000	20 566 000
May	20 358 000	4 258 000	10 568 000
June	20 456 000	820 000	10 451 000
July	20 320 000	650 000	10 328 000
August	20 280 000	4 304 000	10 457 000
September	20 340 000	5 205 000	17 444 000
October	20 250 000	8 431 000	20 568 000
November	20 420 000	8 568 000	34 430 000
December	20 530 000	10 400 000	36 251 000

2. The following extract comes from a report. Rewrite it using a table for the figures. Write a suitable stub heading as well as suitable column headings.

   Sales in 1990 of our microwave ovens showed an increase over our sales for the previous year. The Ace model in three types (Type 60, 45 and 27) sold 535, 420, and 600 respectively in 1990, while our sales for the previous year were 500, 400, and 520 respectively. The sales for our three models in our Double-Ace range for the same three types were 380, 460, and 520 in 1990 and 300, 420, and 500 in the previous year.

3. You have been given the following table. Using the categories and numbers, write a report on sales of vehicles.

YEAR	MOTOR CARS	LIGHT TRUCKS	HEAVY TRUCKS	LORRIES
1985	50	68	40	20
1986	61	70	45	25
1987	63	58	47	20
1988	47	50	35	15
1989	30	40	28	10
1990	20	30	20	5

4. Present the following figures in two ways:
   – As an area graph
   – As a series of bar graphs.

Compare the two. Is one better than the other? Why?

Table 1
Book Sales in Thousands

TYPE OF BOOK	NUMBERS SOLD
Novels	15 000
Textbooks	100 000
Non-fiction	12 000
Reference Books	4 000

5. Using the following figures, draw two jagged-line graphs to compare sales. Make sure that your labelling is very clear.

Table 2
Wine and Beer Sales in Cases

YEAR	WINE	BEER
1987	1 500	9 000
1988	2 000	10 000
1989	3 000	10 500
1990	5 000	11 480
1991	7 000	15 000

6. Choose any company that you know well. Draw a hierarchical flow chart to show how the company is managed.
7. You have been asked to write a short report on the sales of apples in 1988, 1989 and 1990. Draw a pictogram to show these sales.
8. Prepare a flow chart showing a lay audience how to set about writing a bad-news letter of adjustment.
9. Prepare an algorithm for making a local call from a public telephone.
10. You have been asked to explain to someone in writing how to change a motorcar wheel. Draw a diagram to help you instruct a reader who knows nothing about changing wheels.

PART

9

How to Approach a Case Study

CHAPTER 19

How to Approach a Case Study

Summary

Case studies describe situations or incidents in organizations. These cases are used to analyse problems in organizations so that people can learn how to solve them. This chapter covers approaches to analysing:

- a general case
- a specific case.

The approach to analysing a general case should be as follows:

- understand the background to the case
- analyse the problems to be solved
- state the objectives or how the problems are to be solved
- decide on possible courses of action to solve those problems
- analyse each course of action in terms of the objectives
- select the course of action that best meets the objectives.

A specific communication case should be approached as follows:

- Analyse the exact situation in which people are interacting.
- List all communication breakdowns.
- Analyse the sender and receiver in terms of their goals and perceptions.
- Analyse the type of communication that is occurring; for example written, spoken, non-verbal or graphic.
- Analyse the people's communication skills.
- Analyse the people's dress
- Analyse the level of tidiness in the office
- Analyse telephone techniques used.

What is a case study?

A case study is a description of a situation in a company. This description is used to study an aspect of the company such as the management style of its leaders. A case study might also describe an incident in a company. This incident is then analysed in terms of the quality of the communication, for example.

Case studies are useful for studying problems in organizations. They help students, managers and staff to build up a knowledge of business principles by examining real situations.

This chapter covers the following aspects of case studies:

- How to approach a general case study where one major question is asked.
- How to approach a specific case study that focuses on an aspect of communication.

Once these approaches are covered, a case will be presented and analysed. Two further cases are then presented as exercises.

Approaching a general case study

This type of case describes a general situation in which participants have to solve a problem. The reader is then asked:

'What should the Company do?'
   OR
'What should X and Y do?'

The following problem-solving procedure is recommended for this type of case:

1. Make sure that you understand the *background* to the case.
   Ask yourself the following questions:
   - What are the characteristics of this type of organization or company?
   - How do people work together in this organization?
   - Why do they work in this way?
   - What effects do people's relationships have on the organization?
2. Decide on the *problems* that have to be solved. Problems that seem obvious may not be the real problems. Careful analysis is therefore necessary to find out what the real problems are.
   For example, the obvious problem is that the Sales and Product Development Departments do not co-operate. The real problem, however, is that the Managers of these Departments have not been trained in effective problem-solving skills.

3. Once you have established the real problems, then state the *objectives* necessary to solve these problems. Objectives answer the question:

'*What* should the organization do to solve the problems?'

An example of an objective is:

'In order to meet the lack of problem-solving skills the Managing Director should ensure that the two managers are properly trained in these skills.'

4. Once the objectives have been established, decide on possible courses of action to achieve these objectives. For example, a possible course of action to ensure that the two managers are trained is to hold regular seminars on problem-solving.
5. Each course of action should now be evaluated against the objectives.
6. The final stage is to decide on the course of action that best meets the objectives.

Approaching a case study where specific questions on communication are asked

Case studies also cover specific incidents in the field of interpersonal or small-group communication. Often specific questions are asked at the end.

Approach this type of case as follows:

1. Read through the case and analyse the following:
   - The exact situation in which people are working and interacting.
   - The personalities of the people involved.
   - The surroundings in which people are working.
2. List all the communication breakdowns.
3. Analyse each breakdown very carefully. Take into account all the factors that affect the communication. Pay special attention to:
   - The sender's and receiver's goals, needs, perceptions, personality and mood.
   - External pressures on sender and receiver.
   - The messages being sent and received. Are they spoken, written, non-verbal or graphic? What is their content?
   - Any physical or psychological noise distorting messages.
   - Any defences put up by the sender or receiver.
   - Communication skills with the stress on listening and the ability to communicate both information and emotion.
   - Layout of the office with the stress on positions and sizes of desks. Check whether the position and size of a desk are barriers to communication.
   - Level of tidiness as this might affect people's perceptions of others.
   - The way people are dressed, as this will affect communication.

- Use of space with the stress on invasion of others' space.
- Telephone techniques with the stress on handling messages and forming a good relationship with the caller.

Example of a case

Please read the following case and questions. The questions will be answered to give you an idea of how to approach this type of case.

THE INTERVIEW

Nomsu Motsepe had been interviewing job applicants for the trainee manager position since 8.30 am. It was now 4 pm and she was looking forward to a short break before the final interview of the day. She checked her schedule — Gavin Stephens, 4.30 pm. She decided to have coffee sent in to her office, as she didn't have time to go to the canteen.

Unfortunately, Gavin, who had lost his way, was 20 minutes late. As a result the interview began with Nomsu's feeling irritable and Gavin flustered.

Nomsu: Good afternoon, Mr Stephens. Take a seat.

Gavin: Thanks Mrs er Ms Mots . . . er

Nomsu: MOTSEPE. Right. Let's get started straight away. What made you apply for this particular job, Mr Stephens?

Gavin shuffled in his seat and Nomsu noticed that he kept adjusting his tie.

Gavin: Sorry, I'm a bit hot after running here. Phew! Um . . . well I've done a management course at Tech and I . . . this ad. said it was for a trainee manager.

Nomsu: I see. Do you know anything about ABC Ltd?

Gavin: Ja, don't you make toys and that sort of stuff?

Nomsu: You could put it that way. Mr Stephens, we're looking for someone who can think creatively — do you have any hobbies or activities that are creative at all?

Gavin: Um, not really. I surf in the summer . . . But I enjoy working with people.

Nomsu: Can you give me any examples?

Gavin: What d'you mean?

Nomsu: Well, have you worked in a team, or perhaps organized a surfing competition?

Gavin looked around the room for a few seconds. His gaze settled on Nomsu's coffee cup.

Gavin: I must have — I just can't remember now. Um . . . I led a group of scouts on a two-day hike. Oh yes! I was a member of the Debating Society at school. That can be pretty creative!

Nomsu: Right. Mr Stephens, we are hoping to fill this position by the end of October. Would you be available then?

Gavin: Yes. I can't wait to stop delivering pizzas.

Nomsu: Hmm. Well, I think that's it. Is there anything you'd like to ask me about the firm, or the position?

Gavin: Er . . . is there a bar on the premises? I wouldn't mind something cool to drink.

Unfortunately, Nomsu did not find Gavin's attempted joke funny.

Nomsu: Right. If that's all . . .

Nomsu rose briskly and extended her hand, which Gavin shook firmly.

Gavin: Thanks. Sorry I was late. Goodbye Mrs Motsepe.

Gavin left hurriedly, leaving Nomsu nursing her crushed hand.

Questions

1. Analyse the factors that led to a poor start to the interview.
2. Analyse Mrs Motsepe's interview. Did she run the interview properly? Support your answer with examples from the case.
3. Analyse Gavin Stephens' behaviour during the interview. Was he properly prepared? Pay special attention to his answers. How should Gavin have prepared?
4. Analyse the types of questions asked.
5. Analyse the non-verbal behaviour of Gavin Stephens during the interview. How should he have behaved?
6. Write about 200 words on how a good interview should be prepared and conducted.

Answers to Questions

1. The interview started badly because Mrs Motsepe had been interviewing people all day. It seems as though she had not had much of a break all day. The case states that she did not have enough time to go to the canteen to fetch her coffee. She must have been tired.

    Gavin Stephens then arrived twenty minutes late. He was flustered, and Mrs Motsepe was irritated at the delay.

    These factors meant that the interview did not start well.

2. Mrs Motsepe should have started by giving Mr Stephens an idea of the objectives of the interview. She should then have given him some idea of the types of questions she would be asking.

    The interview should have been taken through a set of stages:
    – setting Gavin Stephens at ease
    – preliminary negotiation
    – detailed negotiation
    – closure

    Mrs Motsepe was not able to move through these stages very well because of Gavin Stephens' poor answers. She did, however, try to negotiate with Gavin Stephens by asking him:
    – why he had applied for the post
    – whether he knew anything about ABC Ltd

- whether he had any creative hobbies
- whether he had worked in a team.

However, she did not go into enough detail at each stage. The questions seem disjointed. At the end she should have told Gavin what would happen next. The interview was not well conducted because both people were ill-at-ease.

3. Gavin Stephens behaved poorly during the interview. He was not properly prepared. He was also ill-at-ease, and did not pay attention to his interpersonal behaviour. His first answer was vague. He showed that he had not prepared fully for the interview. He had not studied the job-description, and seemed vague about why he wanted the job. His other answers were vague and unhelpful. His facetious answer at the end left a bad impression.

Gavin should have prepared by:
- studying the job-description very carefully
- finding out as much as possible about the company
- preparing answers to anticipated questions
- finding out where the company is so that he could arrive on time.

4. Mrs Motsepe started by asking an open question to encourage Gavin to start talking. She then asked a closed question. This would have been better expressed as:

'What do you know about ABC Ltd?'

She then asked him a closed question about his hobbies. This could have been better expressed as:

'Please describe your hobbies.'

She could then have asked open and closed questions to find out about his creative abilities.

She closed by asking whether he had any questions to ask. This is an effective way of finding out whether the interviewee has thought about the job.

Mrs Motsepe should have asked open questions with some closed questions to find out details.

5. Gavin Stephens showed signs of nervousness and lack of preparation. Mrs Motsepe would have noticed these signs and probably formed a negative opinion of him.

Gavin's particular behaviour was:
- shuffling in his seat
- frequent adjusting of his tie
- his vague voice
- his hesitant answers
- his poor eye-contact as he gazed at Mrs Motsepe's coffee cup.

Gavin should have answered boldly and fluently. He should have used good eye-contact and sat comfortably without shuffling. He should have avoided fiddling with his tie.

6. *Conducting a good interview*

   A good interview should be well prepared. The interviewer should start with a clear job-description. (S)he should then clarify her objectives for the interview and prepare an interview plan. Once the interview has been planned, (s)he should prepare a set of open and closed questions based on the topics to be discussed.

   Once the interviewee has arrived (s)he should be made welcome. The interviewer should explain the purposes of the interview, and give some idea of the range of topics to be covered. (S)he should do her utmost to set the interviewee at ease.

   The detailed negotiations should then begin. The interviewer should encourage the interviewee to answer freely and openly. Open questions should be used so that the interviewer can form an impression of the interviewee and her or his experience and views. The interviewer should use closed questions to get specific answers.

   The interviewer should bring the interview to a close by asking the interviewee if (s)he has any questions. The interviewer should then close the interview by telling the interviewee what will happen next.

Questions: Part 9

(Answers to these questions are given on pages 589–590.)

Points for discussion

1. How can case studies help students to study problems in business?
2. What six stages should be used in solving a problem in a case?
3. How may a communication model be used in analysing an interpersonal problem in a case?
4. What factors should be taken into account when an interpersonal or small-group problem has to be analysed?

Exercises

Read the following interpersonal case studies. Answer the questions that follow each case.

1. A DAY AT THE APRICOT AGENCY

Thandiwe woke at 08h00 on Monday morning to the sound of the telephone ringing. She groped for the receiver and answered sleepily; "Hello, 7523579". "Hello, Thandi? It's Bob from Apricot. Can you come in today we have an urgent job to be done."

Apricot was an advertising agency that Thandiwe, as a freelance illustrator, worked for regularly.

"Er . . . yes, that should be fine. When should I come in?" "As soon as you can. Thanks. Bye."

As she was getting ready, Thandi remembered that she had a business appointment at 16h30. "Oh, well. I'll sort it out when I get there", she thought.

Thandi arrived at the Apricot Advertising Agency at 09h00. She told the receptionist, Anne, why she was there and waited while Bob was called.

"He says you should go straight to the studio. He'll brief you as soon as he's ready," said Anne.

It was 09h45 by the time Bob arrived in the studio, looking distracted.

"Ah, Thandi. Sorry! Things are hectic today, so let me give you the brief quickly so you can get on with it. I need you to illustrate a new fruit juice box. I want very realistic fruit — strawberries, apples, bananas. Here are my designs, they should give you an idea."

Thandiwe looked through the designs.

"Fine, Bob," she said. "So you'd like individual fruit or perhaps strawberries in a basket, or . . . "

"Yes, yes. That sort of thing. I need the illustrations by 17h00 to show the client. I'll check in on you later — I have to get back to a meeting."

Thandiwe was just about to mention her afternoon appointment, but Bob was already on his way out.

Thandiwe started to work straight away. By 11h30 she had nearly finished the first drawing. She was so absorbed in her work that she did not notice Terry looking over her shoulder.

"Who gave you this brief?" asked Terry sharply.

Thandiwe got rather a fright.

"Er . . ."

"Never mind," said Terry. "It's all wrong. We want fruit TREES. You'll have to do it again."

"But Bob said he wanted fruit," said Thandiwe, "I'd better check with . . ."

"Never mind," interrupted Terry. "We need these by 16h30 today. Do the trees. We agreed about that — he must have forgotten."

With that, Terry left, sighing heavily.

Thandiwe was feeling confused and slightly irritated. She tried to telephone Bob, but he was not available. She wasn't sure whether to re-do the illustrations or wait for Bob. She glanced at her watch — nearly 12h00. She decided to start on the new illustrations or they would not be completed on time.

By 14h00 Thandiwe had finished one illustration and was adding the finishing touches to an apple tree when Bob came into the studio.

"Why the trees? I'm sure I said individual fruit," exclaimed Bob.

"Yes, you did. But a woman came in and changed the brief. I tried to get hold of you, but . . ."

"What was her name?" asked Bob, looking angry.

"I'm not sure," replied Thandiwe. "She had short blonde hair and . . ."

"Terry!" exclaimed Bob. "That interfering #$%^&@! Sorry. Look Thandi, this is my brief. This is what I want," he said, pointing to her earlier illustration. "Can you complete three more before 16h30?"

"I should be able to, Bob," said Thandi "but I . . ." Again, Bob left before she could mention her appointment.

By the time Bob returned to the studio, Thandiwe had finished the work. She had not done as well as she'd have liked, but she'd had to work very quickly.

"These are fine, Thandi," said Bob. "If you could just correct the colour on the apples. I'd like a brighter green."

Thandiwe checked her watch — 16h10.

"I'm sorry, Bob. I have an appointment at 16h30 which I can't cancel."

"Why didn't you say so earlier?" asked Bob.

"I tried to, but you . . ."

"Never mind," sighed Bob. "I'll correct it myself."

"I'm sorry," murmered Thandiwe.

"It's okay. You'd better rush off to your important date," said Bob.

Thandiwe noticed the sarcasm in his voice. She left the agency feeling upset, and wishing she'd been more assertive. As a result, she arrived at her meeting in a bad mood.

Meanwhile, back at the agency . . . Bob finished the drawings by 17h00, which meant that the client had been kept waiting for half an hour.

Questions

1. Analyse the communication between Thandiwe and Bob. Could Thandiwe have handled the communication better? Explain how she could have done so.
2. Analyse the communication between Thandiwe and Terry. How could Thandiwe have improved her communication?
3. Analyse the communication within the Apricot Agency. How could this communication have been improved?
4. Analyse the quality of listening at the Agency. How could Thandiwe, Bob and Terry improve their listening?
5. If you were asked to prepare a plan for effective communication within the Apricot Agency what sort of plan would you draw up?

2. IN A FIX AT SECURE-IT

Selwyn arrived at work early, feeling alert and cheerful. He'd played a morning squash game and had won. He perched on the edge of a desk in the reception area to have his coffee. He liked to chat to the secretary, Stacey, and the receptionist, Beverly, before going to his office in the mornings. Selwyn's outgoing, friendly nature made him an excellent salesman for the firm SECURE-IT, but his ebullience could be a little over-powering first thing in the morning.

He was giving Stacey (Beverly had not yet arrived) a blow-by-blow account of his squash game, when the telephone rang. Before Stacey could get to the telephone, Selwyn picked up the receiver.

Selwyn: Secure-it, good morning.

Caller: Hello, this is Mrs. Musikanth speaking. I have an emergency. Hello?

Selwyn: I'm still here, Mrs Musika.

Caller: Yes, I have an emergency. My husband has . . .

Just then Beverly walked in and noticed that Selwyn was sitting on an important document on her desk. She had slept badly and was feeling tired and irritable. As a result she shouted rather too loudly at Selwyn to get off her desk. Selwyn waved his arm to silence her and knocked his coffee over in the process. He leapt off the desk and tried to mop up the mess with his handkerchief.

Selwyn: I'm sorry, the . . . er . . . line is a bit bad. Could you repeat that Mrs Musics?

Caller: I HAVE AN EMERGENCY. My husband left for a business trip early this morning with the security gate keys. I can't get out of the house! I tried to climb through the window but I can't get through the bars. I need to get to work as soon as possible. Can you send someone round?

Selwyn: Yes, Mrs Music, we have a locksmith. We'll send him round straight away. Don't worry, we'll soon have you sorted out.

Caller: Good! Thank you so much. Goodbye.

During this conversation, Beverly had been frantically trying to salvage her document. She'd managed to save most of it from the coffee — but it would need re-typing.

"Selwyn, you clumsy idiot," she exclaimed crossly.

"I'm sorry," said Selwyn, draping his arm over her shoulder. "But at least I answered the phone for you."

"You're not supposed to answer the phone!" said Beverly, shrugging his arm away.

"If you were here on TIME," said Selwyn, looking at his watch pointedly, "and if Stacey wasn't half asleep . . . "

"That's unfair!" exclaimed Stacey, glaring at him. The three of them started to argue heatedly. They were so busy that they didn't notice Mr Green, their boss, who had come into the room.

"Excuse me," he said loudly, "I have a very upset lady on the telephone. She has been locked in her house for an hour . . . "

Questions

1. What were the barriers to good communication that led to the argument between Stacey, Selwyn and Beverly? Give examples to support your argument.
2. Analyse the telephone conversation between Selwyn and Mrs Musikanth. What did Selwyn do wrong? Give examples to support your answer.
3. How should Selwyn have handled the telephone call?
4. Mr Green has asked you to set up a two-day course in communication to help his staff improve their interpersonal communication. What aspects of interpersonal communication would you put into the course?

PART 10

Writing a Summary and a Comprehension Test

CHAPTER 20

Writing a Summary and a Comprehension Test

Summary

The ability to summarize a message or a group of messages is essential in organizations. Almost every message should have a summary at the beginning. This summary should be so clear that it creates a positive first impression of a message.

A good summary should be so well written and informative that it replaces the original message for the busy reader.

Informative summaries are very important for:

- long proposals
- long reports
- groups of short messages such as letters and memoranda
- meetings.

The writer has to think about two things before she or he writes a summary:

- the purpose of the summary
- how the reader is going to use the summary.

A summary is a reduced version of the original. It does not have a fixed length. A summary may change the order of the original. It may also emphasize certain points and leave out others.

A summary should contain exact figures as well as summary diagrams, photographs or other graphics.

Summaries should be between a quarter of a page to a full page. The length of the summary will depend on what has to be summarized.

Readers need summaries for four main reasons:

- to decide if they need to read the whole original
- to get to the main points quickly and reliably
- to find out the main purposes of the original more easily.

Summaries should be written in a direct style with exact information. The writer should use short, simple and active sentences. The vocabulary should be simple.

Preparing a summary or writing a comprehension test demands the following abilities:

- to grasp the main idea in a message
- to grasp the key points in a message
- to organize the summarized information coherently
- to rewrite ideas in your own words
- to understand the meanings of words in specific contexts.

The following procedure for writing summaries is suggested:

- Decide on the reader's needs and time available for reading.
- Read the passage to find the main idea, and write this down, as well as a title.
- Underline the main idea of each paragraph.
- Decide on the order of information and the proportions of information.
- Decide what you wish to emphasize.
- Prepare a topic outline.
- Decide on summary diagrams and figures, and where they should be placed.
- Decide on the length of the summary.
- Write your first draft in your own words.
- Check your draft and then write the final version.

Comprehension tests are normally set in examinations. They test a person's ability to:

- Grasp the theme of the message.
- Understand what the ideas mean.
- Understand what words in the message mean.
- Understand how the ideas and words connect in the message.
- Write answers that show an understanding of the message.
- Write answers in a clear, formal style.

The following procedure is suggested for answering comprehension tests:

- Read the questions carefully.
- Read through the passage carefully.
- Write down the main idea in the passage.
- Read the passage a second time.
- Underline all key ideas, as well as technical and difficult words.
- Write down the key ideas in your own words.
- Write in your own words the meanings of difficult words.
- Write the answers in your own words.
- Write full sentences in a formal style.

WRITING A SUMMARY AND A COMPREHENSION TEST

Introduction

People in organizations need informative summaries to help them understand the main points of a message quickly. Informative summaries are very important for:
- long proposals
- long reports
- groups of letters or other short messages
- meetings.

An informative summary is a shortened version of the original. The summary should be placed at the beginning of a message so that it prepares the reader for the message. The summary should be so well written that it replaces the original message for the busy reader.

Summary writers have to think about two things before they write a summary:
- the purpose of the summary
- how the reader is going to use the summary.

What is a summary?

A summary is a reduced version of the original. It does not have a fixed length. A summary should be long enough to reflect the main points of the original. It should prepare the reader for the original if (s)he decides to read it.

The length of the summary will depend on the reader's needs. Most summaries will be between a quarter and a full page. Readers will probably be reluctant to turn to the next page. Some organizations expect a 300-word summary. Others expect no more than one page. If summary writers need guidelines for length, then they should aim at 5–10 % of the word-length of the original.

Characteristics of a summary

A summary has the following characteristics:
- It is placed at the beginning and not at the end.
- It has no fixed length — it is as long as is necessary.
- It may include some information and leave out other information.
- It may change the emphasis of the original.
- It may change the proportion of the information.
- It may change the order of the information.
- It keeps the reader's needs in mind.
- It has key summary diagrams and other figures in it.

Plan your summary as follows.

Reports for record

- Use two or three sentences to summarize the Introduction
- Use three or four sentences to summarize the procedure and the findings
- Use half of the summary to give the main conclusions and the recommendations.

Feasibility or investigation reports

- State the recommended action first
- Then state the main reasons for this action
- Then state in about half the summary the main findings. Give exact but selected details of costs, savings and timing.

Proposals for action

- Give a brief background to the proposal in three or four sentences.
- Use half the summary to give the key proposals. Give exact costs and timing.
- In three or four sentences, justify your proposal.

Summary of correspondence

- In two or three sentences, give the background to the correspondence.
- Use half the summary to give the main facts, arguments and discussion in the correspondence.
- Stress the proposed action if there was any.

Summary of meeting

- State in one or two sentences why the meeting was called.
- Give the key decisions made at the meeting. Make sure that you give the exact figures and timings. Give the exact wording of contracts and decisions.

Many summaries are much the same length because most readers are prepared to spend only a few minutes reading a summary. A summary of only three sentences will be too short. A summary that goes on to a second page may annoy the reader because it takes too long to read.

For the above reasons most summaries are between a quarter and a full page. Writers are strongly urged to find out what the readers' needs are.

The length of the summary will depend on what needs to be summarized.

Example

You wish to summarize an investigation of an accident with no single cause, but twelve minor contributing causes. In your summary you would include all twelve contributing causes in a long summary covering one page.

Example

You wish to summarize a report with only one conclusion and one recommendation. Write a short report giving the conclusion and recommendation. Include the key findings, but only briefly. This report should be about half a page in length.

If the original report is only two pages long, then a summary is not necessary. However, two sentences at the beginning telling the reader what the report is about will be helpful.

Problems with terms

Four terms are normally used to refer to summaries:

- Précis
- Executive summary
- Synopsis
- Abstract

Each term will now be briefly explained.

Précis

A précis is a summary. However it keeps the information in the same order. It is essentially a school exercise with a fixed length. This length is normally one third of the original. A précis also reduces the length in proportion. For example, if half the report gives the findings, and only a quarter gives the conclusions and recommendations, then the précis will keep to the same proportions.

Keep in mind that a summary will change the order and the proportions, keeping in mind the reader's needs and time.

A précis is sometimes needed, but summaries should be used for most documents in business.

Executive summary and synopsis

An executive summary and synopsis are the same as a summary. They will be written to suit the needs and time of the reader. Both may change the order and proportion of the original information.

Abstract

An abstract is like a précis in that it is a compressed version of the original, but in the same order and proportion. There are two kinds of abstracts:
- The informative abstract
- The descriptive abstract.

The *informative* abstract is a full-length summary. It gives all the main points from the original. The *descriptive* abstract is written in two or three sentences. It is written to give the reader a brief idea of what is in the original. A *descriptive* abstract normally appears in a *separate* document. Summaries and synopses are always part of the original document.

Writers should use the words 'Summary' 'Executive Summary' or 'Synopsis' for business writing.

Why would a reader need a summary?

Readers need a summary for four main reasons:
- It helps the reader to decide if (s)he needs to read the whole original.
- It helps the reader to get to the main points quickly and reliably.
- It tells the reader the purpose of the original.
- It reminds readers of the key points in the original and helps them to read the original more easily.

Each point will now be covered in more detail.

Decide if one needs the original

People in business cannot read everything. Therefore a good summary will tell the reader:
- whether the original covers special areas that the reader is interested in
- how the original approaches the subject
- whether (s)he already knows the subject
- what the conclusions and recommendations are and how important they are to the reader
- what the key findings or facts of the original are
- whether (s)he needs to read the original.

Helps reader get main points

A summary is a short version for people who do not have time to read the whole original. If managers had more time they would read more than they do.

They have to be very selective. They need to have an overview of a large area of work.

WRITING A SUMMARY AND A COMPREHENSION TEST

A summary is a map of the original. It helps the reader to speed read the original. It stresses important details and picks out the key facts, conclusions and recommendations that really matter.

Purposes of original

A good summary gives the purposes of the original. For example, a reader with a good knowledge of the purposes understands why the original was written. A reader can absorb information if (s)he knows the conclusions and recommendations that the information is leading to.

Reminds reader of key points

A good summary helps the reader to remember the report or proposal, especially at a meeting later on. A summary helps the reader's memory because it repeats points. The reader gets the key points twice.

A style for summary writing

Use an informative style that gives exact figures. Be direct and use exact information to guide the reader. Remember that the informative style helps the reader to gain a complete picture of the original.

Example of vague writing

Tighter ABC specifications on retail grade Flexit 501 require operational changes to improve our product. High temperature oxidation tests have been performed. They have given improved results. However the oxidation jacket has to be changed before even higher temperature tests may be made.

(Note the use of 'high' and 'even higher'. These words are too vague.)

Example of specific writing

ABC specifications for retail grade Flexit 501 now restrict impurities to 3,2 ppm instead of 7,0 ppm. Oxidation tests at 180 °C improved purity. However the oxidation jacket has to be changed before we are able to test at over 210 °C.

(Note the use of exact figures.)

Use short, simple and active sentences. Keep to the most familiar words. Use the range of techniques given in the chapter on readability. Make sure, however, that you do not write in a telegram style. Write full, formal sentences.

Example

Do not write:

> Box mobility poor with 'soft-air'. Air cushion should be used, but system cannot adapt to air pressure changes. Also problems with . . .

Rather write:

> Boxes cannot be moved easily with the 'soft-air' system. The air cushion system should be used. However, this system cannot adapt to changes in air pressure. There are also some problems with . . .

Abilities needed to write a summary

A writer must be capable of doing the following when preparing a summary:

- Grasp the main idea or thesis statement in a passage.
- Grasp the key points in a passage.
- Rewrite these key points in a coherent way so that the reader understands what the original passage is about.
- Organize information and present it coherently.
- Choose words and write them in a clear informative style.
- Present the summary in a highly readable way.

Remember that a summary should be good enough to replace the original message for the busy reader. Use your own words as far as possible. Write any reported speech in the past tense.

Procedure for writing a summary

Use the following procedure for writing summaries:

- Decide on the reader's needs.
- Decide on how much time the reader has in which to read the summary.
- Read the passage or all the correspondence twice to find out the main idea or ideas.
- Write down the main idea(s).
- Write down a title for the summary.
- Read the passage or passages again, and underline the main idea or key sentence in each paragraph.
- Write down what each paragraph is about.

- If you are having difficulty finding the key points, underline the main clause in every sentence. These clauses should give you a good idea of the key points in the passage.
- Decide on the order of information and the proportions of information.
- Decide on what you wish to emphasize.
- Prepare a topic outline of the main and supporting ideas following your new order and emphasizing the most important points.
- Check your outline against your notes and the original.
- Check that you have inserted the right summary diagrams and figures in the right place.
- Decide on the length of your summary.
- Write your first draft in your own words.
- Check your draft against your outline to ensure that you have all the main ideas in the right order.
- Check your draft for style, grammar, punctuation, readability and length.
- Write the final version.

Diagram to summarize procedure

Figure 20.1 summarizes the above procedure.

Example

The following example illustrates the suggested procedure. The original has the key sentences underlined. The theme of the passage is then stated. This is followed by a topic outline and three summaries:

- one third length
- ten per cent of original length
- five per cent of original length.

**THREE FACTORS THAT LEAD TO GOOD
INTERPERSONAL COMMUNICATION IN COMPANIES**

Good communication in companies starts with effective interpersonal communication. Management can devise the finest set of networks and organizational patterns. However, if the people do not work well together these networks will fail. This essay describes three aspects of interpersonal communication that are vital for good communication in companies. The first is good listening, the second is sensitivity to non-verbal behaviour, and the third is effective use of language. This essay will discuss each in turn.

Good listening, or active listening as it is sometimes called, is a mental and physical process. It places demands on the listener's ability to concentrate on the full message. Good listeners should listen both for the facts and the emotions behind those facts. They should motivate themselves to listen, and should be as sensitive as possible to the speaker's non-verbal behaviour. They should show by the position of their body that they are listening.

424　　　　　　　　　　　　　EFFECTIVE COMMUNICATION IN ORGANIZATIONS

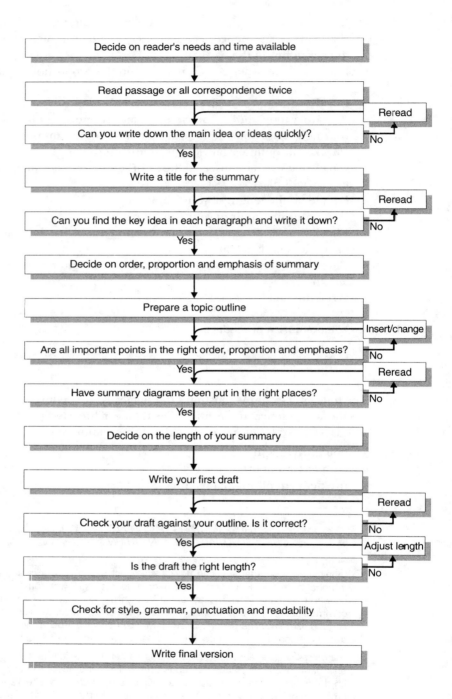

Figure 20.1
How to write a summary

> A good understanding of non-verbal behaviour is essential for effective interpersonal communication. People should be particularly sensitive to the listener's signs that (s)he wishes to join in the conversation. People should show that they are listening. They should ensure that they keep good eye-contact and should be aware of people's space-needs.
>
> The other side of good listening is good speaking. The effective use of language is the third topic of this essay. Speakers should always use language that is simple and geared to the listener's needs. They should not be tempted to use difficult words to impress. All that they will do is confuse the listener and destroy communication.
>
> In conclusion, this essay has stressed three key aspects of good interpersonal communication. Good listening, sensitivity to non-verbal communication and effective use of language will help to ensure that companies are good places in which to work. (302 words)

Stages in summary

What is the main theme of the passage?

This passage is about good interpersonal communication in companies, with the stress on good listening, sensitivity to non-verbal communication and effective use of language.

What are the key ideas?

The key ideas are:

- *Paragraph one:* Good communication in companies starts with effective interpersonal communication.
- *Paragraph two:* Good listening, or active listening, is a physical and mental process.
- *Paragraph three:* A good understanding of non-verbal behaviour is essential for effective interpersonal communication.
- *Paragraph four:* Speakers should use language effectively.
- *Paragraph five:* Good listening, sensitivity to non-verbal communication and effective use of language will help to ensure that companies are good places in which to work.

Topic outline with heading

> EFFECTIVE INTERPERSONAL COMMUNICATION IN COMPANIES
> 1. Good communication in companies
>   1.2 Effective interpersonal communication
>   1.2.1 Active listening
>   1.2.2 Sensitivity to non-verbal behaviour
>   1.2.3 Effective use of language
> 2. Active listening
>   2.1 Mental process
>   2.2 Physical process

> 3. Sensitivity to non-verbal communication
>   3.1 Sensitivity to listener's signs
>   3.2 Show that you are listening
>   3.3 Effective use of eye-contact
>   3.4 Sensitivity to people's space-needs
> 4. Effective use of language
>   4.1 Use simple language
>   4.2 Avoid difficult words

What are the reader's needs?

The reader needs to know the three key points immediately.

How much time does the reader have?

The reader needs to grasp the three key points in a few seconds. These three key points therefore need to be emphasized. They should therefore be placed first.

One third summary

The target number of words is 100, or one third the length of the original. These words include the title.

> **EFFECTIVE INTERPERSONAL COMMUNICATION IN COMPANIES**
>
> Effective interpersonal communication in companies depends on active listening, sensitivity to non-verbal communication and the use of simple language.
>
> Active listening is a mental and a physical process. The listener should concentrate on the speaker's emotions, as well as the facts. People should show that they are listening.
>
> People should be sensitive to non-verbal signs. They should allow each other to speak, and should maintain good eye-contact. They should also be sensitive to each others' space.
>
> Finally, people should use simple language. They should avoid difficult words that are hard to understand. (100 words)

Ten per cent length

The target number of words is 30, including the title.

> **EFFECTIVE INTERPERSONAL COMMUNICATION IN COMPANIES**
>
> Effective interpersonal communication in companies depends on active listening, sensitivity to non-verbal communication and the use of simple language. These will help people to work together. (32 words)

Five per cent length

The target number of words is 20, including the title.

> EFFECTIVE INTERPERSONAL COMMUNICATION IN COMPANIES
> Active listening, sensitivity to non-verbal communication and simple language are essential in companies. (19 words)

The comprehension test

Comprehension stresses understanding. Thorough understanding of a message is essential if people wish to communicate successfully. A thorough understanding of a message also helps people to summarise it more effectively.

Comprehension tests are set in examinations. They test people's ability to:

- Grasp the theme of the passage.
- Understand what the ideas mean.
- Understand what words mean in that passage.
- Understand how the ideas and the words connect together in the passage.
- Write answers that clearly show their understanding of the passage.
- Write answers that show their ability to write in a clear, formal style with good grammar, punctuation and sentence structure.

Procedure for answering a comprehension test

The following procedure for answering a comprehension test is suggested:

- Read the questions carefully.
- Read through the passage carefully.
- Write down the main idea in the passage.
- Read the passage a second time.
- Underline the key idea in each paragraph.
- Underline all technical words.
- Underline all words that you think have a special meaning in the passage.
- Try to write the key ideas in your own words.
- Write in your own words what you think are the meanings of difficult words.
- Write the answers in your own words. Write full sentences in a formal style.

Examples of questions

The following questions are based on the passage already summarized.

Question

What does the writer mean by 'interpersonal communication'?

Suggested answer

Interpersonal communication in this passage means face-to-face communication between people. The writer stresses listening and non-verbal communication, rather than reading or writing.

Question

What do you understand by the term 'active listening'?

Suggested answer

The writer stresses that active listening means that the listener is involved with the speaker. The listener concentrates both on the facts and opinions and on the speaker's emotions. The listener shows that (s)he is listening.

Question

What is the meaning of 'non-verbal communication' as the term is used in the passage?

Suggested answer

'Non-verbal communication' in this passage means messages conveyed by people's bodies, and the distances between them, rather than by the words that they use. The writer mentions eye-contact and people's need for space.

Question

Why should people use simple language?

Suggested answer

People should use simple language because many more people will be able to understand them. Very few people are able to understand complicated language and long words.

Questions: Part 10

(Answers to these questions are given on pages 591–595.)

Points for discussion

1. Why are summaries essential in most messages?
2. What is the best place for a summary in a message?
3. What are the stages through which a writer should go if (s)he wishes to summarise a passage effectively?
4. Why should the writer prepare a topic outline for the summary?
5. What does the term 'comprehension' mean?
6. Why is full comprehension of a passage essential?

Exercises

1. Read the passage below. Then:
   (*a*) Answer the questions on it.
   (*b*) Reduce it to one-third of its length.
   (*c*) Summarize the main idea in 25–30 words.

GETTING THINGS DONE IN COMPANIES

Today, companies in many countries are not moving forward. They are content to carry on their business as they always have. They react to problems and crises, but do not spend enough time and energy on forward planning and innovation. Advances in technology have given companies great benefits. In addition, companies have benefited from a highly numerate and literate population in many countries. They have also built up high skills in problem-solving.

Yet, in spite of all these advantages, many companies are not forward-looking. Why is this?

Companies have not moved forward because they have stressed problem-solving at the expense of innovation. They are afraid to make decisions that involve high risks, or might attract strong criticism. They are particularly nervous of the mass media, because any criticism by these media could lead to loss of business. As a result, managers design decisions to attract the least amount of criticism. These decisions also involve a low risk. Where managers do propose innovative ideas, decision-making groups will often focus on the small proportion of the proposal that is weak or wrong. They ignore the large proportion that is right.

It seems to be easier to criticise and pull to pieces, rather than to praise and be constructive. This general attitude has resulted in lack of innovation and an atmosphere in which the drive to get things done is lacking.

What should companies do about this? First of all, they should try to create a climate of innovation. All staff should be encouraged to move beyond problem-solving to innovation. Regular brainstorming sessions should be held in which staff are encouraged to generate ideas without criticism.

In addition, companies should reward innovation. Mistakes should be accepted as part of the risk of trying out new ideas. Once an idea has been put forward, people should be encouraged to think positively, rather than negatively about it. Companies should be prepared to accept criticism of plans that they believe in. Above all, companies should encourage an atmosphere in which things get done. This ability to get things done should be regarded as an asset, just as literacy and numeracy are.

Companies should look beyond pure efficiency. This implies simply doing things right. If they wish to innovate, they should also strive to be effective. This implies doing the right things.

A spirit of innovation and effectiveness should ensure that companies move beyond problem-solving to getting things done. (408 words)

Questions

(i) The writer states that companies are not moving forward. Explain in your own words the writer's reasons for saying this. (5)

(ii) The writer says 'Companies have not moved forward because they have stressed problem-solving at the expense of innovation'. What do you understand by this statement? (5)

(iii) What do you understand by the term 'a climate of innovation'? (5)

(iv) Why do managers design decisions that attract the least amount of criticism? (5)

(v) What do you understand by a 'brainstorming session'? (5)

(vi) The writer stresses the ability to get things done. What do you understand by this ability? (5)

(vii) Why should the ability to get things done be regarded as an asset, as are literacy and numeracy? (5)

(viii) Do you think that the ability to get things done can be taught? Justify your answer. (5)

(ix) Explain the difference between 'efficiency' and 'effectiveness'. Give examples to explain each term. (10)

2. Summarize the short report on the following page. Decide on the length and on what points should be emphasized. Keep in mind that conclusions and recommendations are important in a summary. Please note that the findings of this report have been shortened.

AN INVESTIGATION INTO FIVE TYPES OF PROBLEMS AT XYZ COMPANY

1. INTRODUCTION

    1.1 Background to investigation

    Mr Douglas, managing director of XYZ, has become increasingly concerned at the number of unsolved problems in the company. These are leading to poor interpersonal relationships and low productivity.

    Mr Douglas called for this investigation in the hope that the problems could be solved.

    1.2 Specific problems to be investigated

    The writer was asked to investigate two specific problems:
    - poor communication among staff members
    - poor understanding of problems that arise.

    1.3 Purposes of this report

    The main purposes of this report are to:
    - Describe the five types of problems that arise at XYZ.
    - Draw conclusions from these problems.
    - Recommend specific action that can be taken to solve the above problems.

    1.4 Procedure used to gather information

    The writer observed all staff for five days during working hours. The writer also interviewed ten senior managers.

2. CONCLUSIONS

The findings of this investigation have led to the following conclusions:

    2.1 Objectives are misunderstood because the person instructing and the person being instructed have different views of what the objectives are.

    2.2 In 30 % of cases, what seemed to be a problem is only a difference between the manager's

view of events compared with what the manager expected to take place.
2.3 In 10 % of cases problems arose that were beyond the control of all concerned.
2.4 In 5 % of cases problems arose because they were unexpected. They were beyond the scope of control of all concerned.
2.5 In 2 % of cases problems arose because of genuine errors. These were well within the scope of authority of subordinates; yet they made mistakes.

3. RECOMMENDATIONS

Based on the above conclusions, the following recommendations are made:

3.1 Make sure that subordinates know the extent of their authority.
3.2 Ensure that all managers give specific instructions. They should make sure that subordinates understand what they expect.
3.3 Ensure that all managers are very clear about their own expectations and perceptions.
3.4 Ensure that managers do not become angry with subordinates over totally unexpected problems.
3.5 Ensure that managers do not over- or underreact to genuine errors.

4. RESULTS OF INVESTIGATIONS INTO PROBLEMS

This section focuses on five types of problems found at XYZ.

4.1 *Misunderstood objectives*

Forty per cent of problems could be ascribed to differences between managers' and subordinates' perceptions of what should have been done. These different perceptions cause friction between managers and employees.

4.2 *No real problem exists*

Thirty per cent of so-called problems arose when a manager expected one thing to take place, and then reacted in anger when something else took place. Once managers had analysed the situation they realized that their expectations had been wrong.

4.3 Unexpected problems

Ten per cent of problems arose from occurrences outside the control of managers and employees.

4.4 Genuine errors

Ten per cent of problems arose when genuine errors were made.

4.5 Poor understanding of authority

Ten per cent of problems could be described as lack of understanding of employees' authority. They did not know what was inside and outside their authority.

PART

11

Mass Communication and Organizations

CHAPTER 21

Mass Communication and Organizations

Summary

Mass communication is defined as the rapid transmission of messages to a wide audience at a relatively low cost to the consumer.

There are three major differences between one-to-one and mass communication:

- Mass communication uses intermediate channels for conveying information.
- Mass communication is virtually one-way communication.
- Any feedback from mass communication messages is limited and delayed.

The mass communication media are able to overcome the barriers of time and space. However, the messages that they send are subject to gatekeeping. This term stresses that messages are subject to control through selection and editing.

The mass media perform three major functions:

- to inform
- to persuade
- to entertain.

This chapter briefly describes four mass media:

- newspapers
- radio
- film
- television.

Newspapers need a literate audience. They carry a wide variety of items designed both to inform, persuade and entertain. They rely on eye-catching headlines and pictures to attract attention and increase circulation.

Films have become a major form of recreation and entertainment. Advertising films are often treated as art-forms in their own right. They are however restricted to cinemas for the best viewing.

Television has had the greatest impact of all the mass media in the twentieth century. Its combination of speech and picture has a powerful attraction for viewers. It has the major advantage of bringing its messages into people's homes.

For these reasons, television has become a major medium for advertisers.

Organizations are increasingly using the mass media in their public relations exercises. These exercises are designed to create a positive image of the organization, and to establish and maintain an understanding between the organization and its public.

Many large organizations also aim their public relations exercises towards their own staff. These exercises are designed to create a good company spirit. Public relations staff use a wide range of media such as films, newspapers, television and radio. They also use brochures, letters, exhibitions, posters and conferences to create a good company image.

Key points

- The mass media are virtually one-way communication.
- Feedback is difficult to obtain. It is also delayed.
- The mass media overcome the barriers of time and space.
- The mass media are subject to gatekeeping.
- The mass media inform, persuade and entertain.

Introduction

Mass communication may be defined as the transmission of messages to a wide audience. These messages are transmitted rapidly and at a relatively low cost to the consumer.

Note that this definition covers five important points about mass communication:

1. The audiences are large, hence the term 'mass'.
2. The audiences are undifferentiated, because it is difficult to know the audience exactly.
3. Messages have to be reproduced.
4. Messages are distributed and delivered rapidly.
5. The cost is relatively low to the consumer.

The major differences between one-to-one and mass communication are that:

- Messages in mass communication are sent from the source to the receivers by means of intermediate channels such as radio, television and newspapers.
- Mass communication is virtually one-way communication, in that feedback is difficult to obtain.
- Any feedback is likely to be very limited and delayed.
- Feedback has to be sent through an intermediary channel such as the telephone line, or a letter to a newspaper.
- The source is inaccessible to the receiver.

Characteristics of print and electronic media

The print and electronic media such as newspapers, magazines, and television share two unique characteristics:

- They are able to overcome the barriers of time and space.
- The messages that they send out are subject to gatekeeping.

Overcoming barriers of time and space

The mass media, particularly television and the radio, enable people round the world to share experiences. News of distant events is quickly conveyed round the world. The result is that great distances are no longer such a barrier.

Messages subject to gatekeeping

The term 'gatekeeping' refers to the control of messages through selection and editing. The audience is, therefore, allowed to see, read or listen to what the Government, owners and business decide.

Each of these groups sets its own standards for:

- what messages contain
- how they are delivered.

Governments may try through laws and the courts to protect the interests of the public, particularly children. They may also try to control the media so that they can use them for propaganda.

Owners of newspapers, magazines and radio stations will also select the messages that they wish to send out. The ways in which these messages are sent out will also be carefully controlled. This gatekeeping will be done according to the owners' policies and their perceptions of the needs of their audiences. Messages must attract and be newsworthy.

Businesses need to advertise. They also wish to pursue public relations policies. They will therefore select the media and their messages very carefully. As they have to buy time and space, they may lay down conditions for the owners. They may, for example, refuse to support a television company if it sends out particular messages. This is, therefore, a type of gatekeeping.

Functions of the mass media

The major functions of the mass media are to:

- Inform
- Persuade
- Entertain

Inform

All the media seek to inform in some way. The diffusion or spread of information depends on the similarity of the receivers. The more similar they are in their beliefs, values, education and social status, the more effective will be the spread of information. The spread of information is often started by people called *change agents*. They are often responsible for creating change. However, such people may not share the same values as their audience. For this reason, they would normally work with an *opinion leader* who shares the values of a group and who is respected by them.

Persuade

All organizations need to persuade customers to use their services, buy their products or make donations. This persuasion is done through a wide variety of advertisements. These advertisements are designed to:

- attract people's attention
- create particular attitudes that lead to action

- persuade people to buy and continue to buy.

These advertisements are based on very careful audience analysis. This is called *demographic analysis*. Every organization has to analyse the needs of its customers very carefully. In addition, advertisements have to be targeted at specific groups.

Entertain

The mass media also seek to entertain. This function serves as a form of escape or diversion. This entertainment function attracts an audience and makes it worth an advertiser's while to advertise.

The mass media described

This section will briefly describe the most widely used mass media:

- newspapers and magazines
- radio
- film
- television.

Newspapers and magazines

Newspapers were originally written to inform. Now, however, they contain a range of content designed to inform, entertain and persuade.

Newspapers rely on the written word, pictures and graphics for their impact. They therefore need a literate audience. Circulation figures are very important for attracting advertising revenue. Newspapers therefore rely on eye-catching headlines, sensational pictures and news items to attract attention. Their readability also needs to be excellent.

Magazines are now targeted at audiences that are more specific than are the audiences for newspapers. Any organization wishing to advertise in a magazine will therefore have to understand its audience thoroughly.

Radio

Radio has been a popular and successful medium for many years. It is especially effective for a non-literate audience. It is also very useful for people who are busy doing work that stops them from viewing television or reading.

The radio is particularly useful for smaller, less wealthy organizations because advertising is less expensive.

Radio is most effective for advertising in which the visual impact is not important. Advertisements offering sales and discounts, for example, are successful over the radio.

Film

The film has become a major form of recreation and entertainment. Films are the most realistic of the mass media. They are often very creative and reach great artistic heights. They have reached a high technical quality, and can be very stimulating. Films are also shown in comfortable and pleasant surroundings.

For the above reasons, advertising films are often treated as art forms in their own right. They are a significant means of advertising, but are restricted to cinemas for the best viewing.

Television

Television has had the greatest impact of all the mass media in the twentieth century. Its combination of speech and picture has a powerful attraction for viewers. It also has a major advantage of bringing its messages into people's homes. For these reasons, television has become a major medium for advertisers. It is especially effective when the visual and the spoken are needed together.

However, because of its expense, companies have to ensure that their audience research is as accurate as possible.

Public relations

All organizations wish to make the public aware of what they have to offer. Apart from advertising their products, companies, for example, undertake public relations exercises. These exercises are aimed at creating a positive image of the company. They are a form of advertising designed to influence the attitudes towards and beliefs about the particular company.

Public relations exercises are designed to establish and maintain an understanding between any organization and its public. These exercises aim to foster trust in the integrity of an organization. They create and maintain an image for the company.

However, the public relations thrust is not only outwards. Many large companies now aim their public relations activities at their own staff as well. These activities have become more important as companies have grown larger. Senior management cannot hope to control or influence every individual in such organizations. Public relations activities are therefore aimed at fostering a good company spirit and a positive attitude towards its customers. Management knows that the reputation of the company built up over many years can be destroyed very quickly.

Public relations staff are involved in a wide range of activities. They:

- Explain an organization's policies.
- Deal with criticism and problems.
- Work with staff to create a positive attitude.

- Stress that the organization is socially aware.
- Stress the company's desire to serve the public and the customer.

These efforts have implications for the mass media. Public relations staff use a wide variety of media to convey their messages. They may, for example, provide speakers at conferences. They could also sponsor a wide range of activities aimed at maintaining and improving the company's image. These activities involve the use of a range of media. They could, for example be:

- brochures explaining the company's policy towards the environment
- films showing the company's contributions towards society
- advertorials in magazines showing how the company recycles all its waste products
- advertising on radio and television
- press releases to local newspapers
- letters to newspapers
- meetings to consult and inform the public
- exhibitions showing the company's activities
- conferences for people with special interests
- posters showing what the company is doing for its staff.

Implications for organizations

All organizations need to be aware of the impact and potential of the mass media. They need to be aware that:

- The general public is becoming well informed about companies' activities because of the mass media.
- They cannot make major decisions, particularly if they affect people or the environment, without consulting the public and advertising their intentions.
- They need to recognise the potential of the mass media to reach specific audiences quickly.
- They need to understand the needs and desires of their audiences.
- They need to undertake careful market research so that their advertisements and other public relations exercises reach the right audience.
- They need to understand that the mass media can help to build up and to destroy an organization.

Questions: Part 11

(Answers to these questions are given on pages 596–598.)

Points for discussion

1. What role can the mass media play in companies' public relations activities?
2. How does mass communication differ from interpersonal communication?
3. Explain why mass communication is described as one-way communication?
4. What are the three main purposes of the mass media? Give examples to illustrate your answers.
5. What are the two unique characteristics shared by the mass media?
6. What advantages does television enjoy over newspapers and the radio?
7. Explain the differences between the radio, film and newspapers in terms of their audiences.
8. Define the term 'Public Relations'.
9. Why do companies need to have public relations exercises?
10. What activities are public relations staff involved in?
11. What mass media do public relations staff use? How do they use them?

PART 12

Grammar, Usage, Sentence Structure and Punctuation

CHAPTER 22

Grammar, Usage, Sentence Structure and Punctuation

Summary

This chapter covers specific problems in the following areas:
- Grammar
- Usage.

It also sets out guidelines for sentence structure, punctuation and clear writing.

The particular areas of grammar and usage covered are rules for:
- number
- case
- participles and gerunds
- defining and non-defining relative clauses
- using 'and which'
- using 'shall' and 'will'
- 'can' and 'may'
- 'may' and 'might'
- 'its' and 'it's'
- sequence of verbs
- 'only' and 'even'
- the split infinitive.

Four different types of sentences are described with examples. They are:
- Simple sentences
- Compound sentences
- Complex sentences
- Compound — complex sentences.

Rules for punctuation are given. They cover:
- The full-stop
- The question mark
- The exclamation mark

- The colon
- The semi-colon
- The dash
- The comma.

Guidelines are given to help people write clearly and concisely. The chapter ends with exercises on grammar and usage.

GRAMMAR, USAGE, SENTENCE STRUCTURE AND PUNCTUATION

Introduction

This chapter has been designed to help you to avoid common grammatical errors in the following areas:

- Number
- Case.

It also covers advice on syntax, with particular stress on defining and non-defining relative clauses and the correct use of participles.

Advice on sentence structure is given. This advice is followed by some rules of punctuation.

The chapter ends with a range of exercises. Answers to these are given.

Rules of number

A verb must agree with its subject in number and person. A pronoun must agree in number, person and gender with the noun to which it refers.

The following rules should help you to avoid common errors in number.

Sentences marked with an asterisk are incorrect; all other sentences are correct.

1. *Singular subject, singular verb*
   The man is talking.

2. *Plural subject, plural verb*
   The men are talking.

3. *Two or more subjects joined by the co-ordinating conjunction 'and' require a plural verb*
   The boy and the man are talking. (Double subject)
   The boy, the girl and the man are talking. (Multiple subject)

4. *When the two subjects form a single thought or have a very closely related meaning, a singular verb may be used*
   My teacher and friend was present. (One person, not two)

5. *Nouns plural in form but singular in meaning require a singular verb*
   Physics is the study of heat, light, sound, mechanics and electricity.
   Mathematics is compulsory.

6. *Subjects plural in form, which indicate a quantity or number, require a singular verb when the subject is regarded as a unit*
   Ten miles is too far to walk.
   Two from five leaves three.
   Twice two is four.
   Five years is a long time to wait for any girl.

7. *Two or more plural subjects joined by 'or' or 'nor' require a plural verb*
   Either the clocks or the timetables are wrong.
   (Alternative subjects)

8. *Two or more singular subjects joined by 'or' or 'nor' require a singular verb*
   Either Mark or Graham is certain to be there.
   Neither Helen nor John was able to go.

9. *If the subjects differ in number or person, the verb agrees with the nearer.* If possible, however, avoid this type of sentence.
   Neither Jack nor the other boys know.
   Either they or I am at fault.

10. *When the subject and the complement of the verb 'to be' are of different numbers, the verb follows the number of the subject*
    Clouds are vaporized water.
    The stars were our only guide.
    Our only guide was the stars.
    Were the stars our only guide?
    Was our only guide the stars?
    The best part of the meal is the coffee and cigars.
    The coffee and cigars are the best part of the meal.
    What has been said is just words.
    What is needed is houses at rents that people can pay.

11. *Always use a singular verb after the expletive 'it'*
    It is the girls who must decide.

12. *After the expletive 'there' the verb is singular or plural according to the number of the subject that follows*
    In the meadow there stands a mighty oak.
    There exist no forces that can help us.

13. *Singular pronouns require singular verbs. These pronouns are singular: 'each', 'every one', 'everybody', 'any one', 'anybody', 'someone', 'somebody', 'no one', 'nobody', 'one', 'many a one', 'another', 'anything', 'either', 'neither'.*
    Each has to go alone.
    Someone is speaking now.
    No one skates better than Mary.
    Everybody has made this mistake.

14. *Note 'None' (literally 'no one') may be followed by either a singular or a plural verb. If a singular noun follows 'none of the', the verb is singular.*
    None of the sugar has been spilt.
    None of the apples have been eaten.

15. *A verb should not agree with a noun or pronoun that intervenes between it and the subject. Red herrings cause the mistakes in the following sentences:*
    – *Each of us are going. ('are' should be 'is')

GRAMMAR, USAGE, SENTENCE STRUCTURE AND PUNCTUATION 451

- *I think almost every one of the Judges of the High Court are represented here. ('are' should be 'is')
- *An immense amount of confusion and indifference prevail throughout the world. ('prevail' should be 'prevails')
- *The cause of all the requests and demands were not apparent. ('were' should be 'was')

16. *The following sentences are correct*
    I, with Robert and Jean, am going. (Singular subject, not a multiple subject. 'With' is not a co-ordinating conjunction but a preposition.)
    The boy, as well as all the members of his family, was determined to go.
    The teacher, accompanied by his pupils, has gone to the museum.

17. *A pronoun must agree in number, person and gender with the noun or pronoun to which it refers*
    Everybody is expected to contribute his or her share.
    Any one who wishes to may bring his or her own camera.

18. *Always use the correct pronoun*
    One does not forget one's own name. (The possessive of the indefinite pronoun is 'one's', not 'his'.)
    One of the children has dropped (his) (her) handkerchief. (Here 'one' is a numeral pronoun.)

19. *Relative pronouns referring to plural antecedents require plural verbs: relative pronouns referring to singular antecedents require singular verbs*
    There is *little* in his statements that bears on the case.
    Each of *those who are* there should play well.
    He is one of the most able *men who have* been in Parliament.
    This is one of the best flowering *shrubs that have* been developed in years.
    He is the *only one* of those present *who plays* well.

20. *A collective noun (noun of multitude) takes a singular verb when the group is regarded as a unit, a plural verb when the individuals of the group are regarded separately.*
    The crew has asked him to appear at the meeting.
    The crew are coming on board in a few hours.
    The family was named Brown.
    The family were seated on the lawn.

21. *If a collective noun is used with a singular verb any pronoun that refers to that noun must be singular too: if a collective noun is used with a plural verb any pronoun that refers to that noun must be plural too.*
    Either:
    The committee *adds* these words to *its* report.
    or

The committee *add* these words to *their* report.

Rules for case

The case of a noun or pronoun refers to the form that it takes if it is:
- subject
- object
- governed by a preposition.

This section deals with pronouns because their forms change. Nouns do not change their form.

Subjective case:
He chased the dog.

Objective case:
The dog chased *him*.

Prepositions

Pronouns governed by prepositions are in the *objective* case. Note the following examples:

*The dog was chased *by* him.*
Between you and *me*, I think that he is wrong.

Who/whom

Note the use of who (subjective case) and whom (objective case).

Who are those people over there? (Subjective)
Whom do you want? (Objective)

Rules for participles

Participles are described as verbal adjectives. They have the forms of verbs but act like adjectives. They may be present or past. The following examples illustrate each type:

Running (present) down the road, the boy fell.
Having run (past) down the road, the boy was tired.
Shattered (past) into many pieces, the precious vase was now worthless.

A participle must be related to the noun or pronoun to which it refers both grammatically and logically. This noun or pronoun must follow after the participal phrase. This phrase is marked by a comma.

Common errors are called *misrelated* and *unrelated* participles.

Misrelated participle

Walking down the road, she met him while she was riding a bicycle.

In the above sentence all the necessary words are present. However, they are in the wrong order. 'Walking' is misrelated to 'she'.
The sentence should read:

Walking down the road, *he* met her while she was riding a bicycle.

Unrelated participle

Wondering irresolutely what to do next, the clock struck ten.

In the above sentence there is no word after the participial phrase to which it can relate both grammatically and logically.

The sentence should read:

Wondering irresolutely what to do next, *he* heard the clock strike ten.

Gerunds, or verbal nouns

Gerunds are similar to participles in form. However, they act like *nouns*, rather than adjectives. The possessive form of a noun or pronoun is used with gerunds.

The following examples illustrate formal usage:

I am distressed at *your* going so soon. (In this sentence, the preposition 'at' governs the gerund or verbal noun 'going'. 'Your' is the possessive form of 'you'.)

They did not like *his* acting in such an arrogant way. (Here 'acting' is a verbal noun. 'His' is a possessive form.)

The *company's* dismissing so many staff in one month was regarded as a disaster. (Here 'dismissing' is a verbal noun. 'Company's' is a possessive form.)

Defining and non-defining relative clauses

A relative clause is an adjectival clause beginning with *who, which* or *that*. It refers to and describes a noun or pronoun.

The following examples illustrate these clauses. They are divided into *defining* or *non-defining* clauses.

Defining clauses are essential to the meaning of a sentence. They are also classified as *restrictive* clauses. Non-defining clauses give extra information. However, this information is not regarded as essential. Non-defining clauses are also classified as *non-restrictive* clauses.

The best way to show the difference between the two is to use *that*, whithout a comma, to introduce a defining clause. 'Which', with a comma before it, is used to introduce a non-defining clause.

Examples

This is the house *that* I bought in 1963. (Defining)
The house, *which* I bought in 1963, has since been altered. (Non-defining)
If 'who' or 'whom' is used then a comma shows the difference between defining and non-defining clauses.

Examples

The man who had a scar on his face was sought by the police. (This is a defining relative clause. It stresses that the police were looking for a man with a scar on his face.)

The man, who had a scar on his face, was sought by the police. (This is a non-defining relative clause. The stress is on the man. The other information is extra.)

Rules for 'and which'

Sometimes two defining or non-defining clauses are used in one sentence. The pair 'and that' or 'and which' should always *follow* a defining or non-defining relative clause.

The following example illustrates this rule:

I like the car that has a manual gearshift, and that is reasonably priced. (Both of these clauses are defining clauses.)

The following use of 'and which' is wrong.

They bought the vehicle at a low price, *and which* they thought was a bargain. (In this example the words 'and which' do not follow from another 'which' clause.)

Rules for 'shall' and 'will'

'Shall' and 'will' are parts of the verb 'to be'. They have different meanings when they are used with different personal pronouns. These meanings show:
- The plain future or simple future. (Future without determination or threat implied)
- The involved future. (Future, plus determination or threat)

The plain future is shown as follows:
- I shall
- You will
- He, she, it will
- We shall
- You will

GRAMMAR, USAGE, SENTENCE STRUCTURE AND PUNCTUATION

- They will

The above use stresses only what will happen in the future. There is no suggestion of determination or threat.

If, however, 'shall' and 'will' change places, then they are being used to express futurity plus determination or threat.

The involved future is shown as follows:

- I will
- You shall
- He, she, it shall
- We will
- You shall
- They shall

Examples

The following examples illustrate the different types of usage.

Plain future:

- I shall leave at five o'clock.
- They will travel to the city when they are ready.

Involved future:

- I will leave at five o'clock whether you are ready or not.
- They shall travel to the city in spite of the threats to stop them.

Rules for 'can' and 'may'

The formal rule is that 'can' has the meaning of 'capability', whereas 'may' has the meaning of 'permission'.

Examples

The company cannot issue the report because the copying machine has broken down. (Here the meaning is that the company is not able to)

The company may not issue the report until permission has been obtained. (Here the meaning stresses permission)

The company can issue the report, but the other companies involved are not yet ready. (This stresses ability)

The company may issue the report, now that all formalities have been completed. (This stresses permission)

Rules for 'may' and 'might'

'May' and 'might' are used to imply permission. However, 'might' is more tentative or hesitant.

Examples

May I leave now? (Here the speaker is asking for permission)
Might I ask you a favour if you are not too busy? (Here the speaker is asking permission, but the approach is more hesitant)

'May' and 'might' are used to refer to present or future possibilities. 'May' however suggests a serious possibility, whereas 'might' suggests a remote possibility.

Examples

We have only ten minutes to get there and it looks as though I may miss the train. (This stresses that there is a serious possibility of missing the train)

There is a remote possibility that we might not be able to get there in time, so we have brought extra food. (Note the stress on the remote possibility)

Past possibilities

When past possibilities are referred to, then only *might* should be used after a main verb in the past tense.

Example

The last time we stayed here we were warned that we might not be able to get a booking at the show.

'May have'; 'might have'

'May have' and 'might have' both show past possibilities. However, 'may have' suggests that the possibility still exists. 'Might have' suggests that the possibility no longer exists.

Examples

She may have been cured earlier, but she was given the wrong treatment. (This use of 'may have' suggests that she is still alive and is cured after receiving other treatment.)

She might have recovered from her illness had the doctors given her the right treatment immediately. (This use of 'might have' stresses the remote possibility of her living. It also stresses that she did not recover.)

Rules for 'its' and 'it's'

The meanings of 'its' and 'it's' are governed by conventions. The form 'its' without an apostrophe shows possession. The form 'it's' means 'it is' when an informal style is being used.

Examples

The company sold its shares. (This stresses that the company owned the shares)
It's not clear what happened. (Informal)
It is not clear what happened. (Formal)

Rules for sequence of verbs

If two verbs are used in a sentence each one should be complete.

The following example is wrong:

I cannot believe that he never has and never will *behave* in such a way. (Behave is correct after 'will', but not correct after 'never has')

This sentence should be re-written as follows:

I cannot believe that he never has *behaved* and never will *behave* in such a way. (Each verb is now complete)

Position of 'only' and 'even'

'Only' and 'even' are used to emphasize words or sections of sentences. They should be placed as close as possible to these words or sections.

Examples

He even worked at night in order to pass the examination. (This stresses that he worked at night)

Even he worked at night in order to pass the examination. (This lays the stress on 'he'. It implies that he is clever, but that he has to make a special effort)

Only that student passed his examination. (This stresses a particular student)

That student only passed his examination. (This stresses that the student passed, but did not do very well)

Not only . . . but also'

'Not only . . . but also' are called correlative conjunctions. They join two items together. These items should be kept as close as possible. The grammatical structures for each item joined should also be the same.

Examples

Compare:

At the end of the year, the company's trade in this country had *not only* increased far beyond the target, *but also* its overseas trade. (Here the section after 'but also' is incomplete.)

with:

At the end of the year, the company's trade *not only* in this country *but also* overseas had increased beyond the targets. (This version stresses that trade in this country and overseas has increased.)

The split infinitive

Formal usage often demands that an infinitive form such as 'to go' should not be split, as in 'to only go' or 'to seldom go'.

It is difficult to make a strict formal rule here because usage varies. Sometimes a split infinitive appears clumsy as in:

'Although critics have suggested that the company takeover was an attempt *to in some way save* it from insolvency . . . '. (Here the infinitive has been split.)

This split infinitive could be rewritten as:

' . . . an attempt *to save* it in some way from insolvency'. (Here the infinitive has been kept together.)

At other times the split infinitive does not appear jarring, as in:

'I did not intend *to even try* to copy what he had done.'

The safest rule is to avoid splitting the infinitive in formal writing, particularly if you know that you have a conservative reader.

Sentence structure

This section describes four major types of sentences that are useful in writing. A knowledge of these types of sentences should help you to improve your writing.

The simple sentence

This is a sentence with one clause in it. A clause contains a finite verb. This is a verb with a subject.

Example

The Manager called a meeting.

This group of words can stand on its own. The word 'called' is a finite verb with the subject 'Manager'.

Note:

The following groups of words are neither sentences nor clauses. They cannot stand on their own.

- *The manager being present at the meeting.
- *The marketing executive running the business.

The words 'being' and 'running' are not finite verbs. They do not have subjects. They could, however, be re-written as follows:

- The manager was (or is) present at the meeting.
- The marketing executive ran (or runs) the business.

They could also form parts of longer sentences as in:

- The manager being present, the rest of the team felt that they could not discuss the problem.
- They were an effective team, the marketing executive running the business while the others carried out the surveys.

The compound sentence

A compound sentence is a sentence that has two main clauses. The clauses are of equal value.

Example

The Town Planning Company did the general planning, and the Engineering Company worked on the details.

(Each clause could stand on its own as a sentence).

The complex sentence

A complex sentence has a main clause and at least one subordinate clause. The subordinate clause is of lower value.

Example

The marketing executive, who was well qualified, managed the company effectively.

(The main clause is 'The marketing executive managed the company.' The subordinate clause 'who was well qualified' is not essential to the sentence.)

The compound–complex sentence

A compound–complex sentence contains at least two main clauses and at least one subordinate clause.

Example

The Manager, who understood the techniques of computer-aided design, ran the team, and her partner, who was not as experienced, worked on a less complex project.

This sentence contains two main clauses:

- 'The Manager ran the team'
- '(and) her partner worked on a less complex project.'

There are also two subordinate clauses:
- 'who understood the techniques of computer-aided design'
- 'who was not as experienced'.

Rules for punctuation

Punctuation has a complex function today, but in general, the aim of punctuation is to indicate the logical structure of sentences. In addition punctuation is used to denote pauses in reading aloud. Punctuation should help one to express oneself in logical, clear language in essays, examinations and all business messages.

The full-stop

The full-stop needs no explanation, but errors in its use, or lack of use should be explained.

(*a*) The use of a full-stop where none belongs, e.g.:
- (wrong): The time drawing near when he was to appear on the stage. He lost his nerve.
- (right): The time drawing near when he was to appear on the stage, he lost his nerve.

(*b*) Omission of a full-stop where one is needed, e.g.:
- (wrong): The people searched the forest they could not find the thief.
- (right): The people searched the forest. They could not find the thief.

The question mark

1. The question mark is normally used at the end of a question in formal writing. Example: What supplies do we need to do the job?
2. Note that a question mark is not used at the end of an indirect question, e.g. He asked who she was.
3. There are occasions when a question mark may appear an internal punctuation, e.g.
   - in parenthetical use:
     e.g. Then Brown (have you ever known such a fool before?) picked up the letter and left the club.
   - to express doubt:
     e.g. Cataline, the Roman conspirator, was born in 108 (?) BC, . . .
   (Questions in series: Who came? Who saw? Who conquered?: that is what he said I needed to know . . .)
4. Question marks are used at the ends of *courtesy questions* such as:
   - Will you please let me know if I can answer any more questions?
   - Would you mind taking your feet off my desk?

GRAMMAR, USAGE, SENTENCE STRUCTURE AND PUNCTUATION

The exclamation mark

The exclamation mark should only be used after sentences or words denoting sudden or extreme emotion. There has been a recent tendency to use it indiscriminately, many people believing that an exclamation mark can amplify the most ordinary idea.

(Right): Quickly now! Jump before the boiler explodes!

(Wrong): Come to Noodnicks smash-bang, skip-the-limit, action-packed cash-o-valurama!!!

Note: Exclamation marks can be used:

- Within sentences, e.g. Poor child! he wanted to go.
- After interjections such as Oh! Help!

Internal punctuation

The colon

The colon is used

(*a*) To introduce the members of a set, e.g. I like the following vegetables: carrots, onions, leeks. (Use a colon only after a complete statement.)
(wrong) I bought: a box of matches, paper, etc.
(right) I bought the following items: a box . . .

(*b*) To introduce examples, quotations and explanatory material.
Example: The Manager resigned from the company: she was frustrated at the lack of opportunity.

The colon may be used with force of 'namely' or 'as follows'; e.g. The general stated that only three choices lay before us: to advance, to retreat, or to dig in.

Note: Modern writing usually lacks at least one of these distinctions because the semi-colon has usurped the place of the colon. For example, the semi-colon has taken over from the colon the role of dividing sentences in half; partly because the average sentence is much shorter than it was in earlier centuries.

The semi-colon

In general, semi-colons separate elements that are too gross for a comma, yet are not necessarily full sentences. The main uses of the semi-colon are:

(*a*) To separate the main clauses of compound sentences that are not connected by a conjunction or a conjunctive adverb.
Example: Certain spices were used as a medium of exchange; early traders were said to have . . . (This could have been written as two

separate sentences, but the semi-colon clarifies the relationship between them.)

(b) To separate main clauses when the second clause begins with a conjunctive adverb such as 'therefore', 'so', 'accordingly', 'hence', 'moreover'.
Example: Poetry is a more difficult art to master than prose; moreover it is an older art.

(c) To separate elements of a set or list if any of the elements contain commas.
Example: The building was filled with eager, nervous applicants; harrassed, irritable officials; and hard-pressed interviewers.

The dash

With the general loosening of English prose style, the dash has come to take over many of the jobs formerly reserved for the colon, semi-colon, and comma.

The dash is more forceful than the comma; it can be used to emphasize phrases that — when set off merely by commas — would not be so noticeable. The dash may be used:

(a) In place of the colon to introduce a list of explanatory remarks.
Example: The Browns brought their whole family — boys, girls, babies and dogs.

(b) To set off parenthetical expressions.
Example: Tom — the idiot — tried to tell her what to do.

(c) To set off phrases or words for the sake of emphasis.
Example: Would you believe it? They found her — asleep.

The comma

The use of commas is largely a matter of common sense. If they aid in the understanding of a sentence, put them in; if they do not, leave them out. Compare:

(a) These incidents, however, trivial in themselves, are liable to lead to more serious demonstrations.
These incidents, however trivial in themselves, are . . .

(b) To separate independent clauses connected by co-ordinating conjunctions.
Example: He went to Australia, and he never came back.

(c) To set off some word, phrase or clause that lies outside the main part of the sentence.
Example: Her father, whom she loved dearly, died last year.

GRAMMAR, USAGE, SENTENCE STRUCTURE AND PUNCTUATION

(d) To set off introductory dependent clauses preceding independent clauses.
Example: When you snore, I have trouble sleeping.

(e) To separate items on a list.
Example: He bought peaches, grapes, and plums.

(f) To indicate an important change in the normal word order.
Example: Like many romantics, he died young.

Writing clearly and concisely

The following rules should help you write clearly and concisely.

1. Avoid circumlocution

Circumlocution is an indirect or roundabout expression, writing and talking round a subject instead of talking about it in a simple, straightforward way. Be brief and to the point.

1.1 Prefer the single word

NOT	BUT
'in respect of'	'about', 'concerning'
'with regard to'	'about', 'concerning'
'with a view to'	'to'
'having regard to the fact that'	'as', 'because'
'on the supposition that'	'if'
'in the event of'	'if'
'in spite of the fact that'	'although'
'in reference to'	'about'
'with regard to'	'about'
'in many instances'	'often'
'on many occasions'	'often'
'in few instances'	'seldom'
'a few occasions'	'seldom'
'the majority of'	'most'

1.2 Be careful of the word 'case'

It is a common refuge of the lazy writer.

NOT	BUT
'in cases when'	'when'
'in many cases the children'	'many of the children'

Compare: In the case of boys and girls under the age of 16, weekly hours of work in factories are limited to 48.

Boys and girls under 16 are not allowed to work in factories for more than 48 hours a week.

1.3 Do not use a verb and a noun when a verb alone will do.

NOT 'He made the suggestion' BUT 'He suggested'
'He exercised an influence' 'He influenced'
'I am under the necessity of' 'I need to'

1.4 Do not use a verb and a phrase when a verb and an adverb will do.

NOT 'He behaved in a disagreeable way'
BUT 'He behaved disagreeably' 'He was disagreeable'

1.5 Particularly avoid roundabout expressions made with colourless abstract words like

nature	extent	degree	quality	description
sort	condition	character	kind	manner

NOT 'His work was of inferior quality'
BUT 'His work was inferior'
NOT 'His views were of an extraordinary kind'
BUT 'His views were extraordinary'

1.6 Avoid circumlocution involving the use of under-statement in a half-apologetic way in order to impress

NOT 'It is not without interest'
BUT 'It is interesting'
NOT 'not an inconsiderable amount'
BUT 'much'
NOT 'possessing an influence by no means to be despised'
BUT 'influential'
NOT 'not infrequently'
BUT 'often'
NOT 'not wholly unconnected with'
BUT 'with'

2. Avoid redundancy

Redundancy is the use of unnecessary words. Get rid of every word that has no work to do, or that is not pulling its weight, or whose omission would not mean the loss of anything significant.

2.1 Unnecessary emphasis of words

Words that can often be dispensed with are:

absolute	definite	perfect	distinct	quite
supreme	complete	exact	positive	remarkable

and their corresponding adverbs of degree.

This is (definitely) so.

I must have (complete) rest.

2.2 Unnecessary modifying or deprecatory expressions

The following words are usually superfluous:

more or less	to a certain extent	practically
for the most part	somewhat	approximately
possibly	probably	rather
a little	in my (humble) opinion	

Words like these should never be used to qualify emphatic adjectives. Do not say 'somewhat infinitesimal', 'rather infinitesimal', or 'somewhat unique'.

2.3 'As to' is seldom necessary

Remove it from a sentence and the meaning of the sentence will not be changed.

It is not clear (as to) what happened.

It is not certain (as to) where the ship will call.

I leave it to your discretion (as to) what course you should adopt.

2.4 Be careful when you use 'up' and 'up to'

You must face (up to) your problems.

2.5 Unnecessary repetition of the same idea (Tautology)

The wool profits were *again* made the subject of another attack by Mr Ellis last night. ('again' is not necessary)

The tribe faced *total annihilation.* ('total' is not necessary)

Her belongings *still remain* here. ('still' is not necessary)

They entered into a *joint partnership.* ('joint' is not necessary)

We are giving you the *true facts.* ('true' is not necessary)

This offer includes a *free gift.* ('free' is not necessary)

2.6 Phrases used to bridge awkward gaps or to give a little more time for thought; trite phrases and catchwords calculated in some way to save the writer trouble

If we examine the case carefully . . .

If I may be so bold as to hazard an opinion . . .

When all is said and done . . .

Let us consider . . .

Let us pass on to the next point . . .

You may take my word for it . . .

2.7 Phrases to get attention or emphasis

Look . . . To be frank with you . . .
You know what I mean . . . Personally . . .
I mean . . . Honestly . . .
You know . . . Literally . . .
Listen . . . I'm telling you . . .
See . . . As a matter of fact . . .
To tell you the truth, it looks like a tiger.

2.8 The stock adjective

The adjective that has been used so frequently with a particular noun that it has ceased to have any special significance.

sickening thud   *subdued* whispers
deafening roar   *uproarious* cheers
actual fact   at *long* last
feverish impatience

Many of these phrases are clichés or stock phrases.

Questions: Part 12

(Answers to these questions are given on pages 599–602.)

Points for discussion

1. What standards of grammar and usage should be set in organizations? Should errors be allowed in official written messages? Justify your answer.
2. Should organizations offer training courses in grammar and usage to staff who need them? What should these courses cover?
3. Should organizations provide written guidelines for effective business writing? What should such guidelines contain? Should they contain guidelines on grammar and usage? What should guidelines on grammar and usage contain?

Exercises

1. Select the correct verb or pronoun from the pair in brackets. Explain why you have chosen that word.
   - (*a*) Three programmers (is/are) necessary for this project.
   - (*b*) One programmer (is/are) all that you need for this project.
   - (*c*) The committee adds these words to (their/its) agenda when necessary.
   - (*d*) What you need (is/are) a pen and paper.
   - (*e*) A pen and paper (is/are) all that you need.
   - (*f*) Either they or I (are/am) wrong.
   - (*g*) A screen, a keyboard and some floppy disks (is/are) all that you need to start work.
   - (*h*) The crew (is/are) coming on board one by one.
   - (*i*) The director and three programmers (is/are) working on the project.
   - (*j*) The director, with all his helpers, (is/are) working on the project.
   - (*k*) They live in one of those expensive houses that (face/faces) the sea.
   - (*l*) Neither the clocks nor the timetable (is/are) wrong.
   - (*m*) Neither the clocks nor the timetables (is/are) wrong.
   - (*n*) Either the clock or the timetable (is/are) wrong.
   - (*o*) The tea and cakes (is/are) all you need for a good afternoon.
   - (*p*) All you need for a good afternoon (is/are) tea and cakes.
   - (*q*) They (is/are) going to town in the morning.

2. Select the correct verb from the pair in brackets — Explain why you have chosen that word.
   - (*a*) The man (is/are) programming the computer.

(b) They (is/are) working on the program.
(c) The director and his assistant (is/are) working in the computer room.
(d) The director and his assistants (is/are) working in the computer room.
(e) Either the director or his assistants (is/are) working in the computer room, but I'm not sure.
(f) Neither the director nor his assistant (is/are) working today.
(g) Neither the director nor his assistants (is/are) working today.
(h) The best part of the journey (is/are) the tea and cakes at the end.
(i) The tea and cakes (is/are) the best part of the journey.
(j) A screen, a keyboard and a computer game (is/are) all you need for a good afternoon's entertainment.
(k) The teacher, with all the pupils, (is/are) going to the match.
(l) The office staff (is/are) all going to the party in separate cars.
(m) The office staff (has/have) elected him to represent them as a whole at the conference.
(n) Six men and a piece of rope (is/are) all you need for a good tug-of-war.
(o) All you need for a good tug-of-war (is/are) six men and a piece of rope.
(p) Either he or she (is/are) wrong.
(q) Neither the girl, nor the boys (know/knows.)
(r) The crew (is/are) coming on board.

3. Fill in the correct forms of the verbs in brackets. Fill in the prepositions where indicated.
(a) They have (broke) the machine and can't fix it.
(b) He ... (broke) the machine before, but he hasn't (change) his method of operating it.
(c) When the operators had (go) home the cleaning crew (start) work.
(d) What have you (do) to these disks? They have not been (format) properly.
(e) Have you (calculate) the figures yet?
(f) They had (walk) for an hour before they (discover) that they had (take) the wrong road.
(g) She has (be) away since last week, but now she has (to come) back.
(h) Have you (work) out the wages program yet? We (to need) it ... the end ... the month.
(i) What did you (to find) out ... the new system? Can we (to adapt) it ... our needs?
(j) They (open) the container, only to find that they had been (to send) the wrong goods.
(k) They had (hope) to attend the conference, but had not (to be) able to.

GRAMMAR, USAGE, SENTENCE STRUCTURE AND PUNCTUATION   469

     (*l*) She (operate) the switch yesterday, but it did not (to work). Now it (work).
     (*m*) Whenever they (run) (past) the program the system (go) (past) wrong.
     (*n*) They had (complete) the program and had to test it before they (use) it.

4. Fill in the correct preposition.
     (*a*) We still have no information . . . his whereabouts.
     (*b*) . . . all he has done for you, I think he has treated you badly.
     (*c*) He persisted in going his own way, . . . my warning.
     (*d*) The bus came . . . the hill.
     (*e*) The secretary glanced . . . the list of names.
     (*f*) They hired a boat and went for a row . . . the river.
     (*g*) The accident was . . . the negligence of the signalman.
     (*h*) The fire started . . . the workmen's dinner hour.
     (*i*) Everyone . . . Smith answered the question correctly.
     (*j*) There were fifty-two people present, . . . the officials.
     (*k*) We have brought a present . . . him.
     (*l*) I am going into this shop . . . some sweets.
     (*m*) We have gone to all this trouble . . . nothing.
     (*n*) The motorist was fined . . . careless driving.
     (*o*) If you wish, we can deliver the goods . . . you.
     (*p*) He is a tall boy . . . eight.
     (*q*) I don't want a person like that . . . a neighbour.
     (*r*) We have been waiting . . . twenty minutes.
     (*s*) A meeting between the two Departments has been fixed . . . next Tuesday.
     (*t*) They made a rush . . . the exit.
     (*u*) The train . . . Cape Town leaves at 13h00.
     (*v*) We paid R5 . . . it.
     (*w*) I mistook him . . . his brother.
     (*x*) You may take my permission . . . granted.

5. Fill in the correct preposition.
     (*a*) He has won the prize . . . the third time.
     (*b*) Had it not been . . . the generosity of his father he would not have studied computer programming.
     (*c*) I long . . . the holidays.
     (*d*) I come . . . Durban.
     (*e*) . . . where we stood, we could see the sea.
     (*f*) It is 20 km . . . Simonstown to Wynberg.
     (*g*) The prices of these computers range . . . R10,000 . . . R20,000.
     (*h*) She took the money . . . her purse.
     (*i*) A lamp hung . . . the ceiling.

(j) All her life she suffered . . . headaches.
(k) We could not distinguish one keyboard . . . another.
(l) The parcel was wrapped . . . paper.
(m) They settled . . . a remote village.
(n) The house was . . . ruins.
(o) Shell House is . . . Cape Town.
(p) They stood . . . a queue.
(q) The child screamed . . . terror.
(r) It is all right . . . theory, but it won't work . . . practice.
(s) There was a curtain . . . the picture.
(t) I stepped . . . the door.
(u) They insisted . . . doing it . . . my warning.
(v) The manager promised to look . . . the matter immediately.
(w) The child was . . . its mother in looks.
(x) They lived . . . a house . . . the park.
(y) Mr Watson . . . Shell went . . . the computer course.
(z) Several . . . the staff climbed . . . the bus.
(aa) The driver . . . the car was drunk.
(bb) The robbed him . . . every cent.
(cc) The children made fun . . . him.
(dd) It is a matter . . . urgency that you attend to this.

6. Rewrite simply and concisely:
   (a) The special difficulty in the case of Mr Smith arises in connection with the fact that he is ignorant as to where he may be sent to work on any particular day.
   (b) Having regard to the fact that other powers are making increases in their armaments, it is high time that this country took the necessary steps to see that it is not left in a position of inferiority to other nations in this connection.
   (c) The factors of climate and geographical position must be taken into account as regards the determination of the character of a nation and both of them will be found to have an important bearing on the question.
   (d) In the opinion of authoritative circles at the higher levels it is considered that the situation is showing an increasing tendency to deteriorate.

7. Correct the following sentences. Explain why you have made the correction.
   (a) In this somewhat unique situation, I am not sure what to do.
   (b) I do not want to only go to the city.
   (c) Flying low, a flock of sheep was seen.
   (d) Being seven years old, my uncle invited me to a party.

GRAMMAR, USAGE, SENTENCE STRUCTURE AND PUNCTUATION

(e) They have a good team and which should be able to solve the problem.
(f) We have no reason to doubt that he will not be able to perform the task.
(g) In our report we have stated that he never has, and never will behave like that.
(h) We are surprised at you resigning so soon after joining the company.
(i) At the beginning of our financial year we found that our projected local expenses had not only increased beyond the budgeted amounts but also our overseas expenses.
(j) We are offering free gifts with every purchase.
(k) They were disinterested in the project, preferring to go to the beach instead.

PART

13

Intercultural Communication

CHAPTER 23

Intercultural Communication

Summary

This chapter covers the very important topic of intercultural or cross-cultural communication. The chapter starts with a number of key definitions of terms used in intercultural communication. The main terms defined are:

- intercultural communication
- ethnocentrism
- cultural stereotyping
- cultural relativity
- world view
- racism*
- affirmative action.

Major barriers to effective intercultural communication are listed below:

- defensiveness
- different world views
- different values and beliefs
- prejudices
- different languages
- different ways of using and interpreting the non-verbal code
- different ways of constructing messages
- unequal power
- failure to allow for individual differences within a culture.

A convergence model is used to show how intercultural communication may be understood and improved. This model stresses the importance of regarding communication as a negotiation of meaning.

The chapter ends with a description of 22 ways in which organizations can improve intercultural communication. The major ways are:

- creating an atmosphere of trust.
- encouraging people to value each other as individuals rather than as representatives of a culture.
- encouraging informal contact among staff.

- encouraging staff to accept differences and similarities among cultures in an open and honest way.
- helping staff to understand that there will be a great deal of variation among people from the same culture.
- helping staff to avoid stereotyping other cultures.
- encouraging communication on a basis of equality.
- helping staff to understand that world views differ.

Key points

- Cultural stereotyping and ethnocentrism are major causes of poor intercultural communication.
- People's world views differ. These differences need to be understood and respected.
- People need to understand the major barriers to intercultural communication.
- People need to recognize that there will be many individual variations within cultures. People from other cultures are not all the same.
- Cultures vary in their approach to constructing messages.
- Cultures vary in the ways in which they interpret non-verbal communication.
- Intercultural communication should be seen as a transaction, or a negotiation of meaning. Communication may not be perfect the first time.
- Companies can take a number of steps to ensure that intercultural communication is improved.

Important definitions in intercultural communication

The following definitions need to be studied and known. They are important for a good understanding of intercultural communication.

Culture

This term refers to systems of beliefs, assumptions and values that people share. This system acts as a set of rules that keep a group of people together. These people will share a view of themselves and of the world. They will use a shared symbolic code such as a language. (See pp. 54–57.)

Culture as applied to an organization

The word 'culture' as it is used in organizations refers to the sharing of a set of ideas, values and attitudes. These values and attitudes develop slowly over time. Members of an organization understand the cultural values of their organization once they have worked there for some time. These values hold the organization together.

However, a major problem may arise when people of a different culture start working in an organization. If the present culture of the company is not flexible enough, then the acceptance of different cultural groups may be difficult.

The climate needs to change first. After this, the culture of the organization will change slowly to accommodate the new intercultural situation.

Cultural relativity

This term refers to people's classification of other cultures in terms of the way in which they view their own culture. Such people are unable to understand the true nature of other cultures because they have a fixed way of describing another culture. This fixed way may be totally inaccurate, but they do not understand this. They judge other cultures as good or bad, from the point of view of their own culture.

Cultural mores

This term describes the customs and habits that cultural groups accept as right. These customs and habits will vary from culture to culture.

Cultural norms

Norms in a culture refer to what people in a culture value as the right way of behaving. These norms are learnt in a particular culture. They will vary from one culture to another.

Note

The term 'culture' has been used here instead of the words 'race' or 'ethnic group'. The word 'race' often has negative connotations. 'Ethnic group' has a similar meaning to 'race'. It is very difficult to make accurate generalizations about racial or ethnic groups. The word 'culture', as used here, suggests that there will be many variations within a racial or ethnic group.

Climate in an organization

This term describes the day-to-day atmosphere in an organization. It refers to the ways in which people behave towards one another. A climate in an organization may change fairly rapidly.

The climate in an organization is determined by the ways in which employees work together in their formal and informal encounters.

The climate will be created according to who speaks to whom, and by people's perceptions of the interactions. The climate will be affected by perceived differences in power between people. These perceived differences in power are especially important in intercultural communications.

If people of one culture perceive themselves to be in an inferior position, they are likely to be defensive. Good intercultural communication has a far greater chance of success between people who perceive themselves to be of equal status.

Affirmative action

Affirmative action is the process whereby organizations take special steps to help, train and employ people of a specific cultural group or cultural groups. These people may have been seriously disadvantaged because they were discriminated against or may have been disadvantaged because:

- they were not allowed access to good education
- they were prevented from having certain jobs
- they were denied access to post-school training and education because they did not have enough money.

Affirmative action could take the following forms:

- bursaries for education and training given to specific cultural groups
- posts in organizations given to people from specific cultural groups
- specific on-the-job training given to people from specific cultural groups.

Cultural stereotyping

This term refers to what people do when they describe people of a specific culture or ethnic group in a particular way. They will classify every member of a culture or ethnic group in the same way. They do not allow for individual differences within the culture that they are stereotyping.

People from one culture who describe another culture in this fixed way will behave as though their stereotyping is true. They may, however, have no evidence.

Such people will label every individual from the other culture in the same way. They may, for example classify another cultural group as lazy or dishonest. Any person they meet from this group will then be classified as lazy or dishonest even if they have no evidence to prove these classifications.

Ethnocentrism

This important term refers to people's unconscious belief in the superiority of their own culture. They believe that other cultures are inferior, even though they have no evidence or proof. They place their culture at the centre of their world. They then measure all other cultures in relation to their own and view them as inferior.

Racism

This describes the belief in the biological superiority of one group over another. A cultural group having racist views may regard other cultures as inferior. They will communicate with them using language and non-verbal communication that make their feelings of superiority clear to the other group.

Racism is based on ethnocentrism, prejudice and feelings of superiority.

A racialistic view may highlight differences between cultures. This approach could lead to conflict.

Intercultural communication

This is a special type of communication in which people from different cultures have to communicate one with another. These people from different cultures may have different ways of seeing the world.

This type of communication can make people very anxious and tense. They find it very difficult to understand other people's ways of thinking.

Intercultural communication involves a high risk. This is because we may have to give up strongly held ideas. We may also have to change attitudes which we regard as very important.

People involved in intercultural communication may be using different verbal and non-verbal codes. Even if they use the same codes, they may attach different meanings to them.

People will, therefore, have to negotiate meanings much more carefully. (See p. 4.) The results of any communication are less predictable. People could also find it much more difficult to plan accurately for other people's responses.

People tend to trust those with whom they share the same values.

Barriers to effective intercultural communication

'Barriers' refer to the ways in which communication is stopped or made difficult. The major barriers to effective intercultural communication are as follows:

- Cultural stereotyping
- Ethnocentrism (See definition.)
- Defensiveness (People are not open to new possibilities. They are reluctant to listen to new ideas. They refuse to change from past attitudes and styles.)
- Different languages
- Different ways of using and interpreting the non-verbal code
- Different ways of interacting (Some cultures place high value on being direct and getting to the point. Other cultures may value a less direct approach.)

- Different values and beliefs (People do not see the world in the same way.)
- Prejudices (People may, for example, have strong negative beliefs about another culture. They will, however, have no proof to support their prejudices.)
- Assumptions (People assume that certain things are true, even though they may not be.)
- Different ways of thinking (People from different cultures may think differently. One culture may, for example, value facts as proof. Another may value intuition as a way of arriving at a solution.)
- Unequal power (If people from different cultures have different levels of power in an organization, they may not communicate very well. A manager from one culture may perceive herself/himself as superior to workers from another.)
- Failure to allow for individual differences within a culture (People from one cultural group may view all people from another cultural group as the same. They do not accept that people are different. This attitude is the same as stereotyping.)
- Different world views (See definition. People holding different world views will find it difficult to communicate one with another.)

World view

A world view is central in any culture. The term refers to any culture's philosophical view of God, man, nature and the universe. This world view is taken for granted in any culture. It runs through all aspects of cultural life.

The African, Asian and European world views are examples. If good intercultural communication is to be achieved, then the world view of each culture needs to be acknowledged and accepted.

The African world view may, for example, value the concept of Ubuntu. This concept refers to the achievement of personhood through participation in the community. This view stresses that an individual has no value unless (s)he has strong connections with other people sharing the same culture.

The Western world view, on the other hand, may value individual enterprise. People are expected to take the initiative and make their own way in life.

Acculturation

This term refers to a person's ability to adapt to another culture. In an organization, acculturation means adapting to the corporate culture.

A convergence model of communication as a tool to understanding intercultural communication

A convergence model of communication is illustrated on page 19. This model is particularly useful for helping people to understand intercultural communication.

This model supports the view that good intercultural communication is a negotiation of meaning. This negotiation of meaning is especially important when people from different cultures are communicating face-to-face.

The sender from one culture encodes a message and speaks to a receiver from another culture. The receiver decodes the message but is not quite sure about the meaning. (S)he then encodes a message to clarify the original sender's message. In this way the two people exchange messages. They keep negotiating until they reach some understanding. This understanding may not be perfect. This is the reason why the sender's and receiver's ellipses on p. 19 overlap only partially.

The two communicators then continue negotiating as they strive to achieve better and better understanding.

The situation above assumes that both people are willing to communicate and have a positive attitude one towards each other. Problems arise, however, when their attitudes are negative. Problems may also arise if they do not understand each other's language.

There are many barriers to good intercultural communication. These have already been discussed and defined. Among the most important are:

- ethnocentrism
- cultural stereotyping
- defensiveness
- prejudice
- different verbal and non-verbal codes.

Intercultural communication often causes great anxiety. People find it difficult to get into people's ways of thinking. This type of communication involves a high risk because people may have to give up ideas that they have held for a long time. They may also have to change their attitudes.

People with different cultural backgrounds are less able to predict how their communication will turn out. They also find it more difficult to predict the other person's responses. Each person's world view might be challenged. In addition, people's verbal and non-verbal codes may be different.

People tend to trust others with whom they share values. People from different cultures may, however, feel that they do not share each other's values. This perception may place a great strain on their communication.

What can organizations do to improve intercultural communication?

This section lists 22 ways in which organizations can help improve intercultural communication. These cover both general and specific approaches.

1. Organizations should strive to create an atmosphere of trust. Trust could be created by helping all cultural groups to understand each others' world view and specific hopes and fears.

    Fear of another cultural group may generate dislike. Where there is dislike, people have greater difficulty acknowledging similarities with other cultures.

    Organizations need to encourage staff to respect other cultures' ways of experiencing life. They need to encourage staff to have a realistic approach to intercultural communication. Both differences and similarities need to be accepted and confirmed. Each cultural group should empower the other.

    Organizations should stress that people do not have to give up their own ideas if they appreciate and accept other people's ideas. All cultural groups in an organization should feel secure in their cultural identities. They should feel acknowledged.

2. Organizations should help people to accept differences between cultures in an open and honest way. They should stress that this acceptance will improve relationships and therefore improve the success of the organization.

3. Organizations should help staff to understand the transactional nature of intercultural communication. Staff should be encouraged to treat communication as a creation of meaning, or a negotiation. This approach will help staff to understand that communication may not be perfect the first time. They need to understand the barriers to effective intercultural communication.

4. Organizations should encourage staff to work at the individual, one-to-one level. People should be considered as individuals, rather than as members of a group. If only groups are recognized, then people seem to classify them as in-groups or out-groups. This approach is likely to encourage stereotyping and to keep prejudices alive.

5. Organizations should help people to learn about other cultures through the personal experience of individual relationships. It is difficult to gain an accurate idea of other cultures. This is why people rely on stereotyping, which may be inaccurate.

    If people work together as individuals, they rely less on information that they have gained at the general level about the other culture. Instead, they gain more genuine knowledge of the other person's nature, values and attitudes.

Organizations therefore need to encourage informal socializing.

6. Organizations should help people understand other people's values. People should become aware of the difficulties, hopes and fears that other people have.

7. Organizations need to stress that there is a great deal of variation within different cultural groups. People should be made aware of the dangers of making generalizations about other cultures.

8. Organizations should make staff aware that in intercultural communication members of cultures are seen as representatives of the whole group. An unfair burden would then be placed on one person to represent the group's point of view.

9. Organizations should, if possible, ensure that there are enough members of each cultural group present. In this way, people will begin to understand that there are individual differences within the group. They will then begin concentrating on the personal, rather than at the group, level.

   People should be helped to understand that there are very many differences within one culture. It is virtually impossible to make general statements about a culture that are totally accurate.

10. Organizations should approach intercultural communication problems directly. These problems should be discussed openly and honestly.

11. Organizations should make staff aware that differences in social class have a significant effect on the ways in which people perceive intercultural communication. People should be helped to understand that the same classes from different cultures may share a large number of values.

12. Organizations should make their staff aware that being rich or poor will have a great effect on how people view intercultural communication. Rich people will see things very differently from poor people.

13. Organizations should help staff to be aware that different occupations and age-groups will have an effect on intercultural communication.

14. Organizations need to make staff aware of the dangers of stereotyping when they interact with people of different cultures. Stereotyping should be openly and honestly discussed.

15. Organizations should encourage a positive attitude to intercultural communication. This attitude will stress that cultural differences are normal. A negative attitude, on the other hand, will stress the difficulties of intercultural communication. It will also stress the dangers of cultural differences. This attitude should be avoided. Organizations should strive to reduce defensiveness.

16. Organizations should do their utmost to change attitudes of superiority and inferiority. Equality in communication should be stressed.
17. Organizations should encourage people to build a sense of identity. Once people are confident of their identities they are more likely to accept others from different cultures. Organizations should strive to reduce fear of one culture for another.
18. Organizations should strive to overcome ethnocentrism. People should be helped to face the challenge of communicating with other cultures. People should be encouraged to interact with other groups.

    They should encourage the following types of contact:
    - equal-status contact
    - friendly person-to-person contact
    - contact in which all present strive to achieve the organization's goals.

    These goals are placed above cultural and individual goals.
    Organizations should provide the administrative support that enables the above contacts to take place.
19. Organizations should have affirmative action programmes. These programmes should go hand-in-hand with changes in attitude. If they do not, then affirmative action could become window-dressing.
20. Organizations should help people to understand that various cultures have different world views. These world views need to be understood and acknowledged in a non-judgemental way.
21. Organizations should help staff in very specific ways to understand different ways of communicating. In particular, staff should understand the following:
    - Different languages
    - Different approaches towards constructing messages. (The Western approach values getting to the point immediately. Other cultures view this as discourteous. They may value gathering all the issues relevant to the messages first and then getting to the point. At the personal level people may exchange pleasantries for a long time before getting to the reason for the meeting. A person with a Western approach would find this delay in getting to the point very irritating.)
    - Different interpretations of non-verbal communication. In particular the following differ from culture to culture:
        - attitudes towards touching
        - attitudes towards eye-contact
        - attitudes towards the amount of personal space one needs
        - attitudes towards the ways in which one's hands are used in conversation

- attitudes towards dress and levels of smartness
- attitudes towards time.

22. Organizations should strive to have a fair language policy. If possible, staff should be encouraged to learn other people's languages. In practice, this is not always possible because of the wide variety of languages spoken.

An international trend is to use English as the language of communication.

Some companies are using what is called controlled English. This is normal English, but with a carefully selected vocabulary of about 2 000 words. In addition, the grammar is normal English grammar, but only simple constructions are used.

Everyone in the organization would be expected to know and use this controlled English in writing and speaking. It is easy to understand because one word has only one meaning. There are two major advantages of using this type of English:
- It is easily learnt
- It is machine translatable with an accuracy of about 70 per cent.

Questions: Part 13

(Answers to these questions are given on pages 603–608.)

Points for discussion

1. What do you understand by the following terms:
   - ethnocentrism
   - cultural stereotyping
   - intercultural communication
   - racism
   - culture and climate in organizations
   - affirmative action
   - cultural relativity
2. From your own experience, discuss the major barriers to effective intercultural communication.
3. If two people of unequal power from different cultures communicate, what are the likely effects of this unequal power on their communication?
4. Discuss the term 'world view'. How will differing world views affect intercultural communication?
5. How may a convergence model be used to describe and analyse intercultural communication?
6. What can organizations do to reduce prejudices in intercultural communication?
7. What specific aspects of non-verbal communication are likely to be different when people from different cultures communicate?
8. How will different approaches to constructing messages affect intercultural communication?
9. What language policy should an organization adopt in order to improve intercultural communication?
10. What steps should organizations take to ensure that their affirmative action policies are successful?

Exercises

1. Work with a person from another cultural group. Ask that person how (s)he feels about communicating with people from other cultures. Pay special attention to non-verbal communication and to approaches to preparing messages.
2. Prepare a communication policy for an organization. This policy should ensure that intercultural communication is as good as possible.
3. Write guidelines for an organization that will help to ensure the success of its affirmative action policy.

4. Prepare a language policy for an organization. This policy should cater for the needs of the different cultural groups working in the organization.
5. Write guidelines for an organization that will help staff understand differences in non-verbal communication among staff from different cultures. These guidelines should be in the form of an in-house journal article.
6. Write an in-house journal article explaining the term 'world view'. Explain how differing world views affect intercultural communication.

PART 14

Answers to Questions

Please note:

The answers given in this section are intended as guidelines. They are not model answers. Students are expected to do their own reading and to investigate situations for themselves.

PART 1 (Chapters 1-2)

Points for discussion

1. *What do you understand by the statement that communication is a transaction?*

   Suggested answer

   The statement above stresses that people have to work together if they wish to communicate successfully. The word 'transaction' suggests that people have to negotiate in order to create a meaning that everyone finds acceptable. This approach to communication is two-way, rather than one-way. Both the sender and the receiver are responsible for the communication. The sender does not simply 'hand over' a message like a parcel that has to be 'unwrapped' by the receiver.

2. *How do people create meaning together?*

   Suggested answer

   People have to take responsibility as senders and receivers of messages. They have to ensure that two-way communication takes place. They also have to ensure that they agree on the meanings of the words that they use. They have to be prepared to give and receive feedback in an atmosphere of trust.

   The above statements apply to face-to-face communication. When people prepare written messages they should analyse the needs of their readers as closely as they can. They should also write clearly and simply, using words that the reader is likely to understand.

3. *What are the main conditions for successful communication in organizations?*

   Suggested answer

   People in organizations need to create an atmosphere of trust in which people feel free to communicate. They should strive to create an atmosphere in which two-way communication is successful. People should ensure that they share the same meanings of words and messages as a whole. They should strive to be sensitive to feedback, and to interpret this feedback correctly.

Managers in organizations should strive to create efficient communication networks that encourage feedback. They should ensure that people are not overloaded with information. People should be encouraged to pass on accurate messages. They should also be encouraged to distinguish between fact and opinion.

Finally, people should be encouraged to be sensitive to differences in cultural values, so that good intercultural communication takes place.

4. *What are the main differences between two-way and one-way communication?*

Suggested answer

In two-way communication the sender and receiver are involved in creating the message. In one-way communication, the sender prepares and sends a message without the receiver's involvement.

Because both sender and receiver are involved in two-way communication, they are likely to trust each other more. They are also likely to be less frustrated. In contrast, in one-way communication the receiver is likely to become frustrated because (s)he is not able to give feedback. The sender does not receive any feedback, and does not therefore know whether the message has been successful or not. In two-way communication, on the other hand, the sender receives feedback. (S)he is then able to gain a better idea of the success of the message. Greater trust is also built up between the sender and receiver.

5. *Is two-way communication better than one-way communication?*

Suggested answer

In most instances, two-way communication is better than one-way communication for the reasons given above. However, one-way communication is sometimes necessary. In an emergency, for example, a leader might have to give orders. If a company is facing a financial crisis, the Managing Director might have to take charge and take drastic steps to survive the crisis. Organizations also use intercom systems to broadcast messages to all staff. If one-way communication is used a great deal in organizations, it can, however, lead to great frustration on the part of the receivers.

Two-way communication, although it takes more time and is more risky, is better in the long run.

6. *Explain the main differences between intrapersonal, interpersonal and small-group communication.*

Suggested answer

Intrapersonal communication refers to the messages that we give ourselves. We talk to ourselves without saying anything out loud. We give ourselves constant messages both positive and negative.

ANSWERS TO QUESTIONS: PART 1 (Chapters 1–2) 493

Interpersonal communication refers to person-to-person communication. It refers particularly to two people communicating. This is called dyadic communication. Interpersonal communication also takes place in groups of more than two.

Small-group communication takes place when three or more people gather together. The communication becomes more complex as people work together to become a good group. If a group meets to solve problems then members of the group have to use interpersonal skills and problem-solving skills.

7. *What do you understand by the term 'public' communication? What are the differences between public and mass communication?*

Suggested answer

Public communication is the term used to refer to public speaking. The speaker addresses an audience by means of a prepared speech. Public communication differs from mass communication in the following ways:

- In public communication the sender and receivers are together when the message is sent. Two-way communication is therefore possible.
- In mass communication the sender and the receivers are not present in the same room. This means that mass communication is virtually one-way communication. The sender finds it virtually impossible to receive direct feedback.
- The audiences in public communication vary in number from a few to many hundreds. Senders are able to assess their needs fairly easily.
- The audiences in mass communication, on the other hand, are very large. Senders have great difficulty in assessing their needs.

8. *Explain the terms 'sender', 'receiver', 'message', 'medium' and 'channel'.*

Suggested answer

'Sender'   The sender of a message is the person, group or organization that starts off with any message.

'Receiver'   The receiver of a message is any person, group or organization that receives a message from a sender. This message will generally take the needs of the receivers into account.

'Message'   A message is any structured or unstructured information that passes from a sender to a receiver. A structured message, such as a report, will be aimed at a specific receiver. An unstructured message, such as non-verbal communication, will not necessarily be aimed at a specific receiver.

'Medium'   A medium is any means by which a message is sent to a receiver. A spoken message is sent through the medium of sound waves in air. A written message is sent through the medium of marks on paper.

'Channel'   A channel refers to any pathway by which messages are sent. For example, telephone and radio messages pass along special channels of communication. Radio and television messages pass along specific wave bands or channels. A speaker might depend on verbal or non-verbal channels of communication. The channels in this case would be the senses of hearing, sight and touch.

9. *What do you understand by the term 'barriers to effective communication'? Explain how breakdowns in communication occur.*

Suggested answer

Barriers to effective communication stop messages from reaching receivers. They also cause distortion in messages. Both senders and receivers introduce barriers into messages. A written message may, for example, be badly organized and poorly written. A receiver listening to a spoken message may be unwilling to listen carefully.

Breakdowns in communication occur because senders do not analyse the needs of their receivers correctly. Senders may also be unable to write or speak effectively. Receivers may not be able to read well, or may not understand the language used by the sender. Receivers may also be unwilling to listen with empathy. Both senders and receivers may be insensitive to non-verbal messages.

10. *How would you ensure the best possible communication between people of different cultures?*

Suggested answer

Establish an atmosphere of trust so that people are prepared to communicate openly. Encourage people to understand each others' cultural values. Strive to avoid attitudes of cultural superiority. Encourage understanding of the non-verbal communication of the different cultural groups working together. If possible, encourage the learning of each others' language.

PART 2 (Chapter 3)

Points for discussion

1. *How can companies organize themselves to ensure the best possible communication?*

   Suggested answer

   The managers who set up the communication systems in companies should strive to achieve the best possible upward, downward and sideways communication. They should ensure that all formal messages, such as reports and memoranda, are properly prepared. All communication networks should be clearly shown and understood. Managers should strive to ensure that messages are correctly passed from one level to another.

   People should be encouraged to pass on messages accurately. They should understand the difference between facts and opinions. People should also be encouraged to understand each other as accurately as possible. They should ensure that they share the same meanings of words.

2. *From your experience, what are the major barriers to effective communication in companies?*

   Suggested answer

   The major barriers to effective communication in companies are:
   - A defensive climate in which people do not trust others.
   - A desire to manipulate other people.
   - Poor interpersonal skills, in particular, poor listening, distorted perceptions of others and insensitivity to non-verbal communication.
   - Distortion of messages because people filter these messages as they pass them on.
   - Lack of understanding of what messages mean because people do not share the same meanings.
   - Inability to distinguish between fact and opinion.
   - Gatekeeping, in which people allow certain messages to flow through the communication channels, but block others.
   - Lack of intercultural understanding.
   - Overloading and underloading of message flows.

3. *Explain the terms 'vertical' and 'horizontal' communication in companies.*

   Suggested answer

   Vertical communication refers to upward and downward communication in a company. Upward communication refers to the communication of messages from the lowest ranks in the company to the highest. Downward communication refers to the communication of messages from top management down to the lowest ranks in the company.

   Horizontal communication is also called lateral or sideways communication. This type of communication occurs between departments of equal rank in a company. For example, the Personnel Department could communicate laterally with the Computer Department. Horizontal communication occurs across a company, rather than upward or downward.

4. *What is meant by the term 'grapevine' as it applies to communication in companies? Is the 'grapevine' a good or bad means of communication? Justify your answer.*

   Suggested answer

   The term 'grapevine' refers to the informal channels of communication in companies. People chat to each other and pass on informal messages in the form of gossip and rumours.

   The grapevine can be useful if the informal messages are based on facts and the truth. However, if the grapevine generates rumours that people act on without checking on the truth then it can be bad.

5. *How do you think people are motivated to work hard? Is it possible to motivate people? Give examples to back up your answer.*

   Suggested answer

   There are many theories of motivation. Some suggest that people's needs drive them to seek satisfaction. Maslow has, for example, suggested a hierarchy of needs that motivate people. Other theories stress that people perceive goals for themselves, and are prepared to work towards those goals.

   Hertzberg's theory suggests that salary and working conditions are not necessarily motivations. People are more likely to be motivated if they perceive their job as worth doing.

   People can be motivated to work hard, but Managers need to understand what their needs and goals are. They need to be helped towards full self-actualization, in terms of Maslow's hierarchy of needs. People should be helped to set themselves goals for which they are prepared to work. They must be given work that they perceive as worthwhile.

   A person might, for example, not be motivated to work very hard if (s)he perceives the work as worthless. Another person may have been set a goal. However, (s)he may feel that no matter how hard (s)he works (s)he will not be able to reach that goal. (S)he will not, therefore, be motivated to work hard.

6. *What is meant by the term 'intercultural communication'? How can companies ensure the best possible intercultural communication?*

   Suggested answer

   Intercultural communication refers to communication between people from different cultures. People from many different cultures are now working together in companies. In addition, many companies are involved in international trade. This means that people from many different cultures have to communicate.

   Companies can ensure the best possible intercultural communication by:
   - Creating a supportive climate in which people trust each other.
   - Encouraging understanding of different cultural values.
   - Encouraging free discussion on how different cultures view situations and approaches to communication.
   - Stressing that different approaches to communication are to be respected.
   - Encouraging discussion of different cultural values placed on non-verbal communication, particularly the use of time, eye-contact and the use of personal space.
   - Encouraging, where possible, the learning of languages spoken by other cultural groups in the company.

7. *Explain the terms 'overloading' and 'underloading' as they apply to information. How would you ensure that they do not take place?*

   Suggested answer

   Overloading refers to a problem when too much information is passed on to a person or department. The person or people involved cannot cope with all this information. The messages are either not passed on accurately, or they are simply ignored.

   Underloading refers to a problem when too little information is passed on to a person or department. The person or people involved may then not receive enough information to be able to do their work properly. They will become inefficient and bored.

   Managers should constantly analyse the directions and numbers of messages flowing upward, downward and sideways. They should check for underloading and underloading. If they find problems, they should devise new channels of communication. They should also discuss with staff how to cope with messages. In addition, staff should be trained in methods of efficient and effective methods of creating, sending and receiving messages.

8. *What is meant by the term 'network' in a company? Give examples of networks.*

   Suggested answer

   A network is any system by which messages are sent or received. A network of managers and staff will be organized so that all of them can send and receive messages along a fixed route. Each person knows with whom to communicate if a message has to be passed on.

   A Managing Director, for example, would send a message to his or her Deputy. This person would then send the message to the next person in the hierarchy. The message would eventually be sent to all the intended receivers. If feedback has been requested, this would be sent along the network until it reached the Managing Director.

PART 3 (Chapters 4–5)

Points for discussion

1. *What do you understand by the term 'organization'? Give examples of three organizations with which you are involved.*

   Suggested answer

   An organization is any group of people working together to achieve the goals of that organization. Individuals would not be able to achieve these goals on their own. In any organization, people do different jobs and have different responsibilities. Each post in an organization may be filled by a number of different people.

   An organization is divided into different sections. These sections depend on each other and work together to achieve the organization's goals.

   The following are examples of organizations:
   - A school
   - The postal services
   - A university
   - A municipality
   - A company

2. *Explain the differences between line and staff divisions in an organization.*

   Suggested answer

   Line staff are the managers who run the company. They make the decisions on the company's policies and goals. However, these managers often need the help of specialist staff so that they can make good decisions. These specialist staff may be experts in public relations, computers, marketing or personnel matters for example.

3. *How would you create an atmosphere of trust in an organization?*

   Suggested answer

   An atmosphere of trust is built up in an organization when Managers show that they are prepared to listen to employees' needs. They are prepared to do something about these needs. In addition, employees are encouraged to listen to each other and to acknowledge each others' worth.

   Open and honest communication is encouraged. Managers have to set the example here. They must be prepared to accept both positive and negative feedback. Managers should encourage employees to do the same.

4. *Explain Maslow's hierarchy of needs.*

   Suggested answer

   Maslow made two major assumptions:
   - People have basic needs. These are arranged in a hierarchy of importance. Only when the basic needs are satisfied are people ready to satisfy the next level of need.
   - Only needs that are unsatisfied can motivate behaviour. Once a need has been satisfied, it no longer motivates a person.

   Maslow identified five levels of need:
   - Physiological needs. These are the basic needs that sustain life, such as food and water.
   - Safety needs. These are the next level of need. They represent the need for protection from danger and job security.
   - Social needs. These refer to the need for companionship and acceptance.
   - Esteem needs. These refer to the need for self-respect and feelings of competence. They also refer to the need for esteem from others.
   - Self-actualization needs. These are at the top of the hierarchy. They refer to people's needs for self-fulfilment and the need to be creative.

5. *Describe four kinds of messages in organizations.*

   Suggested answer

   The four kinds of messages are:
   - Messages used to maintain good relationships
   - Messages containing information about tasks
   - Messages instructing people to do things
   - Messages about the goals, philosophy and ethics of the company.

6. *Describe six major barriers to message flow in a company.*

   Suggested answer

   Six major barriers are:
   - the number of stages through which a message has to go
   - the amount of time allowed for the message to move through the organization
   - lack of understanding of what the message means
   - shortening of messages because people cannot be bothered to share full information with others
   - filtering of messages at each stage
   - deliberate distortion of messages.

7. *Describe six kinds of groups found in organizations.*

   Suggested answer

   Six kinds of groups are:

   - people engaging in small talk
   - tension-releasing groups
   - learning groups
   - policy-making groups
   - problem-solving groups
   - decision-making groups.

8. *Explain what groups are like when they work well.*

   Suggested answer

   When groups work well, there is a supportive climate. People strive to be non-judgemental. They listen well and respect each other. They work towards the group, rather than individual goals.

   The members of the group work well together. Everyone is given a chance to be heard. Ideas are shared. In addition, members of the group use effective techniques to get the job done. They encourage the seeking and giving of information and ideas. They strive to reach consensus.

9. *Describe four leadership styles. Which style do you prefer? Why?*

   Suggested answer

   Four possible leadership styles are:
   - Autocratic
   - Democratic
   - Laissez-faire
   - Bureaucratic.

   The choice of leadership style will depend on the circumstances, the personality of the leader and the people involved.

10. *What are groups like when they do not work well?*

    Suggested answer

    If groups do not work well, there is a destructive climate in the group. People do not allow turn-taking. They also do not value each others' contributions. People try to manipulate the group for personal reasons.

    If groups try to maintain group cohesion at all costs, they could refuse to accept any ideas that might change the group's present position. They will refuse to think critically, and will accept only those ideas with which they can agree. They might also work under the illusion that everyone thinks as they do, and that their position can never be challenged.

11. *Describe the task and maintenance roles in a group.*

    Suggested answer

    The task role refers to what people in a group have to do in order to get the job done. The maintenance role refers to what people have to do to work well together.

    Examples of task functions:
    - suggesting new ideas or approaches
    - encouraging the seeking and giving of information and opinions
    - co-ordinating information
    - summarizing past discussions
    - testing to see if the group is ready to make a decision.

    Examples of maintenance functions:
    - encouraging members to share ideas
    - drawing out quiet members
    - ensuring that everyone has a chance to be heard
    - trying to overcome differences when they occur
    - stressing the value of every contribution.

12. *What do you understand by the term 'conflict'? Does conflict always harm a group?*

    Suggested answer

    Conflict occurs in groups when people do not agree on certain issues. They may also not like each other.

    Conflict may harm a group if it is allowed to be destructive. This occurs particularly if the conflict is allowed to continue at the personal level.

    Conflict may, however, be used constructively if the points of conflict stress the content of messages, rather than personalities. Conflict can be used to clear the air and to generate solutions to problems.

13. *Explain the differences between value conflict and content conflict.*

    Suggested answer

    Value conflict refers to conflict over people's fundamental views of life. This type of conflict is very hard to resolve because people are reluctant to change their values.

    Content conflict refers to conflict over facts, the interpretation of facts, as well as opinions. This type of conflict is easier to resolve provided that personalities are not involved.

14. *Explain the win–win approach to conflict resolution.*

    Suggested answer

    The win–win approach to conflict resolution stresses that both sides are satisfied at the end. They work together to achieve a solution to a problem.

ANSWERS TO QUESTIONS: PART 3 (Chapters 4-5) 503

Neither side tries to dominate the other. Metaphorically, both sides sit on one side of the table confronting the problem on the other side of the table.

15. *You have been appointed Chairperson of a group. You have to run an Annual General Meeting. What would your duties be? What would the duties of the Secretary and Treasurer be?*

    Suggested answer

    These duties have been listed in detail in Chapter 5. The following points summarize these duties.

    Duties of Chairperson

    Before the meeting, the Chairperson should:
    - ensure that an Agenda has been prepared
    - see that the Notice of Meeting has been sent out
    - ensure that the venue has been booked and that everything is ready for the meeting
    - prepare a Chairperson's report and send this out in advance.

    During the meeting, the Chairperson should:
    - ensure that the meeting is properly run
    - ensure that motions are properly put and seconded
    - summarize all decisions at the end of the meeting and ensure that people know what to do next.

    Duties of Secretary

    The Secretary has to draw up the necessary Notice of Meeting and Agenda. (S)he also has to send these out. During the meeting (s)he should write the minutes of the meeting. After the meeting, (s)he should see that all decisions are followed up, and that the Chairperson has been fully briefed.

    Duties of Treasurer

    A Treasurer has to keep records of all the financial transactions of the organization. (S)he should prepare a financial statement for presentation at the meeting.

PART 4 (Chapters 6-9)

Points for discussion

1. *Discuss and define the following terms. Give examples to illustrate your definitions.*
   - Intrapersonal communication
   - Selective perception
   - Frame of reference
   - Stereotyping
   - Dyadic communication
   - Assertiveness

   Suggested answers

   Intrapersonal communication refers to the messages that we give ourselves. We talk to ourselves without saying anything. For example, we might be anxious about an interview for a job in a week's time. We would then give ourselves messages about how we are going to behave at the interview.

   Selective perception refers to people's tendency to perceive what they want to perceive and to ignore what they do not like. For example, you might be listening to a speech containing sections that were both favourable and unfavourable to you. You would be inclined to pay attention to the favourable sections and ignore the rest.

   Your *frame of reference* refers to your system of values and attitudes. This system of values gives you a standard against which you can compare others' actions and ideas. You view the world through your frame of reference. Other people will have different frames of reference.

   Stereotyping refers to people's tendency to generalize about groups of people. For example you might stereotype a group of people as dishonest and lazy. When you meet one person from this group, you assume that that person is dishonest and lazy.

   Dyadic communication refers to two people communicating. Dyadic communication takes place, for example, when one person interviews another.

   Assertiveness refers to behaviour during which a person states her or his feelings and points of view confidently. This behaviour is, however, not at the expense of the other person. You might, for example, be angry with someone because of what she has done. If you wish to be assertive, rather than aggressive, you would say that you are angry and why. You would not, however, attack the other person.

2. *Discuss the effect that your positive or negative self-image has on the way you communicate.*

   Suggested answer

   If you have a positive self-image you will show this non-verbally. Your positive approach to communication will affect other people. They are likely to respond positively to you. If, however, you have a negative self-image you are also likely to show this non-verbally. People will then react negatively to you. This negative approach will affect the way in which you communicate with others.

3. *Discuss the concept of defensiveness. In what ways are people defensive? How does defensiveness affect communication?*

   Suggested answer

   Defensiveness refers to an attitude in which people are unwilling to receive feedback. If there is a defensive climate in a group, people will not be open and honest. People will try to manipulate others and will act in a superior way to other people's ideas.

   A defensive climate will quickly lead to lack of trust and to poor communication. People will not listen to each other.

4. *Discuss the following terms as they refer to the Johari Window:*
   - Open area
   - Hidden area
   - Blind area
   - Feedback
   - Levelling.

   Suggested answers

   The Johari Window is a model that helps people to understand their behaviour and attitudes in relationships.

   The open area refers to what people know about themselves and what others know about them. The hidden area refers to what people know about themselves but others do not. People keep these ideas, hopes and fears hidden from others.

   The blind area refers to what people do not know about themselves but which other people know about them.

   Feedback refers to the information that people receive about themselves and the messages that they send. Willingness to receive feedback is important in interpersonal communication. Levelling refers to what people do when they tell others about their hopes, fears and knowledge. People who are prepared to level with others are likely to communicate better.

5. *Discuss the term 'non-verbal communication'. What part does non-verbal communication play in interpersonal communication? Discuss the approaches of different cultures to:*
    - distance between people
    - eye-contact
    - time
    - touching.

   How could different approaches in the above areas affect communication in organizations?

   Suggested answers

   The term non-verbal communication refers to the messages that our bodies send out. These messages are conveyed by our eye-contact, our hand movements, the distances between people and the way we stand. Non-verbal communication is very important in interpersonal communication. One expert states that non-verbal messages are over 90% of the message in interpersonal communication. In face-to-face communication, we cannot stop communicating even if we say nothing.

   People from different cultures have different 'space bubbles' round them. A Western person might, for example, have a space bubble of about 1 metre. Someone from another culture might, for example, be happy to tolerate a much smaller space bubble.

   Some cultures value eye-contact in communication. Other cultures might, for example, value lowered eyes to show respect. People need to understand these different attitudes to eye-contact if they are to communicate well.

   Cultures view time differently. Some cultures view time as a straight line or a river. Once time has passed it cannot be recovered. Other cultures view time as circular. These cultures view time as renewable. If people with these different views of time work together they need to understand each others' views.

   Some cultures are classified as non-touch cultures. Other cultures tolerate a great deal of touching. If people with these two approaches to touching work together they need to understand these different approaches to avoid trouble.

   People from different cultures working together need to communicate their values to others. If they do not, other people could offend them without knowing. Different approaches to non-verbal behaviour need to be studied and made known. In this way people in organizations should be able to communicate more effectively.

6. *Discuss the term 'active listening'. What steps can you take to ensure that:*
    - you listen actively
    - you are effectively listened to?

ANSWERS TO QUESTIONS: PART 4 (Chapters 6–9) 507

Suggested answer

The term 'active listening' refers to listening during which you are totally involved with the speaker and the message. Active listening is both a mental and a physical process. You would listen for the facts and the speaker's emotions. You would lean forward to listen, and keep your posture alert. You would show that you were listening by giving verbal and non-verbal feedback. If you wish to be listened to, then you should prepare your message carefully. Be very clear in your mind what you want to say. Speak clearly and give your listener a chance to tune in to your accent. Use good eye-contact and effective hand movements to keep your audience listening. If you have a complicated message, summarize the key points at the beginning and the end.

7. *Discuss what is necessary to ensure a good job-interview. Discuss the interview from the point of view of the interviewer and the interviewee.*

Suggested answer

A good job-interview should be properly prepared. The room should be pleasant. A low table with easy chairs should, preferably, be used in a one-to-one interview. If a desk has to be used, the interview should take place across the corner of the desk.

The interviewer should prepare a checklist of the qualities desired in the successful applicant. (S)he should then prepare a set of questions for each stage of the interview. (S)he should make the interviewee welcome at the beginning of the interview. (S)he should state the purposes of the interview and give the interviewee an idea of the range of questions to be asked. (S)he should then take the interview through its various stages. At the end (s)he should give the interviewee a chance to ask questions. Finally, (s)he should state what is to happen next.

The interviewee should prepare for the interview by:
- trying to find out as much as possible about the organization
- preparing answers to questions that could be asked
- thinking clearly about why (s)he wants the job and about what (s)he can contribute to the company
- preparing some questions to be asked at the end of the interview.

The interviewee should arrive on time. (S)he should be well dressed and well groomed. (S)he should strive to answer questions openly and clearly. (S)he should pay attention to effective non-verbal communication.

8. *Give examples of open and closed questions. What are the advantages and disadvantages of each type?*

   Suggested answers

   Example of an open question: 'What do you think of the new financial policy?'

   This type of question demands a broad answer. The main advantages of this type of question are that:
   - it helps to show the interviewee's way of thinking
   - it helps to give the interviewee a chance to construct an answer
   - it shows how articulate an interviewee is
   - it helps to build up a good relationship because the questions do not imply a judgement.

   The main disadvantages of open questions are that they:
   - take time and energy to answer
   - make it more difficult to control interviews
   - make it difficult for the interviewer to record answers during the interview.

   Example of closed question: 'When did you start your studies?'

   Closed questions demand a restricted answer; even 'yes' or 'no'. Their main advantages are that they:
   - save time
   - allow the interviewer to control the interview
   - enable the interviewer to obtain exact information
   - help a shy interviewee to start talking
   - enable interviewers to ask a number of questions in a short time.

   Their main disadvantages are that they:
   - limit replies
   - can turn an interview into an interrogation
   - can make the interviewee defensive.

9. *What should a good letter of application contain?*

   Suggested answer

   A good letter of application should contain the following:
   - A clear subject-line stating the post applied for.
   - An opening paragraph that gives more details about the post.
   - A statement of the applicant's reasons for seeking the job.
   - A statement of what the applicant can do for the company.
   - A statement of the applicant's career objectives.
   - An indication that the applicant knows something about the organization.

ANSWERS TO QUESTIONS: PART 4 (Chapters 6–9)   509

- A reference to an attached curriculum vitae.
- Contact telephone numbers.

10. *What details should be put into a curriculum vitae? How should it be set out?*

    Suggested answer

    A curriculum vitae should contain the following details:
    - Personal details
    - School record
    - Post-school studies
    - Career to date
    - Job objectives
    - Career plans
    - Awards and scholarships
    - Sporting achievements
    - Interests and hobbies
    - Membership of professional organizations and offices held
    - Willingness to be transferred
    - Developed abilities at various stages of your career.

    A curriculum vitae should be highly readable. It should be set out with numbered headings and sub-headings. Lists, short sentences and short paragraphs should be used.

Exercises

7. *Evaluate the letter of application on page 149. Rewrite it to improve it.*

   Suggested answer

   The letter of application may be evaluated as follows:

   This is a poor letter because:
   - There is no subject-line.
   - The opening sentence is too abrupt.
   - The first paragraph stresses the writer's interests, rather than what the writer can offer the company.
   - The second paragraph does not give the applicant's career objectives. It simply stresses what the writer can gain from the job.
   - The writer does not refer to a curriculum vitae.
   - The writer does not give contact telephone numbers.
   - The writer ends off with 'Yours sincerely' instead of 'Yours faithfully'.

The letter could be rewritten as follows:

> The Recruiting Officer
> XYZ Company
> CAPE TOWN
> 8000
>
> Dear Sir/Madam
>
> <u>APPLICATION FOR POST OF SALES CLERK</u>
>
> I wish to apply for the post of sales clerk, as advertised in the Sunday Courier of 10 July 19—.
>
> I believe that I can make a contribution to your company because of my qualifications and experience in sales and marketing. In particular, my qualifications and experience in the following areas will enable me to contribute immediately:
> - My Diploma in Marketing and Sales from the ABC Institute.
> - My experience in marketing during the past three years.
> - My experience as a sales clerk in a supermarket over the last two years.
>
> I plan to pursue a career in sales and marketing, and am at the moment studying for a B.Com. degree part-time.
>
> I attach a curriculum vitae containing the names of three referees. These people may be contacted in confidence.
>
> My telephone numbers are:
> - Work (021) 567835
> - Home (021) 499233
>
> I am available for an interview at short notice.
>
> Yours faithfully
>
>
> P. SMITH

PART 5 (Chapters 10–14)

Points for discussion

1. *Explain the 'Rhetorical Situation'. What are the key factors that affect a message?*

   Suggested answer

   The 'Rhetorical Situation' refers to all the factors that have to be taken into account when a message has to be prepared.

   The following are the key factors:
   - the environment in which the message is being prepared, for example, a memorandum within a business, or a letter to another business
   - the purposes of the message
   - the type of audience, as well as the needs of that audience
   - the planning of the message
   - the way in which the message has been organized
   - the readability of the message
   - the vocabulary suited to the message
   - the style of the message
   - the level of formality of the message
   - the content of the message
   - the format of the message, for example memorandum, letter, report, talk.

2. *What is meant by the terms 'unity', 'coherence' and 'emphasis'? Give examples to illustrate your answers.*

   Suggested answer

   The term 'unity' refers to the need for one major theme to flow through a message. This major theme should be clear to the audience. A message should not jump from one idea to another without warning.

   The term 'coherence' refers to clear flow of sections, paragraphs and sentences in a message. Every section should flow into the next, and every paragraph and sentence should flow into the next. The audience should be able to follow this flow of ideas.

   'Emphasis' refers to the importance of highlighting the key issues in a message so that the audience knows immediately what they are. The points of major emphasis in a message are the beginnings and ends of messages.

3. *Give three examples of good links between paragraphs.*

   Suggested answer

   Paragraphs may be linked by means of:
   - linked ideas
   - a reference to the paragraph below
   - a reference to the paragraph above.

   Two paragraphs may, for example, cover aspects of letter writing. The theme of letter writing would then link the two paragraphs. A writer could also refer to the following paragraph by writing 'This aspect will be discussed in the following paragraph.'. (S)he could also refer to the previous paragraph by writing 'The paragraph above discusses the organization of messages. This paragraph will continue this theme in more detail.'

4. *Explain what a mind-map is.*

   Suggested answer

   A mind-map is a preliminary plan for a message. The sender starts with a blank sheet of paper. (S)he places the key idea in the centre of the page and then writes down related ideas around this central theme. Groups of related ideas are linked by lines. Each group of related ideas is linked to the central theme by means of a line.

   Once the mind-map is complete, the sender should select key ideas from the mind-map and arrange these into a topic outline.

5. *What is the procedure for preparing a topic outline?*

   Suggested answer

   A topic outline may be prepared vertically, down a page, or horizontally, across a page. A topic outline is an outline of key and supporting ideas arranged in a previously chosen order, such as general to particular, or particular to general. These key ideas or topics are numbered by means of a multiple decimal numbering system.

6. *Explain what is meant by vertical and horizontal plans.*

   Suggested answer

   A vertical plan is an outline of key and supporting ideas that is arranged down a page. A horizontal plan is an outline that is arranged across a page that has been turned so that the longest part of the page can be used.

7. *How would you define the term 'message'?*

   Suggested answer

   A message is any fact, idea or emotion passed from sender to receiver. Messages are normally organized with specific purposes and a specific audience in mind. These messages are organized into a format, such as a letter or a report. Non-verbal messages may differ from other messages in that they are not always sent deliberately.

8. *Explain how you would analyse the needs of an audience for a letter or report.*

   Suggested answer

   Ask yourself the following questions:

   - Is my audience a lay, expert, technical or mixed audience?
   - How many people are likely to be reading the message?
   - What is the gender of my audience?
   - What is the age of my audience?
   - What is the intelligence level of my audience?
   - What languages do my readers speak and read?
   - What is the occupation of my audience?
   - What is the position of my audience in the company?
   - What knowledge does my audience have about my topic?
   - Is my audience likely to be positive, neutral or negative towards my message?

   Once you have answered these questions to the best of your ability, prepare your letter or report.

9. *What are the points of major impact in a message?*

   Suggested answer

   The points of major impact in a message are the beginning and end of the message. Senders should strive to create a very good impression at the beginnings of messages.

10. *Explain why a business letter is organized in a diamond shape.*

    Suggested answer

    All letters should be well organized. The opening, or point of the diamond, contains the subject-line and the opening paragraph. This paragraph should prepare the reader for the message.

    The letter then broadens out to give more detail.

    Finally the writer brings the letter to a close at the other point of the diamond. This close should focus sharply on what action is to be taken. The writer could also focus on the main points in the letter.

    The top and bottom points of the diamond are the points of major impact of the letter.

11. *Why is a report shaped in the form of a pyramid?*

    Suggested answer

    A pyramid shape for a report enables a writer to organize the sections of a report so that each section gives more detail than the section above it. The base of the pyramid is the appendices. These give very detailed information. The top of the pyramid gives the summary. This is followed by the Introduction, Conclusions and Recommendations. The Findings of the report follow. The pyramid is completed with the Appendices.

12. *Why are newspaper articles and press releases written in the form of an inverted pyramid?*

    Suggested answer

    Writers use the shape of an inverted pyramid because newspaper articles have to give the main points of the message at the beginning. Readers often glance through a newspaper. They are likely to read the beginning of the message. That is why key points should be placed there.

    In addition, editors trim newspaper articles from the bottom up in order to fit them into the right space. Writers should be careful not to place key points at the end because they could be lost.

13. *Give six different ways of organizing information.*

    Suggested answer

    Information may be organized as follows:
    - General to particular
    - Particular to general
    - Causes to results
    - Time order
    - Space order
    - Simple to complex.

14. *How do words get their meanings?*

    Suggested answer

    Words get their meanings by the ways in which they have been used and are used. Words gain meanings in contexts. On their own words have no meaning. Dictionaries then record the ways in which words are used.

    Senders and receivers should always check that they share the same meanings of words.

15. *Explain the terms 'denotation' and 'connotation'.*

    Suggested answer

    The term 'denotation' refers to the basic meaning or dictionary definition of a word. The term 'connotation' refers to the suggestive qualities of a word.

    For example, if we were describing a person's weight we could say 'He weighs 100 kg'. This fact may be checked. However, we may also say 'He is obese' or 'He is grossly fat'. The words 'obese' and 'grossly fat' suggest disapproval of his condition. These words have strong connotations.

16. *What are four major functions of words in messages?*

    Suggested answer

    Four major functions of words are:
    - To give facts; for example, 'The tower is 50 metres high'.
    - To express personal feelings; for example, 'The tower is ugly'.
    - To persuade; for example, 'Invest in this fine project now'.
    - To express social feeling; for example, 'How are you' and 'I'm fine thank you'.

17. *Explain the differences between 'referential' and 'emotive' language.*

    Suggested answer

    'Referential' language is factual language. The sender tries to give facts, rather than opinions expressed about these facts. An example of referential language is: 'The letter contains six paragraphs'.

    'Emotive' language is language that expresses pure emotion or opinions about facts. The connotations of words are important. An example of emotive language is: 'She rode a magnificent horse'. The word 'magnificent' is emotive.

18. *What is the difference between 'generic' and 'specific' words?*

    Suggested answer

    'Generic' words make general, vague statements whereas 'specific' words give specific information. For example, the word 'building' is generic. It refers to a range of types. On the other hand, 'four-roomed single-storey house' gives more specific information.

19. *Explain what is meant by 'the ladder of abstraction'.*

    Suggested answer

    The ladder of abstraction is a hierarchy, or ladder of words. At the top of the ladder are the abstract words, such as 'labour'. These words give vague and subjective information. At the bottom of the ladder are specific, concrete words such as 'Fitter and Turner named Peter'.

A ladder of abstraction is arranged so that the words on the ladder become less and less abstract as they move down.

20. *What is the difference between 'concrete', 'relative' and 'abstract' words?*

    Suggested answer
    'Concrete' words refer to objects such as 'a desk', 'a chair' or 'a motor car'. These objects may be touched and measured. 'Relative' words are words that have different meanings for different people. They are classified as adjectives or adverbs. The words 'rich' and 'poor' or 'high' and 'low' have different meanings for different people. Abstract words such as 'labour' refer to abstract and vague ideas. These words are the most difficult to define and understand.

21. *What is meant by words that 'pre-judge' a situation?*

    Suggested answer
    Words that 'pre-judge' a situation suggest that the user has a specific attitude towards that situation. This attitude might make it difficult to communicate in that situation.

    A speaker might, for example, describe a meeting as 'boring' even before it starts. Someone else, referring to a man friend as a 'slob', pre-judges a situation. Others might then find it difficult to talk about the person referred to.

22. *Explain the differences between formal and informal words.*

    Suggested answer
    Formal words are used in formal situations, demanding carefully constructed and well written or well spoken messages. Informal words are used in less formal situations in which messages do not have to be as well constructed and written.

    The formal word 'man' could be used in a formal message. However, the less formal 'guy' or 'bloke' might be used in an informal message.

23. *What is meant by the following terms referring to style:*
    - high formal
    - formal
    - consultative
    - casual
    - intimate?

    Give an example of each kind.

    Suggested answer
    The above terms refer to five levels of formality in written and spoken messages. 'High formal' language is very formal language. The relation-

ship between the sender and receiver is not regarded as important. An example is 'It behoves the writer to offer an apology in this matter'.

Formal language is less formal than high formal language. The above example could be rewritten formally as 'I wish to apologize for what has happened'.

Consultative language is more friendly to the receiver. It is more suited to memoranda than letters. An example is 'I'm really sorry about what went on'.

Casual language is more suited to speaking than writing. An apology could, for example, be expressed as 'Sorry pal'.

Intimate language is generally only spoken. It is used by people who know each other very well. One could, for example, simply say 'Sorry' to the other.

24. *Explain the main differences between a personal and an impersonal style.*

Suggested answer

A personal style uses first personal pronouns 'I' and 'we'. It suggests that there is a close or friendly relationship between the sender and the receiver. An example of this style is 'I have pleasure in enclosing my report'.

An impersonal style uses the impersonal pronoun 'it'. This style suggests that there is not a strong relationship between the sender and receiver. The above example could be written impersonally as 'It is with pleasure that the writer encloses this report'.

25. *Explain the differences between an active and a passive style.*

Suggested answer

An active style stresses the doer of an action by placing the doer before the action-verb. This style stresses 'Who does what' as in 'The auditor checked the books'.

A passive style stresses that something has been done by someone. The above example could be rewritten passively as 'The books were checked by the auditor'.

26. *What is mean by 'tone' in messages?*

Suggested answer

'Tone' refers to the attitude of the sender to the receiver. This attitude is expressed by specific words in the message. The tone of a message may be friendly or unfriendly, or pompous or relaxed, for example.

A friendly tone could be expressed as follows: 'I have *pleasure* in attaching . . . '.

An unfriendly tone could be expressed as follows: 'We have *difficulty* in accepting that you knew nothing about the incident'.

27. *Give four elements of jargon.*

    Suggested answer

    Jargon refers to any language that is hard to understand. Four elements that make messages hard to understand are:
    - poor overall organization
    - long paragraphs
    - long, involved sentences
    - a difficult vocabulary of long words.

28. *What is meant by the term 'readability'?*

    Suggested answer

    'Readability' refers to the way in which a written message has been set out to make it easy to read. Readability is achieved by means of a number of techniques such as:
    - short paragraphs
    - short sentences
    - a numbering system
    - headings
    - the use of white space
    - the use of a simple vocabulary
    - good links between paragraphs
    - good links between sentences.

Exercises

1. *Evaluation of letter report*

    This letter report has a poor beginning and end. There is no subject-line to give focus to the report. The opening paragraph is too long. It gives the reader no idea why the report was written. In addition, it does not give the reader an overview of the report. This opening paragraph lacks focus. Is the writer simply reporting on the training course or is (s)he proposing action?

    The final paragraph is too vague. It does not propose action, but merely expresses an opinion. The writer does not make it clear how the model should be used.

    The letter report has been badly organized. The fourth paragraph starts 'In conclusion'. However, the letter carries on for two more paragraphs.

    The writer has written in an impersonal style, but has been clumsy in the first line. The word 'undermentioned' is clumsy here. The writer could have written 'On the 28th and 29th July the writer attended . . . '. (S)he could also have written 'On the 28th and 29th July I attended . . . '.

ANSWERS TO QUESTIONS: PART 5 (Chapters 10–14) 519

The letter-report has been badly set out. The readability is poor. The writer should have used short sentences, a short opening paragraph, and headings to guide the reader.

Suggested version

(Note that this version has been re-written to give the message a focus on action.)

Dear Mr Buthelezi

REPORT ON ABDS TRAINING COURSE – PROPOSED ACTION

I attended the eighth ABDS (Active Budgeting Directive System) training course at Head Office.

The course took place on 28 and 29 July. Six people attended this practical course, which comprised lectures and tests.

This course has convinced me that we should introduce the ABD System into the company.

ADVANTAGES OF ABD SYSTEM

The ABD System has the following advantages:

- It is an easy computer language to use.
- It is very English-like in quality.
- It is very useful for financial, accounting and investment work.
- It can be easily adapted for use in our Accounts Department for solving budgeting problems, especially in the areas of justifications for Expenditure Requests, payouts and the calculation of profits after taxes.

PROPOSED ACTION

I propose that:
- We introduce the ABD System into our Accounts Department immediately.
- We use Mr J. Snyder's model to get the system running.

---

2. *The ten items below are in random order. Rewrite them so that they make a coherent paragraph. Ensure that each sentence flows logically into the next.*

Suggested answer

The following order of items is suggested:

(*b*) The development of scientific thought has often led

(e) to conflict between the proponents of a new idea
(h) and those who follow the established belief.
(g) For example, Galileo, after studying the movement of the moons of Jupiter,
(a) concluded that the earth is a planet
(i) rotating round the sun.
(d) This conflicted with the current belief
(j) that the earth was the centre of the universe.
(e) In an effort to suppress Galileo's ideas
(f) the church had him imprisoned.

3. *Is the following passage coherent? Does one sentence flow logically into the next? Rewrite the passage to improve it.*

   Suggested answer

   The first four sentences of this passage are not coherent. They do not flow one into the other with good linking words. The second-last sentence is, however, fairly well linked to the last sentence.

   Suggested version

   (Note that linking sentences and words have been introduced.)

   Poor storage is potentially the most important source of hydrocarbon emissions in the petroleum refinery industry. Petrol is stored in specially constructed expanding tanks with floating roofs. These floating roofs have to have sealing elements between them and the tank wall, because they are usually 3 cm smaller in diameter than that of the tank. This 3 cm space is usually sealed by vertical metal plates connecting the braces to the floating roof. These vertical plates are fixed with a fabric seal extending from the top of the plates to the inner surface of the tank.

4. *Does the following passage have one unifying theme flowing through it? If it does not, what sentences should be removed?*

   Suggested answer

   This passage lacks unity. It is not clear whether the main theme is 'radar and bats' or 'people's reaction to bats'. The second and third sentences should be removed. If they were removed, the unifying theme of the passage would be 'radar and bats'.

5. *Replace the following words with simple everyday words. Try to use words with as few syllables as possible.*

Original Word	Everyday Word
detrimental	harmful
sufficient	enough
possess	have

numerous	many
remuneration	pay
endeavour (verb)	try
facilitate	help
ascertain	find out
utilize	use
indicate	show

6. *Rewrite the following sentences to improve them* . . .

   Suggested improved sentences

   - This author believes that the company policy may be wrong. (Active verb used.)
     OR I believe that the company policy may be wrong.
   - The Salespeople prepare these reports every Monday. (Active verb used.)
   - The Personnel Department is responsible for the success of this project. (Abstract noun 'responsibility' changed into a finite verb, with Personnel Department emphasized.)
   - A Committee determines the leave dates. (The words 'performs the function of' are unnecessary. 'Determining' has been changed to a finite verb.)
   - The staff reduced the inventory. (The abstract noun 'reduction' has been changed into an active verb.)
   - These reports agree with other evidence. (The abstract noun 'agreement' has been changed into a finite verb.)

7. *The following passage is written at a high level of abstraction. It also has some examples of jargon in it. Rewrite it simply and at a lower level of abstraction. Where possible, replace the general statements with factual statements.*

   This passage has been written simply and at a lower level of abstraction.

   > 'The firm must reduce the money that it spends by 50% in 1993 and 1994. The firm has made 30% less than it planned in 1992. This reduced profit has been caused by staff who did not have the right qualifications or experience for the jobs given to them. We have now appointed three qualified and experienced Chartered Accountants. They will start in 1993, and will help us to reduce our costs.'

8. *Rewrite the following extract from a letter to get rid of the jargon.*

This extract contains the following elements of jargon:
- esteemed favour
- 12th inst.
- refers
- no stone will be left unturned
- enclosed please find
- your goodself.

The letter could be rewritten as follows:

> 'Thank you for your letter of 12 July. I will investigate the incident involving one of our salespersons at once.
>
> I am most concerned about this incident, and enclose a gift token to show our concern. We greatly value your custom.'

9. *The tone of this extract is negative to the point of aggression. The writer implies that the customer is lying.*

Suggested version

> 'Dear Mr X
>
> We are most concerned that your Zing portable radio cannot pick up stations 40 km away.
>
> These radios should be able to pick up stations up to 100 km away. Please return your radio to your nearest agent with this letter. It will then be replaced with a portable radio to suit your needs.'

10. *Work out the fog index of the passage below. Rewrite it to a fog index as close to 9 as possible.*

Suggested answer

The fog index of this passage is calculated as follows:
- 106 words
- 3 sentences

- 35,3 words per sentence
- 22 long words
- 20,75% long words.

The fog index is: (35,3 + 20,75) × 0,4 = 22,4.
This suggests that the passage is very difficult to read.

Suggested version

> 'Early last week the Minister called a meeting between the private sector and the Department of Commerce. This meeting focused on problems in getting and saving fuel. The Government is very keen to reduce the use of the middle distillates.
>
> The use of types of fuels is not balanced. When crude oil is refined, some goes to petrol. Some also goes to the middle distillates such as diesel and paraffin for jet aircraft. Some also goes to heavy furnace oil.'

The fog index is calculated as follows:
- 80 words
- 7 sentences
- 11,4 words per sentence
- 6 long words
- 7,5% long words

Fog index: (11,4 + 7,5) × 0,4 = 7,56.

PART 6 (Chapters 15–16)

Points for discussion

1. *Discuss the range of your purposes when you are giving a talk (a) to a small group, (b) to a large group. Link these purposes to a lay, expert and mixed audience.*

   Suggested answer

   Your purposes when you are giving a talk to a small group could be:
   - to inform
   - to persuade
   - to explain (lay and mixed audience)
   - to entertain
   - to present arguments for and against certain technical issues (expert audience).

   Your purposes when you are giving a talk to a large audience could be:
   - to inform (lay and mixed audience)
   - to persuade
   - to entertain
   - to argue a case (technical audience).

2. *Discuss the range of your purposes when you have to give an oral report to a small group of experts.*

   Suggested answer

   Your purposes when giving an oral report to a small group of experts could be:
   - to inform
   - to persuade by means of facts and conclusions drawn from those facts
   - to record the results of an investigation
   - to propose specific action.

3. *How would you prepare a talk or oral report? Discuss each stage in detail. Pay special attention to your planning methods.*

   The following approach is recommended for preparing a talk or oral report.
   1. Decide on your purposes.
   2. Analyse the needs of your audience.
   3. Decide on your format.

ANSWERS TO QUESTIONS: PART 6 (Chapters 15-16) 525

4. Prepare a mind-map of your key and supporting ideas.
5. Select your ideas that you want to use, as well as supporting ideas.
6. Prepare a horizontal topic outline keeping in mind the beginning, middle and end of your talk or the sections of your oral report.
7. Plan your information to achieve good first and last impressions.
8. Plan your visual aids.
9. Plan the timing of each section.
10. Write your main ideas on cue cards.
11. Rehearse before an audience so that you can be given feedback.
12. Adjust your talk or oral report once you have had feedback.

4. *Discuss the meaning and significance of the following terms:*
   - horizontal topic outline
   - initial credibility
   - derived credibility
   - terminal credibility.

   Give examples.

   (*a*) A horizontal topic outline is a very important planning method. This is called a horizontal outline because it is prepared across a page, rather than down a page. All the information is placed side by side, rather than one item under the other.

   (*b*) Initial credibility refers to the credibility that is conferred on a speaker by his or her audience at the beginning of a talk.

   (*c*) Derived credibility is the credibility that a speaker gains during his or her presentation.

   (*d*) Terminal credibility refers to the credibility given to a speaker at the end of a presentation. This credibility could be different from the speaker's initial credibility.

5. *Discuss a range of techniques that you would use to:*
   - start a talk
   - start an oral report
   - end a talk
   - end an oral report

   A speaker could start a talk using one or more of the following techniques:
   - Asking a question to gain attention.
   - Referring to current events that link with the topic.
   - Using an unusual statement or statistic.
   - Showing a diagram, picture or object.
   - Stating the main points of the talk.

   A speaker could start an oral report by using the following techniques:
   - Giving the Terms of Reference or instructions for the report.

- Stating why the audience should listen to the report.
- Briefly describing the background to the report.
- Giving the purposes of the report.
- Summarizing the key findings.
- Summarizing the main conclusions and recommendations.

A speaker could end a talk by using one or more of the following techniques:

- Summarizing the main points.
- Appealing for action.
- Asking a challenging question.
- Using a quotation, statistic or vivid illustration to sum up the main idea.
- Reminding the audience why the key points are important to them.

A speaker could end an oral report by using one or more of the following techniques:

- Stressing the key recommendations for action.
- Summarizing the main findings.

6. *What techniques would you use to hold the attention of your audience in the middle of your presentation?*

A speaker could use some of the following techniques:

- Attracting and re-attracting the audience's attention with good non-verbal communication with particular stress on good voice variety, hand movements, eye-contact and the way in which (s)he stands.
- Presenting very well organized material.
- Using audio-visual aids to back up key points.

7. *Explain the following approaches to persuasion. Give examples to illustrate each approach.*

- logical appeal
- psychological appeal
- personal appeal.

Speakers use logical, psychological and personal appeals in persuasion.
A logical appeal uses facts as the basis for persuasion. The speaker could, for example, use specific examples as the basis for making a general statement. (S)he could also use a deductive approach. This approach starts with a general approach and then uses specific examples to back it up.

    A psychological appeal is based on the audience's needs, desires and motives. This appeal stresses the benefits to the audience.

    A personal appeal is based on the speaker's reputation and credibility.

ANSWERS TO QUESTIONS: PART 6 (Chapters 15–16)

8. *If you know that your audience is hostile to you, how would you organize your arguments?*

   Organize your message so that you start with points with which they can agree. Then move to your point of view. In addition, make sure that you give both sides of your argument. Always stress the benefits to your audience.

9. *You have prepared your talk, and now have to present it. What techniques would you use to gain and keep your audience's attention?*

   You could use the following techniques to gain and keep your audience's attention.

   - Make sure that you give a good first impression.
   - Prepare your listeners for your presentation by summarizing your main points at the beginning.
   - Use good non-verbal communication. Pay special attention to the way in which you stand, your eye-contact, your hand movements and your voice.
   - Use audio-visual aids to back up your statements.
   - Present a very well organized talk or report.
   - Appear sincere and concerned about your audience.
   - End by going over your main points.
   - Pay careful attention to your dress and grooming.

10. *Discuss the advantages and disadvantages of the following audio-visual aids:*
    - the overhead projector
    - the chalk or white board
    - the flip chart
    - the 35 mm slide projector
    - the tape recorder.

    Suggested answers
    The overhead projector

    Advantages:

    - It can be used with the lights on.
    - It is suitable for large or small venues.
    - The speaker can remain facing the audience.
    - The speaker can prepare transparencies in advance or build up a message during the talk.
    - Transparencies can be stored and re-used.

    Disadvantages:

    - It is subject to power failures and broken bulbs.
    - A good screen at the correct angle is essential for presenting the best images.

The chalk or white board

Advantages:
- It is easy to use.
- The speaker can build up a message during the talk.
- It can be used in a large or small venue.

Disadvantages:
- A white board can take on a glare if the lighting is wrong.
- Poor handwriting and a badly prepared message for the board can destroy the visual impact.
- The speaker is tempted to turn his or her back to the audience while writing on the board.

The flip chart

Advantages:
- It is easily portable.
- It does not need power, and so can be used inside and outdoors.
- The speaker can prepare messages in advance.

Disadvantage:
- It is not suitable for a large audience.

The 35 mm slide projector

Advantage:
- The slides are very attractive and can hold the audience's attention.

Disadvantages:
- The speaker can lose contact with the audience when the lights are turned down.
- It is subject to power, bulb and mechanical failures.

The tape recorder

Advantage:
- It is very effective for illustrating speech or other sound effects.

Disadvantage:
- It will not give very good quality reproduction, especially for a large audience, unless the equipment is of very good quality.

11. *How would you handle the following types of questions?*
    - A very complex question with three parts to it.
    - A question that shows that the questioner has not been listening.
    - A question that has a false inference in it.

- A question that is emotionally loaded.
- A question that is off the point.

A speaker could handle the types of questions below, using the following approaches:

- A very complex question with three parts to it.
  Repeat each part of the question to make sure that you understand each part. Then answer each part as carefully as you can. If necessary, ask the questioner to repeat each section of the question.
- A question shows that the questioner has not been listening.
  Answer the question politely or ask the questioner to stay behind afterwards so that you can then answer the question. Do not be rude to the questioner by pointing out that (s)he has not been listening.
- The question has a false inference in it.
  Politely point out that you would rather not answer the question as it stands because of the inference. Ask the questioner to rephrase the question.
- The question is emotionally loaded.
  Politely point out that you would rather not answer the question as it stands. State why, and ask the questioner to rephrase the question.
- The question is off the point.
  Ask the questioner to stay behind at the end so that you can then answer the question.

12. *What telephone techniques would you use if you had to handle a large number of incoming calls?*

If you had a large number of incoming telephone calls, you could use the following techniques:

- Strive to use your voice so that you sound friendly, interested and concerned.
- Keep in mind that each caller should be treated with the same level of courtesy.
- Keep all callers informed if you have asked them to hold on.
- Write down the key points of each call and read back these points.
- End each call on a positive note.
- Strive to attend to the needs of every caller.
- State what action you are taking.
- Always show that you are listening by making listening noises.
- Ask prompting questions.
- Control calls by being assertive.

13. *What techniques would you use if you wished to be assertive, rather than aggressive or submissive over the telephone?*

If you wish to be assertive over the telephone, use the following techniques:

- Handle the call positively.
- Control the call by using the caller's name.
- Use questions to prompt the caller.
- Speak confidently.
- Do not respond submissively by saying 'I don't suppose I can be of any help.'
- State clearly and confidently what you are doing about any problem.
- End the call on a positive note.

14. *What rights do you have as a telephone user?*

As a telephone user, you have the following rights:

- to know to whom you are talking
- to say that it is inconvenient to take the call at that moment
- to state your needs
- to have your needs properly listened to and responded to
- to ask a range of questions to prompt the caller
- to have your questions answered promptly and efficiently
- to be told what the other person expects of you
- to refuse a request without feeling guilty.

Exercises

Please note that there could be a wide variety of answers to these questions. Only general suggestions have therefore been given below.

1. *You have been asked to give an eight-minute talk on the presentation of persuasive messages. State your purposes, select an audience and prepare a horizontal topic outline. What aids would you use?*

   Suggested audience: A group of 20 salespeople who use a variety of techniques, including talks to specialist members of staff in companies.

   Suggested purposes: Your purposes could be to inform, and to persuade your audience that your suggested techniques are worth using and to entertain your audience with examples.

   Suggested visual aids: Transparencies to give the audience a broad overview of the talk, as well as specific information, flip chart paper to record any reactions from the audience and to write down specific examples. These examples may then be used for revision at the end of the talk.

   Your horizontal topic outline could be prepared as follows. Note that it is not complete.

Introduction	1st Key Point *Logical appeal*	2nd Key Point *Psychological appeal*	3rd Key Point *Personal appeal*	Conclusion
• Importance of using correct techniques of persuasion • Overview of talk to decide on purposes • Analyse needs of audience	• Base logical appeal on reasoning • General to particular • Particular to general	• Base psychological appeal on needs of audience • Stress what the audience will gain from listening to you	• Base personal appeal on your credibility	• Go over main points • Urge audience to use these techniques
(1 minute)	(2 minutes)	(2 minutes)	(2 minutes)	(1 minute)

2. *Analyse the following questions in terms of their difficulty. Explain how you would handle each one.*
   - 'This post calls for long periods away from your family. You don't mind being away do you?'
     – This is a leading question. The questioner is trying to force the listener to say 'No I don't mind'.
     – The listener should state politely that (s)he feels forced to answer in a particular way. (S)he should ask the questioner to re-phrase the question.
   - 'Our company's social upliftment programme is excellent. Would you be for or against spending 50% of our budget to help the wretched people of . . . '.
     – This is an emotionally loaded question. You, the listener, might not agree that the people in question are wretched. You could state politely that you do not agree that the people in question are wretched. You could then ask the questioner to rephrase the question.
   - 'Why do you follow these procedures for answering telephones, when will you consider changing them and what changes will you bring in?'
     – This is a multiple question. Repeat each part to the questioner to ensure that you have heard it correctly. Then try to answer each part separately.
   - 'How can you make your staff more contented so that they will become more reliable?'
     – Point out that this question suggests that there is an implied connection between 'contented' and 'more reliable'. Point out that there is no guaranteed connection. State that you do not wish

to answer the question as it is. Ask the speaker to rephrase the question.

3. *Prepare an outline for an oral report on your investigation into a specific problem.*

A vertical topic outline for an oral report on problems of absenteeism could be prepared as follows. Please note that this outline is not complete.

```
1. Introduction
   1.1 Brief statement of Terms of Reference
   1.2 Main purposes of report
   1.3 Overview of key findings, conclusions and
       recommendations
2. Major findings
   2.1 Absenteeism caused by illness
   2.2 Absenteeism caused by lack of transport
   2.3 Other reasons for absence
3. Major conclusions
   3.1 . . .
   3.2 . . .
4. Major recommendations
   4.1 . . .
   4.2 . . .
```

4. *Prepare an eight-minute persuasive talk aimed at your Board of Directors. You want them to change from a 40-hour working week to a 45-hour working week. What logical and psychological techniques would you use? How would you establish and maintain your credibility?*

You could use the following logical techniques:
- Make a general statement about the value to the company of a 45-hour week.
- Back up this general statement with facts that you have drawn from your reading and from interviews with people in other companies.

You could use the following psychological techniques:
- Stress that a 45-hour week is in the interests of your company.
- Stress what the Board of Directors will gain from it.
- Stress the needs and aspirations of members of the Board.

You could establish your credibility by showing that you have researched the problem thoroughly. You could also show that you are well prepared.

Make sure that you keep up a high standard of presentation. End strongly by expressing your enthusiasm for a 45-hour week. Stress that it is in the interests of the Board of Directors.

ANSWERS TO QUESTIONS: PART 6 (Chapters 15–16)

5. *You have been asked to prepare guidelines on writing bad-news letters. Prepare three overhead transparencies to back up your talk.*

   The following transparencies could be used:

   - TRANSPARENCY 1:
   This could be used during the Introduction.

   WRITING BAD-NEWS MESSAGES

   - Important to maintain goodwill of receiver
   - Show that the writer cares
   - Use a direct or indirect approach
   - Neutral opening called buffer
   - End with a statement of goodwill

   - TRANSPARENCY 2:
   This could be used to illustrate your first main point.

   WRITING BAD-NEWS MESSAGES —
   THE DIRECT APPROACH

   - Neutral subject-line
   - Thanks – buffer paragraph
   - Sorry
   - Because — reasons for refusal
   - Goodwill at end

   - TRANSPARENCY 3:
   This could be used to illustrate your second main point.

   WRITING BAD-NEWS MESSAGES —
   THE INDIRECT APPROACH

   - Neutral subject-line
   - Thanks — buffer paragraph
   - Because — situation in company described
   - Sorry
   - Goodwill at end
   ---

6. *You have been asked to prepare guidelines for good telephone techniques in your organization. Write out these guidelines, paying special attention to:*

- Creating a good first impression
- Stages in handling calls
- Being assertive
- Managing calls
- Taking notes
- Ending on a positive note.

The guidelines could be presented as follows. Note that these have been given in outline only. You are expected to fill in the details.

GUIDELINES FOR GOOD TELEPHONE TECHNIQUES

1. Introduction

- These guidelines should be read by all staff who have to answer the telephone regularly.
- They have been designed to help you answer the telephone efficiently so that you help to maintain our good company image.
- These guidelines have been divided into six sections:
  - Creating a good impression
  - Stages in handling a call
  - Being assertive
  - Managing calls
  - Taking notes
  - Ending on a positive note.

2. Creating a good first impression

- State the name of your company.
- Say who you are.
- Ask if you may help.
- . . .

3. Stages in handling a call

Handle each call in four stages:
- Stage 1: . . .
- Stage 2: . . .
- Stage 3: . . .
- Stage 4: . . .

4. Being assertive

Being assertive means that you control calls without being rude. You state your point of view, but not at the expense of the other person.
. . .

ANSWERS TO QUESTIONS: PART 6 (Chapters 15–16)

> **5. Managing calls**
> Manage calls as follows:
> - Speak confidently.
> - Ask what the problem is.
> - . . .
>
> **6. Taking notes**
> - Prepare a standard notepad (example attached).
> - Take notes during conversation.
> - . . .
>
> **7. Ending on a positive note**
> - Always try to end on a positive note that leaves a good impression.
> - . . .

7. *Write a circular for all staff in your organization, setting out the rights of telephone users.*

This circular could be presented as follows: Note that this is incomplete. You are expected to fill in the details.

> ```
> To:     ALL STAFF
> From:   J. SMITHERS
>         PERSONNEL OFFICER
> Date:   10 January 19—
> ```
>
> SUBJECT: THE RIGHTS OF TELEPHONE USERS
>
> As a result of many requests, I have prepared the following set of points on the rights of telephone users. These rights cover both callers and receivers.
>
> <u>Your rights</u>
> All callers and receivers have the following rights:
> - To know to whom they are talking.
> - To say if it is convenient to take the call at that moment.
> - To state their needs.
> - To have their needs properly listened to.

- To ask a range of questions to prompt the caller.
- To have their questions answered promptly, efficiently and courteously.
- . . .

If you have any comments on this list or any suggestions for improving it I would welcome them.

J. SMITHERS

PART 7 (Chapter 17)

Reports

Points for discussion

1. *What is meant by the following terms:*
   - Terms of reference
   - Conclusions
   - Recommendations
   - Findings?

   Suggested answer

   The *Terms of Reference* of a report are the instructions given to the investigator who writes the report. These instructions, also called the Brief, should contain the following:
   - Who instructed the writer
   - When the writer was instructed
   - Exactly what the investigator was asked to do in point-form
   - When the report has to be handed in.

   The *Conclusions* of a report are the implications drawn from the findings or facts. They are also the insights gained from the facts.

   The *Recommendations* of a report are the proposed actions to be taken as a result of the findings and conclusions.

   The *Findings* of a report are the facts that have been established as a result of the investigation.

2. *What is meant by the pyramid approach to the setting out of reports?*

   Suggested answer

   If the sections of a report are set out in the form of a pyramid, they are organized so that each section gives more detail than the previous section. The base of the pyramid is the Appendix Section. This gives the greatest detail.

   The report pyramid is organized as follows:
   - Summary
   - Introduction
   - Conclusions

- Recommendations
- Findings
- Appendices.

3. *Explain the following types of reports:*
   - Informative
   - Investigative
   - Feasibility
   - Interim
   - Summary.

Suggested answer

An *Informative* report gives the facts of a situation. Somebody might, for example, be reporting on her attendance at a conference. An *Investigative* report gives the results of an investigation into a problem. It could include conclusions and recommendations. A *Feasibility* report gives the results of an investigation into whether something should or can be done or not. It could include conclusions and recommendations.

Interim reports are reports written before a project has been finished. They inform readers of the progress of a project. A *Summary* report is a short report containing the main sections of a report. These sections contain the key points only.

4. *How would you set out the facts in a report?*

Suggested answer

The facts in a report should be set out in a highly readable way. They should be expressed in referential, rather than emotive language. These facts should be divided into numbered sections with headings and sub-headings. The writer should use short sentences, short paragraphs and a simple vocabulary. Facts could also be set out in the form of tables, graphs and illustrations.

5. *What language would you use in the Conclusions and Recommendations of a report?*

Suggested answer

The Conclusions should be expressed in a mixture of relative, concrete and abstract words. They may also be expressed in emotive and referential language, as in 'The writer concludes that the computer system is faulty'.

The Recommendations are expressed in terms of action. The action-words should be written in the imperative form, such as: 'Construct the road . . . ' or 'Reduce the number . . . '.

ANSWERS TO QUESTIONS: PART 7 (Chapter 17) 539

6. *What style would you use when writing a report?*

    Suggested answer

    A report should be written in an objective, referential and impersonal style. This style may, however, change in the Conclusions, as suggested in Question 5 above.

7. *What techniques would you use to make a report as readable as possible?*

    Suggested answer

    The writer should use some or all of the following techniques:

    - Very good organization
    - A multiple decimal numbering system
    - Headings and sub-headings
    - White space
    - Short paragraphs
    - Short sentences
    - A simple vocabulary
    - Key points highlighted
    - Very good layout.

Exercises

1. *You have been asked to investigate customers' complaints about a certain product in a local supermarket. Write a report.*

    There are many different ways of approaching this report. The suggestions below are therefore in outline form only.

    Suggested answer

    TERMS OF REFERENCE

    On the 23rd January 19— Mrs L. Simons, Head of the Customer Services Department, instructed the writer to investigate customers' complaints about Doggo tinned pet foods at the Fancy Supermarket.

    Mrs Simons was concerned about the quality of these pet foods because she had received 23 complaints. Mrs Simons' specific instructions were:

    - to investigate the complaints about Doggo canned petfood
    - to record and analyse these complaints
    - to draw conclusions about whether the complaints are justified or not
    - to recommend specific action
    - to report by 10 February 19—.

SUMMARY

This report describes the results of an investigation into complaints from 23 customers about Doggo canned petfood . . .

(Then give the main points of the following sections of the report in the order below:
- Background
- Purposes of report
- Procedure used to gather information
- Conclusions
- Recommendations
- Findings.)

TABLE OF CONTENTS

Section	Page
Terms of Reference	i
Summary	ii
List of Illustrations	v
1. Introduction	1
2. Conclusions	3
3. Recommendations	5
4. Results of investigation into complaints about Doggo canned petfoods	7
4.1 Complaints about amounts in tins	7
4.2 Complaints about quality of food	10
4.3 Complaints about smell of food	12

1. INTRODUCTION

   1.1 Background to Investigation

     . . .

   1.2 Purposes of Report

     . . .

   1.3 Scope and Limitations of Report

     . . .

   1.4 Procedure used for Gathering Information

     . . .

   1.5 Plan of Development of Report

     . . .

ANSWERS TO QUESTIONS: PART 7 (Chapter 17)

---

2. CONCLUSIONS

   As a result of the findings of this investigation, the writer has drawn the following conclusions:

   2.1 <u>Complaints about amounts in tins</u>
   . . .

   2.2 <u>Complaints about quality of food</u>
   . . .

   2.3 <u>Complaints about smell of food</u>
   . . .

---

3. RECOMMENDATIONS

   As a result of the findings and conclusions of this report, the writer recommends the following action:

   3.1 <u>Quality control of Packing</u>
   . . .

   3.2 <u>Quality of Food</u>
   . . .

   3.3 <u>Smell of Food</u>
   . . .

---

4. RESULTS OF INVESTIGATION INTO CUSTOMERS' COMPLAINTS ABOUT DOGGO CANNED PETFOODS

   4.1 <u>Complaints about amounts in tins</u>
   . . .

   4.2 <u>Complaints about quality of food</u>
   . . .

   4.3 <u>Complaints about smell of food</u>
   . . .

---

2. *Evaluate the example of Conclusions and Recommendations.*

   Suggested answer

   These Conclusions and Recommendations should not have been written together. They should have been written as two separate sections. As they stand, they are muddled, confusing, and difficult to read. In addition, they have been written in the first person, and in an informal style.

The following rewritten version is suggested:

---

2. CONCLUSIONS

As a result of the findings of this investigation, the writer has drawn the following conclusions:

2.1 Cause of fire.
     The fire was caused by an electrical fault in the paint store.

2.2 Condition of main pillars.
     The main pillars are sound. They will not have to be replaced.

2.3 Replacement of asbestos roof.
     The asbestos roof will have to be replaced.

2.4 Replacement of three main roof beams.
     Three of the main roof beams will have to be replaced because they are twisted.

---

3. RECOMMENDATIONS

As a result of the above conclusions, the writer recommends as follows:

3.1 Re-wiring of Factory.
     Re-wire the whole factory.

3.2 Installation of smoke detectors.
     Install sixteen ABC Smoke Detectors in the places shown on the attached sketch.

3.3 Non-smoking area.
     Ban all smoking in the factory building.

3.4 Replacement of roof.
     Replace all the cracked asbestos roofing sheets with new asbestos sheets, rather than with corrugated iron.

3.5 Replacement of twisted roof beams.
     Replace the three twisted roof beams with beams of the same type. The twisted beams are shown in the attached sketch.

ANSWERS TO QUESTIONS: PART 7 (Chapter 17)

3. *Evaluate the findings section of the given report and rewrite it using better headings and a multiple decimal numbering system.*

   Suggested answer

   Note that this has been given in outline form only.

---

1. REPORT ON ADMINISTRATIVE AND MAINTENANCE ACTIVITIES

    1.1 ADMINISTRATIVE ACTIVITIES

    1.1.1 Staffing position
    . . .

    1.1.2 Trade Union Matters
    . . .

    1.1.3 Safety Incident Reports
    . . .

    1.2 MAINTENANCE ACTIVITIES

    1.2.1 Mechanical problems in soap making section

    (a) Soap washing machine 2 has been damaged irreparably. It will be rebuilt by the ABC Company by the end of February 19—.

    (b) Soap washing machine 1 has been sent to the XYZ Company for changes to three water pipes. It will be returned by 30 October 19—.

    (c) Soap washing machine 3 will be kept running until Machine 1 is returned.

    (d) Soap making machine 1 was repaired by the ABC Company on 20-7-92. It is now running well.

    (e) Soap making machine 2 will be repaired by the ABC Company by 30 October 19—.

    (f) Protective plates have been made, and are being fitted to the soap wrapping machine to protect workers.

4. *Evaluate the given example of a summary report.*
   Rewrite it to improve it.

   Suggested answer

   Note that the rewritten version has been given in outline only.

   The Terms of Reference are too vague. The precise instructions were not given. In addition, the writer has written in a personal style, using 'we'.

   The synopsis or summary does not reflect the sections of the report. The synopsis should replace the report for the busy reader. The synopsis should give the main points from each major section. In addition, the synopsis has been written in a personal style.

   The Introduction should be numbered. The description of the background to the report is too brief. The purposes of the report should be given in more detail. In addition, the writer should have given more detail about the procedures used for gathering information. The plan of development of the report is too brief. The writer has not described the scope and limitations of the report.

   The Conclusions should be numbered and divided into sections with sub-headings.

   The Recommendations should also be numbered and divided into sections with sub-headings.

   Outline for rewritten version

   ```
   TERMS OF REFERENCE
   Mr X asked the team comprising A, B, and C on 25
   January 19— to do the following:
   -  . . .
   -  . . .

   SYNOPSIS
   This report describes the results of an investiga-
   tion into why materials dyed with Stayfast Fabric
   Dye do not keep their colour. Conclusions have been
   drawn and recommendations made.

   (The writer should then give the main points of The
   Introduction, Conclusions, Recommendations and Find-
   ings.)
   ```

ANSWERS TO QUESTIONS: PART 7 (Chapter 17)

> 1. INTRODUCTION
>   1.1 <u>Background to the investigation</u>
>   . . .
>   1.2 <u>Purposes of the report</u>
>   . . .
>   1.3 <u>Scope and limitations of the report</u>
>   . . .
>   1.4 <u>Procedure used for gathering information</u>
>   . . .
>   1.5 <u>Plan of Development of Report</u>
>   . . .
>
> 2. CONCLUSIONS
>   As a result of the findings of the report the following conclusions have been drawn:
>   2.1 <u>Washing in clothes washing machines</u>
>   . . .
>   2.2 <u>Method of manufacture of dye</u>
>   . . .
>
> 3. RECOMMENDATIONS
>   As a result of the conclusions drawn, the writers recommend as follows:
>   3.1 <u>Test of materials</u>
>   . . .
>   3.2 <u>Test of Dyes</u>
>   . . .

Letters

Points for discussion

1. *In what ways may letters be used as ambassadors for an organization?*

   Suggested answer

   Letters may be used as ambassadors for organizations in the following ways:
   - They should express goodwill towards the reader.
   - They should be very well set out with a good subject-line.

- Specific people should be named in the address and salutation.
- They should be well organized so that the reader is able to get the answers that (s)he needs as easily as possible.
- They should be written clearly and simply.
- They should state what the reader should do and what the writer will do.

2. *What are the major barriers to effective letter and memorandum writing?*

   Suggested answer

   The major barriers are as follows:
   - No subject-line.
   - Poor subject-line.
   - Confusing first paragraph that gives no idea of what the letter or memorandum is about.
   - Badly organized body of the letter or memorandum.
   - Long, involved sentences.
   - Long paragraphs.
   - A difficult vocabulary.
   - Jargon.
   - A confused ending.
   - Generally poor readability.

3. *What techniques should be used to make letters as readable as possible?*

   Suggested answer

   The following techniques could be used:
   - Address a person, rather than a company.
   - Have a very clear subject-line.
   - Organize the letter very well.
   - Tell the reader in the first paragraph what the letter is about.
   - Write clearly and simply, avoiding jargon.
   - Use headings to guide the reader.
   - Write short sentences and paragraphs.
   - Keep the vocabulary simple.
   - State the action at the end.

4. *What are the characteristics of a good letter-writing style?*

   Suggested answer

   A letter should be written in a clear, friendly style. This style may be both personal and impersonal, depending on the writer's purposes, subject and audience. The style should be formal, but not over-formal. It should not be too casual either. It should be active where possible.

ANSWERS TO QUESTIONS: PART 7 (Chapter 17)   547

5. *What styles should be used for writing memoranda?*

   Suggested answer

   Memoranda should be written in a formal or consultative style. The style could be personal or impersonal. It should be simple and active where possible.

6. *How do the formats for letters and memoranda differ?*

   Suggested answer

   Letters have an address, a salutation and a complimentary close. Memoranda have a 'To' line, a 'From' line and the date. Memoranda do not have a salutation or a complimentary close. Memoranda may be ended with the sender's initials or typed name.

7. *Give examples of the following:*
   - A salutation
   - A subject-line
   - A complimentary close

   Suggested answer

   Example of salutations:

   ```
   Dear Mrs Smith
   Dear Sir(s)
   ```

   Example of a subject-line:

   ```
   DAMAGE TO TEACUPS: ORDER NO. 145 OF 2/6/92
   ```

   Example of complimentary closes:

   ```
   Yours faithfully
   Yours sincerely
   ```

8. *Explain the block style in letter writing.*

   Suggested answer

   If a letter is typed in the block style the addresses, reference, date, subject lines, paragraphs, and complimentary close start at the left-hand margin.

9. *Explain how to write:*
   - A letter of complaint
   - A letter of adjustment

- A letter of enquiry
- A letter responding to an enquiry.

Suggested answer

A letter of complaint should be set out as follows:
- A subject-line giving the details of the complaint.
- A friendly opening that establishes a good relationship.
- A statement of the problem.
- A motivation to the reader to take the desired action.
- A statement of what the writer considers to be fair action.

A letter of adjustment should be set out as follows:
- A subject-line referring to the complaint.
- A friendly opening thanking the writer for calling attention to the problem and expressing concern.
- A statement of what will be done to solve the problem.
- A request to the reader to take certain steps.
- A final paragraph expressing concern and goodwill.

A letter of enquiry should be set out as follows:
- A subject-line giving the request.
- A clear statement of the request.
- Exact details of the request.
- A reinforcement of the request.

A letter responding to an enquiry should be set out as follows:
- A subject-line clearly announcing the subject.
- A statement of thanks for the enquiry.
- A restatement of the request to show that the writer has understood what it is.
- An exact answer to the request.
- An invitation to the writer to state whether (s)he needs any further help.

Exercises

Please note: Since there are many ways of writing these letters, the following examples should not be regarded as model answers.

ANSWERS TO QUESTIONS: PART 7 (Chapter 17) 549

1. Letter to firm of booksellers

Dear sirs

ORDER FOR THREE BOOKS AND REQUEST FOR TITLES

I wish to order the following three titles:

1. Peters, J., How to Write Letters, London, ABC Press, 1992
2. Robertson, S., Reports for Technical Writers, New York, Express Books, 1990.
3. Sampson, B., Communication in Business, Cape Town, XYZ Press, 1991.

Please charge these to my account, number 1234, and post them to my home address.

REQUEST FOR TITLES ON COMMUNICATION IN BUSINESS

I should be most grateful if you would let me have a list of the latest titles of books on communication in Business. I am particularly interested in the field of written communication in business.

I look forward to receiving the books and the list of titles.

Yours faithfully

---

2. Letter to company that has not paid its account

Dear Mr Singh

OUTSTANDING DEBT OF R5 000: INVOICE 567 OF 20/1/92

We have done good business together over the past five years. However, I am now concerned that we have not received payment of R5 000 for goods that we delivered two months ago.

> If you have any problems with this repayment, I shall be very happy to make special arrangements with you.
>
> Please let me know within the next week what arrangements you wish to make about paying us.
>
> Yours sincerely

3. *Letter to local Town Clerk*

> Dear Ms Smit
>
> REQUEST FOR IMPROVED STREET SWEEPING AND RUBBISH COLLECTION
>
> We have always enjoyed a good relationship with the Municipality. Your services have, in the past been excellent.
>
> My company has, however, noticed a deterioration in street sweeping and rubbish collection services over the past six months. The streets round the industrial section are not being swept regularly. In addition, bags of rubbish are being left lying around.
>
> We should be most grateful if you would ensure that
> - our streets are cleaned regularly
> - all our rubbish is collected twice a week.
>
> I shall be very happy to discuss this matter further should you wish to do so.
>
> Yours sincerely

4. *Letter of adjustment*

> Dear Mrs Bhawa
>
> LATE DELIVERY OF, AND DAMAGE TO XYZ TOYS: INVOICE 567 OF 6/10/91
>
> I am most concerned about the inconvenience caused to you by:

- Late delivery of the XYZ toys that you ordered
- Incorrect delivery
- Damage to some toys.

We will do our utmost to see that these problems do not happen again.

<u>Late delivery</u>

We must apologize for this late delivery. Our staff have been under great pressure and we have had to hire temporary staff. One of these staff members mis-filed your order. This led to late delivery.

<u>Incorrect delivery</u>

Our stock clerks decided to give you toys as close as possible to your order because they had run out of the exact type of toy that you had ordered. They believed that their choice of toy would meet your needs.

I must apologize for this. We now have a new stock of toys. Should you wish to return any of the toys we will gladly replace them with the toys that you want.

<u>Damage to toys</u>

We must apologize for any damaged toys. Please return any that are damaged. We will gladly replace them free of charge.

We will do our utmost to ensure that you receive the best service from us in the future.

Yours sincerely

5. *Memorandum asking for extra leave*

To: Mrs J. Zondo
        Personnel Manager
From: Ms B. Sangster
Date: 20 October 19—

<u>SUBJECT: REQUEST FOR AN EXTRA THREE DAYS' PAID LEAVE</u>

I wish to request an extra three days' paid leave, even though I have used up my leave for this year.

My reasons for this request are as follows:
- My father is desperately ill, and my mother has asked me to come and see him urgently.
- My father and mother run a shop. My mother now urgently needs help to organize the business so that she can sell it.
- It is very important that my mother receive a good price for the business because this is my parents' sole source of income.

I should be most grateful if you would consider my request favourably.

B. SANGSTER

6. *Letter asking about vacancies*

Dear Sirs

ENQUIRY ABOUT VACANT POSTS

I am writing to ask whether your company has any vacancies for computer operators. I have five years' experience in this field, and believe that I can contribute to your company.

QUALIFICATIONS AND EXPERIENCE

My qualifications and experience are as follows:

Qualifications

. . .

Experience

. . .

I attach a curriculum vitae for your information.

I am available immediately for an interview. I can be contacted at the following telephone numbers:

. . .

Yours faithfully

ANSWERS TO QUESTIONS: PART 7 (Chapter 17)   553

7. *Unsolicited sales letter*

> Dear Customer
>
> ZIPPY HOUSEHOLD CLEANER:
> TWICE THE POWER FOR HALF THE PRICE
>
> ZIPPY household cleaner is the answer to all your cleaning problems. This new, space-age cleaner offers you the following advantages:
> - Twice the cleaning power at half the price
> - Ozone friendly and biodegradable
> - Easy on your skin
> - Deadly for germs
> - Powerful detergent qualities will move all dirt.
>
> ZIPPY is available as a liquid or cream.
>
> ZIPPY is easy to use. Simply spray or wipe it on. Then wipe if off.
>
> ZIPPY will leave all your surfaces sparkling clean and germ-free.
>
> For more information on SPACE-AGE ZIPPY, simply fill in the attached reply-paid card.
>
> We'll do the rest.

8. The tone of this letter is aggressive and rude. Note, in particular, the words in italics such as 'are', 'you', and 'only'. Note also the words 'General Dogsbodies' and 'completely absurd'.

Suggested re-written version

> Dear Sirs
>
> CONTRACT WITH ABC (PTY) LIMITED
>
> Thank you for your letter of 5 December 19—.
>
> We wish to discuss statements in the second paragraph of your letter.
>
> Unproved items
>
> Your letter states that we have 'alleged' that certain items are 'unproved'. We believe that these items have not been proved in terms of our contract.

> We should, therefore, be grateful if you would obtain written permission for these items.
>
> We wish to stress that our powers are limited, because we are only consultants to the project.
>
> Statements in your second paragraph
>
> We would like to discuss the following statements in your second paragraph:
>
> ...

9. *Analysis of content, organization and language of letter of transmittal*

   Analysis

   The content of this letter of transmittal is good in terms of its discussion of the project. The writer does not, however, use the letter to generate goodwill. In addition, the writer has not mentioned any limitations or problems.

   The organization is weak. The letter has been written as two paragraphs. The first paragraph is very long. There are no headings or short paragraphs to guide the reader.

   The language is a mixture of formal and informal words. The word 'undersigned' is too pompous and stiff. On the other hand, the words 'stuck to' are too informal.

   Suggested version

   > Dear Mr Fish
   >
   > DESIGN FOR PARKING GARAGE FOR 283 CARS: CNR SMITH AND TROMP STREETS
   >
   > Thank you for your letter of 21 June. I have pleasure in attaching my design for your proposed parking garage.
   >
   > Please note the following details:
   > - Capacity of garage: 283 cars
   >   25 motor-cycles
   > - Gross cost   R1 296 000
   > - Cost of housing each vehicle R6 488
   >
   > I wish to apologize for my under-estimation of the cost per vehicle in my letter of 10 April 19—.

PROPOSALS IN YOUR LETTER OF 5 MAY 19—

I have kept to your proposals and have ensured the following:
- The ramp joining the two decks has a very gradual incline of 1:15.
- This ramp holds 40 bays.
- Adequate pedestrian walkways and stairways have been included.
- Emergency exits have been included.
- Angle parking has been used where possible.
- 90-degree parking has been used where traffic flow needs to be improved.
- Public toilets have been included.

The whole concept has been geared for easy manoeuvreability.

LIMITATIONS OF PROJECT

Please note that my design has been limited by City planning regulations and by your two-floor limit.

I have enjoyed working with you. Thank you for giving me this project. If anything is not clear or not to your liking, please let me know.

Yours sincerely

10. *Persuasive letter from marketing manager to customer*

Dear Mr de Beer

XYZ GOODS ON OFFER

We have always had a good business relationship and you have, in the past, ordered a range of our excellent products. We have been able to offer you a most competitive service.

Services offered

Recently, however, I have noted that you have stopped ordering from us. We are still able to offer you excellent service in the following areas:
- A wide range of excellent goods at competitive prices.
- A 15% discount for cash.

> - Same-day delivery if the order is placed before 10h00.
> - Excellent after-sales service.
>
> <u>Catalogue of goods offered</u>
>
> I enclose our latest catalogue showing you what you could gain from dealing with us.
>
> Our salesperson in your area, Ms Jean Townsend, will be calling on you in the next week to discuss your needs.

11. *Short letter to accompany diary*

> Dear Customer
>
> <u>DIARY FOR 19—</u>
>
> I have pleasure in enclosing a diary for 19—. We greatly value your custom and look forward to being of service to you in 19—.
>
> This diary offers you:
> - A page a day for your planning.
> - An alphabetical list of businesses in the City.
> - Calendars for 19— and 19— for forward planning.
> - A wide variety of information of use for businesses.
>
> We wish you a successful 19—.
>
> Yours sincerely

Proposals

Points for discussion

1. *What is a proposal?*

    Suggested answer

    A proposal is a suggestion or request for action to be taken.

ANSWERS TO QUESTIONS: PART 7 (Chapter 17)   557

2. *How should a proposal be organized?*

   Suggested answer

   A proposal should be organized like a report. It should have the following sections:

   - A clear heading
   - A summary of all the key details
   - A background section
   - The detailed proposed action
   - A section justifying the proposal
   - A section reinforcing the proposed action.

3. *What techniques should be used to make proposals highly readable?*

   Suggested answer

   Writers should use the following techniques:

   - Clear headings
   - An effective numbering system
   - Short paragraphs
   - Short sentences
   - A simple vocabulary
   - Key points highlighted in bold.

4. *What information should go into the Background to a proposal?*

   Suggested answer

   The Background should contain the following information:

   - Background to the proposal, including any instructions given by a client.
   - Detailed reasons why the proposal has become necessary.

5. *What information should go into the Justification section of a proposal?*

   Suggested answer

   The Justification section should give detailed arguments backing up the proposal.

6. *What style should be used for a proposal?*

   Suggested answer

   A proposal should be written in a formal, impersonal, active style. The style should be simple and clear. If, however, the writer knows the reader very well (s)he could use a personal style.

Exercises

1. *Proposal for new equipment*

    Please note that this suggested answer has been shortened. An example of this type of proposal may be found in Chapter 17.

    > PROPOSAL TO ALLOCATE R250 000 FOR THE BUYING OF 30 ACE WORD PROCESSORS AND PRINTERS IN 19— AND 19—
    >
    > Summary
    >
    > The writer proposes that R250 000 be spent on 30 Ace Word Processors and Printers for the Insurance Department in 19— and 19—. Fifteen machines will be bought each year.
    >
    > These machines are needed to replace machines and printers that have been used non-stop for the past seven years.
    >
    > The Insurance Department has doubled in size during the past five years. This has placed great strain on the Department's computer and printing resources. The writer estimates that the Department is now working at 50% of its efficiency.
    >
    > Background to proposal
    >
    > This proposal has come about for the following historical reasons:
    >
    > . . .
    >
    > Detailed proposal
    >
    > . . .
    >
    > Justification for proposal
    >
    > . . .
    >
    > Proposed action
    >
    > The writer therefore proposes that . . .

2. *Criticism of proposal*

    This proposal starts with a weak heading. The machines should have been named and the replacement machines should also have been named.

The opening paragraph is too long. The writer makes the reader go through a great deal of material before finding out the details of the proposal. This is bad planning. In addition, the writer does not name the machines or say how many are to be replaced.

Suggested version

Note that this has been shortened.

PROPOSAL TO SPEND R100 000 IN 19— AND 19—
TO REPLACE 8 ABC FOOD MIXERS
AND 10 ZAP MICROWAVE OVENS

Summary

The writer proposes that the Company spend R100 000 in 19— and 19— to replace 8 ABC Food Mixers and 10 Zap Microwave Ovens. These should be replaced with more modern machines of the same brand.

All these machines have been extensively used in our cookery demonstrations. They are now wearing out.

The economy is now improving and we need to break into new markets to survive. . . .

Notices and circulars

Points for discussion

1. *How should a notice or a circular be organized?*

   Suggested answer

   A notice or circular should be very well organized with a good heading to tell the reader what it is about.

   The writer should keep the information simple. (S)he should use headings and lists to highlight the main points. (S)he should use short sentences and a simple vocabulary.

2. *When would you use a notice?*

   Suggested answer

   A notice should be used when all staff have to be given the same information. Very important items should also be sent round to each staff member by means of a circular.

3. *When would you use a circular?*

   Suggested answer

   A circular should be used when an organization wishes to ensure that all staff or customers receive the same information.

4. *What are the differences between a notice and a circular?*

   Suggested answer

   A notice is a message that is placed on a board. It should be designed to attract the attention of people who walk past.

   A circular is a message that is sent to members of an organization through the internal mailing system. A circular may also be sent by means of an electronic mail system. Circulars are also posted to customers. Every circular contains the same message.

5. *What methods should be used to attract readers' attention to recent notices?*

   Suggested answer

   Organizations could:
   - Have a special section of a notice board allocated to 'this week's' or 'today's' notices.
   - Use a large red arrow to attract people's attention to recent important notices.
   - Print the most recent notice in a different colour.

6. *What readability techniques should be used to make notices and circulars more effective?*

   Suggested answer

   Writers could use the following techniques:
   - Very clear headings in capitals and underlined.
   - Lists of items.
   - Items well spaced out.
   - Short paragraphs.
   - Key points printed in bold print.
   - Key points in frames.
   - Message kept simple.

ANSWERS TO QUESTIONS: PART 7 (Chapter 17)

Exercises

1. *Notice about flexitime*

FLEXITIME ARRANGEMENTS FOR ALL STAFF

The Staff Association has reached the following agreement about flexitime.

Whom does this affect?

All staff in Post Grades 1-12.

What does this arrangement mean?

The Staff Association has agreed on the following arrangements:

- WORKING WEEK
  Everyone must work a 45-hour week.
- CORE TIME
  Everybody must be present from 09h00 to 16h00.
- FLEXIBLE STARTING TIMES
  You may choose to start at any time from 07h00 to 09h00.
- FLEXIBLE STOPPING TIMES
  You may choose to stop at any time from 16h00 to 18h00.
- LUNCH TIME
  Lunch is 30 minutes. You may take your lunch from 12h00 to 13h30.
- QUERIES
  If you have any queries about this system, please contact Peter Smit on 5678.

---

2. *Notice on non-smoking. Note that this notice has been shortened.*

AGREEMENT ON NON-SMOKING AREAS IN XYZ BUILDING

Your staff representatives have agreed on the following non-smoking areas in this building.

Please ensure that you:
- Read this notice carefully
- Keep strictly to the arrangements.

> NON-SMOKING AREAS
> - All offices and passages
> - . . .
>
> SMOKING AREAS
> - Specially designated rooms on each floor with the following signs: 'YOU ARE WELCOME TO SMOKE HERE'
> - . . .

3. *Circular telling customers of a move*

> Dear Customer
>
> MOVE TO ABC BUILDING: 20 FIRST STREET
>
> We have moved! Our new shop at 20 First Street offers you greatly improved facilities.
>
> We can now offer you:
> - Twice the floor space
> - All goods clearly displayed
> - A full range of catalogues that you can read in comfort.
>
> Join us at 20 First Street. We look forward to giving you an even better service than before.

4. *Circular on car polishes*

> Dear Customer
>
> NEW IMPROVED SPARKLE CAR POLISHES - THE ANSWER TO ALL YOUR PROBLEMS
>
> We have just unpacked a top-class range of Sparkle car polishes. These polishes have been newly developed in Europe to the highest specification.
>
> They will give your vehicle:
> - Long-lasting protection from harmful ultra-violet rays
> - Rust protection.
>
> These polishes are:
> - Easy to apply - simply rub on and then rub off.
> - Safe to use.

ANSWERS TO QUESTIONS: PART 7 (Chapter 17) 563

> - Easy to store.
>
> Visit our store for a demonstration of this range of excellent car polishes.

Instructions

Points for discussion

1. *What are the purposes of instructions?*

   Suggested answer

   Instructions have the following purposes:
   - to guide people
   - to direct people
   - to command people
   - to help people to work together
   - to help people to do things on their own, but within guidelines
   - to help people to do the same jobs in the same way
   - to tell people what to do and what not to do
   - to help people to get the best use out of products.

2. *Are instructions simply orders?*

   Suggested answer

   Instructions are not simply orders. The purposes listed in answer 1 show the wide variety of purposes of instructions.

3. *Discuss the sections of a good set of instructions.*

   Suggested answer

   A good set of instructions should have the following sections:
   - Title
   - Introduction
   - Theory and principles of operation
   - List of equipment and materials needed for assembly
   - Description of the mechanism
   - Instructions for assembling the machine
   - Operation instructions
   - Precautions and a warning.

4. *What style would you use for instructions?*

   Suggested answer

   Instructions normally start with imperatives such as 'Plug in the ... '. The style should be clear and simple. The writer should keep the sentences and words as simple as possible.

5. *Discuss the uses of the following in a set of instructions:*
   - A flow-chart
   - A logic-tree
   - An algorithm.

   Suggested answer

   Each one of the above is a graphic device to help the reader understand and follow the stages in a process.

   Each graphic is organized logically so that the reader goes step-by-step through a set of stages to a conclusion.

Exercises

Note that these two examples have been shortened.

1. *Instructions on recycling paper*

RECYCLING OF WASTE PAPER

ALL STAFF

Introduction

At the last staff meeting, delegates unanimously voted to recycle all waste paper. They agreed on the following procedure.

Collection points
- Each office will have two special bins for paper to be recycled, a RED and a BLUE bin.
- Place all computer paper into the RED BIN.
- Place all other paper into the BLUE BIN.

Full bins

When each bin is full
- Empty it into the appropriate RED or BLUE BIN at the end of each passage.
- . . .

… ANSWERS TO QUESTIONS: PART 7 (Chapter 17) — 565

2. *Instructions for saving water and electricity*

```
              HOW TO SAVE WATER AND ELECTRICITY
ALL STAFF
As part of the national effort, we have agreed to
save as much water and electricity as possible. The
following instructions show you how to do so.
They have been divided into two sections:
- Saving water
- Saving electricity

Saving water
Please ensure that you:
- turn off . . .
- do not . . .
-  . . .

Saving electricity
Please ensure that you:
- turn off . . .
- do not . . .
-  . . .
```

Press-release

Points for discussion

1. *For what reasons should a press-release be sent out by an organization?*

    Suggested answer

    An organization could send out a press-release to let the public know what it is doing, for example in the area of public service and social responsibility. This is a form of advertising, but it is more informative. It is designed to generate goodwill for the organization, and could be part of its public relations efforts.

2. *How should a press-release be organized?*

    Suggested answer

    A press release is organized in the form of an inverted pyramid. It is organized so that all the key points appear at the beginning. After that, the writer gives less and less important information. The broad base of the pyramid appears at the top, rather than at the bottom.

3. *What are the reasons for this special type of organization?*

   Suggested answer

   A press-release is organized with all the key points at the beginning because that is where newspaper readers read. They are not likely to read the rest of the article with care. In addition, a newspaper editor is then able to cut from the bottom of the article in order to fit it into the newspaper layout.

4. *What style should be used for a press-release?*

   Suggested answer

   A press-release should be written in a formal, referential style. Emotive words should be kept to a minimum.

5. *What techniques should be used to make a press-release as readable as possible?*

   Suggested answer

   A press-release should be very well organized so that the reader understands the main points of the message immediately. The style should be simple with short sentences and short paragraphs. Headings should be used at the beginnings of new sections.

Exercises

Note that only one of the exercises has been done.

1. *Press-release describing a National Week for the Blind*

```
NEWS RELEASE
NATIONAL WEEK FOR THE BLIND


The National League for the Blind is holding a Na-
tional Week for the Blind from 20 March 19— to 27
March 19—. Each region will be running its own
awareness programmes. These will be advertised sepa-
rately. The purpose of this week is to draw atten-
tion to the needs of blind people.

During blind week regions plan to organize a vari-
ety of activities for blind people. These include
motor ralleys with blind navigation, a wide variety
of sporting events, talks and discussions. Fund-
raising events will also be organized.

This week will also focus on what blind people can
achieve. Special attention will be paid to blind
people who hold important positions in organiza-
```

> tions such as the Community Chest. Talks will be
> given by blind students who have gained qualifica-
> tions.
>
> <u>Issued by</u>
> National League for the Blind
> 2 Second Street
> Aceville
> 2345
> Telephone: (045) 123456
> Fax: (045) 123458

Essays and articles

Points for discussion

1. *What are the differences between the format for an essay and a report?*

   Suggested answer

   An essay has a beginning, middle and end, whereas a report has many sections, each with different purposes. An essay is written in continuous writing, whereas a report has numbered sections with headings and sub-headings. An essay is written in a variety of styles. However, a report should be written in a formal, referential and active style.

2. *What techniques should be used to make essays and articles as readable as possible?*

   Suggested answer

   Writers should use some of the following techniques:
   - Very good planning
   - A summary paragraph at the beginning
   - Clear organization
   - Good links between paragraphs
   - A good summary at the end
   - A clear, simple style
   - A simple vocabulary suited to the needs of the audience.

3. *What styles should be used for essays and articles?*

   Suggested answer

   Essays and articles could be written in a range of styles. They could, for example, be written in a personal or impersonal style ranging from very formal to consultative or casual. They could be written in an active or passive style as well. In general, the style should be simple and clear.

4. *What are the purposes of essays and articles?*

   Suggested answer

   Essays and articles are written with some of the following purposes:
   - to inform
   - to persuade
   - to entertain
   - to record facts
   - to impress
   - to argue a case
   - to refute an argument
   - to support an argument.

5. *What is a bibliography card; a note card?*

   Suggested answer

   A bibliography card is a card the size of a postcard. The writer records details of the books, articles, reports and other written documents on a set of cards, one for each document. In particular the writer records:
   - Name of author
   - Title of work
   - Place of publication
   - Publisher
   - Year published.

   A note card is a card used to record notes from any document that the researcher has read. The researcher could use a set of cards for each book.

Exercises

It is not possible to give suggested answers to all the topics suggested. Readers are referred to the appropriate section of Chapter 17 for guidance.

Telegram and telex

Points for discussion

1. *When should a telegram be used?*

   Suggested answer

   A telegram should be used when the sender wishes to reach someone quickly. It should also be used when telephone, fax and telex facilities are not available.

ANSWERS TO QUESTIONS: PART 7 (Chapter 17) 569

2. *What is meant by a cryptic style in a telegram?*

   Suggested answer

   A cryptic style is a style in which only key words such as nouns and verbs are given. Joining words are left out.

3. *What key information should be put into a telegram?*

   Suggested answer

   A telegram should contain the following:
   - Exact information on dates, times and venues.
   - Instructions.
   - Numbers of flights.
   - Names of hotels.

   Anyone receiving a telegram should have exact information and should know what to do next.

4. *What is a telex?*

   Suggested answer

   A telex is a message printed in capital letters. It is a cross between a letter and a telegram.
   When printed, a telex looks like a telegram.

5. *How is a telex sent from one company to another?*

   Suggested answer

   A sender prepares a telex by hand. It is then typed into a telex machine by an operator. A telex machine at the receiving end then types out the message.

6. *How should a telex be set out?*

   Suggested answer

   A telex should be set out with a good subject-line and headings to guide the reader. Headings are not underlined.

7. *What techniques should be used to make a telex as readable as possible?*

   Suggested answer

   A sender should use the following techniques:
   - Good headings
   - Lists where appropriate
   - A clear style that is not cryptic
   - Short paragraphs
   - Short sentences.

Exercises

1. *Telegram to London*

   ```
   FROM: A.Z. THOMAS            TO: B. SMITHSON
         3 FIFTH STREET             208 CORNISH STREET
         CAPE TOWN                  LONDON


   ARRIVING HEATHROW 17H00 FRIDAY 20 JUNE FLIGHT SA
   304. PLEASE PICK ME UP AT PASSENGER PICKUP POINT
   TERMINAL B 17H45.
   ```

2. *Telegram to Branch Manager*

   ```
   TO: MS A. BHAWA              FROM: M. MKIZI


   ARRIVING SMITHVILLE 17H00 22 FEBRUARY 93. PLEASE AR-
   RANGE BOOKINGS BAY HOTEL 22 FEB TO 28 FEB. PLEASE
   ARRANGE INTERVIEWS FOR ME WITH ALL YOUR SALES STAFF
   AT TWO-HOURLY INTERVALS FROM 23 FEB TO 27 FEB. LOOK
   FORWARD TO MEETING YOU.
   ```

3. *Telex requesting permission to run a Sales Conference*

   ```
   PERMISSION REQUESTED TO RUN SALES CONFERENCE 20-22
   JUNE 1993 AT SMITHVILLE BRANCH
   - PERMISSION REQUESTED TO RUN ABOVE CONFERENCE
   - PERMISSION FOR THE FOLLOWING IS REQUESTED:
   - BUDGET = R10 000
   - HIRING OF SECRETARIAL HELP
   - HIRING OF MINI-BUSES
   - BOOKING OF TWO LECTURE THEATRES AND FIVE
     CONFERENCE ROOMS AT SMITHVILLE CONFERENCE CENTRE
   - INVITATIONS TO SIX PEOPLE FROM HEAD OFFICE.
   PLEASE CONFIRM BY 28 FEBRUARY THAT CONFERENCE CAN
   GO AHEAD.
   ```

ANSWERS TO QUESTIONS: PART 7 (Chapter 17)

Advertisements

Points for discussion

1. *What is meant by a classified advertisement?*

   Suggested answer

   A classified advertisement appears in a newspaper or magazine under a specific heading such as 'Cars for Sale'. This type of advertisement gives the facts about what is offered for sale. It is not normally drawn up by an expert, and special advertising techniques do not have to be used.

2. *When would an organization use a classified advertisement?*

   Suggested answer

   An organization would use a classified advertisement when it wished to sell something or advertise its services. It would use this type of advertising when a professionally created advertisement is not necessary.

3. *How should a classified advertisement be set out?*

   Suggested answer

   A classified advertisement should be set out simply and clearly to give the facts. It should be designed to fit into a small space in the classified section of a newspaper or magazine. Special techniques for achieving readability do not have to be used.

4. *When advertising a vacant post, what information should an organization include?*

   Suggested answer

   An organization should include the following information:
   - Name of the organization
   - Type of post(s) offered
   - When posts are available
   - How to apply
   - What details are needed in the application
   - Conditions of service
   - A contact number if people wish to get further information.

5. *Explain the AIDA approach to constructing advertisements.*

   Suggested answer

   The AIDA approach uses four stages. They are:
   - Attention — Cognitive stage
   - Interest — Emotional stage
   - Desire — Emotional stage
   - Action — Action stage

6. *Discuss six techniques that advertisers use to attract the audience's attention.*

   Suggested answer

   Advertisers use the following techniques:
   - Names in capital letters
   - Repetition of words
   - Questions
   - Imperatives
   - Quotations from famous people
   - Headings
   - Lists
   - Attractive photographs and sketches
   - Colours

7. *Discuss six psychological appeals that advertisers use to stimulate an audience's desire.*

   Suggested answer

   Advertisers base their appeals on people's needs for:
   - Pleasure
   - Power
   - Security
   - Beauty
   - A long life
   - Happiness
   - Health
   - Love
   - Social acceptance.

Exercises

1. *Classified advertisement*

   CARS FOR SALE

   Two VW Golfs 1300 1988 Brilliant red. Incl mag wheels. 70 000 km each. Very good condition. Serviced regularly. Phone 7063725.

2. *Advertisement for vacant posts*

XYZ COMPANY

We have vacancies for:

Sales Assistants to work in our retail shop

Applicants should have a matriculation certificate. Sales experience would be an advantage. An ability to work with people is essential.

We offer:
- Good salary and commission
- On-the-job training

These posts offer excellent opportunities for men and women who are prepared to work hard.

Written applications should be sent to:

The Personnel Manager
XYZ Company
P.O. Box 258
Smithville
4186

Faxing and electronic mail

Points for discussion

1. *What precautions would you take to ensure that your fax message is received and read at the other end?*

   Suggested answer

   A typed message or diagram should be very clear with type and lines of good quality. There should be a cover page giving
   - Your fax number
   - The receiver's fax number
   - The total number of pages
   - The number of each page, for example Page 1 of 5.

2. *If your fax-message is hand-written, how would you ensure that it is readable at the other end?*

   Suggested answer

   Make sure that your handwriting is very clear and written in a dark print. All lines should be bold and clear.

3. *What is electronic mail?*

Suggested answer

Electronic mail is any message that is sent from one computer to another.

4. *How does electronic mail differ from inter-office memoranda on paper?*

Suggested answer

Electronic mail comprises messages sent electronically from one computer to another. Messages are not posted. They appear on a screen. Only if the receiver wishes to have a copy of the message is any printing done on paper.

5. *What techniques would you use to ensure that your electronic mail is highly readable?*

Suggested answer

Messages on a screen should be set out in exactly the same way as any message typed on paper.

The sender should use:

- a very clear subject-line
- headings to guide the reader
- short sentences and paragraphs
- a simple vocabulary
- lists of items
- good spacing between lines
- a good, readable typeface
- highlighting for the most important points.

Electronic mail and its effects on communication in organizations

Points for discussion

1. E-mail messages should be typed in a simple style. They should have a good subject-line. The opening paragraph should tell the reader what the message is about. The rest of the message should be well set out with good sub-headings.

    Paragraphs and sentences should be short. A range of readability techniques should be used. These include:
    - lists
    - a serif font
    - 12-point letter size
    - a simple, clear vocabulary
    - technical words explained
    - good spacing between lines.

ANSWERS TO QUESTIONS: PART 7 (Chapter 17)

Messages should not be typed all in upper case lettering. Keep in mind that messages on a screen are harder to read than on paper.

2. E-mail messages are becoming less formal. However, you are advised to keep your messages more formal unless they are intended to be e-chat that does not have to be saved.

    Informal messages could be harder to read than formal messages. Informal e-mail messages may be badly organized with sections removed or out of place. Informal messages may also contain short forms or emoticons that not everyone understands.

3. E-mail messages should be kept short. Generally one screen full is enough. If the reader has to scroll through a number of pages then make sure that you start with a good summary. Use plenty of headings to guide your reader. Avoid large blocks of print.

    Keep the size and number of attachments as low as you can. They can clog up a system.

4. Staff should be advised to check on whether messages cover the organization's policies or not. If they do, then they should be stored. All formal messages that support the organization's mission and goals should be stored for an agreed time. All messages that are going to be referred to should be stored.

    All other messages should be deleted.

5. Organizations should help staff by training them to skim messages to find the key points. Staff should be trained to read subject-lines, opening paragraphs and summaries quickly and efficiently. They should also be trained to read headings and the first sentences of paragraphs.

    Once they have read these, they should be able to decide whether to read in detail or not.

    Staff should be trained to recognize 'junk mail' and to delete it.

    Staff should also be trained to make their messages highly readable so that others can scan them and pick up the key points.

Exercises

1. The e-mail message could be as follows. Please note that this is not a model answer.

    To: All staff
    From: A.N. Other
    Date:

    Subject: Compulsory overtime 3 February to 10 February

    We are now well into our move to our new building. However, we have now fallen behind with our production as a result.

    I am therefore asking all of you to work overtime from 3 to 10 February.

> The details are as follows:
>
> • New hours: 8:00 - 19:00
>
> • Break times: Normal, but supper break between 17:30 and 18:00
>
> • Meals: Lunch and supper will be provided
>
> • Transport: Transport will be provided to your homes if you need it
>
> • Extra pay: All of you will be paid the agreed overtime rates
>
> I will be coming round in the next two days to find out who needs transport.
>
> The directors and management greatly value your co-operation. With your help we will be back into full production by 11 February.

2. These guidelines should follow those given in the chapter. They should cover the following:
   - Construction of messages so that they are easy to read.
   - Readability techniques, with special stress on short paragraphs and sentences.
   - Checking distribution lists to ensure that one person does not receive many copies of the same message.
   - Ensuring that confidential information is not distributed.
   - Ensuring that messages are short.
   - Ensuring that attachments are kept to a minimum.
   - Explaining all technical terms.
   - Not distributing junk mail such as chain letters.

3. These guidelines should stress the following:
   - The organization is responsible for all e-mail.
   - The organization is allowed to monitor e-mail and to take action against staff who send inflammatory messages.
   - E-mail messages are the property of the organization, not the individual.
   - Individual senders of e-mail should take great care over the types of messages that they send. The content of messages can be held against them.

4. The following methods may be used to make e-mail messages easy to read:
   - Good subject lines
   - Good sub-headings
   - Short paragraphs and sentences
   - A simple vocabulary
   - Technical terms explained
   - Messages not typed in all capital letters
   - Good use of opening and closing paragraphs

- Sufficient spacing between lines, for example 1,5 line spacing
- Large enough letters, for example 12 points
- Lists of items

5. The guidelines on storage or deletion should cover the following:
   - Store messages that cover the organization's mission or guidelines for operation, or make copies.
   - Store messages that you will need in the future, or make copies.
   - Store instructions, or make copies.
   - Store reports that could help in future decision-making.
   - Delete all messages that will not be needed in the future.
   - Delete messages that could be classified as e-chat.

Effect of the personal computer and the Internet on communication

Points for discussion

1. In your discussion, cover the following points:
   - Access to large amounts of information
   - Empowerment of the individual staff member in terms of his or her knowledge
   - Ability of the ordinary staff member to communicate more easily with managers
   - Possible changes in managers' attitudes to staff and to negotiation with staff
   - Ability of the organization to conduct business without sending staff on long trips round the country
   - Ability of people in the field to communicate with head office by means of laptop computers
   - Ability of all staff members to call up information and to manipulate that information
   - Possible problems with staff suffering from eye-strain if they look at computer screens all day
   - Possible problems suffered by staff who have to type for long periods.

2. In your discussion of the Internet, cover the following points:
   - Easy access to large amounts of information from many different sources
   - Easy access to expert opinions and information
   - Ability to join discussion groups
   - Ability to advertise on the Internet using a home page
   - Ability to check other companies' home pages to see what they have to offer.

3. When you discuss the use of the Internet in enabling people to work from home, discuss the following points:
   - Ability to use linked computers to receive and send messages
   - Ability to create messages at home and to send these to the office
   - Ability to communicate with the office by means of typed messages that can be rapidly responded to
   - Ability of people to print out messages at the office, that have been typed on a screen somewhere else.

Exercises

1. In this exercise, concentrate on analysing the following:
   - the range of business messages used, for example memoranda, letters, reports, proposals, instructions
   - whether staff make greater use of messages such as memoranda
   - whether the trend is towards short rather than long messages
   - whether staff have problems reading long messages
   - whether staff have problems with attachments to messages
   - whether staff have problems with the readability of the messages that they receive
   - whether staff have problems creating readable messages on the screen
   - whether staff have problems planning their messages.

2. In this exercise concentrate on the following:
   - Use of general key words and how effective they are
   - Use of specific key words and how effective they are
   - Ability to find the information with ease
   - How useful the information is when it has been found.

3. In this exercise, concentrate on the following:
   - Whether staff members looked for general or specific information
   - Exactly what topics they covered in their search
   - Why they look for this information
   - How difficult it was to find this information.

Your reports should follow the recommended report format.

PART 8 (Chapter 18)

1. *What is a graphic device?*

   Suggested answer

   A graphic device is any device such as a table, bar graph, line graph or cartoon. These devices combine numbers, shapes and words. They have to be drawn.

2. *How are graphic devices used in oral and written messages?*

   Suggested answer

   Graphic devices are used to back up written or spoken messages. They show groups of numbers that would be difficult to describe in writing or speech. They also give a quick visual impression that enables a reader to compare amounts quickly.

3. *What are the differences between graphic devices and non-verbal communication?*

   Suggested answer

   Graphic devices are drawn and combine words, shapes and numbers. Non-verbal communication, on the other hand, describes people's body movements, eye-contact, the way in which they stand as well as the distances that they keep between themselves.

4. *What is a table?*

   Suggested answer

   A table is any grouping of numbers and other information set out in rows and columns. A stub heading is a heading at the top of the left-hand column in a table. A column heading is a heading for any other column. Use lines ruled across a table to encourage readers to read across.

   A simple table is suitable for a lay or mixed audience. However, a very complex table should be used for an expert audience. If this type of table is used for any other audience, it should be accompanied by a careful explanation.

5. *What is an area graph?*

   Suggested answer

   An area graph is a circle divided into wedge-shaped sections. These sections show how a whole has been divided up. An area graph is also called a circle graph or a pie chart.

6. *Explain what bar graphs, histograms and gantt charts are.*

   Suggested answer

   - Bar graphs are graphs in which amounts are shown either in horizontal or vertical columns.
   - Histograms are related to bar graphs, but all the bars are grouped together with a continuous base. Only the tops of the bars are shown in a continuous line.
   - A gantt chart is a special type of horizontal bar graph used by project planners. Each bar represents one part of a project. Each bar starts and stops in different places to show when each phase of a project starts and stops.

7. *What is the difference between a jagged-line graph and a bar graph?*

   Suggested answer

   A jagged-line graph is drawn as a jagged line joining points drawn on paper. A bar-graph on the other hand shows vertical or horizontal columns.

8. *Give an example of a curve.*

   Suggested answer

   A curve shows a relationship between two variables when the relationship between the two can be defined. For example if a piece of metal expands evenly over time when heat is applied, then this expansion could be recorded as a curve.

   An example is as follows:

   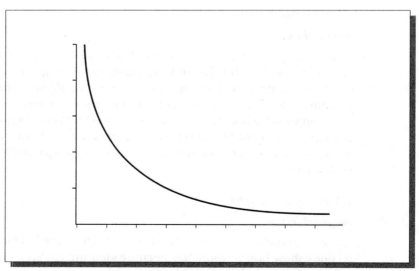

   Figure 1

9. *What is a pictogram? How are pictograms used?*

   Suggested answer

   A pictogram is an outline drawing of a person or object. Pictograms are used to give an audience a rough idea of trends or statistics. They are informal and do not give very accurate information.

10. *What is a hierarchical flow chart?*

    Suggested answer

    A hierarchical flow chart is composed of a series of lines showing how managers and employees in an organization are organized and work together. It shows levels of responsibility and who reports to whom.

    Example:

    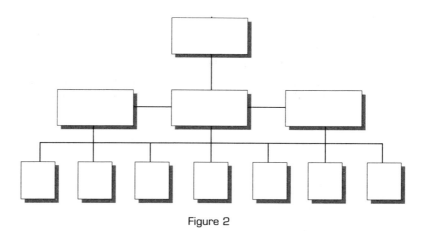

    Figure 2

11. *What is meant by integrating a graphic into a text?*

    Suggested answer

    Every graphic should be placed in the text where it is referred to. Every graphic should have a number and a title. It should be introduced above and analysed below. The writer should tell the reader how to interpret the graphic. Significant figures and trends should be highlighted.

12. *Discuss six techniques that you would use in designing a graphic device.*

    Suggested answer
    - Provide good headings
    - Provide good contrasts between adjacent sections by means of effective shading
    - Use dark lines round bars
    - Write horizontal labels

- Provide a key
- Write clear headings.

13. *Explain how bias may be introduced into a graphic.*

    Suggested answer

    Bias may be introduced by:
    - Choosing a deceptive scale
    - Omitting the zero on a scale and starting with a higher number
    - Labelling ambiguously
    - Selecting only favourable data
    - Drawing pictograms that give a distorted view of trends or numbers
    - Presenting diagrams with the wrong perspective.

Exercises

1. *Graphic for ratepayers*

    (Note that the graphic below is not exactly to scale)

    The jagged line-graphs below illustrate the average monthly water consumption of Businesses, Schools and Private Homes in the City.

    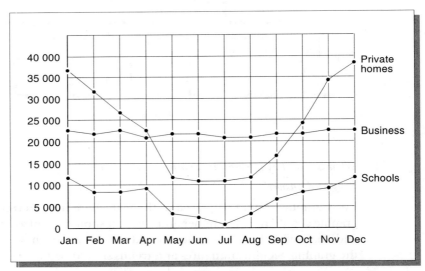

    Figure 3

    The graphs above show that Businesses use about the same amount of water throughout the year. Schools use the least amount of water. They use very little water in mid-winter. Private homes, however, use the largest amounts of water. Householders should, therefore, do their utmost to save water in the hot summer months.

ANSWERS TO QUESTIONS: PART 8 (Chapter 18) 583

2. *Table 1: Sales of Ace and Double Ace Microwave ovens in 1989 and 1990*

Model of microwave oven	NUMBERS SOLD					
	1989			1990		
	Model			Model		
	60	45	27	60	45	27
ACE	500	400	520	535	42	600
DOUBLE ACE	300	420	500	380	460	520

3. *Report on sales of vehicles*

   The figures in this table would form the body of a report.
   They would be set out as follows:
   (Note that this example has been shortened)

---

   4. ANALYSIS OF SALES OF VEHICLES FROM 1985-1990

   4.1 Sales of Motor Cars
       Sales of motor cars rose steadily from 1985
       to 1987. From 1987 to 1990 there was a
       steady decline from 63 in 1987 to 20 in 1990.

   4.2 Sales of Light Trucks
       Sales of light trucks showed the same trend
       as sales for motor cars, but the drop in
       sales started in 1987. Sales rose from 68 to
       70 in 1986. Sales from 1987 to 1990 showed a
       steady decline from 58 in 1987 to 30 in 1990.

   4.3 Sales of Heavy Trucks
       Sales of heavy trucks . . .

   4.4 Sales of Lorries
       Sales of lorries . . .

---

4. *Area graph and bar graph compared*

   Figures 4 and 5 show one set of data represented by different types of graphs. The bar graphs give the reader a better idea of the relative numbers of each type of book sold.

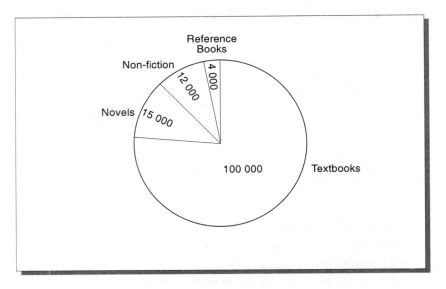

Figure 4
Pie-chart showing book sales by category

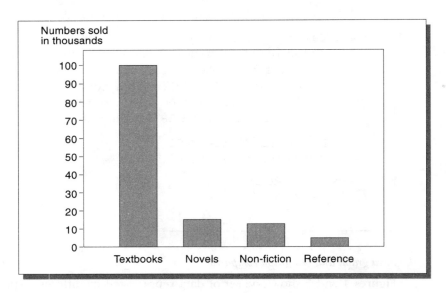

Figure 5
Bar graphs comparing the sales of types of books

ANSWERS TO QUESTIONS: PART 8 (Chapter 18)

5. *Jagged-line graphs to compare sales*

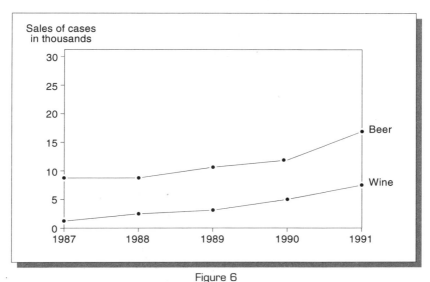

Figure 6
Graphs comparing the sales of wine and beer in cases from 1987 to 1991

6. *There will be a wide variety of answers here. Please use the example in Chapter 18 as a guideline.*

7. *Pictogram to show the sales of apples*

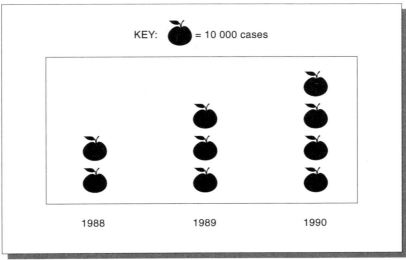

Figure 7
Pictograms showing the sales of apples in cases in 1988, 1989 and 1990

8. *Flow chart to show the stages in writing a bad-news letter of adjustment*

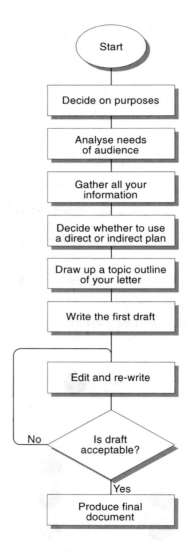

Figure 8

9. *Algorithm for making a local call from a public telephone*

Figure 9

10. Diagram to show someone how to change a wheel.

Step 1
Remove hubcab by using the lever to prise it off.

Step 2
Before jacking up the car, loosen each wheel nut slightly. Turn anti-clockwise.

PART 9 (Chapter 19)

Please note

The answers below have been kept brief. Answers to these questions will vary a great deal. These answers should not, therefore, be seen as model answers.

1. A Day at the Apricot Agency

1. The communication between Thandiwe and Bob was poor. Bob was under pressure because of his meeting. He did not listen to Thandiwe and gave her no chance to discuss the brief. He did not tell her how to get hold of him during the day. Thandiwe did not communicate her needs effectively because she was not assertive enough. There was not nearly enough negotiation.

   Thandiwe could have handled the communication better had she stated clearly at the beginning what her obligations for the day were.

2. Thandiwe could have improved her communication by politely refusing to change the brief until she had contacted Bob. She should have asked Terry to discuss the matter with Bob first. Terry was very domineering and did not allow Thandiwe to discuss the matter with her.

3. The communication within the Apricot Agency was bad on that day. Bob and Terry seemed to be communicating at cross purposes. The communication at the Agency could have been improved had people listened very carefully and made sure that they agreed on any brief.

4. The quality of the listening was poor. Neither Bob nor Terry listened carefully to Thandiwe. Bob and Terry were not listening to each other. They could all have improved their listening by making sure that each person had a chance to speak. They should then have negotiated meanings until they reached agreement. They should have made sure that they heard each other out.

5. An outline plan for encouraging effective communication within the Agency could be as follows:
   - Allocate time each day for careful listening
   - Make sure that each person hears the other out
   - Keep the lines of communication open
   - Make sure that people agree before they take action
   - Listen for the facts as well as attitudes and emotions.

2. In a Fix at Secure-It

1. The barriers to good communication were as follows:
   - Selwyn's attention was centred on himself, rather than on what was going on in the office.
   - Selwyn picked up the telephone when he should not have.
   - Stacey allowed him to sit on the desk. She did not ask him to leave the telephone for her to answer.
   - Beverly came in late and in a bad mood. She then shouted at Selwyn too loudly.

   As a result of this situation the three were not working well together. They were concentrating on themselves, rather than on the situation.

2. Selwyn did not concentrate on the message. He was not listening properly. As a result, he did not listen to the caller's name, and did not take notes. He did not take the caller's name, address and telephone number. In addition, he did not read the details back to the caller. Finally, he had no written message to hand on to the right person.

3. Selwyn should have listened carefully. He should have announced his name and asked if he could help. He should then have taken down the caller's name address and telephone number.

   He should also have written down the details of the problem. He should, finally, have read back the details and assured the caller that help would be on its way.

4. The following aspects of interpersonal communication could be included in a course:
   - discussion of barriers to effective interpersonal communication
   - discussion of principles of effective interpersonal communication
   - active listening
   - sensitivity to non-verbal communication
   - a discussion of why people perceive things differently
   - a discussion of different approaches to communication.

PART 10 (Chapter 20)

Points for discussion

1. *Why are summaries essential in most messages?*

   Suggested answer

   Summaries are essential because they:
   - prepare readers for the message
   - replace the message for the busy reader.

2. *What is the best place for a summary in a message?*

   Suggested answer

   The best place for a summary is at the beginning of a message. This is the point of major impact of a message.

3. *What are the stages through which a writer should go if (s)he wishes to summarize a passage effectively?*

   Suggested answer

   A writer should go through the following stages:
   - Read the passage to gain an idea of its unifying idea.
   - Write down this unifying idea.
   - Write a heading for the summary.
   - Underline the main idea in each sentence.
   - Underline the main clause in each sentence.
   - Prepare a topic outline of the main and supporting ideas.
   - Write a draft of the summary.
   - Check and edit the summary checking that (s)he has the right number of words.
   - Write the final summary.

4. *Why should the writer prepare a topic outline of the summary?*

   Suggested answer

   A topic outline is essential, because the writer can then prepare the message as a whole. (S)he can then check for the right organization, as well as for unity, coherence and emphasis.

5. What does the term 'comprehension' mean?
   Suggested answer
   The term 'comprehension' means 'understanding'. A comprehension test establishes whether someone has understood what (s)he has read.

6. Why is full comprehension of a passage essential?
   Suggested answer
   Full comprehension of a passage is essential because a reader should understand the main ideas, as well as supporting ideas. In addition, (s)he should understand how all ideas inter-relate. (S)he should also understand the meanings of all words in their contexts.

Exercises

1. *The passage: 'Getting things done in companies'*
   (a) Answer the questions on the passage.
      (i) The writer states that companies are not moving forward. Explain in your own words the writer's reasons for saying this.
         Suggested answer
         Companies are not moving forward because they are carrying on business as they have in the past. They react to problems, but they do not plan ahead. They are not devoting enough time and money to research and the development of new ideas.
      (ii) The writer says 'Companies have not moved forward because they have stressed problem-solving at the expense of innovation'. What do you understand by this statement?
         Suggested answer
         Companies are content to solve day-to-day problems. They spend too much time solving problems, and not enough time working on new ideas and plans for the future.
      (iii) What do you understand by the term 'a climate of innovation'?
         Suggested answer
         A climate of innovation refers to the encouragement of new ideas, new approaches and new technology. If there is a positive climate then new ideas and approaches will be welcome. People will be encouraged to put forward new ideas, even though they may seem ridiculous at first. People will also be encouraged to plan ahead.
      (iv) Why do managers design decisions that attract the least amount of criticism?
         Suggested answer
         They do this because they are frightened of attracting criticism, particularly from the mass media. Managers often have to work in

a negative atmosphere, in which people criticize small areas that are wrong, but ignore the large areas that are right.

(v) What do you understand by a 'brainstorming session'?

Suggested answer

A brainstorming session is a session in which people are encouraged to put forward as many ideas as possible without criticism or comment. These ideas are recorded. After the session, people go through these ideas and decide on the ones that they think have merit.

(vi) The writer stresses the ability to get things done. What do you understand by this ability?

Suggested answer

This ability means that people are able both to think and then to apply these thoughts to practical situations. This ability also means that people are able to work with others to ensure that things are done efficiently. All tasks are seen through to the end. The ability to get things done implies that people are able to pay attention to detail.

(vii) Why should the ability to get things done be regarded as an asset, as are literacy and numeracy?

Suggested answer

Literacy and numeracy are regarded as the basis for all good business. People in business have to be literate and numerate if they are to compete in a sophisticated business atmosphere. In the same way, the writer believes that people should have the ability to get things done. In this way ideas will be seen through to their practical conclusions.

(viii) Do you think that the ability to get things done can be taught? Justify your answer.

Suggested answer

The ability to get things done can be partially taught if people work with others who are able to get things done. People can be taught to organize and work with others. They can also be taught to pay attention to detail. Some people, however, are more naturally inclined to pay attention to detail than are others.

(ix) Explain the difference between 'efficiency' and 'effectiveness'. Give examples to explain each term.

Suggested answer

'Efficiency' means doing things correctly. 'Effectiveness', however, means doing the right things. Organizations should seek to be effective first of all. Once they have chosen their tasks, they should do these efficiently.

(b) Reduce it to one-third of its length.
The target is approximately 136 words.

> **ENCOURAGING INNOVATION IN COMPANIES**
>
> Today, companies need to move beyond problem-solving to innovation. They need to encourage an atmosphere in which people take risks, plan ahead and get things done.
>
> Many companies are content to problem-solve, and react to crises. They do not plan ahead. Their staff are not encouraged to plan ahead.
>
> Managers make poor decisions because they are frightened to attract criticism. They often work in a negative atmosphere where people criticize, rather than encourage risks and new ideas.
>
> Instead, companies should encourage and reward innovation and the ability to get things done. Staff should be encouraged to put forward new ideas without criticism.
>
> Companies should accept mistakes, and should be prepared to accept criticism of plans that they believe in. Finally, companies should strive to be effective, rather than simply efficient. (132 words)

(c) Summarize the main idea in 25–30 words.

Companies have lost the ability to get things done. They do not plan ahead. Instead, companies should strive to be effective, rather than simply efficient. They should encourage new ideas. (30 words)

2. *Summary of report*

Note that this summary emphasizes the conclusions and recommendations. The target is 200 words.

```
          INVESTIGATION INTO FIVE TYPES OF PROBLEMS AT XYZ

This report covers an investigation into five types
of problems at XYZ. These problems were causing
poor interpersonal relationships and poor
communication.
The writer observed staff at work and interviewed
ten senior managers.

The main conclusions are as follows:

- Managers and employees have different views of
  the same objectives.
- Thirty per cent of problems are not real
  problems.
- Ten per cent of problems were beyond anyone's
  control.
- Five per cent of problems were unexpected.
- Two per cent of problems were genuine errors.
```

ANSWERS TO QUESTIONS: PART 10 (Chapter 20)

The writer recommends the following:
- Make sure that subordinates know the extent of their authority.
- Make sure that managers and employees understand the objectives very well.
- Ensure that all managers are very clear about their own expectations and perceptions.
- Ensure that managers do not become angry over unexpected problems.
- Ensure that managers do not over- or underreact to genuine errors.

The investigation uncovered the following that cause problems:
- misunderstood objectives (40 %)
- no real problems exist (30 %)
- unexpected problems (10 %)
- genuine errors (10 %)
- poor understanding of authority (10 %).

(179 words)

PART 11 (Chapter 21)

Points for discussion

1. *What role can the mass media play in companies' public relations activities?*

   Suggested answer

   Public relations staff use the mass media to convey their messages about their companies. They could, for example use newspapers, the radio, television and specialist magazines. In addition, they could use brochures and posters.

2. *How does mass communication differ from interpersonal communication?*

   Suggested answer

   Mass communication is generally one-way communication, because feedback is very difficult to obtain. Mass communication is aimed at a large audience that is hard to analyse. On the other hand, interpersonal communication makes immediate feedback possible. Interpersonal communication takes place with a small audience. The sender can, therefore, easily adjust the message to suit the receivers.

3. *Explain why mass communication is described as one-way communication.*

   Suggested answer

   A mass audience is hard to analyse. In addition, direct feedback is very difficult to obtain. The audience is unseen.

4. *What are the three main purposes of the mass media?*

   Suggested answer

   The three main purposes are:
   - to inform
   - to entertain
   - to persuade.

   A newspaper may, for example, have a leading article that informs readers. In addition, there may be articles that entertain. An essay in the newspaper may also attempt to persuade readers of the rightness of a cause.

ANSWERS TO QUESTIONS: PART 11 (Chapter 21) 597

5. *What are the two unique characteristics shared by the mass media?*

   Suggested answer

   These are that:
   - they are able to overcome the barriers of time and space
   - the messages that they send are subject to gatekeeping.

6. *What advantages does television enjoy over newspapers and the radio?*

   Suggested answer

   Television combines the spoken and the visual. This is a powerful combination. In addition, television brings this combination into the home.

7. *Explain the differences between the radio, film and newspapers in terms of their audiences.*

   Suggested answer

   The radio is effective for an illiterate audience. It is effective for people who, because of their work, are not able to view television.

   Film is best viewed in the comfort of a cinema. Films are thus restricted to an audience that can afford to travel to a cinema and pay the relatively high charge to get in.

   Newspapers rely on a literate audience. They rely on sensational methods to attract attention and to increase sales.

8. *Define the term 'Public Relations'.*

   Suggested answer

   'Public Relations' is the creation of messages designed to create a positive image for a company. These messages are designed to influence the attitudes towards and beliefs about the company.

9. *Why do companies need to have public relations exercises?*

   Suggested answer

   All companies need to make the public aware of what they have to offer. In addition, they need to create a positive image that will encourage people to support that company. Large companies also need to create an awareness among their own staff of the company's goals and mission.

10. *What activities are public relations staff involved in?*

    Suggested answer

    Public relations staff are involved in the following activities:
    - Explaining an organization's policies
    - Dealing with criticisms and problems
    - Working with company staff to create a positive attitude

- Making the public aware of the company's social responsibility programmes
- Stressing the company's desire to serve the public and the customer
- Making company staff aware of the goals and mission of the company.

11. *What mass media do public relations staff use? How do they use them?*

    Suggested answer

    Public relations staff use the following media:
    - Brochures to explain the company's policies to the public and to staff.
    - Films showing the company's contributions to society.
    - Advertorials in magazines and newspapers to advertise and to make readers aware of what the company is doing.
    - Advertising of products and services.
    - Press-releases to newspapers to make readers aware of the company's social responsibility projects.
    - Posters to show what the company is doing.

    All these mass media are aimed at specific audiences. They have specific aims in mind.

PART 12 (Chapter 22)

Suggested answers

1. (*a*) are (plural subject)
   (*b*) is (singular subject)
   (*c*) its (committee singular here)
   (*d*) is (singular subject)
   (*e*) are (plural subject)
   (*f*) am (verb follows 'I' because it is closer)
   (*g*) are (plural subject)
   (*h*) are (crew as individuals)
   (*i*) are (plural subject)
   (*j*) is (subject is 'director')
   (*k*) face ('that' refers to 'houses' plural)
   (*l*) is (verb follows 'timetable', singular)
   (*m*) are (verb follows 'timetables', plural)
   (*n*) is (verb follows 'timetable', singular)
   (*o*) are (plural subject 'tea and cakes')
   (*p*) is (singular subject 'all')
   (*q*) are (plural subject)
2. (*a*) is (singular subject)
   (*b*) are (plural subject)
   (*c*) are (plural subject)
   (*d*) are (plural subject)
   (*e*) are (verb follows 'assistants', plural)
   (*f*) is (verb follows 'assistant', singular)
   (*g*) are (verb follows 'assistants', plural)
   (*h*) is (subject 'best part' is singular)
   (*i*) are (subject 'tea and cakes' is plural)
   (*j*) are (plural subject)
   (*k*) is (teacher is a singular subject. 'With' is a preposition, not a conjunction)
   (*l*) are (staff regarded as individuals)
   (*m*) has (staff regarded as a single group)
   (*n*) are (plural subject)
   (*o*) is ('All' is singular subject)
   (*p*) is (both 'he' and 'she' are singular)
   (*q*) know (verb follows plural 'boys')
   (*r*) is (crew regarded as a unit)
3. (*a*) broken

(b) has broken, changed
(c) gone, started
(d) done, formatted
(e) calculated
(f) walked, discovered, taken
(g) been, come
(h) worked out, need, for, of
(i) find, about, adapt, to
(j) opened, sent
(k) hoped, been
(l) operated, work, works
(m) ran, went
(n) completed, used

4. (a) on
(b) in spite of
(c) against
(d) up
(e) at, down
(f) on
(g) due to
(h) in
(i) but
(j) without
(k) for
(l) for
(m) for
(n) for
(o) for, to
(p) for
(q) as or for
(r) for
(s) for
(t) for
(u) for
(v) for
(w) for
(x) for

5. (a) for
(b) for
(c) for
(d) from
(e) from
(f) from
(g) from, to

ANSWERS TO QUESTIONS: PART 12 (Chapter 22) 601

    (*h*) from
    (*i*) from
    (*j*) from
    (*k*) from
    (*l*) in
    (*m*) in
    (*n*) in
    (*o*) in
    (*p*) in
    (*q*) in or with
    (*r*) in, in
    (*s*) in front of
    (*t*) through
    (*u*) on, in spite of
    (*v*) into
    (*w*) like
    (*x*) in, in or near
    (*y*) of, on
    (*z*) of, into
  (*aa*) of
  (*bb*) of
  (*cc*) of
  (*dd*) of

6. (*a*) Mr Smith has a special difficulty. He does not know where he may be sent to work each day.

    or

    Mr Smith has a special difficulty because he does not know where he may be sent to work each day.

  (*b*) Other powers are increasing their armaments. We must do the same to ensure that we are not left behind other nations.

    or

    Because other powers are increasing their armaments, we need to do the same if we are not to be left behind other nations.

  (*c*) Climate and geographical position are important in determining the character of a nation.

  (*d*) Experts consider that the situation is deteriorating.

7. (*a*) In this unique situation, I am not sure what to do. (Unique is an absolute word. It should not be qualified)

  (*b*) I do not want to go only to the city. ('To only go' is a split infinitive. 'To' and 'go' should be kept together.)

  (*c*) Flying low, the pilot saw a flock of sheep. ('Flying' is an example of an unrelated participle. The original sentence suggests that the flock of sheep was flying. 'Flying' must be correctly related to a person here.)

(d) Being seven years old, I was invited to a party by my uncle. ('Being' is an example of a misrelated participle. The original sentence suggests that my uncle is seven years old. The pronoun 'I' should follow the participial phrase.)

(e) They have a good team, which should be able to solve the problem. (In the original 'and which' does not follow from a previous 'which' or 'that'. The word 'and' is a co-ordinating conjunction. It joins words of equal value. The 'and' has been removed from the sentence, and a comma has been placed before the 'which' to show that what follows is non-defining.)

(f) We believe that he will be able to perform the task. (The double negative in the original is confusing. Double negatives should not be used in modern English.)

(g) In our report we have stated that he never has behaved, and never will behave like that. (In the original, the group 'he never has' is incomplete. The word 'behave' goes only with 'never will'. It is ungrammatical to say 'has behave'.)

(h) We are surprised at your resigning so soon after joining the company. ('Resigning' is a verbal noun. In a formal sentence the pronoun 'you', which is linked to 'resigning', should be in the possessive case.)

(i) At the beginning of our financial year we found that not only our local expenses, but also our overseas expenses had increased beyond the budgeted amounts. (The words 'not only' and 'but also' are correlatives. They should join groups of words with equal value. In the original, the groups of words joined by the correlatives are unequal. The corrected version joins 'local expenses' and 'overseas expenses'. The clause 'had increased — amounts' now applies to both types of expenses.)

(j) We are offering gifts with every purchase. (Gifts are free. The word 'free') is unnecessary.)

(k) They were uninterested in the project, preferring to go to the beach instead. (The word 'disinterested' means 'impartial' in formal English. Lack of interest is expressed by the word 'uninterested'.)

PART 13 (Chapter 23)

Points for discussion

1. What do you understand by the following terms?
   - ethnocentrism
   - cultural stereotyping
   - intercultural communication
   - culture and climate in organizations
   - affirmative action
   - cultural relativity

   Suggested answer
   - *Ethnocentrism* occurs when people judge all other cultures from their own cultural point of view. Such people find it very difficult to judge other cultures in a balanced way.
   - *Cultural stereotyping* occurs when people make general statements about other cultural groups. These general statements ignore individual differences within cultures. People then judge anyone from another cultural group according to the general statement. If, for example, another cultural group is regarded as unreliable, then every individual from the group is likely to be classified as unreliable.
   - *Intercultural communication* refers to communication between two or more different cultural groups.
   - *Racism* refers to discrimination against one or more cultural groups by another cultural group that regards itself as superior. The group discriminated against then finds itself at a disadvantage. Members of the group may, for example, be denied access to schooling and to the means of gaining wealth.
   - *Culture and climate in organizations*. These terms refer to the ways in which people work together in organizations. *Culture* refers to the sharing of values, ideas and attitudes in an organization. These develop over time, and gradually become accepted as 'the way we do things in this organization'. These values, ideas and attitudes hold an organization together and enable it to function.
   - The term *climate* refers to the day-to-day atmosphere in an organization. The climate is like the weather. It can change very quickly. The climate is affected by the ways in which employees work together every day. The climate could, for example, be friendly and co-operative but

could change overnight because of one incident in which one person was rude to another.
- *Affirmative action* refers to the giving of special advantages to people who have been discriminated against in the past. Such people may, for example, be given jobs in companies in preference to people from other cultural groups. Such specially favoured people may also be given extra training to help them make up for any lack in their education.
- *Cultural relativity.* This term is related in meaning to *ethnocentrism.* It refers to people's attitudes when they judge every activity in another culture as right or wrong in terms of their own culture. Such people find it very difficult to judge other cultures accurately.

Note

Cultural relativity should not be confused with *cultural relativism.* This term describes a positive approach to another culture. People using this approach try to understand other people's behaviour within the culture in which the behaviour takes place. They do not make any ethnocentric judgements about the behaviour.

For example, in a Western culture ladies would expect to go first through a door followed by the men. In another culture, men would expect to go first. In terms of *cultural relativity*, a Western person might see men going first as wrong and impolite. However, in terms of *cultural relativism*, a Westerner would try to understand why men go first in that culture. Men going first would then be accepted and respected in that culture.

2. *From your own experience, discuss the major barriers to effective intercultural communication.*

   Suggested answer

   Learners are expected to work out their own answers here. They should use the index of this book to give them ideas on barriers.

3. *If two people of unequal power from different cultures communicate, what are the likely effects on this unequal power on their communication?*

   Suggested answer

   Unequal power is likely to have two main results:
   - the person with more power could see herself or himself as superior to the other person. He or she is likely, then, to behave in a domineering manner towards the other person. He or she could also have an ethnocentric view of the other person.
   - the person with less power could become defensive and resentful of the other person. He or she could also take an ethnocentric view of the other person.

ANSWERS TO QUESTIONS: PART 13 (Chapter 23)

These differences in power, coupled with cultural differences, could lead to poor communication or a breakdown in communication. These two would have to work very hard to communicate successfully.

4. *Discuss the term 'world view'. How will differing world views affect intercultural communication?*

   Suggested answer

   The term 'world view' refers to the different ways in which cultural groups view their relationship to the earth, to their creator and to the universe. African, Asian and European world views are examples. Each one of these has a very different world view.

   Differing 'world views' will affect communication because people might not understand each other's actions and statements unless they see them in the context of their specific world view. Poor communication, or a breakdown in communication, could result. The above could easily occur if each person took his or her own world view as correct. Each would then judge the other in terms of her or his own world view.

5. *How may a convergence model be used to describe and analyse intercultural communication?*

   Suggested answer

   The convergence model on page 19 of this book shows how two people keep exchanging messages until they reach some form of understanding. This model suggests that intercultural communication may not be perfect when people from different cultures meet for the first time. The model shows how these people need to work together to create meaning. At first they may share very little meaning. However, as they work together and begin to understand one another, they are likely to share more and more meaning.

   They may find many barriers to their communication. If they are willing to communicate, however, they will overcome these barriers, and will start to share meanings. The shapes for sender and receiver in the model will then overlap.

6. *What can organizations do to reduce prejudices in intercultural communication?*

   Suggested answer

   Part 13 of this book has suggested 22 methods that companies can use to improve intercultural communication. The most important step is to try to create an atmosphere of trust. Companies could then strive to create positions of equal power for staff from different cultural groups. If possible, companies should try to get rid of any feelings of superiority and inferiority among staff. Companies should encourage individuals from different cultures to meet informally so that they can begin to understand each other. Companies can also encourage regular discussions in which people from different cultures describe their customs and values. In this way people will learn to understand other world views.

7. *What specific aspects of non-verbal communication are likely to be different when people from different cultures communicate?*

Suggested answer

The following aspects need to be carefully studied:
- Different values given to eye-contact. Western people, for example, value good eye-contact. They will downgrade people who do not look at them. On the other hand, people from another culture may look down to show respect to people senior to them.
- Different values given to people's space bubbles, or comfort zones. Western people need a large zone around them. This is normally over a metre. Other cultures may, however, prefer a much smaller distance between people when they are talking or working together.
- Different values given to time. Some cultures view time as though it were a river flowing past. Once time has gone past, it cannot be used again. However, other cultures view time more like a wheel. This view sees time as coming back in a cycle. This could mean that if a job is not done on one day, it can be done on the next.

  In one culture, keeping a person waiting could be regarded as an insult. However, in another culture, a person may wish to show how important (s)he is by keeping someone waiting. Keeping a person waiting for a business appointment may be regarded as quite normal in one culture, whereas in another culture this behaviour may make people angry.
- Different gestures are also worth studying in intercultural communication.

8. *How will different approaches to constructing messages affect intercultural communication?*

Suggested answer

Some cultures place a high value on getting to the point quickly. Other cultures may, however, prefer a less direct approach to constructing messages. Such cultures feel that it is rude to be so direct. If people from these two cultures try to communicate, they could find that they do not understand each other. The indirect group could then end up regarding the direct group as rude. The direct group could then regard the indirect group as undisciplined wafflers.

9. *What language policy should an organization adopt in order to improve intercultural communication?*

   Suggested answer

   Organizations should consider using an international language like English to help people to communicate better. This language would be very important for written messages to outside organizations.

   In addition, every effort should be made to give people the chance to learn each other's language.

10. *What steps should organizations take to ensure that their affirmative-action policies are successful?*

    Suggested answer

    Organizations should strive to help their employees understand why the affirmative-action policy needs to be applied. They should then apply the policy with everyone's agreement.

    Organizations should ensure that people employed are properly trained. On-the-job training should be given constantly. Affirmative action should not be seen as 'tokenism' or 'window dressing'. A great deal of attention should be paid to good intercultural communication.

Exercises

1. *When you are working with a person from another cultural group, ask the following questions, among others:*
   - What are your views about eye-contact?
   - Do you like direct eye-contact?
   - Do you respect people who look down while you are speaking to them?
   - What sort of space bubble do you like around you?
   - How far apart should people be if they wish to talk comfortably?
   - What is your attitude towards time?
   - Do you like people to be on time?
   - What is your attitude towards the organization of messages?
   - Do you like people to get to the point quickly?
   - How do you feel about touching other people?
   - Do you like to be touched?

2. *When you are preparing a communication policy, consider the following:*
   - creating an atmosphere of trust.
   - ensuring that people from different cultures are able to communicate as equals.
   - ensuring that people from different cultural groups understand each others' customs and values.

- ensuring that all messages in the organization are clear and easy to understand.
- ensuring that informal communication takes place, in the form of social activities.
- ensuring that the networks in the organization are known by all, and can be effectively used.
- ensuring that listening is of a good quality.
- ensuring that conflict resolution procedures are set up in advance, and are well known to all.

3. *When you are writing guidelines for ensuring that an affirmative-action policy is successful, consider the following:*
    - Make sure that all staff understand the policy and why it is being applied.
    - Make sure that the same standards apply to all staff employed.
    - Make sure that affirmative action is not seen as tokenism or window dressing.
    - Make sure that all staff employed under the affirmative action plan are given on-the-job training to ensure that they can do the job and can communicate effectively.

4. *When preparing a language policy for an organization, consider the following:*
    - Use one language for communicating within the company. This language could, for example, be English.
    - Use a simplified form of English called controlled English. This form would consist of a simplified vocabulary. One word would have one meaning. In addition, the grammar would be simplified.
    - Encourage the learning of other languages in the organization.

5. *This question has been partly covered in Exercise 1.*

    Make sure that you cover the following:
    - Eye-contact
    - Touching
    - Comfort zones between people
    - Attitudes towards time
    - Interpretation of gestures such as hand movements
    - Attitudes towards different body shapes
    - Attitudes towards the ways in which people dress.

6. *When you explain the term 'world view' consider the following:*
    - the Western world view, with its stress on individual responsibility.
    - the African world view, with its stress on working as a member of a group.

    Stress that a world view is a way of interpreting the world used by a particular group.

INDEX

A

abstract 420
   descriptive 420
   informative 420
abstraction, levels of 178, 185–186
accepting differences and similarities among cultures 476
acculturation 480
active listening 109
advertisements 251, 338–341
   AIDA method 338
   classified 340–341
affirmative action 475
   programmes 484
age-group differences in intercultural communication 483
algorithm 325
'and which' 447, 454
anxiety in intercultural communication 481
area graph (circle graph, pie chart) 382–383
articles 250–251, 333
   in-house 251, 333
assertiveness 100, 106
attitudes 157
   long-term 35
   short-term 35
audience analysis 155–158, 168, 174
   expert 157, 173–174
   lay 157, 173–174
   mixed 158, 173–174
   technical 157
audience response
   talking to a sluggish audience 231
audio-visual aids 227
   advantages and disadvantages 227–230
   chalk and white boards 229
   flip chart 228
   models 230
   posters 229
   slide projectors 230
   tape recorders 231
   video machines 230
autocratic leader 72
axis
   horizontal 386
   vertical 386

B

bar graph 377, 382–386
   cumulative 385
   horizontal 383, 386
   key 383
   multiple 383
   reference lines 383
   vertical 383
barriers to effective communication 15–16, 44, 50
   intercultural 475, 479
   major barriers 44
   physical 15
   psychological 15
beliefs, differences in 480
bibliography 163–164
   card 163–164
bureaucratic leader 72

C

'can' and 'may' 447, 455
cartoons 377, 393–394
case 447, 452
case study 401–411
   approach to general case 401–411
   approach to specific case 401–404
   example 404–407
chairperson, duties of 81–83, 90–91
change agent 440
checklists
   for an effective style 200
   for classified advertisements 341
   for electronic mail 352
   for essays 331–332
   for faxing 345
   for instructions 326
   for letters 305
   for memoranda 308
   for press release 329
   for proposals 314
   for readability 208
   for reports 282
   for telegram 337
   for telex 337
   for well-organized messages 175
   forchoosing the right word 188
circulars 249, 316–318, 338

climate
  in organizations 477
code 14
coherence 161, 163, 169–171
communication 3, 5, 21–22, 29, 63, 475
  small groups 3
  activities 6
  assertive style 38
  barriers 15, 22, 44, 50, 52
  conditions under which modern organizations communicate today 155
  content of message 22
  contracting lines of 31–32
  convergence model 18–19
  cross-cultural 22
  customers, with 3
  differences 484
  differences between one-way and two-way 20
  downward 3, 7, 48–50
  feedback 20
  functions 7
  good relationships 43
  grapevine 46
  graphic 377
  horizontal 7
  implications for 42
  in organizations 3–9, 20, 27
  intercultural 11, 54, 475
  interpersonal 11, 20–21, 99
  intrapersonal 11, 20, 22–23, 99
  key points 12
  large groups 3, 5
  lateral 7, 51
  levels of 11, 20
  linear model 13
  main elements 11
  manipulative style 38
  mass 11, 20–21, 437–440
  meaning 3
  need for open 35
  needs and goals 17
  negotiation of meaning 475–476
  networks 46
  non-verbal 115
  one to one 5
  one-to-one 3
  one-way 11
  organizational 11, 20–21
  outward 53
  process 11
  public 12, 20–21
  purposes 14
  relationship of communicators 22
  result 14
  rules 3
  sideways 7, 51–52
  small groups 5, 8, 11, 20–21, 63–76
  small groups‡ 5
  styles 55–56
  transaction 13, 18, 22, 29
  transaction, as a 3
  two-way 11, 20
  upward 8, 48, 50–51
communication system
  electronic 29
company image 438
comprehension test 415
comprehension tests 415–416, 427
  procedure for answering 427
  procedure for writing 416
conflict management 38, 76–78
  lose–lose 63, 78
  needs 63
  win–lose 63, 78
  win–win 63, 78
congruence in messages 14
constructing messages in cultures, different ways of 484
constructing messages, cultural variation 475
continuous writing 327
controlled English 485
convergence model of communication 11, 19
  used in intercultural communication 475, 481
creative pattern 163, 167
credibility 218, 226–227
  achieving 227
  derived 226–227
  initial 226–227
  terminal 226–227
cross-cultural communication 475
cue cards 217
cultural stereotyping 55, 475–476, 479, 481
  avoidance of 476
  major cause of poor intercultural communication 476
culture 56, 477
  as applied to an organization 476
  defined 54, 476
  differences, acceptance of 484
  mores 477
  needs 56
  norms 477
  problems 55
  relativity 477
  stereotyping 478
curriculum vitae 101, 129, 131, 142

INDEX

D

defensiveness   475, 479, 481
democratic leader   72
desktop publishing   343
diagram   377, 390
different languages   479
dogmatism   102
downward communication   49
   barriers   50
   topics   49
   types of messages   49
dyads   104
   roles and rules   104–106

E

echo posture   120
electronic mail   253–254, 343–344, 347–351, 356, 373
   as an effective form of communication   347
   aspects   348
   changes in communication process   349
   characteristics   348
   checklist   352
   construction   347
   construction of messages   347
   legal questions   351
   manners   352
   security   351
   uses in business   347
electronic networks   343
electronic office   252, 342–344
   advantages of desktop publishing   343
   advantages of software programs   343
   advantages of work stations   342
electronic system   27
emotive language   177, 182
emphasis   161, 163, 169, 171
essays   250, 330–333
   checklist for   331–332
   example of   332–333
   preparation   251, 330–333
   readability   250
ethnocentrism   11, 20, 55, 475, 478–479, 481
   overcoming   484
'even'   447, 457
expectancy   41

F

faxing   345
   checklist for   345
feedback   17, 111
   arranging for   17
   direct   18
   indirect   18
   receiving   17
floppy disc   345
flow chart   324, 377, 392–393
fog index   201, 208
   calculation of   206–207
formal meetings   81
format
   for message   14
   for oral report   221
   for talk   219
frame of reference   102
functional literacy   50
function of words   181–183

G

gantt chart   377, 386–387
gatekeeping   437, 439
gerunds   453
goal
   first-level   41
   second-level   41
grammar   447–458
grapevine   28, 47, 52
graphic communication   377–383, 385–386, 388, 391–398
   algorithms   250
   area graph   382–383
   bar graph   377, 382–383, 385–386
   bias   377, 395
   defined   379
   design techniques   377, 395
   diagram   390
   flow chart   250, 377
   gantt chart   377, 386–387
   histogram   386–387
   illustrations   390
   integration into text   394
   line graph   388, 391–398
   logic trees   250
   maps   377
   pictogram   377, 391
   purposes of   379
graphic communication, types of
   bar graph   386
   pictogram   391
group development
   stages   71
groups   65–66
   advantages   66
   defined   65
   formal   66–67

informal 66–67
types 66

H

headings 203
Hertzberg 38
  two-factor theory 38, 40
Hertzberg's two-factor theory 38
hierarchical flow chart 377, 392
histogram 377, 386
horizontal files 344
horizontal outline 222, 224

I

identity, sense of 482, 484
illustrations 390
in-house journal article 333–334
individual differences in cultures 480
  failure to allow for 480
individual level of comunication 483
inferiority, feeling of 484
informal contact among staff 475
information
  downward flow 48
  flow 42
  subordinates 43
  superiors 43
  upward flow 48
information highway 356
instructions 250, 318–322, 326
  checklist for 326
  examples 320–321
  format 250, 319–320
  graphic aids in 320
  language of 319
instrumentality 41
interaction, differences in 477
intercultural communication 11, 19, 54–55, 58, 475, 479
  improving 475, 482
  major barriers 475–476
Internet 256, 353–354
  access 255
  asynchronous communication 356
  credibility 355
  CVs 355
  e-mail messages 355
  groups working together 355
  many-to-many asynchronous communication 355
  one-to-one communication 355
  synchronous communication 356
  usenet groups 354

Worldwide Web 354
interpersonal communication 11, 20, 99, 103–104
  skills 106
interview 129
interview record card 165
interviewee 129–138
interviewer 133, 135–136, 139–140
interviews 101, 129–140
  ability to receive feedback 136
  appraisal 129, 132–133
  candidate scoring grid 137
  characteristics of 131–132, 135
  closed questions 137–138
  definition 131–132
  exit 129, 132–133
  information-seeking 129, 132–133
  job 129, 132–133
  language ability 135
  level of preparation 135
  listening skills 135
  memory 136
  motivation 135
  nature of the job 135
  one to one 129
  open questions 137
  panel 129, 133, 136, 139–140
  perceptions 135
  personal bias and attitudes 136
  phases of 134, 139
  purposes 135
  sensitivity to non-verbal communication 136
  setting 134
  special nature of 132
  structured 132
  thinking patterns 135
  types of questions 135
  unstructured 132
intrapersonal communication 12, 20, 22, 99, 101–102
'its' and 'it's' 447, 456

J

jargon 189, 191, 199
  active or passive 191
  clear or ambiguous 191
  concise or wordy 191
  concret or abstract 191
job application
  curriculum vitae 142–145
  letter 140–141
Johari window 99, 104
  blind area 99

blind section   105
hidden area   99
hidden section   105
levelling   99, 105
open area   99
open section   105
openness to feedback   99, 105
unknown section   105

L

laissez-faire leader   72
language policy   485
leadership
   autocratic   71
   bureaucratic   72
   contingency theory   74
   democratic   72
   designated leader   71
   emergent leader   71
   functional theory   72
   in-group   71–72, 74–75
   laissez-faire   72
   styles   63, 71
   theories of   63, 72–73
   trait theory   72
letters
   adjustment   248, 292, 299–300
   application   101
   application and curriculum vitae   129
   attention-line   289
   audience   284
   bad-news   248, 283, 291–292
   block format   286–287
   body of letter   288
   complaint   248, 283, 292, 297–298
   complimentary close   288
   date   288
   enquiry   248, 283, 292–295
   example of letter   290–291
   formats   248, 286
   good-news   248, 283, 291
   goodwill   283
   heading   286–287
   initials of sender and typist   289
   inside address   288
   invitation   248, 304–305
   neutral   248, 283, 291
   outline plan   289–290
   planning   283–284
   presentation   289
   purposes   283
   readability   286
   reference   287
   reference to items enclosed   285, 289
   refusal of request   296–297, 300–301
   response to enquiry   248, 283, 292, 294–295
   salutation   288
   signature   288
   style   283, 285–286
   subject-line   288
   tone   283, 285
   transmittal   258, 275, 277
   typed name   288
   unsolicited sales   302–303, 338
letters, types of   101
line graph   377, 386–388, 390
   cumulative jagged line   389
   cumulative jagged-line   388
   curve   388
   jagged line   388
line managers   34
linear model   11
   elements   13
listening   19, 21, 101, 109–113, 135
   active   109–113
   difference between hearing and listening   109
   importance   109
   major barriers   109, 111–112
   on the telephone   237
   poor listening habits   109, 112
   speakers' techniques   113
   techniques for effective listening   112–113
listing information   203–205
logic tree   320, 323

M

Maccoby management types   38, 40
   company person   40
   craftsman   40
   gamesperson   40
   jungle fighter   40
management
   participative style   35
manipulation   102
maps   392
Maslow
   hierarchy of needs   39
Maslow's hierarchy of needs   39
mass communication   11, 20, 437
   defined   437, 439
   differences between one-to-one and mass communication   437, 439
   major functions of   437, 440–441
mass media   437–439
   film   437–438, 441–442
   magazine   441

newspaper   437–438, 441
    radio   437–438, 441
    television   437–438, 441–442
    use in public relations   438
'may' and 'can'   447, 455
'may' and 'might'   447, 455
'may have'   456
McClelland'system of needs   39
meaning   3
    creation of   3–5
    of words   22, 179–180
meetings   82–92
    agenda   81, 86
    differences between formal meetings and
        small groups   82
    formal   81–82
    guidelines for speakers   91
    minutes   86, 89–90
    notice of meeting   81, 86
    proposing of motions   91
    rules for conduct   81
    types of motions   92
memoranda   249, 306
    checklist for   308
    copies to   306
    date   307
    example of   307–308
    format   306
    'from' line   307
    of transmittal   275–276, 309
    style of   249
    subject line   307
    'to' line   306
message   27, 31, 35, 42–45, 49, 51, 153,
        155–156, 161, 163, 173, 179
    barriers to flow   44
    beginning of   171
    coherent   153, 156
    congruence   14–15
    contracting lines of   32
    definition   155
    diamond shaped   161, 163, 172–173
    distortion-free   45
    downward   49
    emphasis   153
    flow of   27, 47
    format   14
    goals, philosophy and ethics   44
    good relationships   43
    horizontal flow   47
    in pay packets   32
    informal   47
    instructions   44
    inverted pyramid shaped   161, 174
    last section   171
    lateral   51
    level of formality   156
    middle section   172
    need for information flow   42
    networks   47
    overload   27, 42, 45
    planning and organizing   161–164, 166,
        168–169, 171–175
    planning of   153, 156
    purposes   14
    pyramid shaped   161, 163, 173
    readable   153, 156
    sender   13
    social and productive value   35
    types of   27, 43, 49
    underload   27, 42, 45
    unified   153
    upward   50
    vertical flow   47
    written   247
message pad for telephone   240
messages
    oral   217
microfiche   345
microfilm   345
'might' and 'may'   447, 455
'might have'   456
mind-map   163, 166–167
minds, meeting of   13
minutes of meetings   86, 89–90
    essential elements of   86
    example of   89–90
motions at meetings
    proposing of   91
    types of   92
motivation, theories of   27, 38
multiple decimal numbering   203–204

N

needs and goals of communication   17
negotiation of meaning   475, 481
networks
    all-channels   47
    centralized   46–47
    cosmopolite   48
    decentralized   46–47
    gatekeepers   48
    isolate   48
    liaison   48
    outside link   48
    roles in   48
    stars   48
    wheel structure   47
non-verbal codes, differences   475, 479, 481

INDEX

non-verbal communication   115–124,
    126–128
  clothing and accessories   115, 118, 126
  cultural views of time   116, 118, 128
  differences in   484
  echo posture   120
  eye-contact   115, 118, 121
  facial expression   115, 118, 121
  kinesics   118–120
  major differences between non-verbal and
      verbal communication   117
  need to be sensitive to   117
  objects and environment   116, 118, 126
  paralanguage   115, 118–119
  problems with the interpretation of   118
  proxemics   115, 118, 122–123
  regulators   120
  silence   115, 118–119
  table seating   125
  territoriality   123, 126
  touching   115, 118, 122
norms, cultural   477
'not only . . . but also'   457
note card   165–166
notice of meeting   86–88
notices   249, 315–316
number   447
  rules of   449–451

O

occupations in intercultural
    communication   483
'only', position of   447, 457
opinion leader   440
oral messages   217
  preparing   217
  report   217, 219, 221
  talk   217, 219
organigram (hierarchical flow chart)   392
organization
  communication system   43
  contracting lines of communication   31
  definition   27, 29
  division into departments   31, 33
  flat structure   27, 31, 33
  line and staff divisions   31, 33
  policies and procedures   34
  tall structure   27, 31–32
  theories of   27, 34
organizational chart (hierarchical flow
    chart)   392
organizational communication   11, 20–21
organizations
  communication in   27

mass communication in   437
  writtem messages   247
organizing messages   172
  cause to result   172
  comparison   172
  familiar to unfamiliar   172
  general to particular   172
  particular to general   172
  problem to solution   172
  simple to complex   172
  size order   172
  time order   172
overload   42, 44–45

P

participles   447
  misrelated   452
  rules for   452–453
  unrelated   453
perception   16–17, 101
  frame of reference   100
  improvement of   99, 103
  problems with   103
  selective   101
personal computers   255, 353, 356
  access to networks   354
  and the Internet   354
  power of   353
persuasion
  logical appeal   217, 225
  personal appeal   217, 225
  plan for persuasive message   225
  preparing a persuasive talk   217, 224
  psychological appeal   217, 225
photograph   391
pictogram   391
planning messages   161
  horizontal plan   163
  vertical plan   163
points of major impact in messages   161,
    163, 171
prejudice   475, 480–481
preparing a talk   217, 219–220
preparing an oral report   217, 222
prepositions   452
presenting an oral report   226
press release   250, 327–329
  checklist for   329
  inverted pyramid   327
  who writes one?   329
pressures   17
problem-solving procedures   68–69
proposals   249, 309–312, 314
  checklist for   314

format for 309
non-requested 311–312
public communication 12, 20
public relations 438, 442–443
punctuation 447–452, 454–461
   colon 448, 461
   comma 448, 462
   dash 448, 462
   exclamation mark 447, 461
   full-stop 447, 460
   question mark 447, 460
   semi-colon 448, 461
purposes in communicating 14, 153, 159, 161

Q

questions
   closed 135, 137–138
   controlling 218, 231–233
   difficult 232–233
   open 135, 137–138
   preparing 138

R

racism 475, 479
Readability 201–208
   defined 202
   techniques 201–203
reader 202
   emotional needs 202
   information needs 202
   needs 203
receiver 14
   of message 481
referencing 256, 358, 360
   Harvard system 358–359
   numbered system 358
referential language 177, 181
regulators 120
relative clauses 447, 453
   defining 447, 453–454
   non-defining 447, 453–454
reports 247, 259–268, 270, 272–274, 276–279, 281–282
   audience 259
   evaluative 260
   feasibility 259
   informative 259, 261
   interim 260
   investigative 259, 261
   letter of transmittal 258
   letter reports 278
   logic in reports 281
   purposes 247, 259
   pyramid order 261
   readability of 282
   style of 282
   summary reports 279–281
   technical 260
reports, correct order of sections
   acknowledgements 247, 260, 262
   appendices 248, 261, 275
   bibliography 248, 261
   conclusions 174, 248, 261, 270–271
   feasibility 261
   findings 173, 248, 261, 272–273
   glossary 248, 261, 267
   introduction 173–174, 248, 261, 268–270
   list of illustrations 247, 261, 267
   list of references 248, 261, 274
   list of symbols 248, 261, 268
   procedure 248, 261, 270
   recommendations 173–174, 248, 261, 271–272
   style of 248
   summary 247, 260, 264–266
   table of contents 247, 260, 266
   terms of reference 247, 260, 263–264
   title page 247, 260, 262
reports, correct order of sections
   conclusions 173
reports, correct order sections
   conclusions 173
reports, selections of (in correct order)
   findings 173
result of communication 14
rhetorical situation 153, 155–157
   analysing audience's needs 153
   deciding on one's purposes 153
   turning vague information into communication 153, 155–156
rotary files 344
rules in companies 99

S

secretary 83
   duties of 81, 83–84
self-image 22, 99, 101
sender of message 481
sentence structure 447
sentence types
   complex 447, 459
   compound 447, 459
   compound–complex 447, 459
   simple 447, 458
sequence of verbs 457
'shall' and 'will' 447, 454

shapes of messages
   pyramid 163
   diamond 161, 163, 172
   inverted pyramid 161
   pyramid 161, 173
signpost words 169
small-group communication 11, 20–21, 63
   effective interaction 70
   getting the job done 70
   groups that work well 69
   ineffective groups 75
   stages in group development 71
   supportive climate 69
social class differences in intercultural communication 483
split infinitive 447, 458
stereotyping 482
   dangers of 483
storage and retrieval of information 252
style 189–200
   active or passive 189, 191, 196
   casual 189, 194–195
   clear or ambiguous 189, 191, 197
   concise or wordy 189, 191, 196–197
   concrete or abstract 189, 191, 198
   consultative 194
   definition 191
   formal 189, 193–194
   high formal or frozen 189, 192
   impersonal 195–196
   intimate 189, 195
   levels of formality 189, 192
   personal 195
   personal or impersonal 189, 191
   simple or complex 191
summary 415, 417, 420
   abilities needed 416
   characteristics 417
   example 419, 423–424, 426
   length of 415–417
   planning 417
   procedure for writing 416, 418, 424
superiority, feeling of 484
symbols 5

T

tables 377, 380–382, 394
   audience 382
   column heading 381
   eye across 381
   eye downward 381
   highlighting numbers 382
   stub heading 380
   sub-headings 381

   table number 380
   title of table 380
telephone 235–238
   assertiveness 239
   callers' techniques 241
   choice of words 239
   control calls 239
   effective use 235
   first point of contact 237
   four stages in answering calls 235, 238
   image of organization 235
   listening on the telephone 237
   message pad 240
   prepare for calls 239
   rights of telephone users 235
   showing a positive attitude 239
   taking notes 238
   techniques 238
   use of voice 235, 237–238
   user's rights 240
telex 251, 335–336, 371
   checklist for 337
thesis statement 166
thinking, differences in 480
tone 189, 191, 198
   definition 191
topic outline 166–168
   horizontal 166–168
   thesis statement 166
   vertical 166–168
transaction, communication as 3
transactional nature of intercultural communication 482
treasurer, duties of 81, 85
trust, atmosphere of 31, 35, 475
   creating 475, 482

U

Ubuntu 480
underload 42, 44–45
   solutions 47
unequal power 475, 480
unity 161, 163, 166, 169
usage 447

V

valence 41
values in intercultural communication
   differences in 480
   understanding 483
variation within cultures 476, 483
verbal codes, differences in 481
visible card files 344

Vocabulary 177
    choice of 177
Vroom 38
    expectancy model 38, 41

W

wealth differences in intercultural
    communication 483
'will' and 'shall' 447, 454
words 177–182, 184, 186–188
    checklist for 188
    concrete, relative and abstract 184, 186
    connotations 177, 180–181
    dealing with technical terms 183
    denotations 177, 180–181
    difference between fact and opinion 182
    familiar and unfamiliar words 183–184
    formal and informal words 184, 187
    functions of 181–182, 184
    generic and specific words 183, 185
    levels of abstraction 184–185
    pre-judging a situation 178, 184, 187
    referential and emotive words 183–184
    selecting words for professional messages
        177–179
    simple words 178
    social use 183
    synonyms 181
work pressures 17
world view, differences in 476, 480, 484
writing clearly and concisely 448, 463–465